LOOKING FOR
TROUBLE

LOOKING FOR TROUBLE

An Autobiography –
from the SAS to the Gulf

General Sir Peter de la Billière

HarperCollins*Publishers*

HarperCollins*Publishers*
77−85 Fulham Palace Road
Hammersmith, London W6 8JB

Published by HarperCollins*Publishers* 1994

1 3 5 7 9 8 6 4 2

Copyright © Sir Peter de la Billière

The Author asserts the moral right to be identified
as the author of this work

A catalogue record for this book is available from the
British Library

ISBN 0 00 255245 0

Set in Linotron Meridien by
Rowland Phototypesetting Limited
Bury St Edmunds, Suffolk

Printed in Great Britain by
HarperCollinsManufacturing Glasgow

For Bridget, and all the other wives
who know what it is like
to be left behind

The life that I have
is all that I have
and the life that I have
is yours

The love that I have
of the life that I have
is yours and yours and yours

A sleep I shall have
a rest I shall have
yet death will be but a pause

For the peace of my years
in the long green grass
will be yours and yours
and yours.

Code-poem written by Leo Marks for Violette Szabo when she was Special Operations Executive during the Second World War, and reproduced here by permission of the author.

CONTENTS

LIST OF ILLUSTRATIONS

Our wedding at Holy Trinity, Brompton, 13 February 1965.

Our first child, Nicola, was born on 2 January 1966.

Training the counter-terrorist squad, formed after the Munich Olympics massacre in 1972.

Iranian Embassy siege (*Metropolitan Police Force*).

Joining a Royal Navy guardship of the Falklands, 1985.

Bridget and me outside Britannia House, Port Stanley, with our Igloo greenhouse in the background.

Farewell to the Falklands: boarding a TriStar, July 1985.

With my family at Buckingham Palace after receiving my KBE.

The GOC Wales pioneers the route for the Cambrian Patrol, 1986.

Brigadier Patrick Cordingley outlines his battle plan, November 1990.

Being briefed before the land battle by Major General Rupert Smith in his command vehicle, February 1991.

Discussing the battle plans with Major General Rupert Smith and Brigadier Tim Sulivan.

After the Safwan ceasefire talks, General Norman Schwarzkopf with Prince Khalid.

Carnage at Mitla: military and civilian looted vehicles destroyed from the air as Iraqis tried to flee.

Ticker-tape parade, New York, 1991 (*Associated Press*).

Home at last, May 1991.

ACKNOWLEDGMENTS

Looking back, I realize how much I owe to other people: family, friends and colleagues, both military and civilian. Without their help and advice, my career would have stuttered to a halt decades earlier. To have mentioned everyone would have produced a book far longer than my publisher was prepared to contemplate: the fact that some people do not feature here does not mean that they have been forgotten.

It has always been part of my nature to avoid direct confrontation. Rather than have head-on collisions, I have always sought an indirect approach: whether dealing with colleagues or fighting the Queen's enemies, I have tried to see the other person's point of view. In command, this policy has generally enabled me to work in harmony with others and bring out the best in them. Reliance on other people has contributed more than any other single factor to any success I may have had.

In preparing this book I have been enormously helped by my wife Bridget, and my children Nicola, Phillida and Edward. Not only are their latter-day memories better than mine: they have also read drafts of the typescript with eagle eyes and made many useful suggestions.

As with *Storm Command*, I am much indebted to Duff Hart-Davis for professional assistance. Without his help, this book would never have been written.

I am particularly grateful to the following for reinforcing my own memory with anecdotes and recollections:

Brigadier James and Daphne Alexander, Tony Allen, Angela Ballenden, David Bennetts, Henry Blosse-Lynch, Tony Boyle, Poppet Codrington, Tim and Priscilla Corbett, Major General A. J. Deane-Drummond, Commander A. M. D. de Labillière, Sir John Dellow, Doreen Dunbabin, the Durham Light Infantry Museum, the Reverend Walter Evans, Terry and Maureen

Finney, Lieutenant Colonel Peter Gibbs, Margaret Goode, the Reverend Lance Gorse, Lieutenant-Colonel Neville Howard, Christopher James, Dr Richard Jenkins, Jim Johnson, David Lyon, Brigadier Robert Macgregor-Oakford, Richard Marriott, Peter McClintock, Richard Mercer, Tom Mickley, Colonel Rupert Nicholas, Bill Nott-Bower, Robin Pease, Major Tony Phebey, Lieutenant-General Sir Michael Rose, Anthony Saxton, Brigadier John Simpson, Lieutenant-Colonel Ian (Tanky) Smith, Richard Steel, Baroness Thatcher, Lieutenant-General Sir John Watts, Lord Whitelaw, General Sir Michael Wilkes, Brigadier Michael Wingate Gray, Lieutenant-Colonel John Woodhouse.

PETER DE LA BILLIÈRE, *March 1994*

AUTHOR'S NOTE

I should like to emphasize that this book is my personal story, and that my accounts of military operations do not necessarily reflect official views of the campaigns in which I took part.

For security reasons, and to protect individuals, some names have been changed.

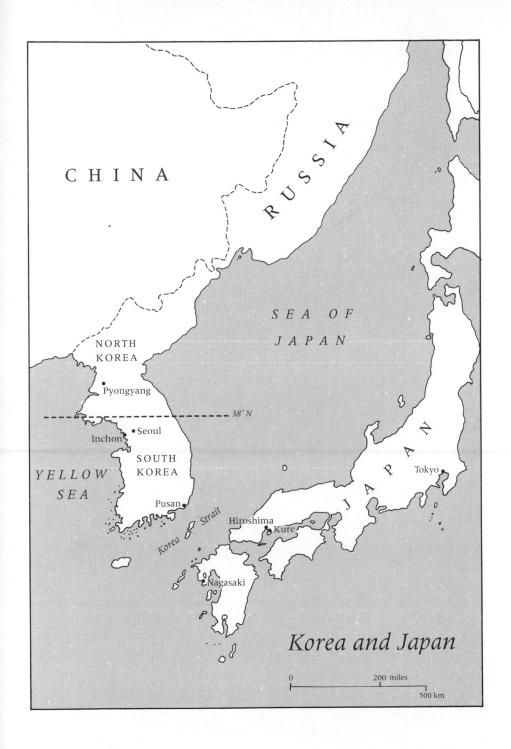

CHINA

RUSSIA

NORTH
KOREA

Pyongyang

SEA OF
JAPAN

38° N

Seoul

Inchon

SOUTH
KOREA

YELLOW
SEA

JAPAN

Tokyo

Pusan

Korea Strait

Hiroshima

Kure

Nagasaki

Korea and Japan

0   200 miles

500 km

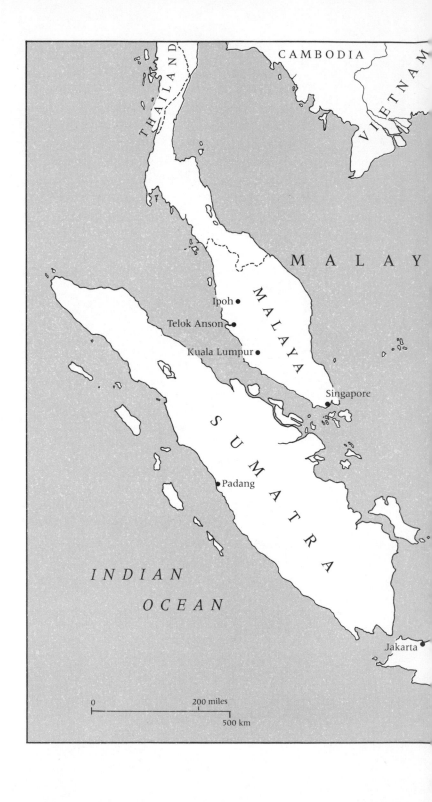

CAMBODIA

VIETNAM

THAILAND

MALAY

MALAYA

Ipoh

Telok Anson

Kuala Lumpur

Singapore

SUMATRA

Padang

INDIAN

OCEAN

Jakarta

0   200 miles

500 km

Malaysia and Borneo

SOUTH CHINA SEA

SIA

Labuan
BRUNEI
SABAH

SARAWAK

Kuching

BORNEO

Kalimantan

JAVA SEA

INDONESIA

JAVA

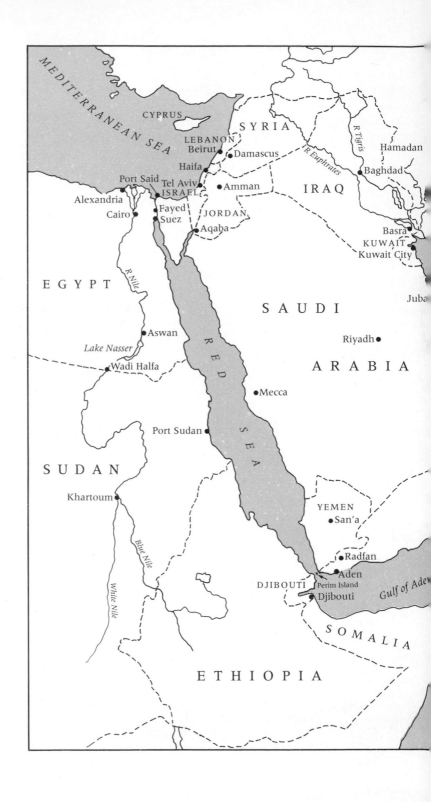

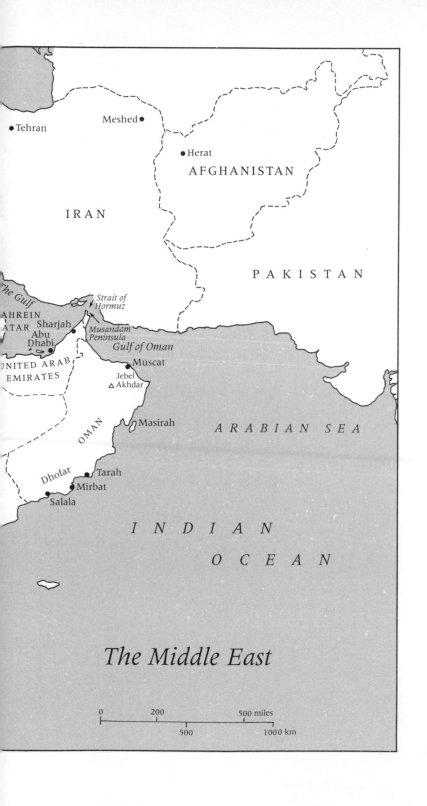

Tehran

Meshed

Herat

AFGHANISTAN

IRAN

PAKISTAN

The Gulf

Strait of
Hormuz

AHREIN
ATAR
Sharjah
Abu
Dhabi
Musandam
Peninsula
Gulf of Oman

UNITED ARAB
EMIRATES

Muscat

OMAN

Jebel
Akhdar

Masirah

ARABIAN SEA

Dhofar
Tarah
Mirbat
Salala

INDIAN

OCEAN

The Middle East

0   200   500 miles
         500   1000 km

LOOKING FOR
TROUBLE

BORN REBEL

1934–42

On a glorious May morning in 1941, not long after my seventh birthday, my mother took me out through the farmyard of our home in Kent and along the grass lane to the paddock. She pretended that we were trying to catch our wild Shetland pony; yet after no more than a perfunctory attempt, during which Polly made off at her accustomed scurrying trot, she gave up and suggested that we should sit down on the grass. It was a perfect early summer's day: there was heat in the sun, the leaves were fully out, and birds were singing. Once we were settled, she said, 'Peter, I've got something sad to tell you.' She hesitated, then went on: 'I'm afraid your father won't ever come home again. He's been killed in the war.' She told me that he had been reported missing, presumed drowned, after his ship, the cruiser HMS *Fiji*, had been sunk by German bombers off the south coast of Crete.

The news did not disturb me greatly. My father, a surgeon in the Royal Navy, had been away at sea for so much of my life that I hardly knew him. Through no fault of his character, but simply because of his career, he had come home so rarely that he had never been a person on whom I relied for help and companionship, or even one with whom I had often played games. I thought of him chiefly as the figure in the photograph on my mother's dressing-table, who would occasionally come to life, stay for a few days, and then disappear again. I had always looked forward to seeing him, but my warm feelings had generally been tinged by the worry that his arrival would mean a return of discipline to the household. And so, as we sat in the field that sunny morning, I felt that, although his death was sad, it was more important that we should catch Polly than spend time grieving.

Looking back, I realize that my father's absences, and his premature disappearance from our family, had a far deeper influence on my life than I could appreciate at the time. I see now that his death had a powerful impact on my personality, and brought out elements of it which might otherwise have remained more moderate or completely in abeyance. In particular, it drew out my sense of individualism, of being a loner, of enjoying my own company. It also gave me and my younger brother Michael a chance to run riot; for although we loved our mother dearly, she was quite unable to control us, and we ruthlessly took advantage of the fact that there was no man about the house to keep us in order. I see now that I was born a rebel, that my rebellious tendencies were fostered by the lack of a father, and that to some extent I have remained a loner all my life.

I was born at 0925 on 29 April 1934 at the Charlton Nursing Home in Plymouth, and weighed 8lbs 8oz. On 29 June 1934 I was christened Peter Edgar Delacour.[1] My father, Denis de Labillière, was then thirty, and a Surgeon Lieutenant Commander in the Royal Navy – a man of medium height and slim build, with a fresh complexion, and bright blue eyes, which he passed on to me. He had trained as a doctor at St Bartholomew's Hospital in London, where he struggled to pass his exams, failing at least once before becoming qualified.

Contemporaries remembered him as a friendly, convivial man, whose slow speech derived partly from his natural reticence and partly from the fact that he had a slight stammer. But he also had a strong sense of humour and an endearing habit of roaring with laughter, which made him excellent company.

---

1. In 'History of a Cevenol Family', a booklet printed privately in 1976, my brother Michael used extensive research by our great-grandfather to trace the de la Billières back to the twelfth century. A branch of the ancient clan de la Cour, they occupied the Château d'Esparon in the Languedoc. Over the centuries the names were spelt in various ways – de la Billière, de Labillière, de Labellière; de la Cour, Delacour – but when I grew up I decided that the first forms were the purest, and elected by deed poll to use them.

He was clearly a good doctor, and deeply interested in his calling;
but I sense that he was easy-going, and preferred play to work.
Although – like me – he had no time for organized games, he
always kept fit, riding whenever he could and walking to the
top of any hill which he found himself near.

He joined the Royal Navy as a surgeon-lieutenant on 1
October 1930, and soon sailed for Shanghai to serve on the
China Station. But in November, before he left, he became
engaged to a girl whom he had known since childhood – Christine Lawley, always known as Kitty. His father Edgar – my
grandfather – was an itinerant priest, who had gone out to Africa
and gadded erratically about the world before settling down as
the Vicar of Llangattock, a rural parish in Monmouthshire. Just
up the road from the vicarage stood Hilston Park, a substantial
house then owned by the Lawleys, a well-to-do family who had
made their fortune from shipping and cotton in Manchester.
There lived the Lawley girls – Kitty and her elder sister Joyce –
with money to spare and servants to look after them; and when
the son of the vicar fell in love with one of them, it must have
seemed a perfect country romance.

Kitty was dark and slim, attractive and full of sparkle. Her
vivacity made her a delight to friends, especially at parties. She
was outgoing and generous, and had inherited from her father
a casual way with money: if she had any, she spent it, and the
family finances were kept in order by her mother, Elizabeth, a
fine woman with an excellent business brain. Yet by no means
all Denis's family were pleased with his choice. His grandmother,
a Ravenshaw, thought it rather disreputable that any member
of her family should, as she put it, 'marry into manufacturing',
and it was said that before he took Kitty to meet her, he made
his fiancée scrub all the make-up off her face. (I daresay that
the Lawleys, for their part, had doubts about their daughter
marrying a man of dubious foreign origins.)

He proposed to her in a country pub – a daring move in those
days; but hardly had he won the promise of her hand when he
disappeared to the Far East for two years, which he spent as
Medical Officer in HM ships *Tern* and *Gannet*, stationed 1500
miles up the Yangtse river, and in their flagship on the China
Station, the new cruiser HMS *Suffolk*. His three-week passage

up-river from Shanghai was full of incident, as the ship was frequently attacked by Communists sniping at them from the banks.

The Navy's principal role was to show the flag: to protect, and if necessary evacuate, the British communities in the Treaty Ports along the river. Denis also put much time and effort into treating members of the expatriate community, especially after catastrophic floods (and consequent cholera) had devastated the town of Ichang. As a token of their gratitude, former patients presented him with a cast-iron British coat of arms, complete with lion, unicorn and the motto 'Dieu et mon Droit', torn down from the British Consulate by rioters during the Boxer Rebellion of 1900. He brought this weighty relic home, and to this day I use it as an ornament-cum-guard in front of the dining-room fireplace.

Returning from China, he married my mother on 8 June 1933: a traditional naval wedding, with colleagues forming an arch of drawn swords as they left the church. Soon afterwards Kitty's father died suddenly of a heart attack while fishing in the Usk: always a great spender, he left large debts, and the family had to sell Hilston Park, moving to Ash, near Midhurst, and then to Old Place, in Sussex. Yet Kitty remained relatively well-off, and during the early months of their marriage she and my father had two cars, which in those days was unusual for a newly married couple – an old black Daimler saloon, and a chirpy little Austin 7 with a canvas top, in which my father used to drive to work.

Deeply devoted from the start, they remained so until my father's death, even if they saw little of each other. In August 1934 he was off again, this time aboard the patrol sloop HMS *Leith*, on a two-year tour of New Zealand and the South Sea Islands. My mother followed him out in November, as soon as she thought I was strong enough, taking with her a nanny and her sister Joyce. In theory our family all lived together in Auckland, but in fact *Leith* was away for months at a time, visiting remote islands, and my father naturally found it frustrating to be separated from his new bride. During the long days and nights at sea he wrote numerous long letters, bringing out many a vivid turn of phrase.

During one of these voyages, a certain antipathy evidently developed between myself and my Aunt Joyce. A letter from my father dated 29 April 1936 makes it clear that our mutual dislike was already well established by the time I was two. 'Peter is growing into a terrific chap,' he wrote to a friend:

> He hated Joyce Lawley while she was here. She thinks she understands children better than Kitty, and has always been bossy and ticking him off. Peter simply laughed at Joyce and used to blow raspberries at her. One day she had been telling him he was a dirty little boy. He took no notice and just ignored her, but a few minutes later he crept up and hit her a bonk on the back of the head with a mallet, and then stood and roared with laughter.

Even if, at the age of two, I could hardly have realized what a tiresome woman Joyce was, my instincts must have been pointing me in the right direction. Yet my own behaviour was far from faultless. 'Peter's hair has suddenly started to curl,' wrote my mother in a letter home from New Zealand. 'It's straight across the front, but the back is a mass of curls which form a sort of halo and make him look positively angelic – until you've been with him a few minutes!' From my earliest days I seem to have had what my grandfather called 'a certain half-humorous delight in disobeying orders', and soon I was known in family circles as 'Peter the Horror'.

We returned to England in 1936, and when my mother found she was pregnant again, early in the New Year, she hoped that her second child would be a girl. Instead, it turned out to be my brother Michael, who was born in August 1937, and whom my mother described in a letter to Joyce as having 'enormous hands and feet, rather like a frog, and a bulbous head and large nose . . . just like Peter at the same age, except he's dark.' Soon Michael revealed a temperament as independent and wilful as mine. One of my earliest and most satisfactory memories is of this horrible little curly-haired monster sitting in his high chair and being force-fed with porridge, but refusing to swallow it, and hurling spoonfuls all round the room. As soon as he was able to toddle, we became accomplices in every sort of petty crime.

In the summer of 1937, before Michael's birth, my father

had been posted to HMS *Pembroke*, the shore establishment at Chatham, in Kent, and my parents moved into The Homestead, a farmhouse in the village of Borden, which was then separated from the town of Sittingbourne by more than a mile of open country. This was the first home of which I have a clear memory: a typical, rambling, red-brick Kent farmhouse, of medium size, lacking in modern comforts, but with a friendly atmosphere. It belonged to a farmer called Mr Hinge, who owned and worked the land all round, although he himself had moved to a new house in Tunstall, nearby. He was a kind and tolerant landlord, even when Michael and I made ourselves an infernal nuisance to him, and the farm, with its large barns and outbuildings, was an ideal environment for boys who liked being outdoors. We had a grass tennis court, a rose garden and an enormous kitchen garden, all looked after by an ancient but green-fingered gardener called Mr Jarrett.

I am sure that my interest in farming derived from that period. We lived in real country, among country people, and our lives were shaped by the rhythm of the seasons. As I walked back from school in Sittingbourne, I passed through acres of orchards: in summer I would strip cherries from the lowest branches and eat them, and the pickers often gave me a bag to take home. The most exciting time of year was the harvest, when primitive binders clattered round the fields of corn, and rabbits rushed about in the diminishing crops until forced to make a break for freedom. In early winter, the high spot was threshing, when rats and mice erupted from the corn-ricks as men lifted the packed sheaves and pitched them into the jaws of the machine.

My Baby Book reveals that I first went to school in October 1937, at the age of three and a half. I have no recollection of the Frobelian School at 58 Park Road, Sittingbourne, but it must have been there that I was forced to write with my right hand. When I naturally began using my left hand, somebody told me that this was a sign of bad character, and compelled me to change over. As a result, my handwriting has always been atrocious.

My memories of my father, sketchy as they are, centre round Christmas, for almost every winter he managed to obtain leave and come home. He loved impersonating Father Christmas, and did so with such imagination that for years I did not connect him with the genial, white-bearded figure who would materialize out of the dark bearing presents. On Christmas Eve the family would be marshalled in the sitting room, with coloured lights glowing on the tree. Then, over a home-made radio system – which must have been difficult to devise with the primitive equipment then available – we would listen breathlessly to a kind of broadcast. Father Christmas was talking to us: he was coming through the air, drawing close to Homestead. Now he was on the roof . . . he had decided to come in from the garden . . . and then suddenly there he was. The French windows would open, and he would appear out of the night, in full regalia, a sledge loaded with presents in tow. We loved the charade, and when we grew up we acted it out every winter for our own families.

One year he gave me a model railway, and we fitted up its circular track so that it could run all round the living room. Then he told me to go and hide behind the sofa while he prepared a surprise. After waiting a few minutes I became restive, but he called out, 'Patience! Patience!' and at last set the train in motion. Round it came, with smoke trailing realistically from a lighted cigarette stuck upright in its funnel – a device which made a tremendous impression on me.

Only once do I remember him chastising me – and that must have been when I was five. Together with Michael, in his pram, I had been packed off for a walk with the nanny of the day, and I had done everything I could to make things difficult for her. I ran ahead on the road, ignoring her orders to come back; I deliberately dropped my gloves; I threw my hat into the hedge. Altogether I behaved insufferably, in the hope that, like several of her predecessors, she would despair and leave. When we reached home she must have reported me to my father, for he gave me a good walloping. My impression is that the nanny did not last much longer; so perhaps I attained my objective, albeit after a certain amount of discomfort.

As early as October 1935, when Mussolini's troops invaded Abyssinia, my father had seen that a major war was in the offing. 'All I hope is that it does not come too soon,' he wrote home.

> It appears to be coming, all right, but war is bloody, and all whoopee stops, and food becomes scarce, and leave is still more scarce. I'm not afraid of war in the slightest. I'm a bit of

a fatalist that way. But I still have a great capacity for enjoying life, and life is too good to want to chuck it away at some dirty Italian dog.

In May 1939 he was posted to the shore establishment HMS *St Angelo* at Malta. When war broke out in September, my mother wanted to join one of the women's services, but he expressly forbade her to do so. 'Whatever would Peter and Michael do,' he wrote, 'if you and I got bumped off?' Somehow he managed to come home for Christmas, and on New Year's Day 1940 he returned briefly to HMS *Pembroke* at Chatham; but at the beginning of March he was appointed to the Colony Class cruiser HMS *Fiji* – and that was the last we saw of him. I have a dim but disturbing recollection of going with my mother to see him off before the ship sailed. At Chatham we seemed to walk through endless corridors to watch him go aboard, and I remember people saying that rats had been seen leaving the ship. Even now I recall a sense of doom as *Fiji* sailed. In a boy still not six years old, it was obviously impossible for that feeling to be very precise – and perhaps I was subconsciously picking up my mother's anguish.

For more than a year my father continued to write, never able to give details of where he was or what his ship had been doing, but always cheerful. For us boys, at home in Kent, under the flight-path of German bombers on their way to London, the war proved a time of high excitement. Much of the Battle of Britain took place above our heads: we constantly watched dog-fights by day, and at night the sky was full of anti-aircraft shells and tracer, looping in red streams through the dark. The long, white fingers of searchlights flicked back and forth, illuminating barrage-balloons and catching aircraft as they twisted. Occasionally one would be hit and go down in flames. In time I became skilled at identifying British and German types: without seeing them, I could pick out the cyclical drone of Dornier bomber engines, and the throaty, guttural roar of the Spitfires and Hurricanes which went storming to intercept them.

Our house was fitted with shutters made of wood and canvas, which we set in place every evening before we drew the curtains, to make sure that no chink of light was visible outside (Air Raid Patrol wardens had the power to fine householders heavily if they allowed the slightest gleam to show). Inside, our cellar was made into a shelter: a steel table was wedged up under the ceiling on posts, in case the rest of the house should collapse about it, and whenever it seemed that a serious air-raid was about to develop, we would be woken up and sent down there for the rest of the night. During the Battle of Britain, air activity was so intense that we slept in the cellar bunks anyway.

In the mornings, defying our mother's orders to stay under cover, and helped by our golden retriever Nell, we would rush out to search the fields for the fall-out of battle: pieces of shrapnel, empty cartridge cases, rounds of ammunition which had failed to fire. Gradually we assembled an immense collection of shredded metal, much of it the remains of anti-aircraft shells fired from batteries round Chatham, which used to clatter down on our roof all night.

The older Michael and I grew, the naughtier we became. We deliberately made life hell for the nannies whom our mother hired – for, as I myself had discovered even before Michael was old enough to be an accomplice in crime, it was easy enough to get rid of them: all I had to do was behave atrociously, and sooner or later they would pack their bags. One victim was the wretched Miss Mason – a thin, ascetic, middle-aged woman, and a bit of a tyrant – to whom we took an immediate dislike. Young as we were, we very soon hatched a plan. 'Ah, Miss Mason,' I said to her sweetly after lunch one day. 'Do let us take you for a walk and show you a bit of the local countryside.' Off we went, down winding lanes and across fields, aiming for some searchlight batteries a couple of miles away. When she had become thoroughly confused, we both took off, left and right, at a prearranged signal, ditching her in the middle of nowhere. Two hours later she struggled back to the house soaked, exhausted and exceedingly cross. To our delight she tendered her resignation immediately, and we never saw her again.

In this rout the one shining exception was a Scot called Christine Turnbull – a large, cuddly, maternal woman who won our hearts and developed a knack of keeping us more or less under control. At first she came to us for a limited period, before going home to her native Dumfriesshire; but we were so fond of her, and her effect on us was so beneficial, that my mother persuaded

her to return, and she became a lifelong friend, always ready to
help in moments of crisis.

The last letter my father wrote, to his parents, was dated 18 May
1941, and must have been posted in Alexandria. It could not
contain detail, for reasons of security, but it brought with it the
smell of the war at sea. His main complaint was about the lack
of family mail. 'It is now two months since I had any news of
you or Kitty,' he wrote:

> We had a pretty hectic time getting here. The enemy attacked
> us for two days and two nights by air. Torpedoes, mines,
> bombs. We shot down eighteen, I think. Pretty hot! That's
> about all I'm allowed to say . . . It's a foul and vile war, this,
> in every way. Those Huns have something to answer for. I sit
> in my Sick Bay during action and fume with rage, and desire
> to hear on the loudspeaker that welcome 'Got him! Down goes
> another one.'
>   I think of you a lot and long for news. Tell me how everyone
> is and where they are. I'm still an optimist and reckon this
> will end before so very long, by the collapse of Germany. Says
> me!
>   Lots and lots of love.
>   Yr loving son, Denis.

Before this letter reached its destination, my father was dead.
Years passed before I learned about the circumstances, and to
this day I am not sure exactly how he died; but I know enough
to be certain that he lost his life through doing his utmost to
save wounded members of his crew from the sick-bay.

HMS *Fiji* had been swept up in the battle for Crete. After
heavy bombing on the previous days, the Germans launched an
immense airborne attack on the island during the night of 20
May 1941. Because British air assets on Crete were minimal,
the Luftwaffe immediately won command of the skies, and
Allied ships were therefore at acute risk, particularly from dive-
bombers. On 22 May *Fiji* was south-east of Crete, steaming in
company with her fellow-cruiser *Gloucester* and the destroyers
Kingston and *Kandahar*, the group's task being to pick up survivors and give air cover.

The German airforce was rampant. During the day *Fiji* survived thirteen hours of continuous attacks: the Captain's secre-

tary, Midshipman Blockley, counted 370 bombs aimed at them, but by violent evasive action the ship avoided them all, until in the end her port side was opened up by near-misses, forcing her to slow down. Then in the evening she suffered a direct hit from a single German aircraft, and the crew abandoned ship just before she sank. The aftermath was vividly described in a letter written years later by Admiral Sir Gerald Gladstone, who in 1941 was on board her as a commander:

> Almost two-thirds of us survived. Some Marines set off swim-ming back to Crete, still in sight but I suppose over thirty miles away. The rest of us tried to gather on or around the various rafts. In the growing dusk it was soon fairly clear where most of us were by the bobbing lights. The Germans left us alone, luckily. All the same, many were disheartened, and I remem-ber seeing one of my pet leading hands drowning himself – well, we'd all had a bashing for two or three days.

The men in the water were mostly equipped with inflatable belts or life-jackets, and the sea was reasonably warm. After four hours, to their unbounded relief, they saw the dimmed naviga-tion lights of two destroyers coming to pick them up. The ships went from torch to torch, and in an hour had collected all the survivors. It was some time before members of *Fiji*'s crew could be sure who was alive, because they were divided between the rescuers; in the end it was established that 520 men had been saved and 244 lost (altogether, in four disastrous days the Royal Navy lost 2400 men).

Among these was my father. Admiral Gladstone reported that he was last seen in the water:

> I don't doubt that he was always trying in his gentle way to go to the help of some neighbouring swimmers in trouble. I'm sure he was pretty exhausted dealing with the wounded, before he even got into the water . . . He was a wholly reliable and respected doctor, and I daresay that his very deliberateness gave the confidence which a hasty man could not command.

That must remain his epitaph. But in the immediate aftermath of the disaster, my poor mother could not accept that he was dead. For weeks she tried to believe that he might have reached the coast of Crete, or an offshore island, and she clung to the hope that our cousin Doreen's husband Tom Dunbabin, who was serving with Special Operations Executive in Crete, might find him alive. When no news came, she must have been plunged into despair; yet she concealed her grief with heroic courage, and our lives carried on much as before.

Only when I grew up did I come to feel a deep sense of loss, mixed with pride at the way my father had conducted himself; and during my own service career his death became a positive advantage to me, in that whenever I had to comfort the family of a man who had been killed, I was able to speak from the heart, as one who had suffered just such a personal loss, rather than offer empty platitudes with no real feeling or understanding behind them.

My father had left instructions that in the event of his death my uncle Hugh Beak (always known as Bill) should become our official guardian. A former officer in the Tank Corps, he had married my father's sister Ruth, and retired in 1934 with the rank of Brevet Lieutenant-Colonel. When the Second World War broke out, he was too old for active service, and became Governor, successively, of the detention camps (known as 'glasshouses') at Sowerby Bridge and Hebden Bridge, both in Yorkshire. Later he was made Governor of Pentonville and Cardiff prisons, and he did indeed take an active hand in our upbringing. Since he and Ruth had two daughters, Daphne and Jennifer, but no sons, Michael and I fitted well into their family, and over the years they were exceedingly kind to us; but in 1941 they were far away in the north, and for the time being my mother was left on her own.

I realize now what efforts she must have made to look after us and keep us in order. To ensure that we had a healthy diet, she registered herself as a vegetarian, which meant that she got an extra ration of cheese and butter, all of which she gave to us. In a way this suited her, because she always took trouble to preserve her elegant figure, and ate as sparingly as possible; even so, at a time when almost every kind of food was scarce, it was a sacrifice for our benefit.

Much as Michael and I loved her, we behaved ever more atrociously. In spring we picked the daffodils growing in Mr Hinge's field and sold them for a shilling a bunch to house-holders in Borden Lane, on the outskirts of Sittingbourne.

(When he discovered what we were doing, he was furious, but lenient.) Worse, we would try to smoke his cigars, which his son Richard filched for us, even though they made us sick.

Some devil in us made us tease our mother most cruelly. Once I rode my bicycle into Sittingbourne, then rang home and in a put-on voice said that I had been hurt in an accident. My mother immediately telephoned the hospital and ambulance service, and became distraught with worry before she found out what I had done. For once she lost her temper and gave me a furious dressing-down, which made me feel small, mean and inconsiderate. Another shameful incident concerned the bottle of ammonia with which I used to kill butterflies destined for my collection. One day I held the bottle out to my mother and said, 'Here, have a whiff of that' – which she did, almost choking on a vicious blast of fumes.

Why did we behave so horribly? I can only imagine it was because we had no one to keep our natural instincts in check – no father present to suppress the thoughtless beastliness of small boys. I think in fact we were fairly normal and exuberant, and got up to so much mischief only because there was nobody to stop us. I suppose, also, that we were rather spoilt, because my mother was too kind to us. Certainly we resented any attempt to impose discipline on us: hence our efforts to dislodge the nannies. Whatever the reason, my mother had an unending struggle to maintain some sort of order among the chaos which Michael and I could not help creating.

The one time she really had us under control was at night, for after she had read to us, we were so worn out by our exertions that we instantly fell asleep. Yet the hours of darkness were anything but peaceful, for the air-war was raging overhead, and one night a fleeing German pilot unloaded a stick of ten bombs which straddled the village. One landed in front of the pub and by a million-to-one chance plummeted straight down the well outside the door, so that the main force of the explosion was contained. Several more fell in the daffodil field, and the blast brought down the ceiling in Michael's bedroom, dumping a load of dust and plaster on his cot. As he was dragged from the wreckage, he made a remark which – even though he had copied it from Nanny Turnbull – found its way into the local paper. 'I'll shoot the boots off that man Hitler!' he cried, and the phrase entered our family vocabulary: from that moment we threatened to shoot the boots off anyone who particularly annoyed us.

I imagine it was no small relief for my mother when the time came for me to go away to boarding school. While my father was alive, he had entered me for St Peter's Court, a preparatory school with a high reputation at Broadstairs, only a few miles from Borden. But on the outbreak of war the school had been evacuated to Devon, and so, when I set off by special train from Paddington, aged eight and a half, in the autumn of 1942, I faced a long journey into the unknown.

CHAPTER 2

RELUCTANTLY TO SCHOOL

1942–51

St Peter's Court had been founded in 1898 by A. J. Richardson, but the man who made the establishment famous was the Reverend Gerald Ridgeway, who joined the staff in its early days and then for many years was headmaster. Under his guidance St Peter's acquired a high reputation, reflected in the fact that it was chosen by the Royal Family for both Prince Henry, Duke of Gloucester, and Prince George, Duke of Kent. The school formed a special relationship with Harrow, and sent many boys there, although some went on to Eton.

In a moral sense Ridgeway was as upright as could be, and he had clearly been a first-class headmaster in his day. But by the time I knew him he was in his seventies, bent by arthritis, and had lost some of his grip. To the boys he was 'Bags' – a reference to the voluminous plus-fours which he favoured – or 'Old Man Ridgeway', to distinguish him from his son Charles, or Charlie, a rather ineffective bachelor who had spent his life in his father's shadow, and in due course took over from him as headmaster. The strongest character in the family was Mrs Ridgeway, known to us as 'Meejay' – a short, friendly, house-wifely woman, who directed the school's administration with tireless efficiency. Although so bossy that no one could argue with her, she was also kind: she addressed the boys as adults, and we loved her.

The Ridgeways' regime was rigidly old-fashioned. My allotted number was twelve (for obvious reasons, no boy was given the number thirteen). I do not remember feeling lonely or dismayed by the severity of the rules: I kept myself to myself, and got on as best I could with whatever task I was set. I had one minor physical problem in the form of warts on the backs of my hands, which led to my being called 'Warthog' or simply 'Wart'. This made me self-conscious, and probably increased the tendency, which I had anyway, to plough a lone furrow. Another factor which confirmed my solitary status was my refusal to take part in bullying, which was rife. I had no taste for gang-warfare, and abhorred the idea of several boys turning on one wretch who could not stick up for himself. In general I was happy with my own company, and made few friends.

One exception was Anthony Saxton, who became a close ally, both at school and at home. In retrospect, I can see that I had already begun subconsciously to follow a policy which has stood me in good stead all my life – to choose as friends, colleagues or subordinates people whose gifts make up for my own deficiencies. At school I saw that I was not particularly bright, and that Anthony was much cleverer. I admired his intellectual ability, and found him good fun to talk to; but I also realized instinctively that he would make a useful accomplice, able to reinforce me in the area where I was weakest. Although I did not know it at the time, he too was a bit of a loner, and glad of a new companion. So for a few years we became almost as close as brothers.

If I remember little of my time at St Peter's, it is because other recollections have been obliterated by the most traumatic event of my schooldays – the fire which destroyed Shobrooke Park in the early hours of 23 January 1945, when I was still only ten years old. The spring term had scarcely begun when I was woken one night, about 0300, by strange clinking and crackling sounds. Slipping out of bed, I felt my way through the darkness of our dormitory, which was on the first floor. As I opened the door, the noises suddenly became louder, and I smelt smoke; but instead of raising the alarm, I thought, 'I want nothing to do with this,' and scuttled back to bed, curling up under my blankets with the instinctive, animal reaction of a small child who hopes that the trouble, whatever it is, will go away.

Moments later the door burst open. In rushed Charles Ridgeway shouting, 'The house is on fire! We can't get down the stairs. Everybody on to the balcony – quick as you can! Take a sheet each.'

Except for the master's torch, the room was pitch-dark. Some boys grabbed dressing-gowns before they struggled out through the window. The rest of us went as we were, in our pyjamas. Three dormitories gave on to the same balcony, and soon forty-odd boys were huddled there, shivering in the icy air. Way below us, the ground showed white, for it was covered with six inches of snow, but we were twenty feet above it, too high to jump safely.

In this crisis Charlie remained commendably calm. Under his direction we tore sheets into strips and knotted them together; then, one at a time, he helped boys over the stone balustrade and on to the makeshift ropes. He had to encourage and guide them individually, for some were so terrified that they could hardly move. Besides, there was another hazard, which he had not foreseen: the sheets were so old that the strips kept tearing through. As every third or fourth boy went over the edge, there would come a yell, followed by a dull thud – and another rope was needed.

All this took time, and with every second the fire was gaining. The clinking noise which I had heard came from the panes of the curved glass dome above the main hall and staircase: the glass was cracking and bursting with the heat. As we waited on the balcony, the sound of the blaze rose from a muted crackling to a roar, and suddenly the whole dome, with its little bell cupola above it, collapsed downwards into the well of the stairs, sending a fantastic eruption of sparks into the sky. Closer at hand, I was astonished to see flames burst into our dormitory and sweep forward across the room: Charlie had closed the door against them, but it offered no defence. Once into the room, the fire devoured everything and began licking the shutters, which we had closed as last-ditch protection.

At first I was not particularly frightened. There was an element of adventure in what was happening: the fire was exciting, and we lacked the imagination to see that a catastrophe was over-taking the school. I myself was distracted by a private anxiety. In the face of strong opposition from my mother, I had brought back to school with me an old and valuable album of stamps collected by my grandfather, containing Penny Blacks, Two-penny Blues, and other rare specimens. My aim had been to impress fellow-pupils, but Bags, seeing how valuable the collection was, had sensibly insisted on locking it away in his study. Now, as I shivered on the balcony, I wondered miserably what was happening to it.

As the fire took a grip of the old building, boys started screaming, and the full horror of it began to sink in. Elsewhere, others were in worse trouble than us. High on the second floor several of the staff were trapped in their rooms. So was Peter Gibbs, cut off with two other boys in a small dormitory. All these people had no option but to jump down on to the flat roof of the kitchen, and thence to the ground. So long were the drops that Peter chipped both ankles and impacted several vertebrae, but shock rendered him numb, and for the time being he felt no pain.

Anthony Saxton was in a dormitory on the first floor, but had no master to direct the evacuation. The captain of the dormitory took charge, and although only eleven, did extremely well. When he opened the door, he walked into a wall of fire coming up the stairwell, so he ordered his boys on to the balcony and told them to throw their mattresses down first, so that if they fell, or had to jump, the impact would be broken. They too made ropes of their bedclothes; but because the blankets were thicker than the sheets, they used them for preference, not realizing that the ancient material was rotten. Anthony, who was heavy for his age, slid down safely as far as the first knot, but then the rope broke and he crashed to the ground. Unscathed, but in a state of shock, he wandered about in pyjamas and bare feet, not feeling the cold.

Richard Mercer, one year older than me, had been asleep in the old servants' wing at the back of the house. His dormitory, also, awoke to find its exit blocked, and when the eight boys tried to escape through the windows, they had to force apart the iron bars put there to confine Victorian domestics to their quarters. The jump from those windows was lower, and they managed it successfully except for a boy called Preston, who impaled his throat on an iron spike and had to be lifted off, pouring blood, but not seriously injured. Richard witnessed the collapse of the main dome; and the sight of boys on the balconies, silhouetted against the flames, has remained with him ever since. As he came back to the servants' wing after a quick reconnaissance, the door flew open, and out ran his friend Peter Charlesworth, on fire from head to foot. Two or three of them smothered the flames, and they carried the boy, by then unconscious, into one of the greenhouses. He was still alive when they laid him down, but he died later that morning. Peter Gibbs remains haunted to this day by the dreadful sight of a boy, whom he had known well, with no hair or eyebrows.

When my own turn had come to go down the sheets, I somehow managed the descent. Perhaps because I was small and light, I reached the ground safely, without the rope parting. Meanwhile – though none of us knew it – an eleven-year-old called Peter McClintock had made an heroic dash to summon the fire brigade. Guessing that the telephone line must have been burnt through, he paused only to pull on a pair of Wellingtons, which he grabbed from an outhouse, and ran into Crediton to alert the volunteer firemen in their station on the outskirts of the town.

Ironically enough, the only reason Peter knew his way to the fire station was that, two days earlier, he had tried to abscond. The son of a Canadian mother, he had grown used to Canadian schools, hated St Peter's, and on the first full day of term had made a bolt for the railway station, only to be detained as he was about to board a train for London. Now he turned his illicitly gained knowledge to advantage, and rode back on the fire-engine. By the time it arrived, however, the house was beyond salvation. He remembered seeing the whole building 'incredibly ablaze from end to end', and the firefighters could make no impression on the flames.

My memories of the rest of the night are hazy. We stumbled about in the snow, half dazed, but not feeling the cold, until members of the staff began to marshal us, some into the greenhouses, and some into the lodge, which stood beside the drive. Three boys – Charles Gurdon, Charles Sheffield, and Peter Charlesworth – and one of the matrons – Evelyn Bell – had been killed, and although many were injured, in retrospect it seems extraordinary that the death-toll was not higher. All of us had lost everything except what we stood up in. My irreplace-able stamp album was only one of a thousand casualties. Later in the morning we were taken down to the Grammar School in Crediton, whose own boys were sent home to make room for us, and ladies of the Women's Voluntary Service, who had been working in Plymouth during the air-raids on the docks, came up bringing us clothes. These thrilled us, for they had been contributed by Americans, and included bright check lumberjack shirts and the first blue jeans we had ever seen.

From the Grammar School the Ridgeways sent out telegrams to the parents of every survivor:

> SERIOUS FIRE IN SCHOOL LAST NIGHT STOP YOUR BOY SAFE STOP PLEASE FETCH HIM AND BRING CLOTHES STOP

For those who survived, that night will never be forgotten. As soon as our own children were old enough, we put them through fire-drills at home, making sure they knew how to leave the house in an emergency. When we began to look at schools for them, our first questions were about fire rules and evacuation procedures. Even now, almost half a century later, whenever I check into a hotel, my first action is to reconnoitre escape routes.

The house was burnt to the ground: apart from the chimneys, little was left of the main block, and only in recent years has it been replaced by a modern structure on the same site. At the inquest, held in Crediton, a good deal was made of the fact that fire precautions and drills had been minimal, but no censure was passed on the Headmaster, and the verdict returned on the casualties was one of misadventure. Parents, far from blaming the school's owners for the tragedy, sent letters of sympathy and substantial cheques, to help replace the books and equipment which had been lost. Among the benefactors was Queen Mary, then the Queen Mother, who was fond of the school and replen-ished the library with many volumes. (At Wellesley House, which later took over St Peter's Court, some of the books bear her name to this day.)

The immediate result of the fire was that, for the rest of that term, St Peter's closed down. With the annual School Notes – a report on the previous year – the Ridgeways sent out a stricken notice listing the names of the four people killed and the message:

> As heavy a blow as can be imagined has fallen on the school and on us. Our sympathy goes out to all those who have lost dear ones in this tragedy. Their deaths leave us ourselves with a memory which can never be effaced. We can only be thankful to God that the loss of life was not much greater, as seemed almost certain when we awoke to find the house ablaze from end to end.

For the summer term St Peter's reassembled at another large country house near Bideford, and then in the autumn – the war having ended – it returned to its original quarters in Broadstairs.

The school's records confirm that I was an undistinguished pupil, winning few laurels either in class or at games. My sole claim to fame is that, at the age of eleven, in company with Anthony, I led a rebellion against one of the masters, a man called Tristram Yelin who joined the staff to teach French in the autumn of 1945.

Our complaint against him was that he threw books at us, threatened us and generally bullied us. I suppose, looking back, that he had just returned from the war, and that to someone who had been in action such minor violence seemed perfectly permissible. To us it was something new and unacceptable: we were not used to being treated in that way, and it frightened us. In self-defence, Anthony and I drew up a petition saying that unless Mr Yelin was promptly sacked, we, the undersigned, would withdraw our cooperation by locking ourselves in the lavatories and remaining there indefinitely. An encouraging number of boys signed our document, and, shaking with apprehension, we took it along to the Headmaster's study.

Never had the passage seemed so long, never the door of the study so far away. We knocked and crept in. Old Man Ridgeway read the petition, looked as though he was about to explode, and sent us away with hardly a word. Later, we heard that he was fearfully shocked by the fact that we had been driven to such an extreme step. Nothing like it had ever been known in the school before. I believe, now, that he wanted to expel us, and would have done so, had we not been saved by the intervention of Meejay. The incident closed without recrimination, but it instantly transformed the behaviour of Mr Yelin, who ceased to throw books and became tremendously nice. In retrospect, I think we were lucky not to pay the penalty for what was at the very least an act of gross insubordination.

From my earliest days in the school, something made me fight against discipline. I wanted to be independent and lead my own life, rather than do what I was told. Inwardly and outwardly, I battled against the pressure and the general need to conform. When someone detailed me to go and play rugby, I resented it bitterly, and took a pathological dislike to the game, which has remained with me ever since.

As I grew older, I gradually became aware that an engaging strain of eccentricity ran in my de Labillière ancestors. A large and ancient Huguenot family, with a tradition of military service, they had come over from France after the revocation of the Edict of Nantes, in 1685, and established themselves mainly in Ireland. In many of them religious faith still burned strongly: according to my cousin Doreen, her grandfather Francis Peter was 'always looking for the Pope under the bed'. My own grandfather Edgar, as I have said, became Vicar of Llangattock, and in 1937 my great uncle Paul was appointed Dean of Westminster – the climax of a successful career in which he had served as Chaplain of both Wadham and Merton (his own college) at Oxford, then during the First World War as Chaplain to the Egyptian Expeditionary Force, and later as Suffragan Bishop of Knaresborough and Archdeacon of Leeds.

One notable eccentric was my namesake, Major Peter Labellière, who died in 1800 at the age of seventy-five. A tall, slender man, who had fought with distinction in the American War of Independence, he returned to England and fell in love – so the story goes – with Hetty Fletcher, daughter of a country parson in Cornwall. When she chose someone else, he travelled in high dudgeon to Surrey and took lodgings at an inn at the foot of Box Hill, where he remained for the rest of his life, going for immensely long walks and becoming ever more reclusive. On 6 September 1799 he returned to base with the news that on the summit of Box Hill he had met the Devil – a tall, well-dressed fellow – who said that he would come back to collect the Major's soul at 4 p.m. on a Friday, in seven months' time. Nobody at the inn paid much attention to this prophecy, but sure enough, at 4 p.m. on 7 June 1800, he died suddenly of a heart attack, and had himself buried in a vertical attitude – head down, feet up – on the summit of his favourite hill. Some said that he arranged this as a protest, to demonstrate that he had been at odds with the world; others reckoned he had an eye on Judgement Day, believing that, when the earth finally rolled over, he would pop straight out the other side. Whatever his motives, a carved stone at the top of Box Hill commemorates him to this day.

My father's generation had eccentrics of its own, not least his brother Cyril, who joined the Fleet Air Arm during the Second World War, then became a mining engineer and went prospecting in East Africa, where he claimed to have discovered a gold mine, but disappeared – murdered (we suspected) by rivals. His body was never found. His sister Madie was another strong character, as impossible as she was good-looking, a frustrated spinster whose fiancé had been killed in the First World War.

On the Lawley side, she was matched by my Aunt Joyce, who also lost a fiancé (or possibly two) in the Great War and remained a spinster ever after. A large and bossy woman, with a gift for creating unrest within the family, Joyce had never been close to her sister, and when Kitty married an attractive naval officer, and produced two obstreperous sons, she became embittered by jealousy. Even when my mother suffered severe setbacks, such as the death of my father, Joyce continued to regard her with implacable envy.

At home during the holidays, I now often had Anthony as a partner in crime, and we launched eagerly into all sorts of minor felonies. Somehow we gained access to Farmer Hinge's store of shotgun cartridges, and amused ourselves by cutting them open and pouring the gunpowder into piles, which, when lit with a match, produced satisfactory flare-ups. We also conducted chemical experiments in a disused outside lavatory, mixing different substances together and setting fire to them. One day we burnt a large quantity of sulphur, and were nearly asphyxiated

by the fumes: considering that we had no idea what we were
doing, we were lucky not to suffer serious injury.

When I developed a passion for films, we discovered the art
of lurking outside the rear exit of the cinema in Sittingbourne
until someone came out, and then, while the door was open,
nipping in without a ticket. At Homestead we would smoke
cigarettes in our hideaway – a garden shed, into which we had
to climb – or out in the middle of a beanfield, and then scrub
our faces in Nell the retriever's coat, so that her smell would
cover us. Our attempts at secrecy were amateurish, and one day
we were spotted in the field by Nanny Turnbull, who was sensible enough not to create a fuss, but succeeded in making us
feel foolish, so that half the fun of smoking evaporated. Nevertheless, we carried on.

Anthony's presence brought about a change in my attitude
to Michael, my brother. The fact that he was three and a half
years younger seemed to put him in a different class; now that
I had a colleague my own age, I saw Michael no longer as an
accomplice, but as a tiresome hanger-on, always trying to edge
in on our grown-up pastimes. In one typically callous episode
we encouraged him to walk about in the loft. Anthony and I
knew perfectly well that one had to keep to joists, and not step
on the plaster in between; but we told Michael he could tread
anywhere – and very soon not just a foot, but the whole of him,
came crashing through the ceiling in a blizzard of crumbled
plaster, high over a dangerous drop down the back stairwell.
Luckily he grabbed a joist and hung there like a small ape, swing-
ing gently in a cloud of dust; but the incident gave him a fright.
(I am glad to say that this phase lasted only a short time, and
that as we grew older, we again became close – which we have
remained ever since.)

I always looked forward eagerly to the holidays, since home
meant glorious freedom from effort and discipline. Once Michael
and I were sent to stay with the Beaks in Yorkshire, and
occasionally we went to my Lawley grandmother, who lived
with Aunt Joyce at Old Place, at Aldwick, near Bognor Regis.
(This large and beautiful house was partly Elizabethan, but most
of it had been built in the early years of this century with
materials salvaged from other ancient buildings.)

Wherever we went, our reputation as juvenile hooligans preceded us, and at one house after another hatches were battened
down in advance to minimize the damage which we could cause.
At Old Place, I once had such a row with Aunt Joyce that I went
home in a rage. She asked me to take some eggs round to a
neighbour about a mile and a half away, and when I announced
my intention of going by bicycle, she forbade it, saying that the
eggs would certainly be smashed. So obdurate was she that in
the end I could not be bothered to argue with her any more,
and just said, 'Right, then. I'm going home' – whereupon I
packed my suitcase, walked down to the station and caught the
next train back to Kent.

At home, all too soon, a new and by no means welcome
element entered my life. Returning to The Homestead one day,
I found a strange man in the house.

I am sure that nobody blamed my mother for forming a new
alliance. Far from it: she was still in her mid-thirties, lively and
attractive. Clearly she needed love, companionship, and above
all help in bringing up her two unruly sons. Yet her choice of
man, which she made on the rebound from my father's death,
quickly proved disastrous.

Major Maurice Bennetts was twelve years her senior – a stout,
middle-aged man with thinning hair, who was then serving in
the RAF Regiment. Obviously he and my mother were in love
at first: they were married at a quiet wedding in Borden Parish
Church early in 1943, and our half-brother David was born in
July the following year. Yet Michael and I took against Maurice
from the start, and never came to like him. At first we resented
him for the very reason that we had resented all the nannies –
because he diverted our mother's attention away from us. In
our view, he was encroaching on our preserves and upsetting
the balance of life which we had arranged for ourselves. Also,
he tried to introduce some discipline – and although our mother
undoubtedly hoped he would restore a normal balance to the
family, for our benefit, it was his attempts to impose order which
annoyed us most of all. A man of greater tact might have managed to win us round, but his method was to shout and bully,
with the result that our relations degenerated from bad to worse.
After the war, when the family moved to Shropshire, Michael

and I went so far as to build ourselves a shack out of packing cases in the garden, so that we could live in that, rather than in the house, whenever Maurice came home.

Fortunately he was often away on military duty, and we had plenty of time without him. When David was born, we at first felt jealous of the way in which the new baby commanded everyone's attention, and constantly had to be pushed about in a pram; but when we realized that nannies did much of the work, and so freed our mother to give us more of her time, our attitude to them at last softened.

At St Peter's I worked my way laboriously up through the school, still making little impression. In my last two years I scraped into the first rugby XV as a forward. I enjoyed boxing, but found cricket plain boring – unless I could be wicketkeeper, and so be guaranteed continuous action throughout one of the innings. In a brief moment of glory I won the Throwing the Cricket Ball trophy with a throw of fifty-seven feet six inches – though this was due more to brute force than to skill. I also enjoyed swimming, but as the pool was unheated, and we were not allowed in until the water had reached a certain temperature, the season was always short.

As my time at St Peter's came to an end, I looked forward to moving on to Harrow, which I thought would give me greater freedom. My mother was scandalized by the fees – £95 a term – and had some difficulty paying them; but in the autumn of 1947 I found myself in The Grove, a large Georgian house at the top of Harrow Hill, next to St Mary's Church, and flanked on its lower side by an extensive wood. My housemaster was the Reverend Lance Gorse (inevitably known to the boys as 'Prickle'), a bachelor scientist and cleric who worked hard to get to know every boy by coming round to our studies and chatting to us in the evenings. Our accommodation was spartan but adequate. For the first two years I shared a study with one other boy, and on winter evenings we took it in turns to light our coal fire – a tiresome but necessary chore, for the house had no central heating, and without a fire, we froze.

I am sorry to say that I took my prejudices with me: a loathing of organized games, and a deliberate intention to do no more work than was absolutely necessary. I was never unhappy, but still I resented authority, and devoted much time and energy to bending or breaking the school rules. I also discovered legitimate activities which I enjoyed, among them squash and rackets. In the summer I earned useful sports points by diving at Ducker, the school's open-air swimming pool, which was then the largest in the country (it has now been filled in and the land has been sold). Diving off the top board won highest points, and was thought very daring, but it held no terrors for me.

My favourite occupation, however, was shooting, which I had begun on a .22 range at prep school. At Harrow all boys had to join the Corps – the Combined Cadet Force. I found the drill very dull, and was not much interested in crawling about the countryside on field days; but I did like the shooting, and soon became proficient at it. The school had a twenty-five-yard range in a hut on the side of the Hill, run by two ex-sergeant-majors, Messrs Moore and Dukes, and there any boy who showed promise could blaze away with old .303 rifles rebarrelled to fire .22 bullets. For full-bore shooting, there were expeditions in summer to Bisley, where we shot on the ranges with Lee-Enfield .303s. With patient coaching from Mr Moore, I improved enough to become a member of the school VIII at the age of only fifteen – and the former sergeant-major also taught me one of the most valuable lessons of my life.

Always an enthusiast, he would praise boys lavishly even if they had not really distinguished themselves; listening to him, I realized that if someone in authority wants people to perform well, praise is more valuable and effective than chastisement – and so I learnt one of the basic principles of leadership.[1]

Much as I enjoyed shooting, its greatest value, in my view, lay in the fact that it was accepted as an alternative to games. So, too, was work on the school farm – an island of open fields miraculously preserved in the middle of endless suburbia. The farm was run by one of the masters, Sidney Patterson, an Irishman and a bachelor who had been at Harrow most of his adult life, but had had agricultural training. It was really an

1. Mr Moore had continuous difficulty with my name, and used to pronounce it – more or less – 'Billiong'. Later, in the Special Air Service, I was called exactly that, because the word was Malay for the small axe much prized by the aborigines.

educational enterprise, and must have been heavily subsidized; but the herd of Friesian cows produced milk for the school every morning – as it does to this day - and there was plenty of hard labour to be done, so that visits to the farm were no sinecure. Whenever our names came up on the milking roster, we had to get up at 5.15 a.m. and be ready waiting in the street for the grey van which collected us. If we missed it, we had a fifteen-minute walk, down off the Hill. Once at the farm, we would wash the cows' udders and operate the milking plant; we also learned to milk by hand, and all volunteers were taught to drive the tractor, so that they could plough, harrow, drill and so on. Back in our house by breakfast time, we would face a full day's school work.

This agricultural work fitted in well with developments at home. Not long after I had gone to Harrow, my mother suddenly announced that she had bought a house near Shrewsbury, in the wilds of Shropshire. Park House was (and is) a plain but friendly farmhouse made of dark-red brick, standing behind low white railings beside a lane, and it suited Michael and myself ideally. The house, which cost £4500, was old fashioned and unmodernized, with primitive plumbing and no central heating; our water came up by hand-pump from a well, and whenever I was at home, it was my job to start the villainous old diesel generator which thudded away in an outhouse to produce our electricity. Cranking it into life was a frightful chore, which might take twenty minutes of hard work before the engine would fire. Yet such minor deficiencies were of no consequence to adventurous boys. More to the point for us was the fact that the house had a field of its own and was surrounded by open country: more fields sloped away at the back, and in front, across the lane, there was a large wood. Another asset was the collection of stables and outbuildings round the old farmyard, with a granary above one of them. Here I began to establish a small-holding, with free-range chickens and pigs – for post-war rationing was still in force, and home-grown meat was invaluable.

Michael became infatuated with horses: he acquired a black pony called Darkie, and during school holidays was constantly on its back. Darkie was one of the meanest characters imaginable. Not only did he throw me at the first fence in the one and only gymkhana in which I took part, he also delighted in chasing children, and several times forced our cousin Daphne to take refuge in apple trees. I, hating horses, developed into a mustard-keen shot, endlessly prowling the fields and the wood in pursuit of rabbits, some of which we ate, and some of which I sold in the village shop at 2s 6d apiece. Whenever I went away to school, the confidence of the rabbits would build up, and for the first couple of days after my return they would sit about like ninepins, offering easy targets; then word would spread, and the survivors soon became wild and wily again.

At first I was armed with a .22 air rifle, but then one famous day my mother took me to the gunsmiths in Shrewsbury and together we chose a single-barrelled .410 shotgun, which became my most prized possession. Under instruction from our gardener, Denis Jones, I also learnt to keep and handle ferrets – how to grab them firmly round the neck and shoulders from behind, before they could sink their teeth into my hand, and how to scoop them up when they reappeared above ground, before they could turn and vanish again. Together with Denis I would take them out in a bag to the warrens which surrounded us and become absorbed in working them.

The big wood across the lane, which was part of the Condover Hall Estate, presented an irresistible challenge, and around its fringes we skirmished with Mr Bell, the gamekeeper, who lived in a cottage close by. With his tall, spare figure, his baggy plus-fours and trilby hat, he looked an archetypal keeper, and he was forever threatening to give us young varmints a good hiding if he caught us poaching on his preserves. I once had a narrow shave when, having flukily killed two partridges with one shot in a field of roots, I was on my way to pick them up when I saw him approaching. Feigning innocence, I said I had missed a rabbit, and although I do not think he believed me, he let me off.

I like to think that by the time I was fourteen I had begun to show some sense of responsibility; and perhaps a faint sign of that emerged in another feature of our life in Shropshire – the week of boys' cricket matches which our neighbours the Corbetts organized every summer. Tim Corbett, my contemporary, became a good friend, even though he had the misfortune to be sent to Eton; and it was his father, Colonel Corbett, who laid the matches on. Boys in the neighbourhood would ask friends to stay, and bring in one or two locals to raise our numbers to twenty-two. Then a succession of captains would pick up teams, and a match would be played each day on a ground in the area – at Shrewsbury School, Shrewsbury Town, or sometimes at private houses like that of the Motleys at Much Wenlock. It may seem odd that someone who until then had found cricket a bore should have enjoyed these games so much; but I did, chiefly, I think, because one year I was called upon to organize a couple of the matches. Finalizing the teams, making sure everyone went to the right place on time, and captaining one of the sides, I learnt some of my first lessons in the art of managing other people.

Another family of whom we saw a great deal were the Nicholases, who lived in the village of Ryton, a mile away, and whose son Rupert was the same age as Michael. He too was mad about horses: he and Michael drove little carts furiously about the lanes with their heads below the level of the body-work, so that motorists would be startled by the sight of apparently driverless chariots hurtling towards them. Rupert's mother, known to us as 'Ma Nic', became a devoted friend of my mother.

By now Michael and I had grown close together again, and it was David whom we regarded as a tiresome interloper. Michael, emerging as the practical joker of the family, once devised a stratagem for keeping David out of our hair. We once put a rug on the kitchen table and told him it was a magic carpet, which would transport him to any place he wanted to visit: all he had to do was sit on it cross-legged, keep quiet, and wish – where-upon he would be whizzed through the sky to his chosen desti-nation. There he sat, wishing and wishing, while Michael and I rolled on the floor with delight in another room.

If I was wild, Michael was a good deal wilder. Once early in the war when we both went to lunch with our Great Uncle Paul in the Deanery at Westminster, and were supposed to be on our best behaviour, he had dived under the table, announced that he was a bear, and refused to come out. Later, in an attempt to defer his return to Harrow, he carpeted the lane approaching our house with broken milk bottles, in the hope that he would incapacitate the taxi summoned to take him to the station (to his rage, the car somehow arrived unharmed). Later again, he caused an eruption at Harrow when the matron who unpacked his clothes at the start of a term found his suitcase loaded with miniatures of whisky, vodka, Grand Marnier and other liqueurs. Then, and on several other occasions, our guardian Bill Beak had to make a rapid visit to the school for a parley with Lance Gorse: without his interventions, Michael's school career would have come to a premature end.

As I grew older, I gradually saw my mother more clearly. She had a wonderful knack of creating fun, which not only made us, her children, love her, but also enchanted our contemporaries. We all looked up to her, admired her and would do anything for her. My memories of life at Park House are of warm happiness and fulfilment. Although she had been brought up in large houses full of servants, she had adapted to simpler forms of country life with admirable resilience. She was a first-rate cook, and saw to it that we always had plenty of good, plain food; she also insisted that we pull our weight in tackling household chores, and our communal washing-up sessions, held in the scullery off the back hall, became part of the fabric of life.

Not only to me, but to my friends, she seemed exceptionally attractive and smart. Once after she had visited me at Harrow I was immensely proud when another boy asked who my girl-friend was; and at home she had an extraordinary ability to appear perfectly turned out, whatever she was doing: she could feed the pigs and clean out the ferrets, and still look as though she was about to set off for Ascot or Henley. In the local com-munity, she became a pillar of organizations such as the Women's Institute and the Women's Voluntary Service.

Alas, her relationship with Maurice had soon turned sour. At the time I was too young to discern what was happening; but later I discovered that even before I had gone to Harrow his affection for her had cooled, and he had begun to spend her money in alarming quantities. We had barely settled in to Park House when things reached crisis pitch. One day when Richard and Miney Wells (the former Miney Edmonds) were staying with us, they ordered him out of the house. My mother had already been trying to get rid of him: now he went, and that was the last we saw of him. I am sure that his disappearance was a relief to her; but to her severe embarrassment, she had to publish a notice in the local newspaper disclaiming responsibility for his debts, and her own finances had been badly eroded by his excesses.[1]

At Harrow, as I moved up the school and became a Thirder, or third-year boy, gaining a study for myself, I branched out into new activities. I adored jazz, and longed to become a member of the school band; but I was never very musical, and had already given up trying to play the violin which my mother had at home. Now I changed to the trumpet, and when that too proved a disaster – more noise than tune – I switched to the trombone and finally to the drums, before I caved in and admitted that music and I were not really compatible. As an extra subject I took classes in navigation, which was taught by one of the housemasters, George McConnell, a former sailor.

Meanwhile, breaking bounds, and breaking rules of all sorts, became an ever-greater challenge. Yet my objective always was not merely to commit minor felonies, but to do so without being detected: not only to beat the system, but also to get away with it. The escapades were never off-the-cuff, last-minute ideas: on the contrary, they were well planned and thought out in advance.

A good deal of mischief could be committed inside The Grove. A trap-door in the ceiling of the room allotted to Robin Pease, a friend, gave access to an attic, where a gang of us could smoke without fear of the smell betraying us. Up in the loft we found the house's cold-water tank, and one day we tied up the ball-cock, so that the supply was interrupted. Only after prolonged investigations had been conducted at ground level did we nip up and remove our tourniquet, just before the official search proceeded to the attic.

Boys were not normally allowed off the Hill, and because we wore a uniform of dark-blue jackets (known as 'Bluers') and grey flannel trousers, we were immediately conspicuous. When

1. Not long after this, he died in a tragic accident.

we wanted to visit the town, we would smuggle sports jackets out of the house, whip off our Bluers at some strategic point, secrete them in the bushes, and proceed in partial disguise. For anyone like myself who enjoyed making illegal visits to Harrow Town, The Grove was exceptionally well placed. Indeed, for a budding specialist in guerrilla warfare, its position was ideal, since the wood came almost up to the building on the lower side, and in a couple of seconds I could disappear into the trees, which gave good cover for the first and most dangerous stretch of the journey. Coming back, I could hover on the edge of the wood until I had made sure the coast was clear.

Soon, however, daylight manoeuvres began to pall, and I con-ceived the idea of prowling the streets at night. To escape from The Grove itself took some planning, for I had to leave a dummy in my bed, evade the monitors, who might be moving round the house until quite late at night, and slip out through the window of some helpful acquaintance, before creeping over a flat roof and down a fire-escape. Luckily Harrow is full of gar-dens, shrubberies, driveways and lanes, many of which run steeply up and down hill, so that a nocturnal rambler has plenty of hideouts into which he can dive if trouble threatens; never-theless, I always took care to think out escape routes and plan them in advance.

As my thirst for courting trouble increased, I began making excursions to London, sometimes on my own, sometimes with a couple of friends. These trips were extremely dangerous – to have been caught would have meant instant expulsion – but that was what made them worthwhile. Having planned our routes and timings in detail, we would climb out of the house wearing sports jackets and flannels, hurry down to Harrow-on-the-Hill, the nearest tube station, and after a quick reconnais-sance to make sure there was no member of staff on the platform or in the carriage, nip aboard the last train to London.

Once we had arrived in the metropolis, we had several hours to fill in, as the first train back in the morning did not run until 0500. On one memorable occasion three of us – Richard Mercer, myself and one other – had seats in the front row at the Windmill Theatre, which in those days was the height of salacity (patrons scrambled furiously forward into any good seats vacated, so as to position themselves closer to the nudes on stage). But usually we just wandered around in the Piccadilly area, window-shopping in Regent Street or Bond Street, for we had practically no money, and no idea what to do. One night we were loitering in a doorway when two policemen appeared and asked what we were up to. Not satisfied with our answers, they took us off to their station for questioning. It seemed to me that telling lies would land us in even worse trouble, so I admitted to the sergeant that we were on the run from Harrow; if he reported us to the school authorities, I said, we would certainly be sacked – so could he please forget that he had seen us? In a moment of inspiration I quoted the punch-line from a song popular at the time – 'Life gets tedious, don't it?' – and this seemed to disarm him. The incident closed with us being given a meal and a cup of tea – a bonus of which we were extremely glad, as it was by then 0330.

Gradually I came to feel that these trips to London were rather pointless, and not worth the risk involved. But then one night, as I slunk along Church Hill in Harrow, dodging from the mouth of one alleyway to the next, I noticed something which had escaped my attention before. At the back of the Old Schools – one of the original buildings, dating in part from 1615 – lay an expanse of lawn. Between the back of the Old Schools and the retaining wall across the end of the garden there was a gap about two feet wide, running away into the hillside at right angles to the street. Although this gap was closed by a cross-wall along the pavement, I spotted a small opening in it, two feet high by one wide, some four feet off the ground. A man's body would not have fitted through the aperture, but I was small and slim.

In a flash I had jumped up and wriggled through the gap. I found myself in a tunnel with an arched brick roof, separating the Old Schools from the garden. Suddenly my adrenalin ran faster. In the wall of the school building was another small opening, blocked by an iron grille. Inside the building, I knew, was the Armoury, where all the Corps rifles were kept. This second opening appeared to lead straight into the Armoury. If only the grille were loose . . .

It was. In a second I had lifted it clear and was wriggling through the aperture. Sure enough, I was in the heart of the

Armoury. I did not switch on a light, for fear that it would be seen from outside; but my torch revealed racks of rifles, standing there unprotected. Because the place was considered as secure as Fort Knox, none of the weapons was locked up. I was immensely excited by my discovery, even if, for the moment, I could not see a way of exploiting it; and after some exploration of the premises I slipped out again, replacing the iron grille behind me.

So taken was I by my breakthrough that over the next couple of weeks I enticed one or two friends into the Armoury with me, among them Henry Blosse-Lynch, who had also been at St Peter's. But I told nobody that I had conceived an ambitious plan. Whenever we had a shooting practice on the .22 range, control of ammunition was slack, and I found it easy enough to carry off a few spare bullets each time. I had already amassed a stock of these, and used to amuse myself by dropping into a boy's room for an apparently casual visit in the evening, surreptitiously scattering a few bullets on to his coal fire, and then taking my leave; a few minutes later, sudden explosions would shower red-hot coal all over his floor.

Now I had a better use for this smuggled ammunition. On a night when a good wind was blowing, I again infiltrated the Armoury, and this time brought a rifle out with me. My purpose was strictly experimental; the expedition was a trial run for a prank which I planned to play at the end of term. For the test run, I selected the room of a boy called David Cazdagli, which was in easy range of the wood below The Grove. By the time I reached the safety of the trees, his light had gone off, and I presumed that he was already in bed; so I took aim and fired a bullet upwards through one of the highest panes.

The crack of the rifle was partially covered by the wind, but to my ears it sounded dangerously loud, and I waited with some anxiety to see what reaction it would produce. Nothing happened. Nobody appeared in the street, and no light came on in the room – not even the flickering beam of a torch. It seemed that Cazdagli was either asleep or terror-stricken and lying low. Disappointed, I wriggled back into the Armoury and returned the weapon to its place in the rack.

Next day a visit to my victim's room, made on some apparently innocent pretext, revealed that the bullet had gone straight through the pane and left only a small hole in the glass before burying itself in the ceiling. Cazdagli had heard nothing, and could not imagine how the damage had occurred. No matter: I saw that my plan was feasible.

On the last night of that term I was abroad again. By then it had become a formality to penetrate the Armoury's defences, and I was soon out on the street armed with a rifle. This time, as my target, I chose a lighted window on the second floor of Rendalls, a house on the lower side of the main road. That night, I knew, Sixth Formers would be having semi-legal parties, tacitly sanctioned by their housemaster; but I also knew that the room I had chosen did not belong to a Sixth Former, and that the party going on in it was definitely illegal. Because the boys had not bothered to draw the curtains, the ceiling light was in view from below.

Having checked my escape routes, I rested the rifle on the railings of the teaching block and took a couple of pot shots. For some reason I missed the bulb, but the revellers, realizing they were under fire, snapped off the light. What I could not know immediately was that they rushed to tell the housemaster that somebody was sniping at them. For a few minutes I withdrew into the wood, feeling rather pleased with myself, and then was foolish enough to return to the scene of the crime for a check on what was happening. Just as I did so, the school clock struck midnight, and to my horror I saw a police car drive up and stop only twenty yards away, with its radio burbling. I hung about no longer, but fled back to the Armoury as fast as safety permitted.

Next day the school broke up for the holidays. I believe that the housemaster, George McConnell, had some inkling of who the invisible gunman might be; but the authorities assumed – as I had planned they should – that the attack was the work of outsiders, and no internal inquiry into the incident took place. In retrospect, I see that firing a rifle into a room full of boys was an exceedingly irresponsible and dangerous act. In self-defence I could claim to have been reasonably expert at handling fire-arms. I could also point out that, by shooting upwards at a steep angle, I was in no danger of scoring a direct hit on anybody. Yet a bullet could easily have ricocheted off the window or something inside the room, and flying glass could have caused serious injury. Later, after I had left the school, my conscience smote me: I felt it was wrong that there should be such easy access to weapons, and I sent the authorities an anonymous note pointing out the flaw in the Armoury's defences. The next time I visited the school, I found that heavy iron bars had been installed to block the entrance to the tunnel – and they remain there to this day.

Success stimulated my imagination, and soon I conceived another felony designed to create a stir but at the same time to draw attention away from the school. After a covert expedition into Harrow Town, where I bought black and white paint and some brushes, I went out one night on a decorating spree, and in four or five places slapped up the motto of our deadly rival, FLOREAT ETONA. On the Head Master's steps the paint was black; on the pillars flanking his front door, white. Elsewhere I used mostly white on the red brick walls.

Next morning the place was in uproar over the outrage, and the Head Master, R. W. Moore, summoned the entire school to Speecher – properly Speech Room, the main assembly hall – for a pep-talk. I went along in some trepidation, prepared to own up if it looked as though a mass punishment was going to be handed out. I need not have worried. In his dry, pedantic and much-imitated voice, the Head Master deplored the fact that Etonians were such vandals, and expressed the strong hope that, gross though the provocation might be, none of us would be so foolish as to retaliate in enemy territory.

Before the offending slogans could be scrubbed from the walls, they were photographed by the local press, and next day the papers were satisfactorily full of reports headed ETONIANS DAUB HARROW WALLS IN JAPE.[1]

As a follow-up, I decided to take a hand in the General Election campaign of February 1950. Since Winston Churchill, the Conservative leader and former Prime Minister, was the School's most famous old boy, I thought it would stir things up if I painted VOTE LABOUR on various walls – which I did, during a suc-

---

1. A distinguished classical scholar, Mr Moore wrote several books with religious themes. He was also reputed by the boys to be a bit of a toper. When *The Moving of the Spirit* went on sale in the school bookshop, it was greeted by a cartoon showing a drayman with a cartload of gin barrels. He died in office in 1953.

cessful night expedition. But the slogans were naturally thought
to be the work of local Labour supporters, and caused a disappointing amount of scandal. At the end of that term I collected
the bicycles of a few senior boys for whom I did not care and
strung them up above the entrance to the school tuck-shop. This
went down well with boys at my level, but in fact it was a pale
echo of an exploit by Anthony Saxton's brother Hugh, a brilliant
climber who somehow scaled the steeple of the chapel and put
a bicycle on top – an extraordinary feat which, unlike mine,
required real courage and skill.

It would be idle to pretend that these extramural activities
were an adequate substitute for the academic work on which I
should have been concentrating. Yet they were in a way useful
training for my later career in the army, since they taught me
to survive on my own. They showed me the importance of
making proper plans, of working out the consequences of my
actions, of having a good story if I were rumbled, of being prepared for the unexpected and ready to deal with emergencies.

In normal school work I did no good at all. I used to dream
in class, paying little attention to the masters: if I found a subject
difficult, I lost interest, and it was no surprise to myself or anyone
else when I failed in my first attempt at the School Certificate
examination. All the same, I dismayed everybody by my spectacular score in French: three out of a hundred. People naturally
found it astonishing that a boy with a name like mine could do
no better in French than that. The only books in which I took
a real interest were stories of war and adventure: Paul Brickhill's
The Great Escape and *The Dambusters*, Eric Williams's *The Wooden
Horse* and so on.

Dreams of travel and adventure filled my head, and although
not much interested in politics, I read the newspapers enough
to become fascinated by the exploits of a Dutch mercenary who
styled himself Captain Turko (or Turk) Westerling. His name
derived from the fact that he had been born and brought up in
Istanbul, and by then – 1950 – he was fighting a guerrilla war
against the authorities in Indonesia, as commander of the rebel
'Forces of the Queen of Justice'. I knew nothing about the rights
and wrongs of the struggle, but that was of little consequence:
Turko Westerling had captured my imagination, and my

ambition became to go out and fight for him. Every day I scanned the papers anxiously for news of him: when his jeep was caught in an ambush but he shot his way out, I was vastly impressed.

Not so Lance Gorse when I told him that I wanted to leave school and go out to Indonesia to join Turko Westerling. The housemaster's response was that after an education at Harrow I should aim for a more ambitious career. He and others tried to persuade me to stay on, and among their blandishments was the chance that, if I did, I might become captain of the Shooting VIII. I have often wondered what would have happened if my father had still been alive. I imagine he would have persuaded or ordered me to stay until the age of eighteen. In the end it was my mother who staunched my restlessness for the moment. With her I struck a deal: if I really got down to work and passed the School Certificate at the second attempt, she would allow me to leave immediately afterwards.

So, in January 1951, I began what I hoped would be my final term at Harrow. With a definite objective in view, I eschewed illegal visits to London, and got up at 0500 to put in a couple of hours' work before breakfast. I beavered away at my Latin, and enjoyed the bawdiness of Chaucer's *Canterbury Tales*, one of the books set for English Literature. I had given up French, but now tackled divinity, as well as history and geography.

Time seemed to pass very fast, and great was my delight when I heard that I had passed the exam: not only that – I had obtained two distinctions and two credits, and had even managed to scrape through in mathematics. I left Harrow, not yet quite seventeen, to sighs of relief from the staff, not least from the Head Master, whose personal efforts to improve my handwriting had ended in almost total failure. I took away with me one benefit which I did not appreciate at the time. Then, as now, there were many overseas students at the school, and in my day the two most notable were Prince Feisal of Iraq and Prince Hussein of Jordan. I did not know them well, for neither was in my house; but I did meet Hussein, who was proclaimed King of Jordan in 1952; and when, much later, my army career threw me into contact with him again, the fact that we had been at school together provided us both with useful common ground.

CHAPTER 3

DISASTER

1951

I came home to Shropshire in the best of moods. I had shaken off the straitjacket of school, and my seventeenth birthday was imminent. Life and its adventures lay ahead. I was pleased to be at home with my mother, in the relaxed atmosphere which her presence seemed to generate. She had retained her looks and elegance, and was not short of admirers. I knew that we had financial problems as a result of her own and Maurice's extravagance, but Granny Lawley had bailed us out for the time being, and there seemed to be no immediate problem. The animals on our small-holding were doing well, and I had a 250cc BSA motorbike on which I could roar about the lanes, hatless and unprotected. Although still not sure what career I wanted to take up, I clung to my determination to travel the world, and to spend seven years in slow orbit.

Practicalities were rather different – the most important being that, as soon as I was eighteen, I should have to start two years' compulsory National Service. This meant that I had just over a year to fill in. Romantic as my dreams of travel might be, I decided that I must do something worthwhile, and gain some useful skill, in the twelve months before my call-up. I therefore enrolled at the Shrewsbury Technical College for a course in secretarial and business skills, which taught shorthand, typing, accounting and the rudiments of management. The only boy in a class of twenty-nine girls, I soon fell for one of the prettiest – Christine Gethin, who was slender and dark, and whose father owned the largest garage in town, down by the Welsh Bridge. She was lively and outgoing – a good foil to my own rather withdrawn nature – and my interest in her sharpened me up, making me dress more smartly.

David, by then seven and a half, was proving to have ten times the brain of myself and Michael put together. He was a different kind of animal entirely: given the slightest chance, he would bury himself in a book with such concentration that nothing could disturb him, and in due course he won scholarships to Winchester and Oxford. I am glad to say that, as we all grew up, we became a closely united family, and we have always regarded David as a full brother, rather than a mere half.

All that summer things went well. Seeing a valuable objective in the diploma which I stood to win, I worked hard at the course and steadily improved my typing. In the evenings, if not taking Christine out, I enjoyed ferreting with Denis Jones and gossiping with Karl Willi, a former German prisoner of war who had stayed on. (In summer Karl used to lock David into the fruit cage, where he happily ate raspberries while the men got on with their work.)

It was symptomatic of my high spirits that when two friends from Harrow, Anthony Saxton and John Gaiser, came to stay in September, we took off on a crazy spree, hitchhiking deep into North Wales dressed in pyjamas and dressing-gowns. Our object was simply to create some excitement – and in this we succeeded, as one person after another decided that we must have escaped from a lunatic asylum and put the police on our tail.

We set off at 1500 one afternoon and walked into the village of Dorrington, where we got a lift on a lorry loaded with beer-barrels. Next an army officer took us on a short distance, but after that we were repeatedly accosted by car-borne police, who had received reports of madmen on the move, and kept drawing up alongside to ask what we were doing. We managed to persuade them that we were (a) sane, (b) out to amuse ourselves, and (c) operating with the sanction of my mother. Presently we got another lift, this time from a nurse driving a van. Yet she too was convinced that we were lunatics on the run, and tried to trap us into revealing which institution we had come from. Eventually she set us down ten miles beyond Corwen, on the fringes of Snowdonia. As it was already 6.30 p.m., we decided to turn for home, and tried to get a train, only to find that none would run until the morning. We spent part of the night in a railway hut, and the rest in a barn full of straw; then, in the early morning, a relaxed lorry driver, who found nothing odd in our apparel, drove us the whole way back to Dorrington. The expedition achieved little, but we enjoyed it, and an illustrated account of it found its way into the local newspaper.

Then at the end of October disaster struck. One evening I noticed that a sow had come into season, so I loaded her into a trailer and drove her along the lane to visit the boar at the next farm. Returning about dusk, and looking forward to supper in the kitchen, I was puzzled to find no lights showing downstairs. David was up in his room, reading, as usual, and Poppet Wells, who was the same age as him, and had come to stay, was somewhere about the place; but downstairs there seemed to be no action.

I went into the kitchen through the back door, switched on the light, and called to my mother. No answer. In the hall I called again. Still no reply. Then I heard a terrible snorting or roaring, as of someone trying desperately to breathe. The door which led down to the cellar was open: in a flash I was at the top of the steps, and saw my mother lying face-down on the floor in front of the boiler – the new-fangled, solid-fuel boiler which we had recently installed to give ourselves central heating.

I dashed down, seized her by the arms and dragged her bodily up the steps, choking in acrid fumes. In the hall I laid her on her back and shouted for David, who came running down. 'Ring Doctor Ballenden!' I cried. 'Tell him Mum's had an accident, and come quick.' David ran to the telephone, dialled the operator, and was put through to Angela Ballenden, the doctor's wife, at their home in the village of Pontesbury, twelve miles away along winding lanes. 'Will the doctor come to my mummy quickly, please,' he said. Mrs Ballenden began to ask questions. I grabbed the receiver and said, 'It's Peter. Mother's been gassed by fumes from the boiler.' She relayed instructions from the doctor – open the doors, keep the patient's head on one side, make sure her tongue isn't blocking her throat – and said he was on his way.

It turned out that Dr Ballenden had two Peters on his roster, and, not certain which had rung, went to the wrong one first. But even if he had arrived in four minutes, rather than forty, it would have made no difference, for the damage had been done. As we later discovered, the chimney had been blocked by a jackdaw's nest: when my mother went down to find out why the water was cold, and tried to stoke the boiler, she had been overcome by carbon monoxide fumes, and she had lain there for many minutes, breathing in the deadly gas, which, being heavier than air, had accumulated at floor level.

In the hall, we had a terrible wait. Obviously she was still alive, but her face was grey and her breathing so laboured that we feared she was going to die. I thought it best not to try to move her, but covered her with a blanket and sat by her on the floor. The doctor, arriving at last, took one look and said she must go straight to hospital. He rang for an ambulance, which rushed her to the Royal Salop Infirmary in Shrewsbury.

Somehow we got through the night, and in the morning I telephoned the hospital, afraid I would hear the worst; yet they told me that she had recovered consciousness, and that I could go in to see her. When I found her lying in bed with her eyes open, my hopes leapt – but an instant later they were dashed, for she did not know who I was. Her brain had been damaged by lack of oxygen, her memory destroyed.

Friends rallied to our help. Poppet's parents, Richard and Miney Wells, came over and stayed with us, running the house for the first couple of weeks. Then Nanny Turnbull arrived from Dumfriesshire and took over, so that at least we were properly fed. But it was soon clear that we could not stay at Park House much longer, for we found that my mother and Maurice between them had run up such debts that the house would have to be sold.

I reacted to the tragedy in the only way I knew – by doggedly making plans for the future. There was no question of my mother recovering quickly. Even when she began to improve physically, she could not remember the simplest details of daily life: she did not know where she lived, and if she had gone out, she would never have found her way home. Indoors she was positively dangerous, for she would forget to switch off electric appliances like heaters and kettles, and could not live on her own.

Nevertheless, I was determined from the start that she was going to recover. Without any real medical knowledge, I reasoned that because the rest of her body was functioning, some at least of her damaged brain cells would renew themselves in time, and her memory would return. For this reason, I considered it essential that she should have the best possible treatment.

The crisis led to a monumental family row – or rather, to years of rows, in which, as always, Aunt Joyce was the prime mover. Now that my mother had been disabled, Joyce moved in for the kill, announcing that Kitty was obviously never going to recover, and should be put away in an asylum, out of sight, for ever. This was more than I could stand. Already I had seen signs of improvement – my mother recognized me and David – and I was determined that when she came out of hospital she should have the most stimulating environment that we could devise for her. It seemed to me that only by being mentally stretched, and confronted with constant small challenges, would she ever make real progress.

This belief threw me into head-on confrontation with Joyce, and we had furious arguments, mostly at Old Place, where she would throw tantrums, shout, and flounce about the house, making such a commotion that meals would be literally hours late and the whole establishment would be thrown into chaos. 'Oh, do quieten down, Joyce,' my grandmother would say mildly, but she might just as well have whispered to a tornado.

Meanwhile, my own life had to go on. For a few weeks I continued my course, and I went on seeing Christine, who now became a much-valued support and to some extent took the place of my mother. But gradually, as the severity of our financial predicament became apparent, I decided I must find employment without waiting for the start of my National Service to come round. Still wanting to travel, I returned to an earlier idea which I had entertained for a while, of going into the merchant navy. In those days merchant ships were far more numerous than now, and I thought it should be easy to get a job on a tramp-steamer. Besides, there was the added advantage that service in the merchant navy gave one exemption from compulsory call-up into the armed forces.

Bitten again by the idea, I arranged an interview with the Benn Line, who agreed to take me provided I passed the standard medical examinations, and soon I was on my way to Cardiff, where selection boards were held. The trip gave me a chance to stay with the Beaks, for Bill had by then become Governor of Cardiff Gaol, and was living in the Governor's House. He and Ruth sided with me in my battles with Joyce and gave me much-needed moral support.

At the medical all went well at first, and it was not until I came to the colour tests that I ran into trouble. To my consternation, I found that when slides were projected on to a screen in a darkened room, I could not make out half the points of coloured light. The tests revealed that I was unable to distinguish between red and green – and this colour blindness alone was enough to disqualify me from service in the merchant navy. The news came as such a shock that I returned to the Beaks in tears.

Bouncing back, I conceived an ambitious, two-stage plan. I realized that if I signed on for three years in the regular army, I could join up at seventeen and a half, rather than wait another six months for National Service. The Korean War was then in its second year, and I made it my first aim to join a regiment which was fighting in it. Not only was the King's Own Shropshire Light Infantry my own county regiment: two of my friends – John Ballenden, the doctor's son, and Tony Pack – were both in it, and in Korea. Both won Military Crosses and became heroes of mine (although Tony, alas, was killed just before his award was announced). The second stage of my plan was that I should move on, via the KSLI, to an organization of which I heard exciting rumours – the Special Air Service.

At that stage I knew very little about the SAS, except that it had been formed in the Western Desert by Colonel David Stirling during the Second World War, and had distinguished itself by blowing up enemy aircraft and vehicles behind the German lines. After the war it had been disbanded, but then it had reformed, and now – the end of 1951 – it was fighting Communist terrorists in the jungles of Malaya. I transferred my enthusiasm from Turko Westerling to this mysterious and – in my eyes

– glamorous regiment, which for me had the added merit of being British. What appealed to me about the SAS was the fact that it operated in small groups behind enemy lines: its soldiers were left on their own for months on end, and had to be able to live with themselves, rather than as part of a structured group.

So my ambition became to join the SAS. But I knew that one could only do that via some other regiment, which one had to join first, and I therefore made my way to the recruiting office of the KSLI in Shrewsbury. The Recruiting Officer was Colonel Bamford, whose three lovely daughters – all older than me – were being pursued by half the young bloods in Shropshire; and it was he who enlisted me. After we had talked things through, and I had signed the necessary papers, agreeing to report for duty in the New Year, he gave me a bit of advice which has stood me in good stead ever since. 'When you're given an order to do something,' he said, 'go away and do it, and see it through to the end. Never pack up halfway. If people can rely on you, you'll go a long way. But if they can't, nobody will trust you, and you'll go nowhere.'

With those wise words ringing in my ears, I went home to the melancholy job of selling Park House. Already the property was on the market, and we arranged that the furniture – some of which had come from old Lawley homes, and was of high quality – should go into store in Shrewsbury. It was typical of Joyce's curious love-hate relationship with her sister and the rest of us that she took enormous trouble to help us pack things up. Every glass had to be wrapped six times and listed in triplicate – but she fussed over family possessions with the best intentions.

For the time being she won the argument over my mother's future. At the beginning of December we moved her to Graylingwell Hospital, a mental institution at Chichester, in Sussex, where she would be within easy visiting distance of Old Place. She hated being there – as I knew she would – but while she was unable to look after herself, we could see no alternative.

With her departure to the south, my world disintegrated. Ever since her accident Michael had been away at Harrow. Now we arranged that in the holidays he and David would live at Old Place, and we despatched their possessions to Sussex. In

Shropshire I gave the ferrets to Denis, and sold the pigs and chickens. In due course Park House found a buyer. Nell the retriever had already died, so that at least I did not have the problem of finding a home for her.

My affair with Christine came to an end without recrimination on either side. I am afraid that in a rather selfish way I decided that girl-friends were a liability, both financially and in terms of the time they took up; of course I did not say so to Christine, because I was still very fond of her, but I became convinced that we must go our separate ways. The problem of how to tell her exercised me greatly: in the end I decided that I would invite her to a slap-up lunch in London, and break the bad news during the meal. We went to L'Ecu de France, and had the best lunch that the place could provide; only as she was about to leave did I manage to say, 'Look. I'm terribly sorry, but I'm afraid this is it. We can't meet any more.' The scene haunts me to this day. I needed every ounce of my courage to get those words out, even though I felt sure that Christine was half-expecting them. But she bore the parting well, and we remained good friends.

When I walked through the high, imposing gates of Copthorne Barracks, on the outskirts of Shrewsbury, on the morning of 2 January 1952, I seemed to have little going for me. My father was dead, my mother in hospital, my aunt and grandmother alienated, my home sold, my own family scattered, my education prematurely cut off. No wonder I went off to a new life with a feeling of quite some foreboding.

CHAPTER 4

FOOT ON THE LADDER

1952–53

When I joined the King's Shropshire Light Infantry as 22774920 Private de la Billière, I had little hope or expectation of promotion, and was determined to make my way in the army from the bottom.[1] I saw myself doing three years as a private soldier, perhaps making non-commissioned officer if things went well, and then coming out.

With nowhere else to live, I needed a roof over my head, and the army offered me a home. So I went in at the start of the year, when it suited me, and I arrived at Copthorne Barracks as an individual volunteer, not part of a draft. I was five foot ten inches tall and weighed just over eleven stone. Since I seemed to be tolerably well educated, I was put to work for the first couple of weeks in the Orderly Room, on the clerical side. I felt lonely, missing home; but the days were busy and passed quickly. Soon the next draft arrived, and I was thrown in with thirty raw recruits. Having been in the army for all of two weeks, I felt slightly superior, as I knew some of the ropes, and could tell the others what to do. We were housed in one of the huge, brick barrack-blocks (which stand to this day); our room had a highly polished wooden floor, and steel lockers between the beds. From the outset I resented the amount of time which we were obliged to spend drilling on the parade ground and cleaning our kit: we blancoed our webbing and polished our boots until

---

1. It was now that I began to spell my name de la Billière, rather than de Labillière, and in 1992, when I was made an Honorary Freeman of the City of London, I confirmed the change by deed poll.

late into the night, and in the mornings our blankets had to be made up into fanatically neat box-shapes, with selected items of kit laid out for the daily inspection. I realized that all this was an inevitable part of army life, yet what I really enjoyed was the outdoor training, the shooting especially, and I became enthusiastic: this in turn made me try hard, and soon I found that I liked the army more than I had expected.

Besides, I discovered that I was at my best working with other people, and that because I had been lucky enough to receive a better education than most of them, the others looked to me for a lead. One morning our instructor was late for the physical training period, and I organized the squad to start some games of O'Grady, in which a ring of people throws a medicine ball at the legs of one man in the centre. When the instructor eventually arrived, expecting us to be rioting or lounging about, he was impressed to find us taking useful exercise, and asked who had arranged the games. I owned up – and I think that as a result of that minor initiative someone picked me out as officer potential.

After six weeks of basic training – in which we learnt to march, drill, salute, shoot and generally keep ourselves clean – a selection board was held: I was chosen for officer training, and sent up to the King's Own Yorkshire Light Infantry depot at Strensall, near York, where potential officers from all the light infantry regiments were brigaded together in the Leader Platoon. Here life was tougher. We had an excellent mentor in the form of Sergeant Harvey – a very presentable and decent non-commissioned officer, ideal for the job of bringing us on – but the tempo of training was more demanding, and living conditions worse. At the end of February the weather was still icy, and we lived in a long, wooden hut – one of a complex known as a spider – with no insulation: there was a dire shortage of fuel, and our coal quickly ran out. To give ourselves more heat in the evenings, we would scrounge duckboards out of the showers, chop them up and stuff them into our cast-iron stove, huddling round so that at least one side of us was warm.

During the day we were under non-stop pressure, with no time to ourselves, constantly scrutinized for our potential as officers. This, of course, was precisely the kind of highly disciplined existence to which (I had repeatedly told myself) I would never submit. Yet now, as at Copthorne, I revelled in the physical side of the training, especially night exercises, and field-firing with live ammunition on the moors at Fylingdales. I found that I could rub along happily with people of every kind, no matter what background they came from, and I enjoyed getting to know them for what they were, not for their antecedents.

As a regular, I was paid seven shillings – thirty-five pence – a day (National Servicemen got from three shillings), and even this pittance was whittled down by compulsory deductions for barrack damages, regimental subscriptions and so on: every week I lost four of my precious forty-nine shillings in stoppages at source. The archaic ritual of the formal pay parade was still in force. The squad would be lined up, and when the duty-sergeant yelled your name, you would shout, '*Sir!*', spring to attention and march up to where the paying-out officer sat at a table. Someone would read off the acquittance rolls that you were entitled to forty-five shillings. The money would be slapped down on the table – whereupon you would sign for it, pick it up, stuff it in your pocket, salute, turn, and march back to your place. (Looking back from the days of computers and credit cards, it is incredible to think how much time all this wasted.)

To eke out my regular pay, I took on the part-time job of operating the projector in the Army Kinema Corporation's camp cinema, for which I earned two shillings a night. Being rather mean by nature, I tried to save what money I had. Every now and then, at a weekend, I would take the bus into York, some-times in the company of Tony Pheby, a friend from the Oxford-shire and Buckinghamshire Light Infantry, Tom Luckock, an immensely tall Old Etonian, and Brian Harris, who was large, with horn-rimmed spectacles. Our favourite rendezvous was the de Grey rooms near the Minster, where regular dances were held; but our chronic shortage of funds, reinforced by natural inhibitions, prevented us from making serious headway among the local girls.

Presently I went in front of a War Office Selection Board, and after two days of initiative and intelligence tests, was told that I had passed. My burning ambition was still to fight in Korea, and I was afraid that the war might be over before I could reach it; so I was naturally eager to move on to the next stage – officer cadet training at Eaton Hall, near Chester. First, however, came an enforced wait of several weeks at Strensall, during which we were given immensely boring fatigues to carry out – peeling potatoes, washing up dishes, clearing rubbish from the camp grounds.

Hating to be caught out with nothing to do, I had already begun looking forward to see what I might take on next, and I found – then, as later – that few people in the army bothered to do this. The result was twofold: first, the authorities were usually glad if someone suggested himself for a particular position, as it meant that one job at least was easily filled; and second, because nobody else was pressing for the post, there was little competition.

So it proved when I applied for the job of projector operator for the camp's training films. The unit possessed a good variety of films, and I more or less had a cinema of my own: provided I showed the training films at the times required, nobody took much notice of what I did in between. One day, poking around in a back room, I found some reels of old film, laced them up and ran them – only to discover that they were of Nazi concentration camps, with ghastly sequences of skeletal human beings being herded into mass graves and shot. That was my first real introduction into the horrors of the holocaust in the Second World War.

At last, in the summer, the time came to move on to Eaton Hall. I thought I had seen some big country houses in my time, but the vast, turreted, Gothic mansion built in dark-grey granite by the Westminster family made all others look like shacks. Opposite the front entrance were the elaborate Golden Gates, made of gilded cast-iron work, and beyond them in the distance, on a rise at the end of a ceremonial avenue, stood the Obelisk, round which defaulters were constantly being sent to double.

The Regimental Sergeant Major of the day was RSM G. C. Copp, MBE, a ramrod-straight Coldstream Guardsman who lost no time in putting us in our place. 'Gentlemen!' he roared when he had us on parade. 'Forms of address! I want to make one thing clear. Here at Eaton Hall, if you're talking to a corporal, you call him "Corporal". A sergeant is "Sergeant".

A staff-sergeant you call "Staff". A sergeant major is "Sergeant-Major". And I'm called "Sir". You call me "Sir", and I call you "Sir". The only difference is that you bloody well mean it, and I don't!'

Once again I enjoyed the outdoor side of life most – the cross-country runs through the rolling Cheshire countryside, field firing at Trawsfynydd in the Welsh mountains, and above all the assault course, on which I pushed myself to the limits of my endurance. Keeping fit was becoming a bit of a fetish: I believed then, as I have ever since, that only by maintaining the highest physical fitness can one be at one's best mentally as well. On the indoor front I did all I could to keep out of trouble – though I did commit one serious error when, for the first time in my life, I became helplessly drunk. Whenever a course passed out, the custom was for members of the junior course to act as waiters at the farewell dinner, their compensation being that it was possible to take surreptitious swigs out of the bottles. I hit the port with such force that in the morning I was quite unable to get out of bed, and had to ask someone to cover for me at the daily muster parade.

My most important discovery was of how valuable it is, in any project or operation, civil or military, to enlist the help and ideas of other people. Whenever I was in temporary command of a group of officer cadets, and we were set a task, I never felt that my own ideas were necessarily right, or the final solution; on the contrary, I reckoned that they were never more than the nucleus of a plan, and that they needed other people's brains to work on them before they became a practical proposition. I realized also that once you have people working for you, you can divide any task up among them; and if you understand their personalities and capabilities, you can make sure that they take on those aspects of the task at which you yourself are least proficient. A team with key people in the right positions is far stronger than the sum of its parts.

With my awareness gradually growing, I thought I was doing reasonably well. It was therefore a shock when an officer from the KSLI came to interview me and told me that the regiment had no place for me, as I was not quite good enough. My disappointment was short-lived, since I was not particularly drawn to any one regiment, and had joined the KSLI mainly because it offered a chance of going to Korea. Already, in September, the Regiment was handing over to the Durham Light Infantry, so I switched my allegiance to the DLI, applied to join, and was grateful to be accepted. In due course I passed out of Eaton Hall successfully, glad to be on my way as a Second Lieutenant.

Before joining the DLI I had some leave, and stayed happily for a few days with the Beaks, who by then had retired to a comfortable country house near Weyhill, in Hampshire. Through Daphne I had come to know another girl, Frances Lowry, the daughter of a doctor, who lived nearby. She was very pretty, and I found myself growing fond of her; but, knowing that I would probably soon go abroad, I was wary of becoming too deeply involved.

Among my immediate family, things were far from comfortable. My mother had recovered physically, and some of her memory had returned. By August she was well enough to leave Graylingwell, but Joyce, typically, refused to have her living at Old Place and arranged for her to be admitted to another sanatorium, the Holloway at Virginia Water. It was characteristic of the relationship between the sisters that, just before Joyce arrived at Graylingwell to collect her on 18 August, my mother absconded and disappeared. Where she went, I am not sure, but she was eventually admitted to Holloway a few days later.

Meanwhile, relations between Joyce and myself were becoming ever more strained. All my life I have made it my policy *not* to have head-on confrontations if I can achieve what I want by indirect means; but the well-being of the family was so vital to me that I could not avoid joining battle over it. David had made a good start at St Peter's Court, yet Joyce was demanding that he be moved to some other school. I was equally determined that this should not happen, and that, if I did go abroad later in the year, Joyce should not gain control of his destiny – or my mother's – in my absence. I therefore took the drastic step, through Miney Wells, of engaging a London solicitor and instructing him to write a letter to my grandmother saying that if she or Joyce made any attempt to remove David from St Peter's Court, I, as my mother's eldest son and David's legal guardian, would take court proceedings against them. This gave the ladies of Old Place such a shock that they cut me out of their wills, and communication between us all but ceased.

I deepened the family rift still further by arranging for my mother's affairs to be taken over by the official Court of Protection, in London. It was obvious that she was going to need professional help for the foreseeable future, if not for the rest of her life, and I was anxious that financial and other advice should come from a sensible, independent source, rather than from an overwrought sister. Luck was with me, in that the court appointed an excellent man to manage family affairs on our behalf: Roy Fieldhouse, an accountant, and a director of the family firm Lawley Everett, who already knew us well, now took charge of my mother's finances. With him in position, I felt more confident about going abroad. Later he handed over to a senior solicitor in the Court of Protection itself, and here again we were extremely fortunate. N. H. Turner, an admirable man, as humane as he was efficient, looked after my mother's money with exemplary care, and became a close friend of the family.

If Eaton Hall was enormous, Brancepeth Castle, the DLI depot near Durham, was (and is) positively colossal. A vast Victorian edifice built of rough stone in the form of a medieval castle, it had peacocks screeching in the courtyard and, in the corner by the chapel, the battered two-pounder anti-tank gun with which Private A. H. Wakenshaw had heroically defended his position at Matruh during the North African campaign of June 1942, winning a posthumous Victoria Cross. My room was three and a half minutes' fast walk from the dining room, which itself was a cavernous chamber forty yards long and thirty feet high, often with only five or six officers eating at its long table. There was no central heating, but a huge coal fire burned all day in the anteroom, and I was amazed to hear that the fuel for this and the stoves in the kitchen cost £35 a week (the equivalent of perhaps £300 today). One of the mess's assets was a full-sized billiard table, on which, in the evenings, we used to play boisterous games of billiard fives (using hands instead of cues to propel the balls). One night, during a particularly vicious tournament, a ball hit the top of a cushion, took off, and flew straight through an oil painting of some venerable DLI officer. As the portrait was dimly lit, we decided to say nothing about the accident, and the damage was not noticed for more than thirty years: only in the late 1980s, when the picture was taken down for cleaning, did someone discover that it had a neat hole punched through it.

As soon as I reached Brancepeth I let it be known that I wanted to join the DLI's First Battalion, which had gone out to Korea. The alternative – the Second Battalion, in Germany – did not interest me. War was what I wanted, and every day in the mess I made my adrenalin flow by scanning the casualty lists published in the newspapers. Family and friends opposed my plans, and tried hard to persuade me to give them up. Anthony Saxton wrote saying that, if I did go to Korea, he would have no more to do with me – but needless to say such threats only increased my determination.

At last, after what seemed an age, but in fact was only a few weeks, my posting came through in the middle of November, and I learnt that I was bound for Korea. There was one slight problem, in that no serviceman was allowed beyond Hong Kong until he was nineteen, and my nineteenth birthday would not fall until 29 April 1953; but I hoped that by keeping quiet I would slip through the net and join the battalion before then.

In those days there were no fast jet aircraft to whisk troops from one side of the world to the other, and travel was much more of an adventure than it is now. The sea journey to the war took over five weeks: thirty-four days to Kure, in the far south of Japan, and then another three days across the Sea of Japan to Pusan in Korea. But the length of the voyage did not worry me: all I knew was that I was off on a great expedition, to fight the King's enemies, in a land unimaginably remote. My fantasies of going to join Turko Westerling and travelling round the world were all about to be fulfilled at a single stroke.

So intensively did I project myself towards Korea that I hardly noticed myself making preparations or going on board SS *Empire Pride* at Liverpool: all at once we were sailing out of the Mersey and on our way. To my shame, I had not told Frances that I was leaving, and although I did write to her from shipboard, I am afraid I was not very chivalrous: in the months that followed, she kept writing to me, but I never answered, so that our affair ended in a mess which I have always regretted. I feel I was unfair to her, and should have been more outspoken early on. The debacle made me decide that I would have no more to do with women for the time being.

Empire Pride was one of the oldest troopships still serving, and exceedingly uncomfortable, with no air conditioning or any such modern luxury; but in those days the disparity between the living conditions of officers and other ranks was much greater than would be tolerated now. We officers lived on the upper deck, three or four to a cabin, but at least in cabins with portholes, and we ate in a dining room where the food was always excellent. Down on the troop decks, by contrast, the men were very crowded and had no privacy whatever. The decks were open, except for supporting pillars, and the men slept on hammocks, which had to be taken down and stowed away in lockers every morning for the ritual of scrubbing-down. At night conditions were thoroughly unpleasant, especially in wet weather, for the ventilation was poor, and the air foetid with the smell of bodies.

With the ship run on a tight routine, we all had particular jobs to do. We were up early, and after breakfast had a muster parade and inspection; then came drill in PT shoes, a run round the deck, and keep-fit exercises. There was also a lot of shooting off the stern at balloons and other targets. Yet much of what the men were given to do seemed to me singularly unimaginative, and designed simply to occupy time. I vowed that later in life I would do something to make training more fun and more worthwhile.

My own job was to look after one of the troop decks and keep it shipshape. This was really my first command, and in my relationships with the soldiers I had to feel my way. They came from all regiments, National Servicemen and regulars mixed together, and their quality varied enormously. At that date the quality of the regulars tended to be very low: people volunteered for the army only if they could find no other employment, and many of those who did join up could not read, write or even sign their names. The National Servicemen, on the other hand, embraced all types, and included many with first-class brains.

Military discipline held sway, as usual, and the stress of living at such close quarters resulted in many a punch-up; troublemakers were locked in the cells, and whenever I was Duty Officer I would have to visit them, deep down in the bowels of the ship.

As the ship headed south, the weather grew rapidly warmer. After a brief stop at Gibraltar, we steamed along the Mediterranean, and at Port Said, in Egypt, I got my first glimpse of the Middle East. We were not allowed ashore, but the Orient paddled out to meet us in the form of bumboat men selling everything from camel-hair rugs to leather pouffes, and gully-gully men, or magicians, who used sleight of hand to conjure chickens out of their noses. The soldiers were warned to watch themselves and their property; nevertheless, several found that they had mysteriously lost their money, even though no Egyptian seemed to have been near them. The bumboat merchants came alongside, threw up lines, and let prospective purchasers draw up whatever objects they fancied; if, after furious haggling, a price was agreed, some piastres or shillings would go down in a bag on the line, and a deal would be struck. In the fierce heat, the jostle of small boats and the buzz of chatter, with other ships hooting and the smell of drains wafting pungently over the harbour, it was easy to lose one's sense of values, and several men succumbed to the wiles of the merchants.

Eventually *Empire Pride* formed into a convoy and started down the Suez Canal. I felt I was leaving Europe behind and heading for another world. Day by day I found out a little more about handling the soldiers. I enjoyed being with them and doing things in their company, and I discovered that if I took the trouble to talk to them individually, and treated them as equals in conversation when not on duty, so that I learnt about their families and problems, they would respond and do their best to support me. Provided I looked after their interests, and arranged minor improvements for them, I could be pretty tough on them – and in fact they almost preferred that I should be. I put much time and effort into taking an interest in the people under my command, and made sure that they got the best of everything my efforts could provide – and I did this throughout my career, whether I was a platoon commander anxious that twenty men should have a proper meal and a good place to sleep, or a general in the Gulf War determined to secure the best possible political and logistic support for a triservice force 45,000 strong.

Our next stop was Aden – then still a British colony – where we refuelled, reprovisioned and delivered some replacements for the garrison. I shall never forget how the dark mass of Shamsan, the extinct volcano, loomed behind the harbour as we came in early one morning. Legend had it that anyone who climbed the mountain three times would never return to Aden; but it was not long before I myself proved the story false, for although I did not go up it on that first visit, I later reached its summit more than a hundred times – and still I went back.

As we steamed on down the Indian Ocean, with the heat now stifling, we began to feel the monotony of our journey. Cut off from the outside world, without newspapers, mail or even any regular radio communication, we lived a very isolated life. The main event of every day was the sweepstake, held on the distance travelled during the previous twenty-four hours, and the announcement of the winner at midday. In the afternoons there was the traditional quiet period, when everyone had to read or write letters or sleep or anyway remain silent. The one day of the week with a difference was Sunday, when we had a church service and did less work. Yet if the days were dull, I ticked them off enthusiastically, buoyed up by the knowledge that every one brought me closer to Korea. Two new friends helped while away the time: Mike Hardy and Mike Campbell-Lamerton, both in the Duke of Wellington's Regiment, and both fine rugby players.

After brief stops at Colombo and Singapore, we made the long haul across the China Sea to Hong Kong. This, for me, was the critical point of the voyage, for I knew that anyone under the age of nineteen was supposed to wait in Hong Kong until he came of age. This of course made me nervous, but during the three days that we remained in harbour, I was splendidly entertained by Geoff Cooke, a DLI staff officer serving in the headquarters of the garrison, who took me into his mess and made me feel thoroughly at home. This was the first positive demonstration I had had of how a good regiment looks after its members: Geoff had never seen me, and knew nothing about me, yet went out of his way to treat me as a friend. In particular, he invited me to the mess for Sunday lunch, for which some magnificent curries had been prepared. He was amused to find that I had never eaten curry, and did not even know what it was; he explained that there were three kinds on offer – mild, medium and hot – and warned me to be careful. The hot, he said, really *was* hot, and he advised against it. I, of course, thought I would go for the best, chose the hot, and took a mouthful. A moment later I was gulping down cold water in a desperate attempt to douse the fire raging in the roof of my mouth. Too proud to give in, I fought my way through the helping. Curiously enough after such a painful initiation, curry became a lifelong favourite, and, in the jungles of Malaya and Borneo, the staple of our existence.

With mounting anticipation we completed the penultimate stage of our marathon, and at last, thirty-four days out of Liverpool, we were steaming into the naval port of Kure. Warships lay in the harbour, and the place had a martial air. We marched stiffly down the gangway, piled into trucks, and were driven to the JRBD (Joint Reinforcement Base Depot), a camp of bungalows built by the British for holding battle casualty replacements (BCRs) until they were called forward to their regiments.

Although the battle zone was still several hundred miles away, war was in the air. The names of those to be posted to Korea went up twice a week on a board in the officers' mess; the glamorous Chinese woman who cut our hair was said to be a spy, noting troop movements – and indeed, a few days after my arrival she disappeared, never to return. After only a week, to my delight and excitement, my name appeared on the list; but then someone did a last-minute check of ages and discovered that I was too young. Later that night I was told that I could not go, that I should not be in Japan at all, and that I would have to wait around in Kure.

I was incensed. For months I had had my sights set on Korea; my battalion was in the front line, and I was within an ace of joining it. The war was running on: if it ended, I might miss a unique opportunity. I felt so angry and disappointed that I could not accept the rebuff: rather than acquiesce, I got hold of a manual of military law, consulted experienced officers, and discovered that, according to King's Regulations, under certain circumstances I might be entitled to something called a Redress of Grievance. Armed with this knowledge, and taking a good deal more care than usual over written work, I sat down and drafted a demand to the Commanding Officer of the base for a Redress of Grievance from the Army Board.

It so happened that the Commandant, a brigadier, was on leave, and my application landed in the hands of his deputy, a not-very-effective lieutenant-colonel. When he began to remonstrate, I told him that he had no right to withhold my plea, but that it had to go forward (I still believe this was correct). Anyway, he sent it off – but all too soon it came back with a brisk retort which said, in effect, 'There's nothing here to have a grievance about. Get a grip!' By then the brigadier had returned from leave, and was not at all pleased to find that his deputy had forwarded my document in the first place. Now he told me not to be an idiot.

Meanwhile I had been given command of a platoon of reinforcements, a mixture of DLI and other regiments. It was difficult to make a coherent unit out of this bunch of individuals who were soon to be split up and sent out in ones and twos, but I saw it as a challenge, and did what I could, enormously helped by two fellow DLI officers, John Burkmar and George Fells. Burkmar was then a captain, and senior to me, but an enthusiastic and bouncy character, with whom I immediately hit it off. Fells was small and terrier-like, with a lively sense of humour. Encouraged by these two, I devised an original programme, with as much shooting, fitness training and cross-country marching as I could cram in.

It soon became apparent that my own map-reading was far from perfect. One morning I took the platoon out for a twenty-mile circular route march, which I knew would stretch us to our limits. Off we went, over the hills and along tracks through the woods; but after seven miles I began to have difficulty relating my map to features on the ground. After twelve miles I was definitely lost, and not sure of the way home; but since we had already gone more than half our full distance, and the men were running out of stamina, to retrace our route was clearly not a sensible option. Studying the map again, I saw that a railway line lay to our east, so I decided to march to that, follow the track to a station, and catch a train. This we managed: at some small country halt I bought all thirty soldiers tickets back to Kure, and the cost was tiny. We arrived home in the dark at 1930, three hours after we had been expected, to find that every-one in camp had been stood-to, and search-parties were about to go out. Luckily the senior officers were so relieved to see us safely back, and so pleased that somebody had undertaken an ambitious exercise, that I escaped without censure.

In general we had little contact with the locals, since we hardly went into the town of Kure. Nevertheless, the attitude of the Japanese amazed me: they were totally impassive, and seemed to have no feelings of guilt about their behaviour during the Second World War. I was disappointed that I never managed a trip to Tokyo, but I did visit Hiroshima, on which the first atom bomb had been dropped in August 1945, effectively bringing the war to an end and saving thousands of Allied lives. Seven years on, the town had been largely rebuilt, but one or two of the original buildings had been retained as memorials, and what made the deepest impression on me were the dark shapes or shadows of humans etched into the wall of the Town Hall – the ghosts of people who had been standing there when the bomb exploded, and whose bodies had shielded areas from the flash. In spite of this haunting reminder, I found it difficult to feel pity for the Japanese: the way they had treated Allied prisoners during the war was too fresh in my memory.

One day in the camp at Kure there appeared Lieutenant-Colonel Peter Jeffreys, Commanding Officer of the First Bat-talion of the DLI, who had come over from Korea for a spell of R&R (rest and recuperation). A lean, chirpy, cheerful man, who immediately inspired confidence, he called me into his office for an interview. The fiasco of my applying for Redress of Grievance had of course percolated through to the Regiment, so I went in some trepidation, expecting a rocket. Instead, I found that the CO had heard that I was becoming despondent about my chances of reaching the war zone, and wanted to reassure me.

'Well, de la Billière,' he began. 'I hear you're keen to get to Korea.'

'Yes, sir,' I said. 'As soon as possible.'

'Right!' he answered. 'I tell you what. I'll get you there on your nineteenth birthday – and that's a promise.'

This brief encounter cheered me up; but for the moment I set my sights on Hura Mura, a field-firing range in the hills six hours' drive to the north of Kure. Hearing that conditions up there were extremely realistic, I wangled my way on to a detachment heading north. Nor was I disappointed. Now once again I was learning, rather than instructing, and the training was really tough and dangerous. I saw for myself the truth of the adage, 'Train hard, live long.' We were allowed to take risks which would never have been countenanced elsewhere: we could operate with only a five-degree safety arc between attacking troops and weapons firing live ammunition on fixed lines, and we could bring down mortar or artillery fire extremely close in front of men on the ground. Small wonder that the casualty rate was high; yet the casualties suffered at Hura Mura were an investment in life later, and I have no doubt that although a few people were killed on the ranges there, the hard training saved numerous lives in Korea.

The low, scrub-covered hills were physically demanding, as we constantly ran up and down them; their greatest merit was that they provided total freedom for troops to give each other close fire-support – something which I came to value highly, and used frequently later in my career. Here I learned how essential it is for soldiers to get a feel for being under fire, and for them to become used to it. I discovered the importance of teaching people what is really dangerous, as distinct from what merely sounds dangerous, and I saw the vital role of fire-support in keeping the enemy under control.

For me, Hura Mura was a godsend – not least because at the weekends I was free to roam the ranges and indulge my passion for detonating blinds, or unexploded shells. On weekdays, the moment we stopped firing, Japanese would appear from nowhere and start frantically digging up the bullets: so poor were they that the collection of lead and brass cartridge cases was a major occupation. At weekends I would join the beach-combers, wandering with a box of explosives, and blowing up any blinds that I could find.

Alongside the British, several Commonwealth units were

training – Canadians, Australians, New Zealanders – and of these none were wilder than the 22nd Royal Canadian Regiment, known as the Vingt-Deux (corrupted by British soldiers to 'Vingt Doos'). We lived in wooden barrack-huts, and one day, after a Canadian had stolen something from another man's hut, the thief set fire to the building purely to forestall a search. Unfortunately a brisk wind was blowing, with the result that a line of huts was burnt to the ground. Another evening three or four of us were walking through the village, and making rather a noise, when a Canadian soldier shoved his head out of the window of what was obviously a brothel. Sighting officers right in front of him, he saluted smartly and popped back in again.

Back in Kure, a good deal wiser, I waited with keen anticipation to see if Colonel Jeffreys was going to keep his promise. When he did, I could scarcely believe my luck. On 26 April 1953 my name appeared on the board in the officers' mess. This time it stayed there. Next day I took ship for Korea, and on the twenty-ninth – my birthday – we sailed into the harbour at Pusan. To our astonishment, we found an American band in full regalia of shiny steel helmets and white crossbelts lined up on the quay to play us ashore. And what song did they choose to welcome us to the war zone? 'If I knew you were coming, I'd have baked a cake'.

CHAPTER 5

BAPTISM OF FIRE

1953

Hurricane lamps flared on tables improvised from packing cases and planks. Rough wooden boards lined the walls. Weapons stood stacked in the corners, and the air in the dug-out was full of atmospheric crackle from radio sets. Yet if the furnishings of the Battalion Headquarters were spartan, the welcome I received could not have been warmer. The Commanding Officer, Peter Jeffreys, came out of his own little corner to greet me. In Japan he had addressed me as 'de la Billière'. Now he asked for my Christian name.

'Peter,' I replied.

'Oh God!' he groaned. 'Not another! We've got four Peters in the battalion already. We can't possibly call you that. What other names have you got?'

'Well – de la Cour.'

'Christ! Nothing else?'

'Only Edgar.' I brought it out reluctantly, having never liked the name.

'That'll do!' Up chirped Oscar Norman, the second-in-command. 'We'll call you Eddie.'

Everyone laughed, and the problem was solved. Within hours of arriving in Korea, I became Eddie; it took me a while to grow used to the new name, and answer to it, but it stuck, and to this day officers who served with me in the DLI call me by it. Soon I acquired a new surname as well: my soldiers, finding de la Billière too much of a mouthful, decided that Smith would be easier. So Second Lieutenant Eddie Smith went to war.

The officers in Battalion Headquarters made much of me, gave

me a cup of tea, and sent me on my way to the front line. Soon
we were slithering through the dark along muddy roads, in a
three-ton truck with no lights on, towards Hill 355, where B
Company was dug in on a vital sector of the front. Flashes from
exploding shells flickered constantly over the humpy skyline
ahead of us. Flares looped up and hung in the night. Whenever
we stopped, we could hear the boom of artillery and mortar fire.
I felt scared and overawed by this menacing new environment:
much as I had wanted to reach Korea, I had not foreseen the
shock of entering a forward battle area for the first time. It was
as if I had dived into cold water and was struggling for breath.

The moment I took command of 4 Platoon, I began an extraordinary, troglodytic existence. Like badgers, we lived in holes
deep underground, and slept by day, emerging into the open
under cover of darkness. Our main quarters were subterranean
bunkers known as hoochies – substantial chambers quarried out
of the hillside, with a minimum of five feet of overhead cover:
earth and rock were filled back in on top of a ceiling of inter-laid
steel pickets, so that they could withstand direct hits during
artillery barrages. Since many of the Durham soldiers were
miners, they could out-perform everyone else when it came to
digging, and we prided ourselves that our earthworks were the
finest in the line.

In these hoochies we lived, slept, washed, shaved and ate.
Our belongings were stuffed into steel ammunition boxes, and
some people hacked into the walls so that they could stand
books or photographs in niches. The dug-outs were connected
by an elaborate system of trenches, seven feet deep and walled
with corrugated iron, which ran for miles around the hillsides.
At every strategic point on the forward slope there was a fire-
trench or weapon pit, big enough to hold two or three people,
and alongside it, round a corner designed to baffle blast, a funk-
hole, or small bunker, with three feet of overhead cover, into
which defenders could dive whenever an enemy bombardment
came down.

By the time I reached the front, the war had solidified into a
static battle of attrition, with the two sides facing each other
from positions of strength across a no man's land which in some
places was only a hundred yards wide. Visiting senior officers

were struck by the close resemblance to conditions in the First World War. In our sector the country consisted of steep, rugged hills, every one of which had a number or nickname for easy reference. At first we were on Hill 355, known as Little Gibraltar. Five hundred yards out ahead of us was a summit known as John, and a hill with spurs running out in a star-shape was christened Alice Springs.

Months of shelling and counter-shelling had blasted all vegetation from the tops and higher slopes of the hills, leaving them bare and brown; but lower down there was scrub, which made a dangerous amount of noise when we pushed through it at night. In the valley paddy fields lay abandoned, encircled by bunds, or retaining banks, two or three feet high – enough to give cover against all but direct hits during mortar attacks. In summer this low ground was alive with frogs and mosquitoes. From our trenches we could generally see nothing of the enemy: for most of the time we were in the curious position of staring out from our observation posts at a blank hillside, which we knew was as deeply honeycombed by slit trenches and bunkers and tunnels as ours, and full of men burrowing away.

Just as movement had slowed to a halt, so tactics had ossified, and scope for innovation had dwindled. Every night we sent out reconnaissance and fighting patrols, and we constantly set ambushes designed to intercept any Chinese patrols heading towards our own line, bluffing and double bluffing from one night to the next over where these traps would be. Sometimes the enemy managed to creep across at night undetected, their aim being to lie up for the day in dead ground immediately beneath our defences, and then, the next evening, suddenly appear on our positions at a time when it seemed impossible for them to have crossed the valley, which we had been watching all day. To launch a major attack, they would put down an artillery bombardment and follow up so close behind it that they were taking casualties from their own shellfire, and, as the bombardment moved over our positions, they would be there, on our parapets, before we could emerge from cover to fight them off. Our tactics were therefore to put down shellfire on the Chinese and gradually to bring the bombardment right back on to our own trenches: only when the shelling stopped would we pop out, with our small arms and grenades, to fight if necessary.

During the months before my arrival I had not followed by any means every twist of the conflict – the first major military confrontation between the Communist bloc and the Western powers – but the main lines of it were familiar enough. In purely geographical terms, Korea is a peninsula of mainland China, an appendix reaching down for five hundred miles between the Yellow Sea and the Sea of Japan. After the Second World War the Russians had imposed Communism on North Korea, above the 38th parallel, and in June 1950 the North Koreans, incited by the Soviet Union, had invaded the south, capturing Seoul, the capital, and penetrating almost to the city of Pusan, in the far south-east.

The reaction of the United Nations was led by the United States and Britain, both of which immediately sent troops to support the south. In September 1950 a seaborne landing at Inchon, on the west coast, boldly conceived by the Supreme Commander of the UN forces, General Douglas MacArthur, took the North Koreans by surprise; after bitter fighting they were driven back into their own territory, and the Americans, pressing on into the north with UN authority, captured the North Korean capital, Pyongyang.

Then in November 1950 the Chinese intervened in strength; the UN lines were pierced, the Communists recaptured Pyong-yang, and early in 1951 re-took Seoul. For the British, the most celebrated action of the war was the three-day stand on the Imjin river by the First Battalion of the Gloucestershire Regiment at the end of April 1951: although surrounded, outnumbered, and reduced by casualties and the loss of prisoners to only one hundred men, the Glorious Glosters held out so valiantly that they retarded the whole Communist advance. After many further offensives and counter-offensives, the Communists were once again forced back behind the 38th parallel in the second half of May, with enormous losses, and peace talks opened in July. Ever since then – for nearly two years – discussions had dragged on, frequently being suspended, then resumed. During all this time fighting had flared intermittently, but the battle lines had hardly changed.

To us at the front towards the end of April 1953, questions
of higher strategy and international politics had no immediate
relevance. Our job was simply to hold our own ground on the
38th parallel, to harass the enemy as severely as possible, and,
by aggressive patrolling at night, to deny the Chinese opposite
us freedom of movement in no man's land. I had been with the
battalion fewer than twenty-four hours when I got my first taste
of this peculiar and alarming activity. While I found my feet, I
was put in the temporary charge of Bill Nott-Bower, a lieutenant
who had been in Korea for about six months. He struck me as
rather reserved, but friendly, and the sort of man who immediately inspires confidence. On a night when there was little moon,
I attached myself to his patrol of ten men. As dark was falling
we blacked our faces, checked our weapons for the third or
fourth time, checked our ammunition, did striker tests on our
grenades to make sure the detonator mechanisms were working,
and at last slipped out through our own defences towards the
low ground in the valley.

The first obstacle to be avoided was our own minefield, and
we picked our way carefully through the corridor known as the
minefield gap, which was guarded by a standing patrol. Then,
down among the paddy fields, we bumped into Chinese. Spurts
of flame spat into the darkness as sub-machine guns opened up
ahead of us. We replied with rifles, Bren guns, Sten guns and
grenades. Shells from our own artillery whistled over from
behind and began to burst just ahead. Chinese artillery opened
up, shells landing very close. The flashes left us temporarily
blinded. The noise was stupefying. I thought we were lost, in
every sense of the phrase, hemmed in by artillery fire between
our own minefield on one side and a stronger, better-sited
enemy patrol on the other.

Several men had been hit, and had to be carried. There was
no alternative but to risk it and hope that we could dance
between our own mines. In the thunderous confusion I rapidly
became aware of two facts: first that I had no idea of what we
were supposed to be doing, and second that I was absolutely
terrified. Then, through the chaos, I realized that Bill was
bellowing at us, in a loud but controlled voice, giving us clear
orders and encouragement. Never for a moment did he falter.

In that nightmare chaos he was a beacon to us all; it was entirely he who, by his example and leadership, prevented the patrol from disintegrating and brought us safely home.

That experience taught me one of the most important lessons of my life. Even as it was happening, I understood that at some time or other all military leaders are frightened, but that they must never show their fear. Still less must they let it interfere with their judgment. I saw that when I myself came to lead, I must never allow my own fears, doubts or lack of knowledge to show through. I appreciated that simply being in a position of command, and holding rank, can never compensate for weakness: if ever I showed lack of confidence or firmness of purpose, I should have failed. I began to understand that leadership is a lonely business: I was going to be on my own, and although I might take advice and listen to suggestions, the decisions upon which success or failure depended would be mine alone.

That night, then, marked a vital stage in my development – and soon my budding powers of leadership were put to a severe test. One day the Commanding Officer told me that he wanted to attach his personal bugler to my platoon so that the man could gain experience in the front line. Corporal Johnson – as I will call him – had an exceptionally high reputation for general smartness and efficiency, and of course he was king of the buglers. As this was his first attachment to a forward platoon, I decided to break him in gently by sending him out on a standing patrol in front of our minefield gap, where all he would have to do would be to lie still and watch for enemy movement.

Just as the patrol was about to leave, my Platoon Sergeant, Sergeant Baker, came into my hoochy with a worried look on his face. 'Sir,' he said, 'that bugger won't come.'

'What d'you mean?' I asked.

'Corporal Johnson. He won't give any reason, but he's refusing to come with us.'

I went out to talk to the man, but could not budge him. At once I was in a leadership crisis. In the front line of a major war, my orders were being disobeyed, and my men were standing round, watching to see what I would do. I thought rapidly. I could seek advice and help from my company commander, Major Reggie Atkinson – but if I did that, I should have failed in a moment of confrontation. The decision must be mine.

I pulled out my pistol, cocked it ostentatiously and levelled it at Johnson. 'Go,' I told him, 'or I shoot.'

He went. But what would have happened if he had stood his ground? Could I have carried out my threat? All I know was that, had he called my bluff, I should have been the loser, whether I fired or whether I dodged the issue. The incident taught me that there are times when any leader has to take unpopular, risky decisions, and that he must face them unflinchingly.

Soon life settled into a topsy-turvy routine. At dawn — one of the most likely times for an attack — we stood-to as the light came up. If all was quiet, we stood-down, and I would have a wash, a shave and breakfast, brought to my hoochy from the cookhouse on the back of the hill by my batman, Private Ainsworth — an excellent man of my own age who had been seconded to us from the King's Own Yorkshire Light Infantry. An intelligent and likeable Yorkshireman — a typical National Serviceman — he cleaned my kit, kept the hoochy tidy and ran errands, leaving me free to concentrate on operational problems. His job as a runner was both important and dangerous, and he had the intellect to think for himself and see what needed doing.

After breakfast I would be longing to go to sleep, because I had been up all night; but there were always daylight tasks to be done — company headquarters to be visited, duty rosters to be worked out, patrols to be planned, reports to be written up. If I was lucky, I would be asleep by midday, still wearing my combat kit, but with boots off, in a makeshift camp-bed fashioned from pieces of canvas and torn-up parachute canopies. After four hours, at the most, someone would wake me with a brew of tea. That was the worst moment of the day. Getting up in the morning, with the light coming and a nice, bright day to look forward to, is bad enough; but to wake up tired at dusk, with only dark and danger ahead, was ghastly. The tea helped pull me round. Then I would have a meal, brief the evening patrols, and check every man to make sure that he was properly equipped. Every night the standing patrol, which guarded our minefield gap, would be the first to slip away; but we also mounted reconnaissance and fighting patrols, all of which were carefully planned on a matrix at Battalion Headquarters.

Most of those not on patrol spent the night digging – for our position needed continuous repair and improvement. As an ordinary, soft-handed public school boy, who had never done sustained manual work, I was amazed by the power and persistence of our Geordie soldiers. Bred from generations of miners, they had huge, broad shoulders, and plundered the ground with steady shovelling movements all night long.

Whenever I remained in our position, I would often pay Company Headquarters a visit during the night, feeling my way along the communication trenches by means of the ropes slung on the walls. Then, before dawn, the patrols would come back in and be de-briefed, and everyone would stand-to until the danger period had passed. Then it was wash, shave, breakfast, and into the same routine again: an existence both mentally and physically draining. When, every ten days, we went back to a base area for a hot shower and a change of clothes, it seemed the greatest luxury on earth.

The DLI was lucky in having highly experienced senior officers. Peter Jeffreys – I soon realized – was an outstanding leader, who had commanded a brigade during the Second World War, and now did wonders in welding together a very green battalion, which contained about seventy per cent National Servicemen. Our Company Commander, Reggie Atkinson, was another veteran of the 1939–45 war, and the holder of two Military Crosses. He was a stickler for the highest standards – something of which I thoroughly approved. 'I don't think I like this,' he would say in his high, querulous voice as he came round inspecting our positions; and his niggling complaints used to enrage us. One of his obsessions was about sand-bagging: the bags had to be made into meticulously rectangular shapes, and laid overlapping each other as neatly as bricks in the wall of a house (this, of course, was absolutely sound, as good building made the walls far stronger). Another refrain was that we must have large supplies of ammunition right forward. 'You never know when you're going to be involved in a battle,' he would say, 'and you never know how long it's going to last.' He insisted that we had 6000 rounds of ammunition for every light machine gun, 1000 rounds for every rifle, and three dozen grenades per weapon-pit – colossal quantities.

Demanding though he could be, Reggie soon won my respect. He was strict and fair, and always said exactly what he thought. He took the trouble to tour our positions every day, inspecting them closely, and I saw that his attention to detail was essential in an operational environment. He did occasionally give praise, but not much, so that if you got any, you cherished it, and knew you had earned it.

I was fortunate, also, in my immediate subordinates. My Platoon Sergeant and right-hand man, Sergeant Baker, was not a very forceful character, but an exceptionally courteous and efficient man, with long experience, on which I could profitably draw. We had plenty of bright sparks among the junior non-commissioned officers, not least the young and able Corporal Collins, and Corporal Cranny, an outspoken, cheeky devil with a very quick brain who could achieve a lot if given the right directions. Needless to say, the soldiers did their best to turn their peculiar surroundings into an exotic replica of Durham by giving everything familiar names: their sector of the front became Little Durham or Brancepeth, the mobile cinema in the base area 'The Geordian', and the bar the 'Cock o' the North', after its original on the Great North Road. Morale was boosted by the flow of gifts which came out from home through the Mayor of Durham's Korean fund: Zenith multi-band radios – the latest type available – were greatly prized, and enough arrived for each platoon headquarters to have one and hear the news regularly.

Even with the stringent precautions on which Reggie Atkinson insisted, we kept suffering casualties. One night a heavy bombardment came down on our position, and we all took refuge in our bunkers – all except one cook, who remained in his tin shack of a cookhouse, on the back of the hill, out of sight of the Chinese, hoping he would get away with it. A shell landed almost on top of him, and he was mortally wounded by shrapnel in the stomach. I have never forgotten how he screamed with agony before he died.

Another night a Chinese bombardment severed the telephone cable which kept us in touch with Company Headquarters.

Because we thought a major attack was imminent, it seemed essential that the gap should be found and the line repaired. The lance corporal who volunteered was a hard-working, dedicated signaller, who took enormous pride in keeping our cable communications going. Out he went, only to be killed by another shell. His death left us feeling particularly low, because he was such a brave and unselfish man.

One evening two new officers were sent up to the front line before last light so that they could have a look at the ground over which they would be patrolling. The man in temporary charge of them was Bob Macgregor-Oakford, another platoon commander, who had been in Korea a few weeks longer than I had, and won a Military Cross for his outstanding courage on patrol. As they were standing in a trench, enemy mortars opened up, and Bob – whose reactions had been honed to a razor edge by weeks in the line – sensed at the last instant that one of the bombs was coming straight for them. With a yell he dived for cover, dragging one of the men down with him. But the newcomers, who had had no chance to learn the deadly sounds of mortar fire, reacted far more slowly. When the bomb landed on the parapet above them, the man whom Bob had seized was wounded in the side, but survived. The other was killed, on his first day at the war.

Worse than any of these losses inflicted by the enemy were self-inflicted battle accidents, and what the Americans called 'fratricide' or 'blue-on-blues' – casualties caused inadvertently by our own side. One relatively quiet evening I was in my bunker when I heard a *crump* from somewhere close at hand. Going to investigate, I found that a grenade had exploded in another hoochy. Four men had been crowded into a small space, and one of them had done a striker test. Somehow he had failed to remove the detonator beforehand. When he let the safety lever go, and heard the fuse fizzing, he dropped the grenade in a panic, and all four men dived for the exit. The leader tripped over the curtain hung as a blackout across the doorway, fell, and fetched down the others on top of him. The grenade exploded behind them and injured all four, two so badly that they had to be evacuated to the United Kingdom.

Another night we heard a sudden burst of Bren and other

small-arms fire from the area of our standing patrol. I called up Company Headquarters in search of information, but no one there had any news. Eventually word trickled back that the standing patrol had been attacked, and that one man had been killed and one injured. Only at the debriefing, after the survivors had returned, did we find out what had really happened. The members of the patrol has been sited fairly far apart, in all-round defence. One of them, becoming jumpy, thought he heard an enemy movement, opened fire, and hit one of his comrades in the back of the head. In the ensuing shoot-out another man was wounded. So, in these two incidents, I had lost six men out of the thirty-two in my platoon: almost twenty per cent casualties.

In the last few days of May, barely three weeks after I had arrived, we were swept up into the desperate struggle which became known as the fourth and last Battle of the Hook. For night after night rumours claimed that the Chinese were about to launch an all-out attack on the Hook – the hill then held by our neighbours, the Duke of Wellington's, and the place where Private Bill Speakman of the King's Own Scottish Borderers had won the Victoria Cross a year earlier, continuing to hurl rocks at the Chinese after he had run out of ammunition. We all thought the assault was coming in on the night of 20 May, for a phenomenal bombardment of 4500 shells rained down on the Dukes' positions; yet no attack followed, and it was not until dusk on the evening of the twenty-eighth that the Chinese suddenly arrived on the parapets in force. The violence of that night's fighting was indescribable: close-quarter and hand-to-hand combat raged for hours on end, and we Durhams, huddled in slit-trenches with overhead cover only a hundred and fifty yards away to one flank, poured enfilade small-arms fire into the attacking Chinese as shells continued to rain down on our own positions. By morning, when the assault was at last beaten off, the Dukes had lost twenty-four dead and a hundred and five wounded – but the bodies, or remains, of more than two hundred and fifty Chinese were scattered about the hill.

Death and injury became part of our lives. Whenever one of my platoon was killed or wounded, I always found it very moving, but at the same time I realized that I must be careful not to appear overcome. In feeling pity for men he has lost, it is easy for a commander to become sorry for himself; yet he must suppress any show of grief. Once they are dead, they are dead, and there is nothing more he can do for them. His job then is to keep everyone else alive, to bolster their morale and keep them going. If the commander cracks up because a body has been carried off on a stretcher, the rest of his unit will not survive for long.

That said, I myself found the night-patrols extremely frightening. They were also very exciting, so that I was always keen to go on them. But I also knew that patrolling was a high-risk activity, and that every time we went out, we were liable to be killed or wounded. A recce patrol, of three or four men, had the advantage of being small: it could move with stealth, and if necessary fade into the background. Yet I always felt more confident on a fighting patrol, ten or fifteen strong, as we were more heavily armed, and numbers gave a greater sense of security, together with the ability to retaliate. In the open, we would move in arrowhead or diamond formation, and I always put a good man at the back, with a Bren gun, to guard our rear, for the Chinese were uncannily adept at slinking up behind you, tagging along, and then suddenly opening fire into your backs.

The confusion and intensity of these night operations can best be indicated by an extract from the official intelligence report covering activities on the night of 24 June 1953:

One contact between ambush patrol and two enemy patrols. Total 1100 incoming mortar and 1500 rounds outgoing retaliation during action.

1. Ambush patrol (officer + 15) posted main strength on reverse slope Alice Springs, with forward element on crest.

2. 2210. Forward person noticed stealthy approach of enemy scout group. These shot whilst calling forward balance of squad. Forward person then doubled back through ambush, closely pursued by enemy, who were completely surprised by resultant fire.

3. Almost simultaneously with above action, further enemy patrol approached ambush from west, and two groups engaged standing patrols.

4. Ambush endeavoured to break contact and circle back to forward defence locations, but was followed, and both parties came under heavy enemy mortar fire. Enemy broke contact and patrol returned directly to company positions.

5. Subsequent sweep patrol at 0045 hours was heavily mortared, but found no enemy casualties. Observation at first light reported at least four bodies, however.

6. Final casualties:
Own 1 KIA [killed in action]
15 WIA [wounded in action] – ambush patrol
7 WIA – sweep patrol
1 KIA 22 WIA (inc two officers)
Enemy Four KIA (counted) plus minimum of ten further estimated.

From our frequent forays, we gradually built up a good working knowledge of no man's land. Our maps were not detailed enough to be of much use – and in any case it was highly inadvisable to switch on a torch, for a look at a map, while we were anywhere near the enemy. We relied more on detailed planning, a study of the route by daylight, and the accumulation of landmarks recognized by all – the lone bush, the big paddy bund, the shattered tree.

Whatever we were doing – reconnaissance or marauding – we were backed by immense firepower, for even I, a mere second lieutenant, had the authority to make direct radio requests for artillery support at any time. I had only to call 'Swan now', or some other agreed signal, to bring down a whole regiment's worth of artillery on a prearranged target (the Americans, in contrast, were reluctant to delegate authority. A patrol leader had to go through so many layers of clearance that, by the time fire-support arrived, the opportunity would have been lost or the position overrun – and many casualties resulted).

Besides artillery and mortars, we also had Centurion tanks, which withdrew behind the skyline during the day, but crawled forward into strengthened firing positions every evening, with only the turret and gun visible to the enemy, so that they could shoot point-blank at any target indicated to them. So accurate were they that they became almost our personal heavy weapons, which we could bring to bear very quickly, right over our own heads. Low-trajectory rounds made a devastating noise, but their effect was spectacular. When not patrolling, I found our own troop of tanks a particularly rewarding place to visit. The commander, Doug Henderson, was an excellent fellow, who always seemed to have a bottle of Scotch about him (we, the infantry, were dry): to climb into a tank, which was deliciously warm, and have a slug of whisky in Doug's light-hearted company, was the high spot of any day or night.

Peter Jeffreys was rarely in favour of mounting large patrols, and I was glad of this, as they seemed to achieve very little. Yet once he allowed Major Johnny Tresawna, an exceedingly brave officer seconded to us from the Oxfordshire & Buckinghamshire Light Infantry, to take out a whole company, more than a hundred strong. Meeting the Chinese head-on, they became involved in a tremendous gun battle, in which Johnny was killed, leading from the front. I thought it an awful waste that someone like that, who had survived the World War with such gallantry, and won a DSO, should die in the futile struggle for Korea. On another night the Australians mounted a patrol seventy strong and penetrated deep into enemy lines with the aim of bringing back a prisoner. They were good, tough, gung-ho fighters, but the Chinese were waiting for them in an ambush, and they were massacred: of the seventy who set out, only a sergeant-major and one other man came back.

As for myself, I had to learn how to command men the hard way. I arrived totally inexperienced, but now I was making plans which involved men's lives: every day I had to convince the men that the plans were good, and then ensure that everyone stood by what we had agreed. Commanding men – I began to see – is actually a question of getting them on your side, over a period of time, and working to bring them together as a loyal and coordinated team.

I thought it would help if I started a platoon notebook, in which I wrote down everyone's name and family background, adding more information as I discovered it, and I made particular efforts to visit all the men in their hoochies. We were living an extremely limited existence, isolated from the rest of the world in our little warren of bunkers, yet tied to a tight routine, busy for every minute of our waking hours, and all the time fighting the cumulative exhaustion brought on by strain and danger. In such conditions it was hard to find the time or energy to talk to the men: yet I forced myself to go and sit in their hoochies and chat to them, breaking down the formality of rank-structure, until I understood them and they understood me. I also made a point of briefing down, or passing on any information I was given to everyone in the platoon, so that they all knew what was going on. This may sound obvious – but in our contorted existence it was far from easy. By the time I came back from Company Headquarters in mid-morning, half my men would already be asleep; and when I myself woke up in the afternoon, feeling awful, I would face a frantically busy evening. In learning man-management, and in taking decisions, I was enormously helped by Bill Nott-Bower, whose hoochy (on Hill 355) was sited on my way down to the minefield gap, so that it was easy for me to drop in for a chat as I went past.

After a stint of three weeks at the front, we would go back for a spell in reserve, during which we dug positions in what had been nicknamed the Kansas Line – a second, defensive line which the UN forces would occupy if a ceasefire came into force and a demilitarized zone were established. Back there, five miles from the tension of the front, life was much easier, and people even found time for the occasional pleasantry. There were a few wild pheasants about the fields, and a story was told of how, one day in the winter, Peter Jeffreys had been out after them, easily recognizable as a British officer from his uniform. When a bird got up and he missed it with both barrels, an Australian private soldier lounging by the road shouted out contemptuously, 'I could have hit that bastard with a fucking *stone!*' Another night DLI men were guarding Pintail, one of the bridges over the Imjin, and a sentry stopped an American truck driven by a great big black soldier who could not remember the password. For a few moments there was an impasse: the Geordie held out, and the American glared down at him from his cab. Then suddenly he cried, 'You ever seen a goddamn black Chinaman?' and roared off across the river.

Even at the front there was the occasional frivolity. As 2 June, the day of the Queen's Coronation, approached, Bill Nott-Bower was busy preparing a surprise for the Chinese. He laboriously

stitched together some blue and orange ground–air identifica-
tion panels made of fluorescent cloth, two feet wide by six long,
to form the device E II R, covering about quarter of a tennis
court. On those rugged hills there were very few smooth patches
which could be seen from our own lines, but after scrutiny with
binoculars we had spotted one, and Bill made for it in the dark.
Snaking silently up to within a few yards of the Chinese sentries,
he pegged the panels down and withdrew – and in the morning
we found to our delight that the banner was in full view from
our own position. Better still, it was obviously not visible to the
Chinese, as it remained undisturbed for the rest of that spell in
the line. In fact the enemy realized that 2 June was a day of
celebration for us, and when our guns shot off red, white and
blue smoke shells, our men all gave three cheers, and our tanks
raised their guns to maximum elevation for one vast, simul-
taneous volley, their reaction (as a regimental report put it) 'was
for once phlegmatic', and they entered into the spirit of the
occasion by holding their fire all day, so that people on both
sides could move about in the open with a freedom impossible
at normal times.

In all we occupied three different positions – first Hill 355, on
the right of the line, the feature controlling that whole sector;
then Hill 287; and then the hill called Yong Dong, which was
further away from the Chinese than the other two. On our right
on 355 we had a unit of ROKs – Republic of Korea troops –
who were good fighters, but exceedingly physical, with a regard
for human life and dignity which by no means matched ours.
A man who committed some minor offence would be put into
full battle order and doubled up and down one of the very steep
hills until he dropped, whereupon he would be beaten back into
activity. One day we found that some chickens had disappeared
from our cookhouse; we lodged a complaint with the ROK platoon next door, and that evening we heard that the thief had
been identified and was about to be shot for minor theft. I
quickly went round and persuaded the ROK platoon commander to be lenient.

I was lucky in reaching Korea when the winter was over. The
rest of the Battalion had had to live through bitter cold, with
deep snow and temperatures so low that no standing patrol

could remain on station for more than half an hour without serious risk of hypothermia setting in. During my time the temperatures were never uncomfortably high or low, and the main meteorological enemy was rain, which turned our trenches to rivers of mud and flooded our hole-in-the-ground latrines.

In the final days of the war, fierce fighting flared up all along the line as the Chinese tried desperately to make last-minute gains – for everyone knew that the peace talks in progress at Panmunjon were close to a settlement, and that, when the end came, the frontier would be established according to the final positions of both sides. Little was achieved by these terminal battles, but heavy casualties were sustained, particularly by the Americans and Chinese.

By then the DLI were in reserve and helping to build the Kansas Line: the Battalion had done eleven months of its year-long stint, and was about to hand over to the Royal Warwickshire Regiment. Building hoochies for other people to occupy, in a reserve position which might never be needed, was an exceedingly tedious occupation, which I hated. There was some compensation in the fact that summer had arrived, and we were living in tents rather than in holes. When the ceasefire at last came into effect on 27 July, we were having a dinner party in our mess-tent, with candles on the tables and bottles of champagne: the instant the news arrived, we rushed outside and stood in awe, listening to the silence. For the first time in three years, the thunder of artillery had ceased to rumble across the hills. We all felt prodigious relief – and perhaps it was because people let their guard down that, the very next day, a man was killed when he walked on to a mine.

Soon it was time to leave for our next posting, Egypt. But before we took ship at Pusan, we went by train to visit the war cemetery at Seoul. Nobody remained unmoved by that experience: our own casualties had been high enough – in a year the Battalion had lost twenty-four dead and one hundred and forty-four wounded – but they were as nothing compared with the immense losses – over 33,000 dead and over 100,000 wounded – suffered by the Americans.

My first experience of combat had lasted barely three months, but it had been extraordinarily intense. I had discovered that war is immensely exacting, but rarely clear-cut: everything had been muddle and confusion. Trying to analyse my feelings as we left, I found I had no personal hate for the Chinese. I saw that for them, as for us, fighting was a job which had to be done: their political masters had sent them into the field, just as ours had sent us, and the enemy soldiers must have been going through much the same experiences and emotions as we were. Nevertheless, they had done their best to kill us, and the only way of stopping them had been to shut them up. The North Koreans were another matter – a cruel and evil lot. Unfortunately it was they who had guarded most of our prisoners.

If I had learnt one rule of survival in war, it was this: when someone is out to kill you, you had better get him first, or at least keep out of his way – otherwise you will not be thinking about the problem for very much longer.

CHAPTER 6

FROM DESERT TO DURHAM

1953–56

Sailing to Egypt aboard the troopship *Empire Orwell*, I began to think about home. For more than four months I had had no news of my family. I had written several letters to my mother, but I had not expected any answers, as I knew she was incapable of replying. I had also written to my grandmother, but – with relations so strained – I was hardly surprised to have heard nothing from her. I assumed that Michael was too busy bending the rules at Harrow to find time for correspondence, and that David was applying himself studiously to his lessons at St Peter's Court. The only person who had made contact at all was Nanny Turnbull; I was glad to hear from her, of course, but as she wrote from her home in Dumfries, she sent no word about events in the south of England. The lack of contact did not worry me: my upbringing had reinforced my natural independence, and I was immersed in my army existence. Nevertheless, I should have liked to know how my mother was progressing.

We had hardly steamed out of Pusan when tension began to rise, for the ship was carrying many British prisoners recently released by the Communists, and among them were a few who had tried to curry favour with the Chinese, or even worked actively for them. Conditions were difficult anyway: the troop decks were crowded, with soldiers milling around everywhere, and it was hard to keep them occupied. Up to the surface, inevitably, welled all the gossip, malice and sheer hatred which had been festering in the prison camps: fingers began to be pointed, and rough justice to be meted out.

Most of the former prisoners belonged to the Gloucesters

and the Royal Ulster Rifles, and they included the legendary Lieutenant-Colonel J. P. Carne, the Gloucesters' Commanding Officer, whose extraordinary courage and leadership during the stand on the Imjin won him the Victoria Cross. On shipboard the job of the DLI was to run the troop decks, and it proved no easy task. Our main problem was that, although we were in charge, we did not know the men, or what individuals had done. Besides, the soldiers themselves were demoralized and uncoordinated, for in captivity they had been separated from their officers, and their guards had done all they could to break down unity among them. With the exception of Anthony Farrar-Hockley, the Gloucesters' Adjutant, who had attempted to escape from the Chinese nine times and still had phenomenal energy, their officers were not in a fit state to spend time on the troop decks. Carne himself seemed very withdrawn – which was not surprising, after the ghastly privations which he had suffered during eighteen months of solitary confinement, much of it spent shut up in a box like a coffin. The result was that we felt we were sitting on a time-bomb.

In this awkward situation Farrar-Hockley was a priceless asset. Such was his spirit that he seemed almost as if he had just returned from leave, refreshed, and his help prevented any number of fights and injuries. With his guidance we identified men who were definitely guilty, and known to be, of siding with the Chinese. These we weeded out and put into the cells on the lowest deck, purely for their own protection; but by the time we reached Hong Kong, it had become clear that animosity against them was so strong as to make it dangerous for them to remain on board. Those known to be threatened – either because they deserved it, or simply because rumour had pointed at them – were therefore put ashore and left behind to cool off at a camp up in the hills.

The rest of the voyage to Egypt was more relaxed, and I was able to spend time with my own platoon. By now I felt that it was not just my job to command them: having come through a searing experience with them, I had grown to love them. The men were my life, and they meant a tremendous lot to me. Working with them, getting the best out of them, seemed almost a calling. Thinking the matter through, I always came back to the same conclusion: that the more I did for them, the greater my own reward. This theory, constantly proved in practice, became part of my philosophy in life: if you really look after people – which does *not* mean being soft with them, but taking more trouble about them than you take about yourself – they quickly appreciate your efforts on their behalf. You win their respect, and a special relationship develops. Talking to them on the boat, I conceived the idea of staging a platoon concert – and this proved a hilarious success, with everyone who had the slightest talent taking part. My own contribution was a direly tuneless rendering of 'The Blaydon Races', for which I had to learn the words.

By the time we were ferried ashore at Fayid, on the Great Bitter Lakes in Egypt, many of the soldiers had been away from England for a year, and they faced the prospect of two more years abroad before they saw home again. In those days, however, such long postings were routine, and nobody thought of complaining. Although we did not like to admit it, we were in effect an army of occupation, whose task was to guard British installations along the Suez Canal against an increasingly hostile native population. Over the past few years strong nationalist tendencies had boiled up: in the summer of 1952 King Farouk had been deposed, and in June 1953, only weeks before we arrived, General Neguib had proclaimed Egypt a republic, with himself as President and Prime Minister. The British were becoming more and more unpopular, and the Arabs took every chance to show their resentment of our presence, especially along that emblem of imperialistic capitalism, the Suez Canal. In those days, before the advent of long-distance jet aircraft, the canal was still of the highest strategic importance, since it cut thousands of miles off any journey to the Far East, and the Egyptians dearly longed to take it over.

St Gabriel's Camp consisted almost entirely of tents pitched over concrete bases; the camp was surrounded by high wire and patrolled at night by armed sentries: a necessary precaution, since the Egyptians, besides being anti-British in general, were astonishingly clever thieves – as one incident will show. The officers' mess and individual tents stood in a compound of their own, floodlit at night, and fenced in by ten-foot wire patrolled by armed guards. It seemed impossible that any intruder could penetrate this small area unseen; yet one night some Arab, by an amazing feat of agility and fieldcraft, slipped in through the wire and carried off everything portable from the Commanding Officer's tent while he was asleep inside it – not only his uniform and belongings, but even his dressing-gown, which had been lying on the end of his bed.

By then the CO was Lieutenant-Colonel P. H. M. 'Crackers' May, who had succeeded Peter Jeffreys when the battalion left Korea. The nickname Crackers was thought to derive either from his short-fused temper, or from the craziness of the daring which he had shown leading patrols in the Second World War. Either way, it suited him perfectly. He looked every inch an officer – always very well turned out, with hair immaculately brushed and moustache neatly trimmed – and he was certainly explosive enough for us to be a bit frightened of him; but he was also a first-class leader.

Naturally he was not pleased by the theft of his kit. Apart from the personal loss, it reflected poorly on the alertness of the battalion. But his reaction to the outrage was original and constructive: he asked me to highlight the weaknesses of the officers' mess compound, and to write an appreciation of how, if I were a thief, I would break into the camp. 'Study it from the enemy's point of view,' he told me – and in so saying he taught me a valuable lesson: that a commander should always try to put himself into the mind of the opposition, and think through any confrontation not merely from his own end, but from that of the enemy as well.

Out in the flat desert beyond the wire, I studied the camp from all angles and worked out a way of beating the defences. I then suggested various small improvements, such as changes in the lighting; and even if I could not come up with any very original ideas, the exercise made me feel that perhaps I had something to offer the battalion. I daresay that in giving me the task it was Crackers's aim all along to boost a young officer's confidence.

Our life was uncomfortable, to put it mildly. The heat was barely tolerable, the flies infuriating. We were on guard at least three nights a week, and we had no ready-made entertainment:

no telephone, no radio, still less television or videotapes. In those days recreation was seen as a privilege, not necessarily always available. The desert began immediately outside the camp wire: flat at first, it stretched away to low hills in the distance. The nearest native community was Fanara, a village of mud huts about a mile away, and the nearest town, Fayid, five or six miles off, had little to attract us. Cairo was five hours' drive to the west, and in any case out of bounds. Even in our own area the movement of military personnel was governed by strict rules: nobody was allowed into a civilian area alone, as there was always a risk that Arabs would try to cut the throat of a solitary Briton.

My own reaction to these privations was to create novel forms of entertainment for the men. The first was judo. As no mats were available, I commandeered some reject mattresses, which had been urinated on, and sewed several together into enormous mats. Then I found a non-commissioned officer who was a judo Dan, persuaded him to run classes, and soon had quite a few soldiers interested.

My next venture was into camel racing. As anyone who has dealt with camels knows, they can be quiet and friendly, but equally they can be wilful, and they tend to work best for their owners. When I hired half a dozen from the surrounding villages, I knew we were in for a lively time. In front of a strong turn-out from the battalion, volunteer riders found that merely to mount a camel is quite a performance. The beast kneels down, and the jockey has to scramble on to its back, which is still quite a way off the ground; then, at a command, it stands up with a violent rocking motion, back legs first, front separately, so that the rider is bounced vigorously up and down.

After copious advice had been yelled at the jockeys, we had six of them on board. A few bets were placed, and away they went on a course that was supposed to be roughly oval. One or two owners entered into the spirit of the occasion, hoping that they might win some money, or at least that their animals would establish a local reputation for speed. Others, however, were not interested, and soon lost control of their camels, which headed out across the desert towards their home villages, with soldiers jolting desperately on their backs, too far from the ground to jump off easily, and knowing that if they suddenly arrived in some strange settlement, the natives would almost certainly be hostile. In the end most of them opted for bruises and jumped, and altogether the afternoon proved such a success that two more meetings were staged, by popular demand.

An equally enthusiastic response greeted the concerts which I initiated. Here my experience of staging the show on shipboard proved a good foundation: again, we had to depend largely on our own talent, but the high spot of every performance was the belly dancer, hired from some sleazy local source at minimal expense. Anywhere else, the sight of a fat Egyptian woman, rotating her rolls of stomach in time to peculiar Arab music, might not have created much of a stir; but here in the desert the soldiers, who had been starved of female company for months, greeted even the blowsiest harridan with an amazing cacophony of wolf-whistles, howls and groans, and every show was packed.

Soon we developed a more dangerous addiction – to cross-country motorcycling. With some justification the DLI prided itself on being a leading polo regiment, but polo and horses were anathema to me, and motorbikes had far greater appeal. At first I borrowed a 250cc BSA from the MT department, which was run by my old friend John Burkmar, and rode about the desert behind the camp purely for fun. Then I found that several of the soldiers were equally keen, so we formed ourselves into a group and built up a cross-country scramble team. When we heard that the army ran an annual scramble competition, we entered for it and began to train hard, getting up at dawn and riding out into the hills before sun-up – with the result that, to the slight incredulity of everyone else in the Regiment, we won the Suez Canal Zone championships. By then I myself had dropped out, because some of the men had become more skilled than me; but when the team went forward to the Middle East championships in Cyprus, it did brilliantly and came second – an achievement which silenced the sneers of the polo players and earned the Regiment no small amount of credit.

These extra activities meant that every moment of my days was full; they also meant that I had to get up very early in the morning – and the consequence was that I found it impossible to stay awake in the evenings. I came to dread mess nights –

the official dinners held two or three times a week, for which everyone had to appear in dress uniform – and soon I established a reputation for falling asleep between the main course and pudding. Seeing that I was nearly infallible in this respect, Crackers May once came to dinner with a noisy, old-fashioned alarm clock; when he saw me nodding, he wound it up, set it to go off in a few minutes' time, and passed it down the table to one of my neighbours, who secreted it in a piece of regimental silver in front of me. When suddenly it jangled into life, I leapt up with a frightful start, thinking dawn had come, and sent everyone into paroxysms of laughter.

More to my taste was to escape from the camp altogether and take my platoon down to Bir Udeib, a training area on the edge of the Red Sea, about sixty miles to the south. That was a wonderfully remote place, which gave us marvellous freedom: we had the sea for swimming, the beach, flat desert, and then empty hills rising inland to the west, in which we could manoeuvre and fire live ammunition without interference.

Crackers May was very good about giving me my head at Bir Udeib: seeing that I was enthusiastic and unorthodox, and always made training as adventurous and realistic as possible – sometimes at considerable risk – he let me go down there and get on with it for weeks at a time. Inevitably we had several narrow scrapes, but all were instructive. Once I took a truckload of soldiers up a very narrow track which climbed at an angle across the face of a mountain. Halfway up, the inner side of the wagon began to grate against the rock; the outer wheels were on the edge of a precipice, and for several minutes it seemed certain that the vehicle must topple over. I ordered everyone but the driver out, and somehow he managed to claw his way to the top. Another day we went off on a wide, clockwise sweep through the desert, intending to end up at the port of Suez, twenty miles north of our camp; but because I refused to trust my compass, we became lost and almost ran out of petrol in the middle of the desert, with sixty men and very little water. That episode taught me once and for all that the basic essential of map-reading and navigation is to believe what your compass is telling you.

Living this full and energetic existence, I found that the

months passed with astonishing speed. Crackers May several times discussed the possibility of my switching from a short-service to a regular commission, and I am sure I puzzled him with my attitude to promotion: I told him, truthfully enough, that I was not in the least worried about what rank I achieved. I was more interested in finding things to do which I enjoyed, and at which, because I enjoyed them, I had some chance of succeeding.

My over-riding ambition was still to become a member of the SAS, and Crackers, like everyone else I consulted, tried to talk me out of it, saying that to join such a shoddy organization would finish my career prospects in one quick move – a kind of sudden death. The reputation of the SAS was then at an all-time low. The Regiment had been disbanded after the Second World War, but had been reformed in 1952 from the Malayan Scouts, a body of volunteers raised a year earlier by 'Mad' Mike Calvert to fight Communist terrorists in the jungle. Calvert's idea had been to release men from gaol and put them to soldiering; but although his Scouts were far from ineffective, they were also very wild and undisciplined, and won themselves a bad name through their cavalier approach on operations and their riotous behaviour off-duty in Kuala Lumpur.

At this stage the SAS was not in the Regular Army order of battle, and thus, however successful one might have been in it, the Regiment could not offer any long-term future. Yet by the time I was in Egypt, in 1953 and 1954, a new era was already dawning, for an outstanding officer called John Woodhouse had set up a selection process which had begun to produce a far higher standard of trooper. But the Regiment's poor image persisted, and there was a good deal of sense in the advice I was receiving. All the same, I remained entranced by David Stirling's visionary concept of the unit, and how it should work, and I persevered in my determination to become a member. In the end Crackers made a deal: he promised that if, at the end of our Egyptian tour, I went back to the DLI depot at Brancepeth and put in a year training recruits, the Regiment would release me to have a shot at joining the SAS.

He also pressed me to try for a regular commission, as the Regiment was short of officers. I myself was still uncertain about how long I wanted to stay in the army; but in due course I yielded to friendly arguments and travelled back to the United Kingdom to take my Regular Commission Board at Westbury, in Wiltshire. Naturally I wanted to succeed, as a matter of pride, but it was with mixed feelings that I tackled the written tests, interviews and obstacle courses. When I heard that I had passed, the brigadier in charge told me that it would be good for my career if I went to Sandhurst. The idea of a two-year training course appalled me, and, with what must have seemed atrocious arrogance, I replied that I was not prepared to do that under any circumstances. What the brigadier made of this, I cannot imagine; but I did switch from a short-service to a regular commission, and, although I did not realize it at the time, this proved a decisive step in my career.

My second year in the Middle East was enlivened by trips to Jordan and the Lebanon. I was delighted when I heard that my company was to go on detachment to Aqaba, then a tiny settlement at the head of the Gulf of Aqaba, just inside Jordan's border with Saudi Arabia. Reggie Atkinson had moved on, and the company was now commanded by Major Francis Greenwell, who became a good friend (and later asked me to stand godfather to his son Robert). We steamed southwards down the Gulf of Suez and then northwards up the Gulf of Aqaba, to the point where the British army was maintaining a tented camp which housed one infantry battalion and a detachment of artillery. We had strict orders not to stray over the frontier into Saudi territory, but as the border was not marked, we naturally wandered across what we took to be the line of it, just to be able to say that we had done so.

Aqaba was another extremely remote spot, ideal for training, as it was well away from any other unit, and the village consisted of nothing but a few huts (today it is a thriving port). One of the joys of life there was the swimming, for a magnificent coral reef extends two or three hundred yards out to sea, only a few feet below the surface, before dropping away sheer as the face of a mountain, hundreds of fathoms into the dark-blue depths of the Gulf.

Our equipment was primitive – we had only the most basic face-masks – but the first time I swam out over the reef I became so absorbed that, before I noticed what was happening, my back had been severely sunburnt. For a week I was in acute discomfort, and that, combined with treading on a sea-urchin and getting its spines embedded in my foot, brought home to me the importance of educating one's men in the dangers of living in the tropics, and of teaching them how to protect themselves against natural hazards. Thus we had strict rules about when men were and were not allowed to take their shirts off, and we made sunburn an offence, because it was avoidable.

From Aqaba I had a chance to visit Petra, the ancient capital of the Nabataeans, and one of the archaeological wonders of the world. All who went were astonished by the splendour of the site, which one approaches through a narrow gorge hundreds of feet deep, and by the tombs, temples and other buildings carved out of the rose-red sandstone cliffs. Today the place is a major tourist attraction and heavily frequented; forty years ago, it was deserted, and the absence of people powerfully increased its mystery.

One tragedy marred our otherwise idyllic months at Aqaba. I made friends with Jeremy Cockburn, a Gunner officer the same age as myself; a very able and likeable fellow, he too had a passion for exercise, and together we used to run up the nearest mountain after work had finished every evening. Then, soon after we had left, he was suddenly struck down by poliomyelitis – the scourge of young people at that time, before the Salk vaccine had become available – and within a week he was dead.

Another chance to escape from St Gabriel's came when two officers were posted for a fortnight to the Lebanon, learning to ski. Probably Crackers May thought it was time I had a change and a rest: at any rate, he nominated me as the DLI candidate for one of the places. Together with an officer from the Royal Artillery, John Barnard, I flew to Cyprus in a military aircraft, and then on by civil air to the Lebanon. At a lovely resort called The Cedars, high in the mountains on the border with Syria, we were taught to ski by a first-class French instructor, Louis Conte, and had a fantastic holiday, with perfect snow, hot sun, and good food in a comfortable Lebanese army mess.

Even in the Canal Zone there were places in which one could escape the drudgery of routine at St Gabriel's. One was Jebel

Maryam, an ammunition dump in the middle of a lake near Ismaelia. The only means of reaching the site was by landing craft: once there, with a guard the size of a strong platoon, one was totally cut off from the outside world, with no possibility of a surprise visit from any senior officer, since anybody who wished to cross the lake had to send radio warning of his approach. This, to me, was bliss, as it meant that I could arrange the guards to my own liking.

In the spring of 1955, as our tour drew towards its end, the tide of Egyptian nationalism was rising steadily. General Neguib had lasted less than a year as President: in April 1954 he had been deposed by a revolutionary council of army officers, who ruled the country for the time being. But the man whom outside observers were watching with the greatest anxiety was Lieutenant-Colonel Gamal Abdel Nasser, head of the military junta. A violently outspoken opponent of colonialism, he was waiting with undisguised eagerness for the British to depart, and stirring up feeling against us by any means he could devise.

Incidents round our camps, already frequent, kept increasing, as intruders tried to break in and steal things, or merely sought to annoy us. One of their most brilliant and outrageous coups was made at Abu Sultan, an immense ammunition dump out in the desert, with a perimeter of some twenty-five miles, which needed most of a battalion to guard it. A week or two before the British were to withdraw, a bulldozer disappeared, and it seemed that someone had stolen it from under the noses of the guards. Nobody could understand how they had managed this – and only an airborne reconnaissance, flown over the site, revealed what they had done. They had dug a large hole in the desert, driven the bulldozer out there, parked the vehicle in the pit and covered it over with sand, intending to return and exhume it once we had left. Unfortunately for them, although they had obliterated most of the tracks, they had left a few, and their ruse was unmasked.

At last the day came for us to leave. On 26 May 1955 – a month after my twenty-first birthday – the regimental flag was lowered for the last time over St Gabriel's Camp, and we marched out to the nearby railway siding to board a train for Port Said. There we embarked on Her Majesty's Troopship

Lancashire, and set off on the relatively short, ten-day voyage back to England. As many of the soldiers had been abroad for three years, excitement ran high, and the trip was made memorable by a short, sharp incident. One afternoon, during the statutory quiet period, Crackers May was snoozing peacefully in a deck chair, clad only in sailing hat, dark glasses and bathing trunks, when a Bengali deck-hand accidentally dropped a tin of white paint on him from above. The ensuing explosion delighted all ranks, and next day at the children's fancy dress party, the first prize – given away by the Colonel – went to a very small boy wearing only a sailing hat, dark glasses and bathing trunks, smeared all over with white cream, and carrying a notice which read: 'The first man who laughs gets twenty-eight days'.

On 6 June, under overcast skies, we steamed up the Mersey amid triumphant blasting of horns to a grand welcome from regimental families and friends assembled on the quay. After the heat of Egypt, England seemed extraordinarily cool and green. Because a strike had brought the railways to a standstill, a fleet of buses had been laid on, and these took us to the depot at Brancepeth, where we sorted ourselves out before proceeding on leave.

At home – insofar as I had a home – things had improved slightly. My mother was still in hospital, but, little by little, her memory was returning, and she was pleased to see me. She had put on a lot of weight, and her face had lost much of its fineness – but this seemed a small price to pay for her partial recovery. At Old Place I found to my relief that I was back on speaking terms with my aunt and grandmother: I had softened them up with a continuous bombardment of letters from abroad, and they could hardly help being curious about my experiences. It was good to hear that David was doing well at St Peter's Court, and that Michael had left Harrow early at his own request to join the Fleet Air Arm. Nevertheless, our fundamental family problem remained unresolved. Joyce's animosity towards her sister was unchanged, and she was determined that my mother should stay in hospital indefinitely. I still felt that we must bring her out into a more stimulating environment, if ever she was to have a chance of making a full recovery.

After a week or two I began to find leave rather boring, as I had nothing particular to do, and I was glad to return to Durham, where I took over as Training Subaltern in charge of the new recruits who came into the Regiment in drafts. Still my sights were set on the SAS, but for the moment I had a challenging job which I soon began to enjoy.

It was fascinating to see what changes a basic course could make in lads coming raw from civilian life. They arrived as over-grown boys, with gangling limbs and long hair, straight from school or from the pits, lacking in discipline or motivation. Ten weeks later they were smart, fit and confident: they had developed a fierce competitive spirit, which left them in no doubt that their platoon was superior to all others, and they marched off the square proficient young soldiers. To achieve this transformation with one intake after another gave me no mean satisfaction.

Fortunately for me, the course was not rigidly fixed or centrally directed, so that I had plenty of scope for innovation. Better still, I came under the wing of two first-class senior officers – Major Jim Collingwood and his successor, Major Gill Maughan. Gill was short and bouncy, a great enthusiast himself and a strong supporter of other enthusiasts, who let his subordinates get on with things. Jim Collingwood was entirely different – much quieter and more phlegmatic – yet even more willing than Gill to stand back and let young officers have their head.

By now I had built up a useful bank of experience: things I had seen in Japan, Korea and Egypt came together to give me a clear idea of how I could make training realistic by introducing a degree of risk and danger. I had become a strong believer, for instance, in the value of firing live ammunition, and of giving the men a feel for what being under fire is like. On the thirty-yard range inside the camp I used to make them crawl through a pit which ran across in front of the targets, so that they had to pass two or three feet beneath a stream of bullets pouring into the bank from light machine guns. Of course it was highly illegal, and if there had been an accident, I should have had no excuse; but I felt that if we always stuck to the rules, life would be very dull, and nobody would learn anything.

Out on the ranges at Whitburn, I did what I could to make

shooting practice more interesting. It seemed self-evident that, to become effective infantrymen, soldiers must fire large numbers of rounds in training, and I managed to squeeze ever-greater amounts of ammunition out of the system. Rather than the dull, standard practices, in which one lay down and fired five or ten rounds at a stationary target, I built in as many innovations as I could devise – snap-shooting at moving targets, running down the range between firing-points, and so on. It all sounds obvious now, but in those days such novelty was rare.

I also introduced more night training. In the past the army had been reluctant to lay on night exercises, partly because they disrupted daytime routine; but my tour in Korea had taught me that, whereas fighting by day is relatively simple, combat in the dark requires a much higher standard of training. Above all, it demands confidence, which can only be built up by continual practice. Most of our recruits had never been out at night alone: we had to overcome their fear of the dark, and of being unable to communicate visually. Night-fighting in the dry moat of the castle, section patrols and ambushes – all this was strange to the men, but most of them found it exciting and enjoyable. In general I tried to create opportunities for people to use their initiative and develop their imagination.

Looking back, I realize that I must have become a bit fanatical about training. In the winter, when we had a blizzard, and some of my men were taken for snow-clearance, I had quite a serious row with my superior officers because my recruits were missing valuable training time. The immediate result was that I got a rocket, but because I made such a nuisance of myself, the Commanding Officer in the end found it easier to use someone else's soldiers for shovelling snow, so that mine were left alone. Here was another lesson: that a person who makes a justified fuss often gets what he wants, because it is simpler for the authorities to pester someone else who has not bothered to complain.

Perhaps my blood had grown thin after two years in Egypt; but that winter seemed bitterly cold. Once again I was living in Brancepeth Castle, and if I was lucky, my batman would light a coal fire in my room; but the place was still so icy that I bought a one-bar electric fire and plugged it in illegally. At least the hot water was always scalding, and one could soak luxuriously in the vast, cast-iron baths.

With my eye on the SAS, I was more and more concerned about physical fitness. When my platoon was due to go out to the ranges at Whitburn – a blasted heath on top of the cliffs, over which the north-east wind howled in from the sea – I would speed-march out, leaving camp in the pre-dawn darkness to cover the twenty-odd miles by the time the soldiers' bus arrived. I had acquired another golden retriever, also called Nell, who used to plod around the camp with me; one day I took her on my speed-march, but she became exhausted long before we reached the ranges, and when the troop bus came past, I had to bundle her aboard. Altogether, I must have grown rather intense in my preparations, for I cut pieces of scrim off a camou-flage net and sewed them on to my cotton overalls – to the delight of my platoon.

As always, I was packing every minute of every day with activity, and I tended to work right through weekends, preparing the next week's lectures. About once a month I would take a day off and go into York, but I was still very poor, and most of my shopping consisted of staring wistfully through store windows. By dint of saving and scrounging, by being exceed-ingly mean and never buying drinks in the mess, I did eventually manage to buy my first car, a black, second-hand Hillman coupé, for which I paid £300; being elderly and well-used, it gave a certain amount of trouble, but it also gave me a degree of inde-pendence, and the ability to travel south on leave.

The year which I had promised Crackers May I would serve at Brancepeth soon passed – and it was a long enough period in which to train recruits. Satisfying as it was to see the changes that the basic course could bring about, the work would have become very repetitive if I had continued with it. I was therefore glad on every count when October 1956 came along, and the DLI released me to try my luck on the SAS selection course.

CHAPTER 7

SAS RECRUIT

1956

This regiment was different: that much was immediately clear. Instead of being formed into a squad and paraded about, with shouts ringing in our ears, we were left to our own devices. At once we were introduced to the fundamental SAS principle of delegating responsibility to the lowest possible level – and in this instance the lowest level was each individual candidate for selection. Nobody could imagine a greater change from the rest of the army, which tends to over-organize men and make sure they have no chance of putting a foot wrong: here, it was every man for himself – and I rejoiced, because that was what I wanted.

With some difficulty, and in a state of considerable tension, I found my way to a tin hut tucked away at the back of a barracks in Aldershot. There, in a shabby office, I was greeted by a friendly but owlish man, with large, horn-rimmed spectacles and lank black hair slicked down over his head. He was quiet and charming, and seemed to be welcoming me to a unit with a nice, gentle atmosphere. His manner eased my nervousness, and as he took down my details, I felt better. Little did I know that Major Dare Newell had a formidable record of fighting behind enemy lines, and was one of the postwar architects of the Regiment which I had set my heart on joining. A man absolutely devoted to the SAS, and modest to a fault, he could be exceedingly tenacious, and indeed quite ruthless, when promoting the Regiment's interests or defending it against detractors, and his placid exterior concealed a core of steel. Somehow I sensed this at our first meeting: though his demeanour was courtesy itself, he made a deep impression.

Soon I had been issued with a bergen, or rucksack, and a railway warrant to Brecon, a garrison town in the mountains of central Wales. Nobody shepherded us to the station: we were simply told that we should catch a certain train. As we trundled westwards across England, I knew that everything hung on my performance over the next two weeks. Could I measure up to the challenges ahead? And who were all these people with whom I was going to tackle them? Glancing round the faces in the compartment, I could see that everyone was in the same state of apprehension, heightened by the fact that all were strangers to each other. I assumed that, like me, they were individualists who wanted to break away from the formal, drill-machine discipline which obtains in the army as a whole, and have a chance of living by self-discipline, the touchstone of the SAS.

At Newport we changed trains and rattled northwards on a single-track line into the hills. Suddenly I realized how much I was on my own. So far in the army, I had been swept along by general organization, but now I was responsible for myself. If I had missed the train, I should have had no one else to blame; if I did not arrive in Brecon on time, the fault would be mine alone. The thought was invigorating, but it had the effect of increasing tension still more.

At last, in the evening, the train stopped at a bleak little station in the mountains. We piled out on to the platform, and because the authorities had deliberately not sent any transport to meet us, we walked the short distance to Dering Lines, where we were put into a barrack room for the night. We knew little about what was going to happen to us, and the staff told us almost nothing, as it was part of their policy to confront us constantly with new challenges at short notice. Our only instructions that evening were to be on parade immediately after breakfast in the morning.

Thinking that it would be sensible to start the day with a hearty meal, I tucked into porridge, bacon and eggs. Almost at once this proved a mistake. The first thing we were required to do was double up and down the slope at the back of the camp until we could double no more. Inevitably, after the first two ascents and descents, my breakfast blew back at me and came to rest on the hillside – after which I went on grimly, feeling chastened and trying not to become annoyed. Dimly I saw that there was method in this apparently senseless slogging up and down: right at the start it was eliminating a few scroungers, and others who had underestimated the task they had set themselves, leaving the staff time to concentrate on serious candidates.

After that leisurely initiation, life became steadily tougher as we were despatched into the mountains, one by one, on a series of endurance marches which lasted on and off for the next twelve days. In these trials of stamina and initiative every man travelled alone, with no companion in whom he could confide his fears or from whom he could seek advice. Some of the marches were purely against the clock: each of us had to reach a rendezvous in a certain time, doubling over the hills for twenty-four or thirty-six hours with heavy bergens on our backs. Other trials were also of speed and endurance, but all incorporated map-reading, and most included minor tests of initiative, such as the collection of information from fixed points. During these marathons I found that there was no time for rest: I just had to keep going and going. Still less was there time to cook: whenever I felt faint from lack of food, I hacked open a can of compo rations and choked some calories down cold.

At least the season and the weather were on our side. In mid-October, there was as yet no snow on the mountains, and the temperature was never uncomfortably low. Although we had some wet days and nights, it did not rain by any means all the time. Nor were the nights so long as to mean that most of our movement was in the dark.

Nevertheless, conditions were gruelling enough. I thought I was fit when I arrived, but soon discovered my error: weight-carrying in the mountains demanded an altogether higher level of physical efficiency. Operating at or beyond my normal limit, I was plagued by the constant worry that in the rain, mist and darkness I might not be able to find the next rendezvous. One night my mission was to recover information about the trig-point marking the top of a certain mountain. Rain was falling; the darkness was intense. I was not even sure that I had found the right hill: the ground over which I was stumbling seemed too level for a summit, and my morale sunk to its lowest ebb. I was on the verge of asking myself whether I really wanted to go on – whether this whole endeavour really was for me. Then a miracle occurred: suddenly, five yards ahead of me, there was the trig-stone looming up in the murk, and I was able to read off the information I needed before hustling on, rejuvenated, to the next check-point.

Only when I reached each rendezvous did I discover where the next was, so that, if I missed one, I was effectively grounded: besides, the check-points were open for a set length of time, and if I arrived late, the truck manned by a member of the directing staff would have gone. Sometimes the truck – usually a three-ton lorry – would have a welcome brew on board, sometimes nothing; but always I would be told that, if I wanted to, I could climb into the back and be driven off to barracks. Indeed, I was almost encouraged to give in: several people succumbed to these weasel words – and that was the end of the course for them. Again, the key to survival was self-discipline.

The course was full of surprises, mostly unpleasant, and all designed to increase the pressure. At one rendezvous we were sent on to another; at the next we were given a report to write; at the next we would be sent back to barracks – but we never knew how long we would remain there. It might be for a night, a few hours, or only a few minutes. At one point I had to cross the Wye in the middle of the night: the river was flowing fast over rocks, and the water was very cold. Had I fallen over and hurt myself, I would soon have become numb in that icy torrent – and nobody knew where I was.

In one exercise after another we were dropped off individually into areas designated enemy-occupied territory, and required not only to cover long distances without using roads, but also to garner specific information, produce sketch maps of particular areas, and report any untoward incidents. Immediately after each exercise we were de-briefed about what we had seen or failed to see. In the early days our bergens were filled with thirty-five pounds of sand, but later the loads were increased to fifty-five pounds, so that the straps cut savagely into our shoulders. (Our packs were liable to be weighed by the supervising staff, who had scales at the rendezvous points.) As the pressure increased, man after man dropped out. Some days and nights we spent in the Black Mountains, but the climax of the course came in the Brecon Beacons, where we made our first close acquaintance with Pen-y-Fan, known simply as 'The Fan', the mountain whose outline is said to be engraved on every SAS man's heart.

The cumulative strain of all this had a most debilitating effect. Early one morning I was still on the march at about 0630, and so exhausted that I fell asleep on my feet. I did not realize what had happened until I heard a screech of tyres and woke up to find car headlights flaring in my face. Seconds later I was lying in the ditch, shaking, lucky not to have been knocked down.

At last the marathon came to the end. Back in barracks with the final march over, I collapsed into a hot bath and enjoyed a large meal, luxuriating in the knowledge that I should not have to take to the hills next day. Thinking back on the hardest two weeks of my life, I decided that in a masochistic sort of way I had enjoyed the experience; but it had taken toll of my physical strength and determination. I had lost fifteen pounds, and eaten into my body's reserves.

During that traumatic time I had formed close bonds with several fellow candidates. One was Ian Cartwright, a quiet Royal Fusilier with an off-hand sense of humour, who was already a first-class commander. He and I found ourselves much in agreement, and managed to share some of the problems on the course. Another interesting figure was Harry Thompson, who was several years older than me and already a captain in the Parachute Regiment. Prematurely balding, with a fringe of red hair round his smooth cranium, and a temper to match, he was immensely keen and dedicated; and if he was liable to explode from time to time, he would recover his composure just as quickly. (When he reached the Regiment, the soldiers immediately christened him 'Skinhead'.)

Talking among ourselves in odd moments, we had put together some information about the men in charge of us. Dare Newell had joined Special Operations Executive's Force 136 to fight behind the lines in Albania and the jungles of Malaya during the Second World War, and had seen a lot of action. Back in Britain he had become the SAS's link man in London: at that stage the Regiment had no firm base, and its entire administrative staff consisted of Dare and a couple of clerks. Even now, in 1956, its base facilities were minimal, and it relied heavily on help from the Parachute Regiment – for instance in providing office accommodation at Aldershot.

On our selection course Dare's principal assistant was Sergeant Paddy Nugent, an Irishman of experience, energy and drive. With a strong sense of humour, which rose easily to the surface, yet also with the highest standards, he epitomized the mix between a non-commissioned officer of the regular army and a senior NCO of the SAS.

Our ordeal, we realized, had been designed to identify people with the right personalities and characteristics for the specialized SAS community, but no attempt had been made to train us. Today, Special Forces deploy all over the world, but in 1956 the SAS was active in one theatre only – Malaya – and the Regiment needed men specifically for jungle operations. The aim of the course was to make sure that we could operate on our own, but also work with other people under stressful conditions, perhaps for months on end: then, as now, the emphasis was on modesty about personal achievement, on the ability to keep things to yourself, and above all on the ability to feel at home with your own company.

Just because we had survived the physical rigours of the course, it did not mean that any of us had passed. We still had to face a final interview, and then jungle training in Malaya. I myself knew that I had made plenty of mistakes. What I did not know at the time was that the SAS was desperately short of recruits, officers particularly: the Regiment's reputation stood so low that the commanding officers of other units were making it difficult for their people to go on the selection course.

When I went in and sat down opposite Dare Newell at a bare table, he asked how I thought I had done – and at once I was in a quandary. If I reckoned I had done well, he would surely slap me down; if I said I had done badly, he would retort that I was not a very good advertisement for myself. Somehow I talked my way out of that awkward corner. Dare murmured: 'Well, we've had a good look at you,' and proceeded to list a whole string of errors that I had made. Then suddenly I heard him saying, 'Nevertheless, the Regiment will accept you.'

My heart leapt. Blood drummed in my ears. That was all I needed to hear. Here was the turning point of my life. I knew instantly that I would stay in the army for the foreseeable future, and go out to Malaya almost immediately.

Back at Aldershot we handed in our kit, were told to report for duty in a few days' time, and went off on embarkation leave. Knowing that I would be away for at least a year, and possibly several, I did everything I could to make sure that family affairs were in order. My mother was still in the Holloway Sanatorium, and reasonably content there, and her affairs were being ably managed by Roy Fieldhouse. Michael gave me no cause for worry: with his natural ebullience, his spicy sense of humour, and his engineering bent, he had found his feet in the Fleet Air Arm, and needed no support from me. (Oddly enough, just as the DLI officers decided to call me Eddie, so Michael's colleagues re-christened him Fred – by which name he is still known in naval and family circles.)

The member of the family who concerned me most was David. He was then twelve, and about to go to Winchester (Joyce having refused to risk a third fiasco at Harrow). At school he was more than capable of looking after himself, but during the holidays he had to live at Old Place, where he was subject to Joyce's overpowering personality. Michael and I had both managed to escape this by (in effect) running away; David, not yet old enough to leave, had to put up with his aunt's obsessions, among them the idea that he was chronically undernourished. Because he was naturally slim, Joyce decided that our mother had starved him in infancy, and she conceived it her duty to feed him up. He was thus continually faced with colossal meals, which he neither wanted nor needed. Luckily he had one impregnable defence against outside irritations: the gift – which Michael and I never possessed – of being able to withdraw into a book and dissociate himself from the uproar going on all round him.

It so happened that at the outset of my SAS career there occurred another campaign in which I should have much liked to fight: Suez. In Egypt President Nasser had seized the canal at the end of July; during August and September Britain and France had built up an invasion force in the Mediterranean, and on 31 October – at the very moment when we were finishing our selection course in Wales – the RAF had bombed Egyptian military airfields in the opening of the campaign to recover the canal. As the world now knows, the attempt proved disastrous: yet at the time, having served in Egypt, and knowing the environment well, I could not help wishing that I had a chance of taking part. No matter: I had achieved my ambition, and an exciting tour lay ahead.

CHAPTER 8

JUNGLE WARFARE

1956–58

In 1956 long-distance air-travel was still a novelty. It was also slow and uncomfortable: our journey to Malaya took three days, with two overnight stops, and straddled Christmas, with the result that we were served Christmas pudding in an improbable setting, 20,000 feet above the Indian Ocean. When I finally arrived in the steaming heat of Kuala Lumpur, I could have done with a good night's sleep; instead, I found that the officers' mess – a nice old house in Ampang Road – had been cleared of furniture in preparation for a Boxing Night party. I felt rather disillusioned: I had come all this way to hunt down terrorists in the jungle, not to play wild mess games, and my first twenty-four hours with the Regiment were rather a disappointment.

Doubts soon vanished. After an interview with the Commanding Officer, Lieutenant-Colonel George Lea, things began to happen fast. Hardly had I been issued with jungle kit when I was despatched on a three-week training course – which was also a live operation – run by the formidable John Woodhouse, then in command of D Squadron. Gossip told us newcomers that we were about to be put through it – and gossip was right.

Together with Harry Thompson and Ian Cartwright, I flew in a fixed-wing aircraft to Ipoh, some hundred and fifty miles to the north-east, and then on by helicopter. The Sycamore skittered at tree-top height over an endless sea of forest before sinking into the LZ (landing zone), a natural clearing which had been artificially enlarged. Under orders to shift ourselves, we scrambled out and were grabbed by the LZ party, who hustled us into the cover of the trees as the aircraft lifted away. In a few seconds we were moving cautiously in single file, led by one of the D Squadron regulars, through a magnificent forest. Trees two or three hundred feet tall towered above us, their canopy shutting out the sun; in the humid shade beneath them the under-storey of smaller trees and shrubs was so thick that visibility was limited to fifteen or twenty yards. Birds called and monkeys hooted.

The squadron's headquarter camp was perfectly laid out, with every man's basha, or bivouac, facing outwards round a perimeter guarded by trip-flares. Everything blended into the background so as to be practically invisible, and the immaculate nature of the arrangements reflected the perfectionism of the man who had caused them to be created – John Woodhouse.

Like Dare Newell, Woodhouse was deceptively quiet and unassuming; but also, like Dare, he had done very well in the Second World War, winning a Military Cross, and he too was steel to the core. In appearance he was not particularly impressive, having a slender, gangling figure and what we called a bergen stoop; but his reputation was that of an outstanding leader who always drove himself to his limits, put the welfare of his men before his own, and expected the highest standards from everyone.[1]

His renown was enough to make any new recruit nervous, especially as we knew that we were still very much on trial: this jungle course was a further period of selection, which we had to pass before becoming fully fledged SAS officers. Woodhouse gave us a gruff but friendly greeting, and he did me a particularly good turn by putting me in the temporary charge of a Hong Kong Chinese non-commissioned officer, Corporal Ip Kwong Lao. Ip, as I soon discovered, was a remarkably brave and resourceful soldier. In December 1941, when the Japanese occupied Hong Kong, he had walked from there the whole way to join Orde Wingate in Burma – a distance of more than a thousand miles. He had joined the Malayan Scouts in 1950, and then

---

1. Once when he was Commanding Officer he took part in an escape and evasion exercise, wearing no badges of rank. The opposition knew that he was a runner, and had offered a case of beer as a reward for his capture; but when he was caught, there was some doubt as to his identity. As he was being brought in by Military Police, he wiped his nose on his sleeve, and the officer in charge said, 'No officer would do anything so disgusting – it can't be him.'

22nd SAS. Now he became my mentor and instructor, teaching me how to live in the jungle.

At this he was a natural. With typical Chinese ingenuity, using mess tins over an open fire, he could conjure delicious curries and pancakes out of army rations, and when it came to building comfortable bashas, he was second to none. He showed me how to pitch a poncho, or groundsheet, between two trees to make a roof, and how to fashion a sleeping bag from old parachutes. He taught me how to deal with the ubiquitous leeches – never to pull them off, as this would leave their jaws embedded in the skin, which would then fester – but to touch them with salt or a lighted cigarette, which made them let go. He showed me how to get water from the giant vines which climbed into the forest canopy: if you simply hacked into them, back-pressure would stop the liquid running out, but if you cut out a strip, there was room for air to flow in, and the water poured out.

The task for which we were training was to combat the Communist terrorists (known as CTs), who were using the deep jungle as a base from which to launch attacks on tea-plantations, villages and military convoys round the edges of the forest. Their aim was to put fear into local communities, so that they could not, or would not, cooperate with the government; they were trying to extort food from the local people, and the government was making strenuous efforts to control supplies. The terrorists' favourite tactic was to lie up in the jungle and put pressure on outlying hamlets, where friendly agents would provide them with food and information. Anyone who refused to cooperate or stepped out of line would be executed – and so the system of control by fear built up. The only effective answer was a Draconian policy of resettlement, introduced by Lieutenant-General Sir Harold Briggs, Director of Operations until 1951: whole communities were moved to sites which could be guarded, and people were allowed out to work the land only during the day.

When I reached Malaya in 1956, the struggle had been going on for eight years, and the tide was turning in our favour. The decisive factor had been the introduction of the SAS, who alone had the ability to patrol for long periods in the deep jungle to which the terrorists had retreated. Our role was to kill or capture the enemy if possible, but in any case to deny them the use of the jungle, to restrict their freedom of movement and to cut off their access to the aboriginal tribes. Our operations, by their very nature, were largely negative: the number of enemy was relatively small, and the area of dense cover vast, so that the chances of confrontations were low. Nevertheless, our first requirement was to be able to live in the jungle for weeks on end, to move through it silently in patrols of three or four men without leaving any trace of our presence, and to be ready to engage enemy at any moment.

Extracts from a paper written by John Woodhouse hint not only at how we lived and what we were trying to do, but also at the precision with which he had thought his methods through:

INTRODUCTION

These notes are guides to action, not orders. It is the duty of all SAS commanders to think out and apply new tactics and to introduce frequent variations on existing methods.

The essence of operations in a guerrilla war is that they should be unpredictable.

A base is a hive, NOT a nest.

BATTLE DISCIPLINE

1. Stand-to. Purpose is to rehearse rapid manning of pre-arranged defensive positions. It is never to take place at set times. Regular habits and regular soldiers are God's gifts to guerrillas. No prior warning of stand-to will be given.

At night, positions will be within five paces of bashas, which are to be sited tactically and not comfortably. On a night stand-to, all ranks will kneel or lie. No man will move once in position. Anyone seen moving will be shot without warning from the closest range possible. The firer will do all he can to fire at a rising angle. On no account will fire be returned unless the enemy can be seen. 'The answer to noise is silence.'

So his curt recommendations went on for five typed pages, all eminently sensible. Under the all-important heading of 'Command' he quoted Napoleon's maxim, 'There is no such thing as a bad soldier: there are only bad officers'.

  a. You have the best soldiers in the army under your
command. This means exceptional standards of work and
efficiency are expected from you. It does not mean you can
relax and let them carry on.

  b. You are responsible for obtaining the best possible conditions for your soldiers and for ensuring efficient administration in all matters concerning them. Unless you are
genuinely interested in their well-being, you had better find
a job as far away from them as possible.

  c. 'The best form of welfare is training.' Field Marshal
Rommel.

If you look after your soldiers, you can and must expect
them to work to the extreme limits of human endurance
on operations. If you do the former, they in turn will not
fail you. Insist on meticulous observance of battle discipline,
especially when you and your men are tired. This is a matter
of will power – yours, not your soldiers'.

Another maxim of Woodhouse's was that in any crisis – when
a man is wounded, for instance, and the natural impulse is to
rush off and take some immediate action – the best course is to
sit down for a few minutes and think before reacting, as such a
pause for reflective planning may save hours later. During the
months ahead I often marvelled at the truth and wisdom of his
thought; but at the outset we had a tremendous dose of new
information to swallow and assimilate. To help us find our feet,
he had devised a programme of lectures – which took place in
jungle clearings – and practical instruction. His teaching made
a deep impression on me, and the principles of warfare which
he instilled in us have remained with me for the rest of my life.

  On our first short patrol, for half a day, we were led by an
instructor who showed us how to move in the jungle and taught
us the rudiments of navigation. Our speed of advance depended
partly on the tactical situation: whenever we suspected we were
close to enemy, we would go for a few yards, then stop to listen
and watch before moving on. Usually, however, progress
depended on the terrain and the density of vegetation in any
one area. Compared with movement in the open, it was always
extremely slow. On a good, level track, we might cover 2000
yards in an hour; going up or down the steep-sided *bukits*, or

hills, without a path, we might do only half that; and in really thick jungle, through which we had to cut our way, we might manage no more than 500 yards. Secondary jungle, which had been felled for agriculture and then grown up again, could be almost impenetrable, but the worst of all was bamboo, through which we had to hack every yard of our way. (Another of Wood-house's precepts was to cut as little as possible: cutting made a noise, increased visibility, and left indelible evidence which a skilled tracker could interpret all too accurately.)

Navigation in the jungle was an art which could be mastered only by experience. Our maps were sketchy affairs, made up from air-photographs transferred to map-paper and overlaid with a grid system of lines five hundred yards apart, rather than with contours. Some features, like hill-tops with trig-points on them, and *kualas*, or river junctions, were accurate, and gave us a useful basis on which to work; but much was inaccurate or simply missing. Other features might have been obscured by cloud when the photographs were taken, and small streams were often concealed from the air by the jungle. Maps thus gave only a general idea of the topography, and we had to find our way by navigating, rather than simply map-reading. Sometimes by climbing a tall tree on a ridge one could gain a view of landmarks ahead, but generally there were no outstanding features by which to steer. Furthermore, the sun was hardly ever visible from beneath the canopy of the trees, so that we could not take sightings. Rivers, cliffs and impossibly steep hillsides usually meant that we could not go straight in the direction we wanted. In this terrain navigation was not so much a precise science as a question of judging how much progress one had made in a particular direction during a certain time. On the whole it was best to follow ridges, but choosing the moment to drop off a ridge and transfer to another, or go down to a stream, became a skill in its own right. Gradually, by trial and error, we acquired a feel for the country, and instinct began to pull us to the right place.

Thanks in part to Corporal Ip's tuition, I soon felt at home in the jungle. Some people found it claustrophobic, and could never relax in that dim, green world; others were positively frightened of what the undergrowth might contain – principally armed terrorists, but also snakes, monkeys, wild pigs, elephants, bears, scorpions, hornets, bats, crickets and frogs. Yet to me the jungle was never hostile: on the contrary, it struck me as a friendly place, in which one could make oneself quite comfortable.

Of course it had disadvantages, among them the wet. In the rainy season, deluges poured down every day, and if we were in the open, we were immediately soaked to the skin. This did not much matter – provided we were not too high up in the mountains – for the heat was such that being wet was no hardship, and if we were not drenched by rain, we were sodden with sweat. Another hazard was the mosquitoes, which would settle on us in swarms as we were moving and bite through our jungle-green fatigues; at night, if we showed our noses outside our parachute-canopy sleeping bags, they would whine in to dive-bomb us relentlessly (the greasy, foul-smelling repellent with which we were issued was effective while it lasted, but kept getting washed off by sweat or rain). Leeches also abounded, fastening on all over our bodies. Yet all these were minor irritations, with which one learned to deal.

Not that my introduction to the jungle went smoothly. Trying to show keenness by acting as leading scout of my patrol as we came back into camp, I walked into one of Woodhouse's trip flares. Everyone had to stand to in case it signalled a genuine intrusion, and I was obliged to apologize for my carelessness, getting only a grunt in response. When the same thing happened again a few days later, Woodhouse was down by the stream, shaving, so that he had to drop everything and rush back to his stand-to position. Right, I thought: never again am I going to lead a patrol back into any camp run by John Woodhouse. Like everyone else, I was haunted by fear of the ultimate punishment – being RTUed, or Returned to Unit. For anyone in the SAS, that was the final disaster and humiliation. I therefore moved about the camp with extreme caution – but by sheer bad luck I came to grief yet again. On the track leading from the camp to the LZ Woodhouse had a wire set at thigh-height: you could either climb over it, or crawl under it, and on this particular journey I chose to crawl, in case I should slip and fall. All would have been well, had not the handle of my *parang* (jungle knife) been sticking upwards from my belt. Inevitably, it caught the wire, and the whole camp stood-to once more.

This time Woodhouse was furious, and threatened that if it happened again, he would RTU me. In the meantime, he said, he would put a pound of plastic explosive on top of each flare, just to help me concentrate. It so happened that the next trip was caused by a visiting general; but luckily for him – and perhaps for Woodhouse too – there had been no time to carry out the threat.[1]

Somehow I survived, and our three-week training period came to an end. By then we were very tired: we had patrolled for miles through the jungle, and spent nights stuck on the sides of hills so steep that there had been nowhere to sling a hammock or even to stretch out. Once I had had to sleep propped against a tree and, if I moved at all, I began rolling down the slope. After such an exhausting introduction, it would have been a relief to fly out to Ipoh by helicopter; but Woodhouse decreed that Harry, Ian and I were to march out with some soldiers – so we set off on the long trek. After three weeks under the tree canopy, our skins were white and pasty, and we had to take care not to expose ourselves to the sun as we came back into the open.

Eventually we reached Ipoh, and there on the school playground stood a helicopter, about to take off for Kuala Lumpur, on a flight scheduled to last not much more than an hour. Since the alternative was a six-hour drive along diabolical roads, a place on the aircraft seemed highly desirable. There were only three seats spare, but to my surprise I was allocated one of them, and I was about to climb aboard when along came Harry, who pulled his superior rank on me and turned me off. The pilot was a Pole, Peter Pekowski, a brilliant flyer widely experienced in that theatre – but this was not one of his days. He ran up his engine, took off with difficulty, and failed to gain height. For a terrible moment it looked as though he must crash into a group of children playing; but he just managed to keep going in level flight, cleared them, and smashed into the scrub beyond. By

1. A story was told of how Woodhouse, returning to camp in the evening, was fired at by one of his own sentries. He immediately put the man on a charge, for missing.

some miracle the aircraft did not catch fire: the machine was written off, but we got everybody out alive, although some had broken bones and were badly shaken.

I was a now a full member of the SAS, except that I had not yet learned to parachute – and this deficiency was soon made good by a three-week course at Changi airfield, in Singapore. After the privations of the jungle, the RAF officers' mess seemed the height of luxury, and the parachuting itself most enjoyable. We began with the usual ground training, in how to deploy our parachutes, how to land, and so on, then did six daylight and two night jumps out of Hastings aircraft, after which we were allowed to wear the coveted dark-blue and silver SAS wings on our sleeves. That brought a powerful feeling of achievement: so many people had failed at one stage or another that we survivors felt part of an elite.

My euphoria did not last long. Back in Kuala Lumpur, I was assigned to B Squadron, in command of 6 Troop (in theory a troop consisted of sixteen men, but shortages and postings had reduced ours to twelve). Within a few days of my taking over, we were sent into the jungle on an operation lasting three and a half months – and so began one of the most testing periods of my life.

Not only did I have to cope with jungle existence, of which I had only just grasped the rudiments: I had also to lead and control an extraordinary bunch of men. All very tough, all individualists, all strong minded, they had been in the jungle far longer than I had, and were sceptical about having an inexperienced young officer placed in charge of what was already a fine troop. Besides, they were all a good deal older: I was twenty-two, and the rest of them averaged twenty-five or twenty-six, with one or two real old sweats of thirty or more. My sole advantage was that I had fought in Korea, which none of them had done.

Chief among them was Lawrence Smith, my troop sergeant. In every way a typical SAS non-commissioned officer, he was extremely fit, quiet, firm and positive, but he did not tolerate fools. If he disliked something that I proposed to do, he told me so, and why – but he always did it in such a charming fashion that it was impossible to take offence. In due course he became a loyal friend, and my Sergeant Major in 'A' Squadron.

Another forthright character was Bill Mundell, whose strong Scots accent matched his will. Though quiet and unassuming, he was an able leader, who led through personal example and completed many successful forays in the jungle; but he was also outspoken if he did not like the way things were going, and stubborn about arguing his point. One of our principal needs was for linguists who could communicate with the natives, and we had a brilliant one in the lanky form of Corporal Tony Allen. Always known as Lofty, because he was six foot three inches tall, he had great long legs and carried his bergen as though it was full of feathers. He too had an independent cast of mind, and his original way of thinking constantly acted as a stimulus to the troop.

The fourth outstanding member of the team was Corporal Ian Smith, always called 'Tanky' because he had been a gunnery instructor in the Royal Tank Regiment. Another Scotsman, with dark hair and light blue eyes, he was built on the lines of a bear, with broad shoulders and deep chest – definitely not the sort of man you would want to confront, in the jungle or anywhere else, but a terrific asset on one's own side. Less tactful than the other NCOs, he was outspoken to a fault: if he disagreed with me, he said so without mincing his words, and usually followed up with a few verbal punches, just to make sure that I had got the message. It so happened that he was away on leave when I took over, but he was very much present by reputation; when he returned I had no small difficulty controlling him, and it took us several months to reach an understanding – which has lasted to this day.[1]

I had only two or three days to get to know members of the troop, brief them on our forthcoming operation, and organize myself for a long stay in the jungle. Although we knew we would be re-supplied from the air after a fortnight, it was essential to pack everything we might need into our bergens, and to stow

1. The quality of these men can be gauged from the fact that three of them – Lawrence Smith, Bill Mundell and Tanky Smith – became Lieutenant-Colonels, and that Lofty Allen joined the police force and rose to high rank before becoming a solicitor.

things in the right order, so that those likely to be wanted first were at the top. Our most basic necessity was food, and the standard Woodhouse ration, enough for fourteen days, was made up as follows:

7 12oz tins corned beef
4lbs rice
3lbs sugar
10 packets army biscuits
20 Oxo cubes
14 chicken noodle soup packets
1 bottle Ovaltine tablets
8oz tea
4oz egg powder
8oz cheese
8oz potato powder
1lb oatmeal

To this everyone added his own favourite extras, principally curry powder, spices, salt and onions. Our perennial problem was weight: we had also to carry ammunition, grenades, poncho, field dressings and spare clothes, and yet to keep the weight of our bergens down to a level at which we could retain our efficiency as fighting soldiers, and move through the jungle at full combat readiness, rather than just as beasts of burden.

For my first full-scale operation I was assigned a huge area of primary jungle and given a free hand to patrol it. Flown by helicopter into a clearing, we moved off briskly to put distance between ourselves and the dropping-zone, and then, deep in the forest, established a base from which I sent out patrols of two or three men. Some went for one day, some for as many as ten, our object being to build up a thorough knowledge of our area, and to detect any enemy movement within it.

After the comforts of the officers' mess, it was a shock to plunge back into the jungle and the primitive existence there, during which we were on duty twenty-four hours a day. At first, as I slogged along, I kept thinking of regular meals, beer in the evening, time off, swimming pools and other sybaritic delights; but gradually these faded into the background as other priorities established themselves. What mattered now was

whether we were going to find a good spot in which to basha
up, and so have a comfortable night.

Yet physical difficulties were small in comparison with the
problems I had in controlling my troop. Not for nothing was B
Squadron known as 'Big-Time B'. Its members thought they
knew it all, and at once we had differences over the siting of
bashas: I, freshly imbued with Woodhousian principles, insisted
that bashas be deployed tactically, in defensive formation, round
any camp-site. The old-stagers of B Squadron, who had been
doing things their own way for years, preferred more comfortable and sociable lay-outs, with the bashas clustered together.
They knew, better than I did, that in thick jungle at night it was
impossible for enemy to approach a camp without being heard,
and that this fact of life obviated the need for nocturnal sentries.
Nevertheless, I insisted on tactical deployments, and this caused
a good deal of friction. Later I learnt that the NCOs and troopers
thought I was behaving like a typical young infantry officer,
trying to impose alien practices on them in typical infantry
fashion. They did not realize that I was only applying what
Woodhouse had laid down so firmly – yet at the same time it
was clear that I had not mastered the subtleties of command
which prevail within the SAS.

To be thrown into the jungle with people as independent as
these was no easy assignment. We wore no badges of rank.
There were no other officers from whom I could seek advice or
support. There was no mess into which I could escape. Like it
or not, I had to live and work with my troop for the next fourteen weeks. I realized that the only thing to do was to communicate with them as much as possible. Instinctively I came to the
conclusion that it was better to thrash everything out and solicit
ideas, than to take the more defensive line of issuing orders and
instructions – which you *can* do in the army – in such a way
that there could be no argument. Had I tried this, I should very
soon have been isolated and ostracized, and lost control of the
troop. In talking things through, I unconsciously promoted the
SAS tradition of what are known as Chinese parliaments – pow-
wows in which everyone has his say about a problem before
the commander takes a decision.

Even when I pursued this policy, relationships were difficult at first. I deliberately did *not* address the men by their Christian names: I stuck to surnames – as was the general practice in those days – unless I had got to know someone particularly well. The men, for their part, never called me 'Sir' unless they wanted to be rude. The acronym DLB came into use quite soon, but generally they used the standard SAS form, 'Boss'.

I saw that the only way to win them over was to follow Woodhouse's recommendation, and do as much as, or more than, they were doing – whether it was patrolling, setting ambushes or mundane tasks like fetching water. I also made immense efforts to talk to individuals in the evenings, as I had in Korea. I used to brief them all together in general terms about what was happening, but I made a point of going round the bashas at night and talking to every occupant. It was tough work, because some of them did not want to talk to me, and resented my intrusion. All the same, I persisted in asking about their families, homes and backgrounds until I understood more about them; and because they saw that I had a genuine interest in them, in the end I began to evoke the inevitable human response, even from the most hardened soldiers.

So, by trial and error, we settled in to my first operation. Some of my mistakes were due purely to inexperience – as when I had an argument with Tanky Smith about the best way to reach a point on the end of a ridge. To me the obvious route was straight across country, down one hill and up the next; but Tanky, who knew what those *bukits* were like, insisted that it would be quicker to stick to the ridges all the way, even though the route would be longer. When a showdown threatened, he suggested that I should take one man and go the way I wanted, while he took another along the ridges, and that we should see who reached the rendezvous first. When I and my partner arrived, exhausted by a ferocious climb, Tanky had been sitting comfortably at the RV for the past two hours. As he remarked, he did not mind if I made ten mistakes a day, provided I made them once only.

Near the equator, where we were operating, day and night were more or less equally divided, twelve hours apiece. Dawn and dusk came quickly. In the mornings we had to be up for stand-to before it was light, and that meant rolling out of our home-made hammocks by about 0530, when a single hand-clap sounded through the jungle. Generally we had nothing to eat in the mornings except a biscuit and a brew of tea, which we boiled up over our little solid-fuel stoves. Then we would be on the move all day, returning to base, or setting up a one-night camp, at dusk.

In choosing a site, we were always driven by our greatest need – to be able to communicate with base. We needed a spot from which our radio would work – and if it didn't, we would move on until we found somewhere better, or until dark overtook us. My signaller Jock Baird, a short and irascible but likeable Scots Guardsman, was a skilled and determined professional, who would not even contemplate making himself a brew until he had rigged his aerial and established contact. Sending messages was a laborious process, partly because of atmospheric interference, and partly because everything had to be encoded before being transmitted in Morse. Even though transmissions were kept as short as possible, to frustrate enemy direction-finding equipment, Jock might have to spend four or five hours on the set every evening.

These evening calls formed a key part of the whole operation. Unless each patrol came on the air regularly, headquarters had no means of telling where it was or what had happened to it – and in case of trouble we had an elaborate system of overdue drills and fall-back rendezvous. If a patrol missed its evening call, no action would be taken; but if no call came the following morning, an alert went out. If silence still prevailed after thirty-six hours, a helicopter would stand by to go out on search. A patrol might put up smoke, or a balloon, to indicate that its radio had failed, or proceed to a rendezvous agreed in advance, and there meet another patrol.

Another essential in the evenings was water, but we never bashaed down close to a stream, because the noise of running water might cover potentially dangerous sounds; rather, we chose sites as close to streams as possible, but above them, on any level patches that we could find. Once settled, we brewed up our one full meal of the day. Thanks to Corporal Ip's tuition, I became expert at cooking curry, which always turned out slightly different and became like a drug – something on which my well-being depended. If I had any onions, I would fry some up in ghee, which came with our rations, add water, curry powder and chillies, and mix the sauce with meat from my compo rations. The rice was easy: I would put two or two and a half handfuls into the smaller of my mess-tins, fill the tin with water, add a good deal of salt, and fit the larger tin over the top as a lid. By the time the surplus water had boiled away, the rice would have absorbed the rest and be cooked. Sometimes, if we were in particularly dangerous areas, cooking had to be banned, because the smell would have given us away – in which case we had to settle for a cold compo supper.

We were meticulous about leaving no trace of our presence. We tried to avoid tracks, to leave no footprints, and to move as unobtrusively as possible. In camp, we removed every scrap of litter, burning paper and sinking tins underwater or taking them with us. Personal hygiene was of vital importance. No health parades or inspections were held – as in other units – to make sure that people looked after themselves: it was up to every man to make sure that he did not suffer from foot-rot, skin infections, stomach complaints or (above all) malaria, which could be kept at bay by taking one Paludrine tablet every day.

No matter how careful one might be, occasional setbacks were inevitable. One evening, as I sat on a log eating my curry, dressed only in a pair of the thin, green underpants known to the army as 'drawers, cellular', I was stabbed by a sudden pain in the buttock. My curry flew one way and I the other, before I established that I had been stung by a scorpion. The pain was excruciating, but luckily the scorpion was only a baby, and no great damage was done (Lofty Allen was later paralysed by a scorpion sting, and had to be evacuated by helicopter). Another night, asleep on the ground, I was woken by a burning pain in my midriff. I leapt up to find that I had lain down across a main termite route, and that the insects were marching over me, taking bites on the way. We were on such a narrow piece of flat ground that there was no other spot on to which I could move, so I ringed my position with an oval of foot powder, which I knew termites did not like, and for the rest of the night they marched round me.

As we moved stealthily around our allotted area of jungle, we came to know every yard of it – every *ulu* (stream), every *kuala* (confluence), every ridge, every headland, every track, every broken twig. Living in the forest for day after day, speaking in soft voices, we developed an uncanny ability to detect minute changes and deduce information from them: a single footprint, a bent stalk, a crushed leaf – any of these would tell us how many people had passed that way, how big they were, whether they were men or women, and how long ago.

Whenever we did come on recent traces of the enemy, excitement rose and we proceeded with extreme caution, talking in whispers, not using the track, but making loops into the jungle and coming back to the path at intervals, in case an ambush had been set. Once we found the site of a camp which had been used so recently that I decided to set an ambush on the track approaching it. We made a camp of our own some two hundred and fifty yards away, and for the next six weeks we maintained the ambush from dawn to dusk, in two shifts, changing over with the utmost stealth in the middle of the day. That was an extraordinary experience: in the camp we had to maintain silence, except for whispers, and no cooking or smoking were allowed until after dark. In the ambush position, the task of keeping up concentration was incredibly exacting. To sit for hours on end, gazing at walls of vegetation, with visibility limited to fifteen yards, and in the knowledge that if people did come, they would be on top of you without warning – all this, though physically less demanding than being on the move, was a tremendous mental strain. No terrorists ever did return, but we emerged from that operation more exhausted than from any other.

The fact that we made so few contacts was disappointing, but it did not mean that we were losing the battle. On the contrary, we were definitely winning the social and political struggle, which had become known as the Hearts and Minds campaign. Quite apart from killing terrorists, our purpose was to wean the aborigines away from the Communists and bring them on to our side.

The aborigines formed a vital part of our operation. Delightful little people – at the most about four foot six inches tall – clad only in loin-cloths, they lived up in the hills in long-houses

raised off the ground on stilts, tilling small areas of cleared land
before moving on to a virgin site. Many had never seen white
men before, but they responded well to friendly overtures. Our
job was to get to know them, explain the government's point
of view, and, as far as security allowed, live with them from
time to time, our aim being to make sure that they passed on
information about enemy movements and that they were working for us, rather than for the opposition. This was a difficult,
long-term operation, based on the slow build-up of understanding and personal relationships between ourselves and the jungle
people. One of the special skills in which the SAS takes pride is
languages, and in 6 Troop the master of contact with the Abos
was Lofty Allen, whose fluency in Malay was such that he could
communicate with them even if they spoke outlandish dialects.
A few Abos were paid to act as porters, and they were invaluable
for carrying our heavy radio sets and batteries. Contact with
these primitive but attractive people had an influence on our
own behaviour: we all picked up a smattering of Malay words,
and we imitated the Abos in their habit of gesturing with lips
and heads, rather than with hands – for to them facial expression
was all-important, and to point with your hand was an insult.

After three and a half months in the jungle, everybody was
run down. We had all lost weight, and our efficiency was diminishing as our physical and mental reserves dwindled: it was time
for a spell of rest and recuperation and a few days' leave. And
yet, tired as the soldiers were, the effect of returning to civilization, to alcohol and women, was explosive. We were supposed
to shave off our beards, but some of the men managed to bypass
the regulation and head straight for Singapore. There the red-
light district, Bugis Street, was out of bounds, but the Military
Police who regularly raided the area mistook the hirsute creatures for Scandinavian seamen on leave, and failed to arrest
them. In Kuala Lumpur wild scenes took place in Nanto's, the
bar which had become 'B' Squadron's favourite watering hole:
the Military Police had a busy time there too, for high-flyers
often ran through four months' pay in a week or ten days.

Even in the officers' mess (which by then had moved to
Wardieburn Camp) things could become pretty lively. The Regiment was at its greatest-ever strength, and had five squadrons:

three of its own, one from the Parachute Regiment and one from New Zealand. As the squadrons rotated in and out of the jungle, one could never be sure who would appear in the mess on any given evening; but if New Zealanders were present, the friendly rivalry between them and the Brits was always liable to boil over in riotous games. The Commanding Officer of 22nd SAS, George Lea, and his wife Pam – both much loved by the Regiment – had managed to have the entire mess refurbished. The walls were only of *attap* – the leaves of a jungle tree, woven together – but they had been given a smart new lining, and new covers and curtains lifted the tone of the place. One night, when games became excessively boisterous, some of the Brits grabbed a Kiwi and threw him clean through the wall. In the ensuing riot the room was reduced to chaos, and Lea, though an equable man, became furious – the only time we ever saw him lose his temper. After that we were banned from holding parties for the time being, and sent back into the jungle early.

After another outbreak of horseplay, one of the troop com-manders, Peter Raven, rang up the local newspaper and said that a fellow officer, John Slim, had become engaged to the daughter of the Commander-in-Chief. Since John's father was Field Marshal Viscount Slim, then Governor-General of Aus-tralia (and one of my heroes), the news was printed at once: the story was picked up by Reuters, and flashed round the world. Soon a signal arrived from Government House in Canberra:

FIRST I'VE HEARD OF THIS STOP IF TRUE
CONGRATULATIONS STOP IF NOT WHAT THE HELL'S
UP QUERY

Of course it was pure invention. Poor John had a great deal of unravelling to do.

George Lea – a Northumberland Fusilier, and a splendid man – was trying to instil some formal discipline into the Regiment, and to that end he imported a new Regimental Sergeant Major, Sid Reed, whose zeal did not endear him to the soldiers. One day his pace-stick – emblem of his authority – disappeared from his office; he soon spotted the end of it protruding from the flower-bed outside, but when he pulled it up, he found to his rage that only about eight inches of it remained. On another memorable occasion he inspected a parade, and as he stalked along the ranks he came on a man with a crucifix slung on a chain round his neck.

'What's this?' he cried. 'What the hell is this?'

'It's a cross, Sar'nt Major,' said the soldier stoutly. 'I'm Church of England.'

'Are you, be Christ!' roared Reed. 'Well, I'm church of bloody Egypt, and I don't wear the f***ing pyramids round my neck. Do I?! Get it off!'

Operational soldiers though we were, we could not escape the occasional formal parade, and once when the Duke of Edinburgh was due to visit the Regiment, panic threatened: there was a tremendous outbreak of what the army calls bullshit – white-washing tree-trunks, sluicing down road surfaces, painting kerbs – the very activity which people had joined the SAS to escape. Preparations evidently struck one member of the Regiment as excessive. Our VIP was due at 1500, to inspect the guard of honour, and we hovered nervously in our Pea Greens, the smart tropical uniforms which we had invented for ourselves. At 1459 an ox-cart laden with manure and driven by a tiny Indian came creaking to a halt outside the guardroom. The guard commander was horrified and tried to shoo him away, but the Indian refused to move and, becoming indignant at the efforts to shift him, demanded to speak to the CO. 'Very important telephone call this morning,' he piped. 'CO tell me he need big load of bullshit, delivered to guardroom at three o'clock precisely . . .'

The last major operation in which I took part was also the most difficult and unpleasant. This was in the Telok Anson swamp – a vast, low-lying area of jungle near the west coast, with a river running through it. The swamp was harbouring a persistent terrorist gang whose leader was thought to be a man called Ah Hoi. So deeply was this gang entrenched in the swamp that Harry Thompson – now in command of 'B' Squadron – conceived a novel plan for outflanking them: a substantial force would be parachuted in at first light and take the enemy in the rear.

Parachuting into trees two or three hundred feet tall is an

exceedingly hazardous procedure. The idea is that your parachute becomes hooked in the top of a tree, and you abseil to
the ground. In practice, men are liable to be injured or killed by
striking branches, or, if their chutes do not lodge and hook up
firmly, by crashing through the jungle canopy and free-falling
the rest of the way to earth. The SAS had used this method
before, but it had always resulted in casualties: Oliver Brooks,
George Lea's predecessor as Commanding Officer, had broken
his back and been crippled for life.

We did a good deal of special training, to make sure we could
steer our parachutes into the top of any good tree we found
beneath us when we dropped, and we sought to eliminate as
many hazards as possible by careful planning. We were going
to jump from Beverley transports – the first time these aircraft
had been used in such an operation. The planes would make
one pass only: they would fly from many miles out at parachuting speed, so that there would be no change in engine-note
when we dropped, and they would carry straight on, making it
impossible for anyone listening to tell that there had been a drop
at all. We would take in three weeks' rations, so that there
would be no need for a quick resupply.

So much for the planning. At 0500 one morning in February
1958 we fitted our chutes and filed on to the Beverleys in stick
order. After a short flight – no more than half an hour – as
we were approaching the DZ, we hooked up and stood in the
doorway. The loadmaster went through his routine of hand-
signals, shouted commands and coloured lights: 'Red on . . .
green on . . . *Go!*' Out we went into the grey dawn sky. The
light was coming up, and I could see the uneven, grey-green
sea of forest stretching away below us. My extra-heavy bergen,
strapped in position beneath my feet to protect me as I hit the
branches, made my chute steer clumsily and increased the speed
of my descent. In a few moments the tree-tops were coming up
fast to meet me. I aimed for a thick-looking patch: with a sudden
rush I shot through leaves and branches and came to a stop
with a tremendous jerk. My chute had lodged securely, and
seconds later I was on the ground, having abseiled down more
than a hundred feet.

I soon found that we had one major casualty. Trooper Jerry

Mulcahy lodged in a big tree, but before he could abseil, the branch holding his parachute snapped, and he plummeted to the ground, landing on tree-roots and breaking his back. Unable to move, and in severe pain, he needed immediate evacuation – and so, with the operation barely launched, we had to bring a helicopter in, blowing our elaborate security precautions. Mulcahy presented a bizarre sight, for after a wild party the night before his colleagues had shaved his head bare, and as he lay waiting to be lifted out, his skull gleamed white in the gloom of the jungle. With him safely airborne, we moved off towards the river which my troop had been detailed to patrol; but the accident emphasized the risks of that kind of parachute drop, and, so far as I know, it has never been attempted again.

The swamp proved a hellish environment in which to live and move. Because it was so low-lying, the heat was relentless. In most places no ground was visible: the mangrove trees were standing in water, into which their roots plunged. To make progress, we either had to slosh through waist-deep, dark-brown liquid, making a dangerous amount of noise, or hop from one root to the next – a laborious and exhausting process which wore the arches of our feet raw. The leeches were unspeakable. At night there was no ground to sleep on: we had to sling hammocks between trees, and we cooked crouching on the flattest root that could be found.

Gradually we realized that not even the terrorists could stand such ghastly conditions, and that they were living on drier ground round the fringes of the swamp and along the river. Realizing this, we too moved out into slightly more comfortable areas. Although my troop never clashed with the enemy, we found many traces of them near the river – freshly abandoned camp sites, with the shells of turtles which they had cooked and eaten – and radioed back information which enabled Harry Thompson to deploy other units in a more precise pattern and gradually tighten a cordon on the gang. Eventually we put such cumulative pressure on them that they gave up: one morning I received a signal saying that a surrender had been arranged, and suddenly, after three weeks, the operation came to an end.

Lofty Allen, who had been invalided out of the jungle after his scorpion-bite, but had recovered and returned to patrolling on the periphery, witnessed the initial moves in the surrender, at which he acted as interpreter. Out of the jungle at the agreed rendezvous came not Ah Hoi, but his messenger, a tiny woman called Ah Niet, who first demanded large payments for each member of her team. Told that there would be no deal, she slipped back into the jungle, and at dusk that day Ah Hoi came out into a paddy field, together with some of his men.

So ended the Telok Anson operation. After that I was taken out of the jungle and acted for a while as liaison officer at Ipoh, before being posted to the Operations Room in the SAS headquarters in Kuala Lumpur. I have no clear recollection of why these moves came about; but they were certainly due to Harry Thompson, who for some reason had formed a poor view of me. Harry, as I have said, had a volatile temper, and rounded on most of his subordinates sooner or later. In Tanky Smith's recollection, he came to visit our jungle base one day, and, arriving in a foul mood, took exception to our arrangements. When we defended them, he lost his temper and said, 'Right, I'm going to RTU the pair of you.' I cannot vouch for the accuracy of Tanky's memory, but he himself certainly finished up in the jungle training base, and I in the Operations Room. What I know for sure is that Harry complained about me to 22nd SAS's new Commanding Officer, Lieutenant-Colonel Tony Deane-Drummond; he, however, stuck up for me, and instead of sending me home, as Harry demanded, put me to work in the Ops Room.[1]

This I enjoyed a good deal, as I was at the nerve-centre of our entire deployment, and I was able to keep my jungle skills honed by slipping away, every now and then, for a short patrol. Deane-Drummond proved a fascinating, if exacting, commander for whom to work. A tall, neat-looking man with sandy hair and moustache, and a good, experienced soldier, he came to the Regiment with a reputation for outstanding courage, and with a ready-made nickname, 'The Cupboard'. This derived from his astonishing feat, after the Battle of Arnhem in 1944, of hiding for

1. Thompson was killed in a helicopter crash in Borneo in 1963. I hope and believe that his strictures about my conduct were ill-founded – and I am encouraged in this belief by the fact that, after the Telok Anson operation, I was awarded a Mention in Despatches.

thirteen days in a cupboard in a house full of German soldiers. By the time I knew him he had developed a propensity for making sudden, radical changes of plan: he would ask me to lay on complicated arrangements for him to visit forward troops in the jungle – fixed-wing flight to Ipoh, helicopter in to the LZ, raft downriver to meet a patrol – and then at the last minute cancel everything in favour of some more pressing engagement. For me this was at least good practice in maintaining flexibility of mind.

As my time in Malaya began to run out, I did not feel keen on going back to normal regimental soldiering. I had nothing against the DLI, who had been extremely good to me: it was just that, after a taste of life in the SAS, no other form of soldiering appealed so much. I decided, therefore, to use my position in the Far East as a springboard for travelling home overland. A study of maps suggested that most of the route was feasible, except for the stretch through Burma, which at that time was in political and economic disarray. I could see that crossing the Irrawaddy would present a problem, but I thought that the way to overcome it would be to travel by motor scooter, which I would be able, more or less, to pick up and carry aboard any small boat that became available. I therefore bought a Lambretta, learned to ride it, and arranged evening classes in maintenance and repairs. I also set about acquiring the necessary visas, and got them all, except the one for Burma, whose embassy made no sense at all.

Then suddenly a thunderbolt blew my plans apart. Sitting in the Ops Room on the morning of 28 October 1958, I read a highly classified, coded signal from London which set the hair on my neck crawling. It came from Major Frank Kitson,[1] in the Planning Branch at the War Office, and asked the Commanding

---

1. Kitson had served with distinction against the Mau Mau in Kenya, and against the Communists in Malaya in 1957, and had an original mind; but in social circles he had the reputation of being very hard to talk to. One evening in 1979, when, as a general, he was Commandant of the Staff College, a young wife who had been placed next to him at dinner attempted to open a conversation by saying, 'I've been bet £5 that I can't get you to say more than five words.' To which he replied, 'You've lost,' and never spoke to her again. He was Commander-in-Chief, UK Land Forces from 1982 to 1985. He was knighted in 1980. Thanks to his and Deane-Drummond's advocacy, the SAS was finally incorporated into the regular army's order of battle.

Officer urgently to appraise the possibility of deploying the SAS into Oman, where rebel leaders had established themselves on top of a mountain called the Jebel Akhdar.

I had never heard of the Jebel Akhdar, and I knew practically nothing about Oman. But here, surely, was a tremendous opportunity for action. At once I began mentally replanning my future: if I could secure a place in any unit sent to Arabia, I would cancel my scooter trip. I would give up the four or five weeks' leave which I had intended to spend travelling, and serve on instead.

I took the message in to Deane-Drummond, who seized on the opportunity as eagerly as I had, though for different reasons. He saw this not merely as another operation, but as a chance for the SAS to prove to the world that it could fight effectively in environments other than the jungle. Because the Regiment had been in Malaya ever since its reformation, its soldiers had become known to outsiders as 'Jungle Bunnies', and the general assumption was that all we could do was to creep about in thick cover. Moreover, many people believed that when the Malayan campaign came to an end, the SAS would be disbanded. As Deane-Drummond at once realized, Oman would give us another chance.

I said that, if it were in any way possible, I should love to take part in the campaign. To my amazement, he more or less agreed that he would find room for me if anything developed. Signals flew back and forth between Kuala Lumpur and London. Frank Kitson came out on a flying visit and met Deane-Drummond in Bahrein. Together the two went on for a reconnaissance in Oman, where they met Colonel David Smiley, then in command of the Sultan of Oman's armed forces.

In short order, and largely on Deane-Drummond's initiative, the decision was taken that the SAS would deploy a squadron into Oman immediately. The unit chosen was D Squadron, then under the command of the redoubtable Johnny Watts, who had taken it over when John Woodhouse moved on. At that stage I had met Johnny only once or twice, but I had immediately recognized him as an exceptional leader. Short, stocky, with an engagingly crumpled face and a deep voice, he cared nothing for his appearance, and generally had a home-rolled cigarette dangling from one corner of his mouth. But he was tough and determined, a real soldiers' soldier, with terrific energy and drive, and a fine, bold imagination. Before joining the SAS he had worked as a bodyguard in South America and served in the Parachute Regiment, and one factor which contributed to the decision to send him to Oman was his family background: he had been brought up on the North-west Frontier in India, where his father had served in the army, and for years he had eagerly studied mountain warfare.

It so happened that when Kitson's message arrived Johnny's squadron had just launched a major operation in Perak, in the far north of Malaya, almost on the border with Thailand. Ever ready with novel schemes, Johnny had dreamed up the idea of using elephants to transport the squadron's stores into the jungle, and it had fallen to me, as Operations Officer, to hire the animals. After a struggle I had managed to line up enough elephants – only to find that the wretched creatures were a total failure, because they were simply too big for the jungle, and as they moved through the forest, kept losing their loads, which were swept off their backs by trees. In the end everything had to be reloaded on to aircraft and dropped in. Johnny was thus not my favourite colleague at that moment, and I expected some favour from him in return.

Summoned back to Kuala Lumpur at zero notice, he came roaring into the Ops Room demanding to know why he had been recalled. The moment I told him what was afoot, he lit up. I pretended that, unless I was included in the party, the whole expedition might be unhinged. (Of course I had no power to unhinge it, but this was all good banter.) In he went to see Deane-Drummond, and in a short time everything was decided. 'D' Squadron would be pulled out of the jungle and despatched to Oman as soon as possible. I was posted to 'D' Squadron, and, to the infinite chagrin of my friend Ian Cartwright, who had led it until then, I was given command of 18 Troop, with the rank of acting captain. It was pure bad luck for Ian that he had chosen that moment at which to get married, and my good fortune that I happened to be in the right place at the right time (I was best man at his wedding, just before we left).

The pace of life had been hectic. Now it became frantic, as the squadron re-trained against the clock for combat in an altogether different environment. Instead of lurking in the green twilight of the jungle, able to see as far as we could throw a grenade, we would be out in blazing sunshine on open mountains, with visibility extending for thousands of yards. In place of our short-range weapons, we would need the new ·762 self-loading rifles (SLRs), three-inch mortars and rocket-launchers. Rather than move by day in small groups, close together, we would operate in larger units, spread out, at night.

I sold my scooter, closed my files on the overland trip home, sent a signal to the DLI saying that my return would be delayed, and eased myself out of the Ops Room to train with 'D' Squadron. Outsiders who saw us thought we had gone crazy. The SAS behaving like regular infantry? What did we think we were doing?

Until the last moment our destination was kept secret. Then, at a briefing, the squadron heard an outline of the operation, not to be passed on, and on 18 November we filed into two Beverley transports. The flight plan – itself a carefully arranged deception – stated that we were bound for Aden and Khartoum; apart from ourselves, only a handful of people knew that our destination was neither of those places.

CHAPTER 9

ARABIAN NIGHTS

1958–59

We landed at the RAF airfield on Masirah, a small, low island off the south-east coast of Oman. To preserve security, the aircraft turned round and flew back to Colombo and Singapore, under the cover that an emergency rescheduling of services had suddenly proved necessary. Barely two years after the fiasco of Suez, Britain's name stank in much of the Middle East, and any suggestion that British special forces were launching a campaign in Arabia would have set off a diplomatic storm, with Nasser orchestrating the denunciation. Our deployment was therefore top secret.

We arrived at the coolest time of the year: even so, the daytime heat was formidable, and the camp at Masirah was a dump. The officers' mess had only outdoor showers, and the whole island seemed desolate. We heard a story that a British ship had been wrecked off the coast earlier in the century, and that when some of the crew reached the shore, local people had slaughtered them. The Sultan of Oman, it was said, became so angry that he condemned the islanders to isolation, and had left them destitute ever since.

Luckily we spent only one night on Masirah. Next day another Beverley came in from Aden and lifted us northwards on to the mainland, putting down on the dirt strip at Sib. There we piled into trucks with floors sand-bagged against mines, and were driven to a tented camp, which Sappers were still building, outside the capital city, Muscat. That same evening, in a large tent which also served as dining room, Deane-Drummond and Smiley briefed us on the situation.

This was more easily described than dealt with. The Ruler of Oman, Sultan Sayid bin Taimur, was despotic and reactionary, but had been supported by Britain, with whom Oman had had treaties of friendship for centuries. A recluse, who rarely appeared in public, he had long been unpopular among his own people, and now he was in serious trouble. Three rebel leaders – Sheikh Ghalib bin Ali, his younger brother Talib bin Ali, and Sheikh Suleiman bin Himayer – had established themselves on top of the Jebel Akhdar – literally Green Mountain – a massif with a flat top 8000 feet above sea level, and all efforts to evict them had been in vain. The prime mover of the revolt appeared to be Ghalib, an *imam*, or religious leader, who had defied the Sultan; but Talib had had military experience, and was thought to be in command of the dissident army. Suleiman was Paramount Sheikh of the Bani Riyam, the principal mountain tribe. All three were being financed and armed by Saudi Arabia, who had sent them arms, mines and gold. Their troops were said to number six or seven hundred men: they were living in caves, and coming down at night to harry the forces of the Sultan round the base of the mountain, as well as to mine the dirt roads.

The plateau measured some twenty miles by ten, and formed a phenomenal natural fortress, protected by the precipitous steepness of its sides and by the fact that there was no road leading to the top. Only half a dozen paths, negotiable by men and donkeys, wound their way up wadis, or dry valleys, so steep and narrow that each could be effectively guarded by a small detachment. On any one track half a dozen men with rifles and a machine gun could keep a company at bay and inflict severe casualties. Even without opposition, the sheer physical difficulties of climbing seven or eight thousand feet in very high temperatures would have been formidable: other units trying to patrol the mountain had lost several casualties to sniper-fire but more to heat-stroke. Small wonder that no foreigner had conquered the top of the jebel since the Persians in the tenth century.

To us, this was a terrific challenge. Senior officers had estimated that a force of four battalions, including a parachute battalion, would be needed to clear the mountain of rebels – but any such large-scale operation had been ruled out by political constraints. We had about sixty fighting men, and aimed to do the job with a stiletto rather than with a bludgeon, not causing so much as a ripple on the surface of international waters. One vital point, emphasized by Deane-Drummond, was that we could not afford casualties: it was essential that none of us fell into enemy hands, alive or dead, since possession of a prisoner or a body would enable the rebels to create a political storm. The Commanding Officer's top-secret Operational Instruction No. 1 remarked that 'a number of larger operations have been planned and turned down for political reasons. This could also happen to the "D" Squadron operation if a fuss were made in the UK.'

We had four days in which to draw new kit, sort ourselves out, train with our long-range weapons and start acclimatizing ourselves to the dry heat. It soon became clear that we were in an extraordinarily backward country, where little had changed since the Middle Ages – for the Sultan had decided that the best way of keeping control was to suppress all forms of development. Muscat itself was a medieval city, surrounded by a high mud wall, its houses built of mud and wood. Neither there nor any-where else in the country was there a tarred road; the only cars were those few which the Sultan kept locked away in his palace. There were no schools, no hospitals or other medical facilities, all of which were forbidden. There were no telephones or postal services, no electricity or piped water. Islamic law was rigorously applied, and anyone convicted of thieving had his hand cut off. Lesser crimes, such as smoking in public or walking about after dark without a lantern, were liable to land offenders in the Jelali, a fortress-gaol which according to rumour contained a pit thirty or forty feet deep. Into this prisoners were thrown, remaining there at the Sultan's pleasure, and receiving no food except what their relatives might bring and lower to them on a rope. Out-side, agriculture had withered, and the people had a depressed, harassed look.

All this we took in as we made our preparations. The delay was a godsend to me, as it gave me a chance to become better acquainted with the members of my new troop. I was glad to be back with 'D' Squadron, in which I had done my jungle training. Probably I myself had gained confidence from my experience in Malaya, but I found its members, who were mostly younger than those of Big Time 'B', less argumentative and more prepared to do what they were told.

Now my Troop Sergeant was Darkie Davidson, a tough and efficient man, not altogether popular with the soldiers because he expected so much of them and drove them so hard, but invaluable to me. Another outstanding non-commissioned officer was Corporal Tindale, who later became a regimental sergeant major: a Geordie, quiet, good-looking and dark, he did an immense amount of work without fuss. Among the troopers, Dicky Dunn was outstanding – a real old reprobate, the size of a flea but as tough as an ox, whose bergen looked bigger than its bearer: the sort of man who kept the troop's sense of humour in good shape with his sudden asides. Another long-serving soldier was Bob Creighton, who in the end reached the rank of major, but also blew off two fingers while experimenting with explosives in Hereford. I was delighted to find that Tanky Smith had also been posted to 'D' Squadron, although he was now in 19 Troop, rather than in mine.[1]

As we prepared for the interior, we started to learn the rudiments of a new language. The opposition were no longer CTs but *adoo*, the Arabic for enemy; in no time at all we were referring to the mountain as 'the *jebel*', and the mountain rebels as *jebali*, and we began saying '*Insh' Allah*' (God willing) or '*Allah karim*' (God is generous) as if we had used those expressions all our lives.

Meanwhile, Deane-Drummond was organizing an efficient supply operation, to bring in everything needed for the campaign, either from Aden, which lay fifteen hundred miles to the south-west, or from Bahrein, which was six hundred miles to the north. At an early stage it became clear that a large number of donkeys would be needed for transporting ammunition, food and other stores up the mountain; and when the War Office discovered that Somali donkeys could be bought for £3 apiece,

---

1. One day just before we left Malaya, Harry Thompson had spotted Tanky and myself walking through the camp. 'Ah, Corporal Smith,' he began magnanimously. 'I've forgiven you. You can join "D" Squadron and go on the new operation.' To which Tanky replied, 'With all due respect, sir, you can get stuffed. I've been posted already.'

whereas a single Omani animal cost £40, they decided with characteristic parsimony to ship two hundred donkeys from Africa. These arrived at Muscat in a landing-craft and had to be swung ashore in nets, five or six at a time. What the mandarins in Whitehall had failed to appreciate was that the Somali animals were much smaller, and could carry only about fifty pounds – half as much as their native counterparts. Besides, they were used to eating cereals, whereas the Omani donkeys lived on dates. The final straw was that the immigrants were not accustomed to heights, and after climbing a thousand feet or so simply lay down. Altogether, it was a disastrous experiment and led to boundless frustration.

On the fifth day we boarded three-ton trucks and set off inland. Even down on the plain, the extent of the rebels' domination was apparent: wrecked vehicles littered the desert, and in the course of a sixty-mile trip we lost three more to mines. By extraordinary bad luck our Anglo-Indian medical orderly, Bill Evans, was on every truck which was blown up. First, after about twenty miles, his lorry had a wheel blown off and he landed in the desert. No sooner had he transferred to another vehicle than that too went up. When it happened a third time, he himself, though uninjured, became shell-shocked, and nobody wanted to have him as a passenger.

Eventually we reached Nizwa, a village in the foothills not far from the southern edge of the Jebel Akhdar. It was a pretty place, with a fine, circular mud fort, handsome trees and a clear stream running through – exactly what we hoped Arabia would be like. Yet it was not the village which seized our interest. Now for the first time we caught sight of our objective – and some sight it was. Through the heat and dust haze on the northern horizon loomed a tremendous massif of grey-brown rock. It might be called Green Mountain, but at that time of the year little green was visible: through binoculars, we could see dry scrub dotted over its tawny flanks, but otherwise it looked barren.

That first glimpse gave us some idea of the mountain's peculiar construction. Its sides seemed to consist of vast rock-slabs laid at precipitous angles: smooth-looking sheets rose for thousands of feet at angles of fifty or sixty degrees before ending in small cliffs, which fell away vertically to the foot of the next slab. It was as if the mountain were clad in gigantic tiles, overlapping each other. Rudimentary maps and air photographs showed that various steep-sided wadis wound their way up into the massif, but that the high plateau itself, lying between seven and eight thousand feet, was reasonably level.

After a few hours in Nizwa we drove on to Tanuf, a village ten miles to the north-west, right at the foot of the mountain. The place had been attacked by the rebels so often that most of the people had left, but a small garrison of the Sultan's forces was established there with a 25-pounder gun, with which they would blaze away at the mountain as raiders came down in the evenings. Here we again settled into a tented camp to prepare for our assault.

In his Operational Instruction No. 1 Deane-Drummond had laid down that

> 'D' Squadron 22 SAS will carry out an offensive recce on all slopes leading up the mountain and on the plateau with a view to
>   a. Gaining knowledge of all possible routes up the mountain.
>   b. Ambushing and killing pickets on the wadis or anywhere else.
>   c. Killing Talib.

This was our brief. Before we arrived, things had been going badly for the government forces. In the words of an SAS report, operations had been 'of a haphazard, unmilitary, valueless and sometimes almost suicidal nature'. The initiative was 'very definitely held by the rebels'. One fact which immediately became clear was that we would do no good patrolling by day. For one thing, the heat was lethal; for another, the rebel pickets guarding the high ground would pick us off at their leisure. We therefore began aggressive patrolling at night, learning how to move and fight on the mountain in the dark, and collecting information about possible routes up to the plateau.

Half the squadron – 16 and 17 Troops – drove round to the northern side of the massif, to reconnoitre that, under the command of Captain Muir Walker, a larger-than-life Scotsman with flaming hair, known to his fellow officers as 'Red Rory' and to the soldiers, paradoxically, as 'Black Abdul'. After a successful reconnaissance patrol they established a base high up in an area called the Aqbat. The principal feature of the mountain there – strongly held by the rebels – was a pair of peaks which were soon officially named Sabrina, after a well-endowed actress of the day, but which became known colloquially as the Twin Tits. Other prominent points also acquired nicknames for easy reference: Pyramid, Ambition, Cassino, Nanto's.[1]

My patrol remained in Tanuf, exploring the slab and the wadi above the village. By day the heat was ferocious, and even at night, when the air temperature fell sharply, the metallic rock remained hot to the touch. A greater change from Malaya could hardly have been conceived – and yet many elements of our training in the jungle now stood us in good stead.

We were used to moving silently, in dim light, using hand-signals instead of spoken commands, and above all we were fit as gypsies' dogs. Soon we were going up and down the mountain – as Tanky put it in one of his inimitable phrases – 'quick as a whore's drawers'. In no other campaign have I known sheer physical fitness play so important a part: without it, we could not have succeeded.

One evening in our camp at Tanuf, Tanky played a master-stroke. He had already seen that our Bren guns lacked the range for this environment: the spaces were huge, and the rebels had quickly discovered that at distances of a thousand yards or more our chances of hitting them were very small. We needed a more powerful weapon, and Tanky spotted one in the form of the ·30 air-cooled Browning machine guns mounted on the armoured cars belonging to the detachment of Life Guards quartered with us. From his days in the Royal Tank Regiment he knew that these were excellent weapons, with an effective range of 3000 yards, and he suggested to Johnny Watts that we should borrow a couple from the cavalry.

---

1. One of Muir Walker's principal recreations was playing the bagpipes, and he was famous for the occasion on which, as a mob stormed the British Embassy in Jakarta, where he was on the military staff, he marched up and down outside, squalling out a lament. Later, in 1959, he hit the headlines by setting a fast time in the early stages of a London–Paris race organized by the *Daily Mail*.

Strolling across to the Life Guards commander, who was smoking a big cigar, Johnny put up the idea. The cavalryman replied superciliously that the Brownings were too complicated for mere infantrymen to handle. Johnny, as usual, was smoking one of the filthy cheroots which he had got from some bazaar in Malaya, and the Life Guards major bet him ten decent cigars that none of his men could dismantle one of the guns and reassemble it. With a gunnery expert at his elbow, Johnny took the bet – whereupon Tanky spread out a groundsheet, stripped a gun and put it together again in a few minutes. The cavalryman was astonished, but paid up, so that they all had a good smoke. Far more important, he lent us two of the weapons – and Tanky's initiative, which began as little more than a joke, may well have saved my life.

Just as we were beginning to find our feet on the mountain, Johnny went down with a raging fever, apparently malaria, and lay in his tent pouring sweat, his temperature dangerously high. So ill did he feel that he thought he was going to die – and so did we. To this day he swears that what made him turn the corner was the sound of myself and someone else, outside his tent, discussing in low voices who should take command of the squadron when he expired. This so enraged him (he claims) that he immediately began to feel better.

Becoming bolder, we conceived the idea of thirty-six-hour patrols: ascending the mountain one night, lying up at altitude during the day in sangars, or small strong-points made of rocks, so that we could observe enemy movement, and coming down the next night. The first such patrol which I led succeeded – but only just. The daytime heat proved incredibly fierce: the iron in the rock seemed to attract, absorb and intensify the sun's rays, so that it became too hot to touch, and breathing demanded conscious effort. Even with strict discipline, we needed every drop of the water which we had laboriously carried up with us. By the time we returned to base late on the second night, we were dehydrated and close to the point of exhaustion.

Every patrol brought home to us the fact that we were up against a skilful, bold and determined enemy. The *adoo* might be barefoot, and some of them might be armed with ancient, smooth-bore Martini-Henry rifles; but the majority had relatively modern Lee-Enfield .303s, with which they were extremely accurate. They also had .5 heavy machine guns and two kinds of mortars, three-inch and eighty-one millimetre – formidable firepower. Besides, they were fit and agile, and knew every yard of their ground.

Their efficiency became all too apparent in an incident on 26 November. The night before, 19 Troop had sent up two five-man patrols, which established themselves on high ground and lay up for the day. At about 1400 the patrol under the command of Tanky Smith saw a single Arab coming up the wadi from below, hallooing to comrades in the rocks above. Tanky waited till the man was within two hundred yards, gave him a wave to bring him to a halt, and shot him dead with a burst from his SLR.

That one quick fusillade brought the mountain to life. About twenty rebels opened up, and bullets flew in all directions. The second patrol were some six hundred yards away, and when they heard the disturbance, prepared to move over to give covering fire; but as one of them, Corporal Duke Swindells, stood up, he was instantly shot in the chest by a rebel hidden in the rocks only two hundred yards below him. Swindells died within half a minute, and a gun battle raged for half an hour before the rebels withdrew. In the end the SAS were able to pull back, carrying Swindells's body. Why he – an experienced man from the Middlesex Regiment, and holder of the Military Medal – had stood up on the ridge as he did, skylining himself, no one could explain; but the disaster emphasized how sharp the Arab snipers were. Swindells was buried in a small, secret graveyard on the shore, which was difficult to reach from the landward side, and where, in earlier days, the crews of ships had laid their dead to rest. To this day there is no access from the land, except by scrambling down a cliff, and it is just the sort of place in which I feel he would have wished to lie.

'As for the enemy,' wrote Johnny in a letter to Deane-Drummond, who had temporarily returned to Malaya, 'they are a much tougher crowd than was thought, especially the hard core, whose minor tactics – fire and movement – are first class.' He might have added that, at this early stage, they were also confident, not to say cocky. When they knew they were far enough away to be safe, they would stand in the open and wave at us – a practice which made the soldiers utter fearful imprecations.

Piece by piece, we built up a picture of the rebels' dispositions, and soon I identified one particularly promising target. As we lay up in the rocks during 26 November – the same day as the Swindells incident – some 6000 feet above sea level, we watched a good deal of coming and going around the mouths of caves in a sheer rock face. From the quality of the Arabs' clothes, it was clear that men of importance were living there. A frontal assault was impossible, because the rock face was vertical, but I saw that if we approached under cover of darkness, we should be able to position ourselves on an outcrop only two hundred yards from the caves. From there, we could open fire on the inhabitants at first light, as they emerged from sleep.

As soon as we returned to Tanuf that night, I put up my idea to Johnny – and it was lucky for me that he was still half-comatose: I believe that, had he been himself, he would have vetoed the plan as carrying too great a risk of casualties. Ill as he was, he let it pass.

On the night of 30 November we set off at 1930 with two full troops: my own, 18 Troop, was to carry out the assault, and 19 Troop was to give us cover from a higher outcrop. Tanky Smith was carrying the main part of his .30 Browning (his partner Curly Hewitt carried the tripod for it, and hence was known as 'Legs'). We were all heavily laden with water bottles, extra ammunition for our SLR rifles and rockets for the 3.5-inch launcher.

It was a dark night, with little moon, but enough ambient light for us to pick out salient features. The ascent was uneventful but tough: to be sure of reaching our assault position in the dark, we had to press on hard, but at the same time make no sound. Even with Commando boots, this was difficult, for as the rubber soles wore down – which they did at an astonishing rate – the screws securing them grated on rock. After a while the troops separated, each heading for its own objective.

Steep escarpments delayed our advance. Several times I feared we had lost our way. The moon went down, leaving us in deeper darkness. But by 0530 we had reached what seemed to me the right place, so I sent a couple of men forward to make sure that the position was the best available. A few minutes later they came back, affirming that all was well. I crept forward and placed every man, spaced out in a line, with a party to guard our rear.

The ground was ideal for our purpose, with plenty of big rocks to give cover. All we had to do was wait. Having sweated pints on the way up, we now began to shudder in the icy pre-dawn air. I pulled on the thin jersey which was all I had in the way of extra clothes, and still kept shivering. The sky started to lighten. We were facing north, so that dawn stole up on our right. I thought about Tanky, somewhere above us, and hoped that the strike by Venom fighter-bombers, which I had laid on with the RAF, would come in on time.

As the light strengthened, I was disconcerted to find that we were farther from the caves than I had hoped. The distance which during our reconnaissance I had reckoned as two hundred yards turned out to be three hundred, the limit of accurate fire for our weapons. Still, we could not move.

The sky paled. Light stole on to the mountain. Now at last I could see the black mouth of the main cave, with smaller openings beside it. The air was absolutely still. The cold bit more fiercely than ever. My watch said 0610 . . . 0615 . . . 0620. At last a white-robed figure appeared in the cave-mouth. The Arab looked round, yawned and stretched. When he spat, we heard him as clearly as if we had been in the same room. He moved off to one side to urinate. Another man appeared, then another.

I looked to right and left. Everyone was poised for action. The rocket launcher crew, Troopers Goodman and Bennett, were on their feet behind a rock with their weapon levelled. I waited until four or five Arabs were in view together, then at last gave the signal.

Pandemonium erupted. With a *whoosh* the first rocket flew straight into the cave. A flash lit up the entrance, and the boom of a heavy explosion came back at us. The rattle of our small-arms fire echoed harshly round the rock walls. Several Arabs fell, and for a few seconds we had things to ourselves. Then suddenly the whole mountain came to life as shots began to crack out from above us on both sides. What we had not realized was that other caves high in the rock faces were also inhabited.

Far from bolting when taken by surprise, the *adoo* counter-attacked with commendable resilience.

The ricochets were prodigious: bullets whanged and whined in every direction, and chips of rock flew. All at once we were in trouble. Where were our Venoms? From high on our left came the comforting, heavy rattle of Tanky's Browning, firing in short bursts. Then I heard the roar of jets, and saw a pair of Venoms high overhead. I put up a Verey light to indicate the enemy, and within seconds the aircraft made their first run. Cannon-fire and rockets tore in, helping to keep the enemy's heads down.

With the advantage of surprise gone, the battle degenerated into a long-range sniping match, as both sides took snap shots at fleeting targets. With fire and movement, one group covering another, we pulled back. Still from above came the hammer of the Browning. So great was the noise, and so intense the fire, that when we reached a relatively safe position, over a ridge, I was amazed to find that we did not have a single casualty. Except for cuts caused by flying rock splinters, nobody was any the worse. By then we were short of ammunition, and in no state to run into an ambush. Once on to the big slab, we spread out well and hurried down, reaching base at 0800. After more than twelve hours on the go, everyone was exhausted; even so, we held an immediate wash-up, or debriefing, sitting in the sand, to make sure we recorded everything of importance while events were fresh in people's minds. Then we had some food and went to sleep.

The raid went down as a major success. Early reports indicated that we had killed twenty of the enemy, including the rebels' chief expert on the .5 machine gun. Later it seemed that the number of dead may have been exaggerated; even if it was, the attack gave the enemy's morale a jolt. We had taken them by surprise in one of their strongholds, an area which until then they had thought impregnable, and we had given them an unpleasant glimpse of what we could do.

Meanwhile, that same night, Muir Walker's people had been having equal success on the other side of the mountain. In one memorable encounter a five-man patrol under the command of Sergeant John Hawkins was attacked by a force of thirty or forty rebels firing light machine guns and rifles. With outstanding coolness, Hawkins held his fire until the enemy were only a hundred and fifty yards off. Then his patrol opened up, dropping several Arabs immediately. Still the rebels kept closing in, but the patrol withdrew under cover from its Bren gun as dark was falling, and escaped unscathed, leaving between nine and twelve enemy dead.

All through December, for night after night, we continued our aggressive patrols from both sides of the mountain. On 5, 6 and 7 December my troop stayed out for three nights and two days, with only two water bottles apiece to keep us going. When at last we returned to base, each of us immediately drank six pints of water, straight down. By 10 December we had established that there was some kind of rebel headquarters at the head of the Wadi Sumait, due north of Nizwa, and we planned to attack it in strength, leaving on the night of the fourteenth; but the raid proved inconclusive. Next, 16 and 17 Troops stepped up their pressure on the enemy around Sabrina, harassing them at night with sporadic mortar fire; and at last light on 24 December Muir Walker led both his troops out for a sustained attack. This went in on the night of 27 December and proved a notable success, with 16 Troop scaling the right tit by rope. The engagement began at 1715 and raged all night, at distances from 1200 yards down to twenty. At one point the SAS were held up only a few feet below some of the enemy across a very steep ravine, though covered by rocks. As they searched for a way across, the rebels realized they were there, and one of them called out in broken English, 'Come on, Johnny!' In reply the SAS men sang, 'Why are we waiting? Oh, why are we waiting?' to the tune of 'Oh, Come, all ye faithful'. As Muir later remarked, 'It was Christmas, after all.' Having captured Sabrina's right tit – a powerfully symbolic achievement – he withdrew to his base-camp; partly by luck, partly by skilful use of fire and movement, he had suffered no casualties at all.

On the other side of the mountain at Tanuf, we had a quieter Christmas. Thinking that a religious service would be good for morale, I arranged for a padre to fly down from Bahrein. I knew that on the whole the SAS was rather agnostic, and that people did not often go to church; but I also knew that whenever a member of the Regiment was killed, and a memorial service was held, the church was packed. At Christmas I did not order anyone to attend: I simply told my troop that the padre had flown six hundred miles to be with us, that I intended to go along myself, and that I hoped they would support me. The service was held out in the sands: the altar was a six-foot trestle table with a sheet draped over it, and a few chairs were put up facing it. I arrived in good time, to set an example; but when the padre was about to start, I looked round and found that the only other person who had bothered to come was Darkie Davidson, who, being Anglo-Burmese, was a Buddhist anyway.

By the turn of the year we had established a certain ascendancy over the rebels: by showing that we could tackle them on their own high ground, we had given them a fright. Our regimental record reflected a big change in their attitude. 'Rebels obviously jumpy and firing at shadows,' said a note on 2 January. 'They continued firing all over the place, and at each other, for three hours. They are much more cautious, show no fires at night and do not move by day.'

The exhilaration of operating successfully in this tough environment had sent our own morale soaring. Even by our own high standards we were incredibly fit: people's skins were peeling and splitting with sunburn, but most of us had faces and arms tanned the colour of horse-chestnuts, and we rejoiced at the challenge of the hard climbing with which the *jebel* presented us. In every way this was an ideal operation for the SAS. Unlike in Malaya, where we had hardly ever set eyes on the enemy, here we saw *adoo* every day: once we were up the mountain, pretty well any Arab was fair game.

Nevertheless, we were also stretched to our limits. We could not tell how many men the enemy thought were opposing them: probably they imagined we were hundreds strong. In fact we had barely sixty fighting men, and no reinforcements available. Appreciating the extent of the operation, Deane-Drummond, still in Kuala Lumpur, had urgently asked the War Office for permission to bring in a second squadron, and after the usual bureaucratic delays this was at last granted on 29 December. At once he set about pulling 'A' Squadron out of the jungle, and he himself arrived back in Oman on 1 January. One of his first moves was to set up a tactical headquarters at Nizwa, to control not only the SAS, but also the units of the Life Guards, the Northern Frontier Regiment and the Trucial Oman Scouts who were supporting us.

Together with Captain John Spreull, an exceptionally able man who had recently joined the Regiment from 21st SAS, and who now came from Malaya to act as Operations Officer, he began planning our final assault on the *jebel*. We felt sure that if we could once establish ourselves on the plateau, the rebels' resistance would crumble. If we could set up a firm base on the top, we could be resupplied from the air and occupy the mountain in strength. The problem was still to gain access to our objective, which now became known as Beercan. It was clear that when we launched our main assault, we must reach the plateau in one night: if we failed to do that, and were caught short on the way up, we should be in serious trouble, with the enemy able to look down on us and snipe at their convenience. Other considerations made it imperative to move quickly: summer, with its intolerable heat, was approaching, and everyone was nervous that, if we remained in Oman for much longer, our security would be breached.

Our patrolling had led us to the conclusion that the best route up to the plateau was from the south, the shortest and most direct approach; and one day, poring over the latest air-photographs, we spotted something which we had failed to notice before: a faint scratch, looking like a track, across what until then we had thought was a vertical cliff at the back of the main slab leading up this route. If it was possible to scramble down that precipice, this was our way.

For an all-night march of the kind we anticipated, we would need a good moon, and the next full moon was due on 25 January. D-Day was therefore set for 26 January. From the moment the date was chosen, we concentrated on building a deception plan designed to lure the enemy away from our selected line of approach. The plan had two elements: first, to persuade the rebels that our main attack would be launched from the north, from the direction of the Aqbat and Sabrina; and second, to make them believe that there was another serious threat from the direction of Tanuf, in the west. While preparations were in hand, we therefore maintained a high level of activity in both these areas.

In the middle of January the troops changed places for a while. While 16 and 17 came back to Tanuf, we in 18 went out and did a stint on the Aqbat. 'A' Squadron, commanded by Johnny Cooper (who had been David Stirling's driver in the Western Desert), reached Oman on 12 January, and had only five days' intensive training before some of them were despatched to the Aqbat to relieve the 'D' Squadron troop there and keep up the pretence that our sights were set on a major attack from the north. At 0330 on D–2 (24 January) they launched an all-out assault on Sabrina, this time capturing the whole feature. Until the last possible minute, 'D' Squadron maintained vigorous patrolling above Tanuf.

Donkeys and their handlers also played an important role in the deception scheme. It was clear that when, or if, we reached the top, we would need water and food, and perhaps also more ammunition. An air drop was planned for 0645 on the morning of D-Day + 1, but if for any reason it should fail, we would depend on stores brought up the wadis. A large number of donkeys was therefore marshalled, and loads prepared. On the evening of 25 January Deane-Drummond gave four of the leading handlers a special briefing. He opened by saying that the information which he was about to divulge was top-secret, and that they were not to pass it to anyone else, on pain of death. He then told them that although a feint was to be made up the Wadi Kamah, the real assault was to be launched from Tanuf, and the donkey-trains would be going up that way. (Our knowledge of the local intelligence system suggested to us that this information would reach the top of the *jebel* in very short order – and so it proved. We learnt later that an accurate account of our phoney plan reached the rebels within six hours.)

It was difficult to sleep, or even to relax, on D-Day, for I could not stop my mind dwelling on the supreme physical effort that lay ahead. Giving his orders in the evening, Johnny Watts nominated my troop as lead-troop. I was delighted: I had pressed for this – an honour of a kind – as I was determined to be the first foreigner on to the top of the *jebel* since the Persians in the tenth century. But Johnny, who had still not fully recovered from his fever, and was determined not to hold up the ascent, left me with a typically paradoxical final instruction. 'Whatever happens,' he said, 'bloody well keep going. Even if I order you to stop and rest, ignore me.'

We left Tanuf in lorries, after last light, at 1930 and were driven to Kamah, due north of Nizwa. There we waited for half an hour until the moon rose, and then drove on the short distance to our start-line, which we crossed at 2030. So began the toughest night of my life.

Away we went, climbing hard, not up any of the wadis, but straight up the face of the slab above us, our first objective being a feature known as Pyramid. Two troopers ranged ahead to warn of any enemy and make sure that the bulk of the squadron did not waste time by going up blind alleys. The first hour or so was the most daunting. We were all carrying very heavy loads – some bergens weighed 90lbs – and we knew we would have to keep climbing all night, without any chance of a proper rest, still less of a restorative brew. At first the air was very hot, and we poured with sweat. So steep was the face of the slab that some of the squadron could not stand the pace and fell back, left to come on as best they could. Every hour, on the hour, I stopped for a couple of minutes to let stragglers catch up, but otherwise we went on and on.

Away in the distance to our right front we heard 4 Troop of 'A' Squadron putting in a diversionary attack on the Aqbat, but closer at hand everything was quiet, and for seven hours we met no opposition. Then, at about 0400, as we were approaching the point where our slab ended in the small precipice, our leading scouts came hurrying back to meet us. They had found a .5 machine gun covering a natural bottleneck leading to the point at which the track went down the cliff. The gun was fully set up, but the crew were not in sight.

The better part of the scouts' news was that the cliff, though steep, was not very high, and negotiable. Johnny and I held a rapid, whispered conference. We could not knock out the machine gun crew without making a noise which would advertise our presence to half the *jebel*. The best plan seemed to be to slip past without waking the enemy. But we also had a bigger problem: we were running late, and if we continued at the pace which we had managed so far, it seemed unlikely that we would reach the plateau before daybreak. I suggested to Johnny that we should take off our bergens, cache them, and leave them in the charge of a small guard-party, who could also deal with the machine-gunners when they returned. This idea had the added merit of making our descent of the cliff easier and quieter: for men rendered clumsy by ninety-pound loads on their backs, it would have been both noisy and dangerous.

Johnny agreed, and detailed twenty-two of us, including himself, to press on; so we silently extracted bandoliers of extra ammunition from the tops of our bergens, slung them about our shoulders, dumped our packs, and went on in light order, with only our weapons and belt kits. First we crept past the machine gun. To this day I can see the moonlight shining on its barrel and belts of ammunition as it poked out of a small cave, in an ideal position to cover the approach. Then we came to the cliff, which proved to be only thirty or forty feet high. There was a track of sorts, but very sheer, and dangerous in the dark, especially for men already tired and thirsty. With the stars paling, it was agony to stand at the bottom and wait for twenty men to feel their way down.

When the last of them reached the bottom, we set off fast to our left, along a track which ran up a wide wadi. Then we came onto another slab – the final one, we hoped. As we scrambled up it, the sky was lightening rapidly on our right. Far back to our left, fires twinkled out of cave-mouths in a cliff-face as the machine-gun crew brewed up their breakfast coffee. Soon a burst of firing and the distant boom of grenades told us that an SAS party had put paid to them.

Our stamina was ebbing away. Up we went, over one false crest after another, hoping fiercely that each was the last. As we grew weaker, the light grew stronger. But then suddenly we came over one more ridge and saw that the mountain hardly rose any more: the slope eased off into a rough, rocky plateau. Elation gave us one final burst of energy. At the last moment Johnny Watts appeared from behind me, and we sprinted neck and neck to be first to the top – a race which I reckon I won by a short head.

Dazed with exhaustion, we hurled ourselves down behind

rocks on the highest piece of ground we could see, expecting to
be attacked at any moment. Johnny set us out in ten pairs round
a rough perimeter, told us to die where we stood, and positioned
himself in the middle. The ground, though rough, was nearly
level, and we could see five or six hundred yards.

We lay and watched, catching an occasional glimpse of movement among low mounds in the distance, but nothing closer at
hand. Then we picked up the blessed drone of engines, and in
came three Valettas to make our air-drop, dead on time. Jerricans of water, banded together with tough webbing straps,
crashed down among the rocks; Johnny had left his knife in his
bergen, and had a struggle to free the cans, smashing and kicking
at the straps to tear the bundles apart. Then he came scuttling
to each of our positions, with a can for every pair, and at last
we could slake our thirst.

More of our own people began arriving, among them Deane-
Drummond. Dazed though I was, I was hardly expecting to see
the Commanding Officer so far forward – but it was typical of
him, and he was, after all, the architect of the assault. As the
sun climbed and the heat built up, it became clear that few
enemy remained anywhere near us: our deception plans had
worked magically, and we were in possession of the plateau.
Some of the soldiers found it an anti-climax: they had been
hoping for a good battle, and felt cheated. I saw their point: it
was hard to believe that our monumental efforts were over. In
fact further violent exertions awaited us, for we had to go down
in relays, recover our bergens, climb back to the top, and then
begin despatching patrols to determine the state of affairs farther
out on the plateau. Three troopers in 'A' Squadron had been
wounded on the way up – and two of them later died – after a
bullet had detonated a grenade in one of their bergens; but these
were our only casualties.

The campaign was as good as over. Once we were established in
strength, with air support available, the rebels' guerrilla methods
were no longer much use to them. Lacking the strength or
organization to dislodge us with an infantry-type attack, they
simply melted away. To our slight disappointment, we did not
manage to kill or capture the three rebel leaders, all of whom

fled for sanctuary into Saudi Arabia. Nevertheless, their insurrection was at an end, and we had some small compensation in that we found Suleiman's cave, which had been hastily abandoned. This was a marvellous complex in the face of a cliff, with a big outer hall used by the Sheikh's bodyguard, retainers and slaves; at the back of it a low entrance, through which we had to crawl on hands and knees, led to an inner sanctum. As Johnny and I went through it, we could smell pungent women's perfume; inside, our torch-beam lit up rugs on the floor, and rows of tin trunks stacked round the walls.

Wild with the elation of our victory, we tore these open, hoping to find them loaded with Maria Theresa silver dollars or other money; but they contained nothing more exciting than clothes and ancient, illuminated books in Arabic. I pocketed a French-made MAB six-millimetre pistol, which I later gave to the SAS museum in London. Johnny carried off two swords, an old-fashioned bandolier inlaid with silver, and – prize possession – Suleiman's stick, which the Sultan was said to have laid across the door of the house, to bar all-comers, whenever he was exercising his *droit de seigneur* among girls in the villages.

The inhabitants of the plateau were in a wretched state: their villages had been wrecked, their fields left untilled. The ancient *falaj*, or water-conduit, system was in ruins, and the people themselves had been living miserably in caves. For the next three weeks the SAS carried out a programme of flag-marches, trekking all over the *jebel* in half-troops, each accompanied by a couple of donkeys and an officer from one of the native regiments. According to Tanky, who took part, it was a wonderful time: they visited lovely oases lying seven or eight thousand feet above sea-level, with running springs, and fig trees and limes flourishing. Alas, I myself missed this exercise, because I had overstayed my period of leave and felt I must hurry back to the DLI.

The Jebel Akhdar campaign proved a turning-point in the history of the SAS. We had shown that we were a flexible force capable of adapting quickly to new conditions. We had demonstrated that a small number of men could be flown into a trouble spot rapidly and discreetly, and operate in a remote area without publicity – a capability much valued by the Conservative

Government of the day. Above all, we had proved that the quality of the people in the SAS was high indeed, and that a few men of such calibre could achieve results out of all proportion to their numbers.

No word of our involvement in Oman reached the public until April, when *The Times* at last broke the secret with an article fed to the newspaper by Deane-Drummond. Knowledge of what we had done pervaded the army long before that, of course, and our success had a material effect in keeping the Regiment in being. Until we stormed the Jebel Akhdar, the probability was that, despite the efforts of George Lea, Dare Newell and Tony Deane-Drummond, the SAS would be disbanded when it came home from Malaya; but now this victory gave it a new lease of life.

CHAPTER 10

DURHAM AND DEVON

1959–60

After the heat and action in Arabia, it was a shock to return to England, cold and grey in February. Muir Walker and I travelled back together, reached London feeling rather full of ourselves, and went to stay a night with Dare Newell and his wife Hazel at their flat in Balham. There we deluged Dare with stories of our adventures; and he, who had fought his way through the Second World War, found it thoroughly amusing to hear these two young captains holding forth about what to him was a minor operation. Later, he pulled our legs about it mercilessly, but on the night he gave us a grand curry washed down by plenty of beer, and after supper, sitting on the floor, I inevitably fell asleep.

I was thrilled to find that my mother had made real progress. Two years earlier, in 1957, she had finally left hospital and gone to stay in a private house. Although still slow in her reactions, and not able to initiate a conversation, she was beginning to show stirrings of independence. Relations with Joyce and my grandmother were as edgy as ever; but in August the family was temporarily jolted out of its feuds and rivalries by the news that for my work in Oman I had been awarded the Military Cross. The announcement gave my mother a strong lift, and by the time I went to Buckingham Palace for the investiture in November, she was well enough to accompany Michael, David and myself.[1]

---

1. The SAS won eight awards in the Oman campaign. Tony Deane-Drummond received a DSO; Johnny Watts, Muir Walker and Tony Jeapes all gained MCs, Sergeant Hawkins the DCM, and Trooper Cunningham the MM.

Bill and Ruth Beak were as welcoming as ever, and I spent several happy weekends at their cottage at Rambridge, in Hampshire; but still, at the age of twenty-five, I had no home. On the social front, I remained determined not to become involved with women, and to keep them at bay I had grown a horrible moustache, which, being orange, bristly and unattractive, seemed to be having the desired effect.

Somehow I had to settle down to conventional soldiering again. Back at the DLI depot in Brancepeth Castle, I once more trained recruits; but by then National Service had come to an end, and intakes were less frequent. In one of the gaps between drafts, I turned my attention to training the permanent staff of the camp. Having learned a good deal during my travels, I modified my methods according to various new ideas, several of them derived from John Woodhouse. In general, I encouraged people to think for themselves, and not to be bound by conventional discipline and routine. I also sought to broaden their interests by including some instruction in world affairs, concentrating on countries in which Britain still had interests, and in which we might have to go and fight.

One day I decided to teach the trained soldiers a little about demolitions, and announced that the subject would be introduced during the first period in the afternoon. Now, I thought, the essential of any good lecture is a brisk start, particularly after lunch: kick off with a bang, and make sure that everyone is awake. I decided, therefore, to launch my lecture with a small detonation. Had I been honest with myself, I would have admitted that I did not know much about explosives. I had amused myself blowing up blinds on the ranges in Japan, and in the SAS I had been on a short explosives course under Alan Julius, a former Royal Engineer officer. I knew how to make up a charge and place it on a railway line or a bridge – but I was *not* well informed about the finer points of the effect which explosives can have in confined spaces.

To prepare for my lecture, I put half a pound of plastic explosive on the ground outside the back of the building and fitted the charge with detonator and time-fuse, cut to a length that would give me just long enough to walk into the building and take my place at the lectern. At about 1358 my students filed into their places. As they were sitting down, I nipped out, lit the fuse, and strolled back in. After shuffling my papers for a few seconds I cleared my throat and announced, 'Right. What we're going on with now is the theory and practice of explosives . . .'

Hardly had I uttered the word, when *BANG!* A gigantic blast made everyone leap from their seats. The wall behind me cracked from top to bottom and bulged inwards. I had no option but to evacuate the building in a hurry. Outside, the tinkle of falling glass betrayed the fact that many windows had been blown out, and from every side came yells of indignation. Not for some time did I learn that the greatest outrage had been suffered in the Officers' Mess: the blast-wave, whipping across the moat, had blown in many of the windows on that side of the castle, and as the senior officers of the DLI sat drinking their coffee after lunch, they had received a nasty shock.

Such was the damage that I could not possibly pay for the repairs, and – rather as when I had set off the third trip-flare in the jungle – I decided that the only thing to do was to own up. So I told the quartermaster, Darkie Davidson, what had happened, and his reaction was magnificent. He found the accident highly amusing, and took control without demur. 'Don't let it worry you,' he said in avuncular fashion. 'Leave everything to me.' How he managed to lose the costs involved, I never knew; but although I escaped any financial penalty, the incident persuaded my senior officers that I was a liability at the depot, and they soon despatched me to the DLI's other barracks at Honiton, in Devon, to which the First Battalion was about to return after a tour abroad.

I put it about that I was being sent to Devon to cut the grass round the Officers' Mess; but in fact I was put in charge of arrangements for the battalion's return, and this dull task did not last for long, as the Commanding Officer, Lieutenant-Colonel Charles d'Arcy Irvine, saw that I needed a reasonably challenging job, and posted me as second-in-command of the training wing under an old friend, Major David Dunn, to help run courses for junior non-commissioned officers. This suited me perfectly, as it gave me a chance to put into practice ideas developed in Korea, Egypt, Malaya and Oman.

In the SAS I had found that the delegation of responsibility to the lowest possible level produces results out of all proportion to the risks involved in letting junior people have a measure of independence and authority. At the same time, I had seen that you cannot simply delegate without knowing your people: you must make sure that you have people whom you trust, and who trust and can work with you. Furthermore, a leader must obviously lead by example, and with knowledge: the man on the Bren gun, for instance, does not expect his commander to be better on the gun than he is, but he does expect him to know its capabilities and limitations, so that he, the gunner, is not given tasks which are beyond him and his weapon.

Clearly in any military organization there must be an element of discipline and authority, and these should be based on firmness, fairness and understanding; but experience had taught me that the best kind of discipline is self-discipline, when a commander instils into his men the will to do things, which they want to see done well, because they have been given the responsibility for carrying them out. Anyone delegating in this way has to take risks. Some of your people may let you down, and some may make mistakes; but if they do blunder, you must be prepared to back them. If you jump on them every time something goes wrong, they decline to commit themselves next time round, and you never create the mutual trust essential in achieving self-discipline.

All this had come out in my time with the SAS, where there was a wonderful freedom to make experiments, and the quality of people was higher than in other regiments. Yet when I returned to the DLI I was fascinated to find that I could apply the same principles to normal soldiers, provided I was prepared to ride out an initial period of adjustment. The experiments I made were very simple. For instance, when giving orders, I would leave people to carry them out, and not check and double-check that they were doing as told. In the matter of punishment, I never approved of putting people on orders or charging them in the conventional way; I always preferred to impose a punishment which was practical and short-lived, and left no mark on a man's record. Further, I believed that officers should be subject to roughly the same discipline as other ranks, and not get away with offences. If someone was late, for example, when the transport set off for an exercise on Dartmoor, he would be left behind and expected to find his own way out to the rendezvous, whatever his rank. When this happened once or twice, and the people concerned found their predicament both tiresome and slightly demeaning, they made sure that they were not late any more. In general, all ranks appreciated having trust put on them, and responded.

One minor obsession of mine was with the importance of kit, clothes and ammunition. I had learnt that, when you are fighting, everything counts, and you must not waste anything. If you fail to look after your kit, and constantly need reissues, you throw a strain on the logistic system which is supplying you, and are liable to have an adverse impact on the whole operation. I was therefore very fierce with anybody, including myself, who lost something, and always ruthlessly made him pay for it. Once I initiated this practice, people began to look after their kit with a great deal more care.

Whenever possible, I myself avoided parades (which I loathed, and on which my performance was an embarrassment to the Adjutant and the Regimental Sergeant Major) by organizing far-flung exercises on Dartmoor; several times I took contingents to my favourite haunts in the Brecon Beacons, and I once arranged for the journey back to Devon to take the form of an initiative exercise. Men were dropped off lorries in pairs, each with 12s 6d (about sixty pence) in his pocket, and told to find their way home to Honiton in thirty-six hours, with the added requirement that on the way they were to make a sketch of the Clifton Suspension Bridge, over the Avon gorge in Bristol. Some of the sketches were first class, and showed the bridge in astonishing detail. I myself joined in with a partner: we left Brecon at midday on Saturday, and after securing several lifts reached base at 0500 on Sunday.

As a side-line, I became Food Member in the Officers' Mess, in charge of catering. By putting in a lot of work, I managed to bring our budget under control, with the result not only that we ate extremely well, but also that I saved a substantial amount of money. When I came to hand over, four months later, I found that our account was £700 in credit; and, rather than pass the balance on to my successor, I arranged a grand dinner in the mess, to which we invited all the people who had helped us in the area. Our guests were amazed to find themselves sitting down to a nine-course meal, of which the *pièce de résistance* was a whole roast sucking pig, marched round the dining room on a silver salver by the chef before he ceremonially carved it. The dinner lasted four hours, and by the time we staggered up from the table at midnight, everybody was stupefied.

All this was enjoyable and rewarding; yet at the bottom of my heart I was always hoping that somehow I could return to the SAS. Like malaria, the bug had entered my system, and nothing could get rid of it. Luckily for me the Regiment was short of officers, and the chances of rejoining seemed reasonably good. Then one day late in 1959 George Lea, now a brigadier commanding the brigade of which the DLI were part, came to visit the Regiment at Honiton. Still better, he summoned me to see him. There he was, as huge as ever, with his welcoming smile, his big, booming voice and all his old charm. When he asked if I would like to become Adjutant of 21st SAS, the Territorial regiment, my heart leapt. No matter that this would be fundamentally a desk job, and in London: I needed no second invitation.

Once again, the DLI was generosity itself. Other regiments were often awkward about letting people return to Special Forces; but the Durhams had correctly discerned my bent. They saw that it would be far better for everyone if they let me stay in the army doing something which I wanted to do, rather than force me into posts which I did not care for, and they made no fuss about letting me go: perhaps they were even rather pleased.

CHAPTER 11

ADJUTANT 21ST SAS

1960–62

Because 21st SAS had long since been amalgamated with another distinguished (and much older) volunteer regiment, the Artists' Rifles, its official title was 21st SAS (Artists').[1] Its headquarters was a Victorian drill hall in Dukes Road, Euston – a vast building put up in about 1870, and in its day the last word in modernity, but looking slightly run down ninety years later. In spite of dingy yellow and green paint, the hall itself had a certain style, with the names of illustrious officers inscribed on boards round the walls; but the offices attached to it were small and dark, and the whole place was rather dreary.

This became my base for the next two years. Having never before worked in an office, or in London, I was not certain how much I was going to like it; but various factors combined to ensure that I had an interesting and enjoyable tour. The first, sad in itself, was the illness and death of our Second-in-Command, Hugh Mercer. He was off-duty, sick, when I arrived, and although we did not at that stage know how ill he was, he was soon diagnosed as having cancer, and died not long afterwards. His absence meant that I became not only Adjutant but also, in effect, Second-in-Command and Training Major, with the result that I was able to escape from the office and take

---

1. The Artists' Rifles were founded in 1860 by Edward Sterling, an art student who formed a volunteer corps of painters, sculptors, musicians, architects, engravers and actors. The combined 21st SAS (Artists') Regiment came into being in 1946. It has always seemed a happy coincidence that the founder of 22nd SAS should also have been called Stirling.

part in planning and running exercises far more often than at first looked likely.

The second factor was that I found an excellent place in which to live. Another Territorial officer, Mark Milburn, told me that a room was going spare in the basement flat where he was lodging in the Little Boltons, South Kensington, and I was able to move into it at once. The flat belonged to Phemea Cazenove, a lady of powerful character who had done wonders as a nurse in the Second World War, winning the Royal Red Cross, and who now looked after her tenants as if they were patients, letting us rooms at ridiculously low rates. I paid £3.50 a week for a good big room, including breakfast, which I cooked for myself; if we left the flat in a mess, Phemea would come down and give us a rocket, but when we returned exhausted from exercises, she would fuss over us and put us to bed with hot-water bottles and scalding whisky toddies. Although we referred to her with mock formality as 'The Landlady', she became a good friend, almost a second mother, and her flat made a perfect base.

The Commanding Officer of 21st SAS was then Jim Johnson, a tall, smooth City man of no mean originality and wit, who worked in Lloyds. During the war he had served in the Welsh Guards, but now was a volunteer, and so came into the office only two or three times a week, to sign letters and make sure that everything was running smoothly. This meant that I had to draft most of the letters; and in all the time I was working with Jim, he only twice altered one of my drafts. This, I thought, showed extraordinary self-discipline on his part: provided a letter made sense and said what he wanted, he would let it go, unworried by the fact that it might not be couched exactly in terms which he himself would have chosen. This impressed me a great deal, and taught me a lesson in the value of delegation.

To run our Orderly Room we had 'Wolly' — Mr Wolland — the Chief Clerk, a delightful little man, polite, courteous and owl-like in appearance, with horn-rimmed spectacles. A beaver for work, he stayed on far past office hours every night, even though paid a pittance. The stores were in the charge of Ned Pinnock, the Quartermaster, who came from the Rifle Brigade — a bit of a tyrant, and rightly so, for in the Territorial Army it is extremely difficult to maintain control of clothes and equipment.

People draw complete sets of kit and keep them at home – and as long as they continue to serve, there is no harm in this habit. Trouble sets in when a man leaves, and – whether through idleness, negligence or mild dishonesty – fails to return everything that he has on loan: the cost of bergen, sleeping-bag, poncho, set of mess-tins and other equipment adds up to a formidable amount, which the Regiment can ill afford to lose. Ned kept his stores immaculate, and was brilliant at not letting people get away with carelessness or petty larceny.

The territorials with whom I was now working were an impressive bunch, quite different from any of the soldiers I had come across before. I felt privileged to be dealing with such able and intelligent men, whose originality dragged me well clear of the rut of the professional army. Instead of hard-bitten regulars, I now had company directors, bankers and solicitors among the troopers (for everyone had to come in at the bottom, no matter what rank he might have held in other regiments) – and I was pleased to find how dedicated these people were, giving up their weekday evenings and weekends to train. (A second TA regiment, 23rd SAS, was also being built up at this time, from its base in Birmingham.)

Yet I soon discovered that an unpleasant amount of antipathy smouldered between the regulars and territorials of the SAS. The regulars looked on the part-timers as amateurs, and tried to unload poor instructors on them, at the same time claiming that to be posted to the TA was the kiss of death. This was nonsense: the TA were, and are, the cream of society, in that besides their innate ability they all have exceptional energy and determination. Why else would they devote their spare time to activities which are often exceedingly strenuous and uncomfortable?

What worried regular soldiers was the fact that the territorials were unorthodox – yet this in itself was a virtue. Discipline was not as tight as in the regular army: things tended to get done slowly, because the soldiers were part-time, and standards could never be the same, with people not working at them seven days a week. Nevertheless, levels of achievement were high, and the people thoroughly competent.

When I saw this, and realized how antagonistic feelings were,

I became determined that our regular servicemen should understand the capabilities of the TA. Later, when I was Commanding Officer of 22nd SAS, I made it a rule that nobody could be promoted beyond the rank of sergeant unless he had had a successful TA tour – and I am glad to say that the attitude of the regulars gradually changed from one of scorn and horror to one of respect. In time, people began to see that the territorial SAS were first class, and enhanced the reputation of the whole Regiment in a special way of their own.

A regular pattern of activity made weeks slip away. On drill nights, held two or three times a week, people would arrive in the evening wearing city clothes, change into denims, and work at weapon training, unarmed combat, vehicle recognition and so on. As the weekend approached, they would draw kit and equipment and begin planning exercises, and then on Friday night they would rush off for Dartmoor, the Brecon Beacons or some overseas training area, often parachuting in during the early hours of Saturday. Occasional dinners would be held in the Officers' Mess, which we shared with the Artists' Rifles. There, post-prandial pastimes were of the usual high intellectual calibre: competitive diving off chairs, circumnavigation of the room without touching the floor, and the game known as High Cockalorum, a form of piggy-back jousting.

In the early 1960s 21st SAS began to develop a new and important role. The concept of operations in Europe at that date was basically that we, the NATO forces, were on the defensive. We never expected to attack the Russians, but we did expect them to attack us. Our plan in that event was to withdraw, consolidate, hold the enemy on a given line and destroy them with nuclear weapons. To implement this plan effectively, the British Corps Commander needed an organization which could send back accurate reports of Russian movement from far enough out in front of his own troops to enable him to identify the main enemy thrust and deploy his reserves accordingly, as well as to help target his own nuclear weapons. That organization was 21st SAS. If Soviet forces did launch a pre-emptive strike, our task would be to go to ground behind enemy lines and report troop movements back to British Corps headquarters.

Our aim was to place our people on the ground before the

Russian advance began, in such a way that they would be over-run, and remain *in situ* for as long as seemed necessary or proved possible. The idea of lying hidden beside arterial roads for days or even weeks on end did not at first appeal. This seemed a rather passive intelligence-gathering task, and far removed from the SAS's original, gung-ho role of roaring about the Western Desert in heavily armed vehicles. In the early days of the concept the plan was hard to sell to people who were essentially aggress-ive and fit, who enjoyed their independence and wanted to move around on offensive operations, and whom we had delib-erately encouraged in these tendencies during training.

But the fact was that the Corps Commander did not want us rushing round Germany in gun-buggies; and, as people per-ceived that our new commitment had a fascination of its own, they began to work out means of discharging it with character-istic inventiveness. Indeed, many of them became absorbed by the intellectual challenge of remaining alert and useful while hidden underground, and obsessive about the detail with which they camouflaged their hides.

After many experiments, we reached the conclusion that what we needed were underground bunkers, strong enough to with-stand nuclear, biological and chemical attack, and big enough to house teams of six people (the minimum, if two were to be on duty twenty-four hours a day). At the same time, the shelters had to be compact enough for all the component parts – princi-pally a long, hooped sheet of corrugated metal for the roof – to be carried in a trailer towed behind each team's vehicle. From the shape of the metal roof, they became known as 'wriggly holes'.

In the development and siting of these hides, we owed a great deal to David Lyon, a tall, sandy-haired man in his twenties, then working in Courtaulds (and, to our delight, designing brassières and selling them by the thousand), who had served as a second lieutenant in the Rifle Brigade during his National Service and fought against the Mau Mau in Kenya, winning a Mention in Despatches. Very few of the SAS volunteers had commanded men in battle, and the fact that he had done so made him all the more valuable. Besides enormous energy, he had an exceptionally clear mind, and was constantly questioning received ideas – qualities which made him an ideal scout for 21st SAS's new venture. One summer he set out on his own and spent two weeks in Germany identifying on the ground positions which the three Regiments could take up in the event of war. The project was ranked top-secret, and at the headquarters of the British Army on the Rhine he found himself treated with gratifying deference; after a briefing there, he drove off in a civilian car and pin-pointed nearly thirty sites, some of them almost on the frontier between West and East Germany, and looking straight into Communist territory. All were chosen so that clandestine teams would be able to watch the main roads and bridges which the Russians would use to move forward.

Back at home, David dug and built a shelter in a wood behind his cottage in Berkshire, and lived in it for a week with three companions. They found themselves at intimately close quarters: in spite of a primitive ventilation system, the air in the bunker became foul, and the atmosphere highly claustrophobic. The experiment showed that the SAS's new role would need all the Regiment's typical character and endurance, and that it would require extraordinarily strong nerves to allow the enemy to run over you, and sit there passively reporting events.

Trials of this kind were repeated in many training areas in England and Wales. One patrol remained underground for three weeks and emerged sane, defying predictions that by then they would all be off their heads. At least once a year SAS teams took part in the big ten-day or two-week exercises in Germany, digging themselves in at locations close to those which they might occupy in a real emergency. We learned to site our observation-posts in depth, so that if units of the Red forces (simulating the enemy) were advancing to contact down a road, not one report, but a whole series, would come back by radio, and the speed of the advance could be worked out precisely. Again and again we demonstrated the crucial importance, in intelligence work, of having human beings on the ground. No matter how sophisticated spy aircraft and satellites may be, they are no substitute for pairs of alert eyes, which function whether the sky is clear or cloudy, at night as well as by day, in rain, snow and even fog – and we proved this so many times that after a while the Corps Commander came to regard us as indispensable. Time after time on the major exercises ninety per cent of the best intelligence emanated from our hides, and we became so popular that we could not furnish enough teams. (This experience was repeated in the Gulf War of 1990–91, when, although the Coalition had the largest air force ever assembled, and satellite surveillance, in the open environment of the Iraqi desert the SAS became the most reliable means of identifying mobile Scud ballistic missile launchers.)

The most vital skill needed was the ability to recognize vehicles, tactical signs and pieces of equipment immediately, without reference to manuals, and to pass information back to command posts with minimal delay: hence in our training recognition had a high priority. Another prerequisite, as always, was good signalling: since speed was of the essence, and all reports had to be transmitted in Morse, we laid emphasis on signal training, and had an entire Signals Squadron based near the White City in west London.

When sending people in behind enemy lines, one essential principle is that a commander must not commit them to operations from which there is no hope of recovery. In Western military terms, it is simply not acceptable, either morally from the point of view of senior officers, or in terms of the morale and welfare of the units in the field. In other words, our surveillance teams had to have some realistic hope of extricating themselves after a nuclear exchange, and in consequence their training concentrated on techniques of escape and evasion. Of course it was impossible to tell who or what would survive a nuclear battle; but we had to make sure that our patrols had the best possible chance of making their way back to our own lines. We saw this as essential, partly because we genuinely wanted our people to escape, and partly because we could not have them feeling that they were being condemned to a pit in the ground, never to be seen again.

One problem which we never solved was that posed by the Champ – the jeep-like vehicle in which each team rode, towing their trailer full of equipment. It was generally agreed that in the event of war the Champs would have to be abandoned, and burned, at least 5000 yards to the rear of each hide – and this meant that the teams would have to make their way back on foot.

Our escape and evasion exercises trained people for such an emergency, and most of them took place on Dartmoor. They were extremely arduous, particularly in winter, and laid emphasis on resistance to interrogation. Participants would be given a scenario which laid down that they were on the run in enemy territory: they would be required to break away from a truck or a train in the middle of the moor, with minimal rations, and move across country to the first of several rendezvous, using only skeleton maps and escape compasses. If they were caught – as they usually were – they were brought into an interrogation centre manned by the Military Police and specialists from the Joint Services Interrogation Wing.

Our people were trained, methodically and in depth, *not* to answer questions, and to resist interrogation. The theory behind their training was that they should know what to expect, and therefore be frightened by nothing. They would know, for instance, that an interrogator who seemed to be friendly was just lulling their suspicions, and that a hostile questioner was behaving in an aggressive manner because that was the pose which the enemy had chosen to adopt at that moment.

Nevertheless, prisoners had a tough time of it. One of the fundamental objectives of each exercise was to wear down their will to resist by keeping them short of food and sleep, and sending them on strenuous cross-country marches, so that by the time they were caught, their resistance had already been lowered. Once captured, they were taken down still further by various aggressive methods: the rules definitely precluded physical violence, but not more subtle kinds of maltreatment. Prisoners were made to stand for hours in stress postures, leaning against a wall with their hands above their heads; they were disorientated by having hoods put over their heads, and confused by sustained loud noise known as 'sound white-out'; sometimes they were stripped to their underpants and put out in the snow, and at others led to suppose that they were about to be swamped with water.

Such practices were acceptable in moderation: our aim, after all, was to train people for capture in war, and if we did not make interrogations fairly realistic, there was no point in them. Unfortunately the leader of the JSIW, Wing Commander George

Parker, would occasionally allow himself to be carried away and take things too far. A highly able man, but dark and dour-looking, he created a sinister impression. As an RAF bomber pilot he had been shot down, taken prisoner and tortured by the Germans during the war, and his own experience seemed to have convinced him that even in peace-time he must push his victims to their limits. The result was that one or two nearly had nervous breakdowns: the Press got hold of the story, and serious complaints were made, both in the newspapers and in the House of Commons. We carried on, although with tightened rules. In the end we built escape and evasion into the selection course for newcomers to the Regiment, because we felt that if a recruit could not take the isolation which goes with interrogation, and come through it and keep his mouth shut, he was probably not the right sort of man to have working behind the lines, where he might easily compromise his colleagues.

I myself was always surprised at the way people gave in. While I was Adjutant, I would often go out and act as a runner, or escaper, and I was frequently caught; but I always took the view that this was just another exercise, that in forty-eight hours it would be over, and that all I had to do was to hold out for that time, secure in the knowledge that nothing really bad could happen to me. Interrogation never bothered me. On the contrary, I regarded it as an interesting diversion from the boredom of captivity: it broke the monotony of sitting in a blacked-out room, or being assaulted by noise, or standing propped against a wall. It also gave me a chance to look at possible escape routes, and generally brightened up the day.

Perhaps it was repeated experience which gave me this confidence. Whenever I was caught, I made it a rule to start planning my escape immediately: the sooner I broke out, the less well prepared my captors would be, and the shorter would be the distance which I would have to travel to reach some safe area. Escape was the subject which kept me absorbed during periods of detention.

On one exercise in Singapore during my time in Malaya we had been marching through the night to place demolition charges on a target, and due to my stupidity in letting the troop stop to have a smoke, we were seen, surrounded, captured and put into gaol in one of the RAF base camps. Experience had taught me that the best way of preparing to break out was always to feign injury or illness, as this made my captors feel obliged to look after me, and also reduced their vigilance, since they thought I was physically incapable of making off. On this occasion I pretended I had sprained my ankle, hopping about as though unable to put any weight on it. Presently a doctor came along to examine it, and the supposed injury exempted me from having to stand in the normal prisoner position against a wall.

Eventually, at night, I saw a chance to escape over some wire on top of a wall. After this first break I was still inside the main RAF camp − a vast place, with a perimeter several miles in diameter, the whole of which was wired, lit and patrolled by guard-dogs. Rather than try to slip out that night, while the hunt for me was on, I headed cautiously towards the centre of the camp and in due course found my way into the Officers' Mess. There, at about 0300, I discovered dozens of breakfasts laid out and waiting to be cooked, so I grabbed myself a quick meal before creeping upstairs and going to ground in an empty room, where I spent the next day comfortably stretched out under the bed. When night fell again, I came out and escaped over the wire.

During 1961, as always, I was living partly in the future, enjoying my present work greatly, but looking ahead to see what my next job, my next posting, my next country might be. Had I wanted promotion in the conventional way, I should have aimed for a job on the staff. That, however, did not appeal to me. Nor was I keen on returning to the regular army. I decided that what I really wanted was to go abroad again − and a secondary ambition, which had haunted me for years, was to find a post in a distant country so that I could sail out to it in a small yacht. I therefore began looking round for overseas posts, and discovered one for a Military Intelligence Officer in Uganda. More than a year before my tour with 21st SAS ended, I worked up an application, and to my surprise landed the job.

Now suddenly I was consumed with thoughts of sailing out to Mombasa, on the coast of Kenya, or possibly to Aden. Two small snags lay in my path: one was that I had no experience of sailing, and the other that I could not afford to buy a boat.

The second problem was solved – for the time being, at least – when I applied to my bank, Coutts, for a loan of £1500, and was granted one without difficulty. The answer to the second problem, I thought, was to recruit a companion with nautical experience who would join me for the voyage. I therefore placed an advertisement in one of the Routine Orders emanating from Headquarters, 1 British (BR) Corps in Germany: under the heading 'AFRICA OR ADEN' I announced that a captain was required for a small boat sailing out in March 1962. I received only one answer, but that was enough: it came from Julian Howard, a captain in the Royal Artillery then serving in Germany. As I remarked later in a report for the family, 'he replied expecting a rich officer with a large yacht which he wanted positioning out there. When he found that the advertiser not only had no yacht but had never sailed and was colour-blind, he was not a little surprised.' Nevertheless, he rose to the challenge, and, without even meeting, we became partners.

After much correspondence and the exchange of many ideas, we decided that the only yacht which would answer our financial and nautical requirements was one of the new, twenty-two foot, four-and-a-half-ton fibre-glass Crystal Sloops designed by Alan Buchanan and built by Stebbings of Burnham-on-Crouch. In June 1961 Julian flew over from Germany: together we travelled to Essex to visit Stebbings's yard and discuss the modifications which we would need to adapt a basic production model to long-distance cruising. Julian turned out to be dark-haired and very good looking, with the exuberance of a true extrovert – a great man for telling a yarn, and not one to worry too much about the petty rules and regulations of life. He was so different from me that I immediately felt confident that we could work together. In the choice and fitting-out of the yacht, as later at sea, his experience proved crucial: he had spent half his life in boats, and knew them from stem to stern. I was glad to find that he insisted on having the yacht fitted with all the latest safety equipment, including special flotation devices in the hull, which meant that she could not sink even if she was swamped.

In August Julian and I went to Burnham again, this time to take delivery of our new baby. We had named her Cape Albacore, after the sporting game-fish found off the coasts of South Africa (Julian's mother is South African); and as we saw her lying in the Crouch we were struck by her gracefulness and charm. Inside, she was fairly cramped, and we could not stand upright in the cabin, but the space was adequate for two. To try her (and ourselves) out, we sailed her round the south coast, down the Channel, across to France and back to Falmouth, in Cornwall, where we laid her up for the winter in Thomas's yacht yard. The voyage lasted ten days, for most of which I was horribly sea-sick, but thanks to Julian I learnt the rudiments of handling the yacht, and I returned to London confident that we would form a serviceable crew.

Living and working in the south of England, I was able to give more attention to family affairs – and this was just as well, since I was determined to make the best possible arrangements for my mother before I set off on another long tour abroad. Besides, Aunt Joyce had become even more tiresome than usual. Whether or not she resented my mother's partial recovery, I cannot say, but that was certainly how it seemed, and she behaved with a mixture of petulance and malice which was extremely unsettling. Although it was jealousy of her sister which goaded her, she devoted much time and energy to attacks on me, persistently running me down to friends and relatives.

Roy Fieldhouse, who had served us nobly as Receiver, acting on behalf of the Court of Protection, wished to retire, and in the summer I made arrangements for my mother's affairs to be handled directly by one of the Court's own solicitors. While this change was being prepared, Mrs Reynolds, with whom my mother had been lodging, decided that she must give up taking paying guests. We therefore had to find new accommodation, for which we advertised in *The Times*, *The Lady* and other journals.

The immediate cause of our open warfare with Joyce was Lassie, a Sheltie or miniature collie which my mother had been given by Mrs Reynolds. As soon as she got the dog, I felt certain that it would be of immense benefit to her – and so it proved: a placid companion with whom she could share her life, it gave her something to love, something to worry about, and a reason for going on frequent walks. In short, it was exactly the stimulant she needed. For both physical and emotional reasons, Lassie became an invaluable asset, and set such a precedent that my mother owned one dog or another ever after – so much so that in due course my own children called her 'Granny Doggy'.

Joyce, however, took violently against the animal, and used it as a pretext for venting her general spleen. '*What about the dog?*' she bellowed in a letter to me on 3 September. 'I should have it destroyed, as by advertising and giving it away you will waste time and money, and it will probably be returned endlessly.'

The acrimony poisoning our relationship caused me no slight distress. I loved my grandmother dearly, and respected her enormously; it was thus with the greatest reluctance that I felt obliged to write her the following letter:

> Dear Granny,
>   Many thanks for ringing up yesterday. As we all lost our tempers, I have decided to tabulate what we were attempting to discuss:
>   (a) That Mummy should be settled in a pleasant, happy home where she will be well cared for.
>   (b) That she should be sufficiently near Bognor to be able to get over and see you regularly on a day visit.
>   (c) That she should keep her dog.
>
> We all agree on points (a) and (b), and there is only (c) left to discuss. I just can't believe that even Joyce puts so little store on Mummy's personal feelings and happiness as to wish to take from her without cause the one real joy and sense of possession which she has.
>   I am sorry, Granny, that we have to have these sordid and distasteful family quarrels. I do my best to keep my temper, and in the past have continually suffered insults on the rest of the family and myself, and said nothing, in order to try and keep the peace. But I feel very strongly on this point.

Alas for my good resolutions. With nothing better to do, Joyce spent her days deliberately fomenting trouble. 'Dear Peter,' she wrote from Old Place on 5 September:

> I am afraid you have a great deal to learn yet as regards handling your mother, and obviously understand her very

little. The prospect of being left to cope with her for three
and a half years with the help of Fieldhouse was hard
enough, with all my other responsibilities, but this dog is
just the last straw.

   We shall not make any plans for visits [from your
mother] while you are away, as it will be too much trouble
and expense parking the dog. Don't trouble to get her too
near here, and do not lead anyone she may go to to suppose
that I shall be able to support them in any way.

There followed pages of recrimination about my failure to get rid
of the dog while I had the chance – and as the days went by,
Joyce's obsession with Lassie seemed only to increase. On 15 September she wrote to my mother with a characteristic mixture of
threats, sarcasm, innuendo, exaggeration and cajolery:

Dearest Kitty,

   It was most unfortunate that Mrs Reynolds decided to pack
up . . . It is also v. unfortunate that you have seen so little of
David these hols, but as we understand from Peter that you
developed a sudden phobia [she meant 'passion', the opposite]
for one of Mrs Reynolds's dogs, the chances are that you will
see a good deal less of David and all of us in the future, because
it is impossible to find a nice house for you, where they will
take you and the dog. David and I have spent all the holidays
hunting, writing and interviewing for you without success, so
Peter now says he will send you anywhere where they will
take the dog.

   I hope you will not miss your visits to Beryl (who will not
have a dog, you know) or us at Xmas, and other amusements
such as theatres, concerts etc too much, because you either
cannot take the dog, or else you cannot leave it as it barks too
much! It will be pretty lonely never seeing anyone you know
when you are far away from here, Michael at sea and Peter
in Africa for four years quite soon. However, Peter seems to
think you will like this. David feels a bit sore, and thinks he
ought to be worth a bit more to you than one dog, which
really belongs to someone else! Anyway, it's your choice –
David and everyone else or the dog . . .

   Mother is not at all well. Peter's mismanagement of everything worries her, and she will be sorry not to see you again,
too! So goodbye, we may see you in the distant future, but as
I am tied to Mother, who cannot be left, and as Mother is tied
here by health and blindness now, we cannot go far away to
see you.

It must be some dog to be worth all this!! Goodbye again from all – with love – Joyce.

Fortunately this volley of malice went over my mother's head, leaving her unmoved, and on 21 September one of our advertisements brought a reply which secured her future – most happily – for the next five years. From the Old Mill House at Withyham, in East Sussex, Mr Edwyn Lyte wrote recommending his premises as the kind we wanted; and after a visit of inspection, we decided that my mother would be well looked after there. So it proved: the Lytes were exceptionally accommodating, and she at once felt at home in their comfortable house, where she had a room of her own, and some of her own furniture. The dog, needless to say, posed no threat to anyone. 'Your mother seems to have settled down very easily, and I would say she was very happy,' wrote Mr Lyte in October. 'Lassie has made friends with everyone. She is a dear little creature, and beautifully behaved.'

Far from soothing Joyce, the news that my mother had found a good base positively incensed her. In a sixteen-page broadside to Dumfriesshire she unnerved Nanny Turnbull, criticizing everything I had done and claiming, among other lies, that 'Mummy is now four hours from Bognor'. (In fact she was barely one hour away.) 'Dear Peter,' Nanny wrote to me in some anxiety, 'I pray you won't take Lassie from her, it's her great companion. Try to be nice to Aunt Joyce, for peace sake.' On 21 October I grew so exasperated that I sent Joyce, by recorded delivery, a broadside of my own:

Dear Joyce,
   I am receiving a continuous stream of complaints from various friends and relatives that you have been pestering them with long phone calls or letters. A great many of the facts you quote on these occasions are either distorted half-truths, or completely untrue. Further, a large number of things which you say are libellous.
   I consider your actions to be those of a vindictive and spoilt child, and I find it difficult to attribute them to a woman of your age and upbringing.

I was sorry not to be at Old Place to witness the impact of this guided missile; but it must have been considerable, for it evoked a protest from my poor grandmother, and the following follow-up from me:

> I cannot and will not ever accept that my mother is either a lunatic or a zombie without any feelings or views of her own, and this principle has been my guide in everything I have tried to organise for her. Joyce and she have never got on and never will get on. I am afraid that Joyce's visits to my mother, although they are well intentioned, cause her nothing but distress. Therefore I must insist on one point quite categorically, and that is that as from now the Court will be entirely responsible for my mother's affairs and private life.
>
> The next thing is my letter to Joyce. I make no excuses for this. I am afraid Joyce has quite deliberately and cold-bloodedly set out to poison my friends and relatives against me. I am a very patient and even-tempered person, but even I have my limits, and I cannot accept anyone, least of all a relative, making such vicious attacks behind my back.

Armoured though she was with a hide like that of a rhinoceros, even my aunt was cowed by this counter-attack, and when the Official Solicitor formally took charge of my mother's affairs on 2 November, she was left to fume in vain.

My own life grew busier than ever. Not only was I preparing for the voyage: I had also begun to learn Swahili. I enrolled on a course (which the army paid for) and went off twice a week to a marvellous old lady who, having spent most of her life as a missionary in Uganda and East Africa, spoke fluent Kiswahili, the classical form of the language.

I had also developed an engrossing new hobby – free-fall parachuting. In those days free-falling was a novel sport. Nobody had done much, and it was impossible to buy sport parachutes. The only chutes available were blue-and-yellow American T–10s, designed for aircrew baling out: we used to buy these for £10 a canopy, cut holes in them and patch them up to our own specification, to induce variable levels of drift. Mark Milburn and I together became heavily involved in the free-falling world.

Our main problem was finding aeroplanes: it was a question of begging or borrowing a pilot who would take us up, and we spent hours hanging about airfields, waiting for the weather to come right or an aircraft to become available. There was no Service free-falling then, so that all our jumps were made with civilian clubs. We did many from Thruxton, near Andover, and whenever we had a spare weekend, we would hurry down there. Over Christmas and New Year the weather turned freezing cold but brilliantly clear, and we managed to put in several exhilarating jumps. Much free-falling was then done from Tiger Moth biplanes, which were numerous, and cheap to fly, but could take only one passenger in the open cockpit, and had a ceiling of 6000 feet. In spite of these limitations they were the greatest fun: after we had climbed, I would ease myself out of the cockpit, scramble on to the lower wing and stand there clinging to the struts and directing the pilot to the spot over which I planned to jump. Once we had reached it, I would merely step back off the wing and drop away.

The sport was fairly hazardous, because parachutes were primitive and difficult to control: as we were free-falling, we had to assess what the drift would be when we opened our chutes, but our calculations did not always work out, and we were liable to land on roads or greenhouses or other undesirable spots. The leading exponent, Mike Riley, himself was killed when he landed in the sea and was dragged by his chute so that he drowned. Yet techniques and equipment advanced fast, with the French leading the way. Mark and I went on a course at Chalon-sur-Saone, where they had a Rapide which could lift six jumpers to 10,000 feet, and I managed fifteen descents in a week.

My enthusiasm derived partly from sheer excitement: every jump was a tremendous thrill. But I also saw that here was a means of launching troops from an aircraft at such a height that the plane could not be identified by people on the ground, except possibly with radar, and I began to advocate free-falling for military purposes.

What with free-falling, keeping fit, running 21st SAS, preparing for the voyage, learning Swahili and trying to suppress Aunt Joyce, I had not a waking minute to spare, and no social life to speak of (my moustache was still proving effective). As our boat trip was to last five months, I had to scrape together all the leave I could muster, and also undertake to serve for a period without pay. Then at the last moment came a setback. Towards the end of 1961 Uganda took a decisive step towards independence (which was eventually proclaimed on 10 October 1962). As colonial rule drew to an end, the British began to pull out, and the post for which I had been heading disappeared. Suddenly I had no job to sail to. At once I made contact with the Officers' Posting Branch, explained what had happened, and asked if they could find me another job in roughly the same area. The response was magnificent: they came up almost immediately with a post for a Staff Officer, Grade Three, Intelligence, working for the Federal Regular Army in Aden. I jumped at it gratefully. My hard-won Swahili was useless, but the voyage was on.

In December 1961 David Lyon and I stirred up a hornets' nest within the SAS by publishing a brief article in the Regimental journal *Mars & Minerva*. I always found David a powerful stimulant, and now we combined in an attempt to give the Regiment a verbal boot into a new era. The article appeared anonymously, and to throw sleuths off the line it was written partly in the first-person singular, as if by one author. In calling it '*J'ACCUSE*' we deliberately borrowed the title of the open letter sent by Emile Zola to the President of the French Republic in 1898, and published in the Press, which exposed the official attempt at a cover-up in the Dreyfus affair. A few quotations will show that our own communication did not lack punch:

'J'Accuse'

Look round the three regiments. In 21st SAS we find a collection of hard-core conservatives trying desperately to cling on to tactics, methods and ideas which were out of date at the end of the last war . . . Let 21st SAS get out of its Lewis-gun-lumbered jeep rut, button up its present task and look to new horizons and employment in the future . . .

22nd SAS are sliding backwards fast . . . How many of them are still reluctantly living in the present with out-of-date jungle operations befogging their brains? . . . I detect the desire to rest on past operations and laurels. These are out of date . . . Don't stagnate in the desert or jungle, or become a subsidiary of Cook's Tours . . .

Last, but by no means least, the youngest addition to the SAS fold, 23rd SAS. One would think that they would be possessed of the unbounded enthusiasm for the job and the

future which goes with youth . . . but perhaps in 23rd SAS
we have the greatest number of die-hards in our ranks . . .'

Tough stuff, this attack produced a furious reaction. All three
Regiments were in uproar: *Mars & Minerva* was deluged with
letters from individual members, and there was also some official
disquiet, not least from Lieutenant-Colonel Dare Wilson, Commanding Officer of 22nd SAS, because the article suggested that
the whole Regiment was doing poorly, whereas in fact it was
doing fine, and we had deliberately exaggerated faults in order
to stir things up. Dare Newell, who edited the journal, came
under pressure to reveal the identity of the author; but he was
a man of no mean moral courage, who had dedicated his life to
the SAS, and also a demon for intrigue – so he steadfastly refused
to give us away.

Thus my tour with 21st SAS ended in a buzz of controversy,
which did us all good. I had found my time with the TA
thoroughly stimulating, and, largely through the backing of Jim
Johnson, I felt that we had achieved a good deal. But now, as
winter came down and we began to load *Cape Albacore* in Falmouth, my thoughts were turning more and more to the sea.

CHAPTER 12

TWO MEN IN A BOAT

1962

Because we had not been able to afford an engine, we were entirely dependent on the wind, and on the evening of 16 March 1962, after waiting two days for a gale to subside, we slipped our mooring at Falmouth. As we left the Black Rock astern in the gathering dusk, and watched the lights of England drop away, we were content to sit silently in the cockpit, each busy with his own thoughts. In the ship's log, which Julian kept, we formally entered our roles as 'Julian – Skipper and Navigator', 'Peter – Mate, Cook, Purser and Owner'. We were both apprehensive about the first leg of our trip. Julian – although he never admitted it at the time – was worried by my lack of experience; and I, while having every confidence in him, was afraid that I would be so debilitated by sea-sickness that I would not be able to support him properly. Before we left, we had agreed never to sulk if we argued, but always to apologize afterwards, whether we thought we had been right or wrong.

A wave of good-luck messages had launched us on our way, among them one from my mother, and one from 21st SAS in Dukes Road. 'Sir,' read the note signed by Mr Wolland, 'Best wishes for a safe and successful journey from Orderly Room Staff.' Muir Walker, signalling from Sutton Coldfield, was less respectful: 'Refer you Genesis 6, verses 15–16. Trust you have complied.' Luckily we had a Bible on board and could look up the reference, which was part of God's instructions to Noah on how to build his ark:

> And this is the fashion which thou shalt make it of. The length of the ark shall be three hundred cubits, the breadth

of it fifty cubits, and the height of it thirty cubits.

A window shalt thou make to the ark, and in a cubit shalt thou finish it above; and the door of the ark shalt thou set in the side thereof; with lower, second and third storeys shalt thou make it.

Our little ark was more modest than Noah's; but we had done all we could to make her seaworthy, scrubbing her bottom and coating it with anti-fouling paint, cleaning and greasing all screws, snap-hooks and other adjustable fittings. We had varnished every one of the two hundred and thirty-six tins of food supplied by the NAAFI, to prevent them rusting, and stowed them carefully so that they could not break free and roll about in bad weather. On 13 March Julian had ceremonially given up smoking by throwing half a packet of cigarettes into Falmouth Harbour – a decision which he revoked next day when we shipped our duty-free supplies, including a dozen bottles of whisky at 8s 9d (42p) each.

The start of the voyage confirmed my fears about sea-sickness. For the first day we ran before a fresh easterly wind in fine weather, and made over a hundred miles – more than we had dared hope for. Nevertheless, I was miserably sick, and could not keep even a glass of warm water down. Then on the second day the weather began to deteriorate: our radio warned of gales imminent in our area, and in the evening they hit us, bowling us forward under bare poles over mountainous green seas topped with foam, without respite for the next three days and nights. We paid out two hundred and fifty feet of rope astern, in the hope that it would stabilize us, but the warp was only partially effective, and the yacht kept trying to broach-to. The result was that one of us had to man the tiller the whole time; neither of us got much sleep, and so many waves broke over the deck that our clothes and bedding became soaked through. Several times the man on deck was saved from being swept overboard by his safety harness, anchored to a strong-point in the cockpit. I felt so weak that, whenever I went below, I could do nothing but lie flat, and Julian had to cook for himself such food as he was able to keep down. Our one consolation was that *Cape Albacore* lived up to her name and rode the storm without any sign of distress.

When the gale at last abated, in the early hours of 21 March, a sudden crisis roused us from our apathy. At 0330 I had just completed a watch and gone below when I noticed that Julian had switched on our navigation lights, which indicated that he had seen another ship. I took no particular notice until suddenly he yelled at me to come on deck quickly, and bring the Verey pistol (for signalling). When I stuck my head out of the hatch, I was appalled to see a large merchant vessel bearing down on us. As we were still under bare poles, we had no steerage, and could not change course. The ship was about half a mile, or three minutes' steaming, from us – and without sails we were practically invisible in the dark and heavy seas.

With commendable calm Julian waited another thirty seconds, then sent a red flare arching across the ship's path. A few moments later she heeled over as the helmsman gave his wheel a violent spin, and she passed across our stern a few yards to windward. The near-miss left us shaken, not least by the realization that, if the ship had hit us, she would almost certainly have ploughed on her way without the crew noticing that anything had happened.

Next day the weather at last brightened, and so did our spirits. With my appetite restored, I went to work in the galley and began to apply some of my curry-making techniques learnt from Corporal Ip in the Malayan jungle.

For the next three days, as we headed south and the air grew steadily hotter, not much happened – and it was just as well, because we were both worn down by lack of sleep. We had tried to arrange our watches so that each of us got eight hours of sleep, in two four-hour batches, out of every twenty-four. But the gale had played havoc with our routine, and we found that six hours' sleep were the most that each of us could achieve. The result was that we were deeply tired, and, whenever we did manage to lie down in our bunks, we passed out.

On the morning of 27 March, eleven days out of Falmouth, we were about a hundred miles west of Lisbon when over the horizon appeared the graceful and majestic lines of an aircraft carrier. As the day wore on, more and more warships came into sight, but not until we reached Gibraltar did we realize that we had sailed through the middle of the biggest NATO exercise of the year, in which more than sixty vessels were taking part. More fascinating to us were the whales – colossal creatures, larger than the yacht, which kept pace with us effortlessly, diving, rolling on the surface and blowing jets of water to a great height. From wave-top level and a distance of a few feet they looked even more magnificent than when seen from high up on the deck of an ocean liner. We were also accompanied by dolphins, which gambolled for hours beneath our bows, as though to assure us of their friendliness.

Soon after lunch on 31 March we sighted our first land since leaving England. Cape Spartel on the Moroccan coast, to starboard, and Cape Trafalgar on the Spanish shore, to port, came up simultaneously on either bow. It was a moving moment for both of us, but particularly for Julian, whose navigation had brought us twelve hundred miles and made a perfect landfall almost to the minute which he had predicted. Dusk found us sailing into Tangiers harbour, with lights twinkling from the town, the sky aglow behind it, and tantalizing Moorish smells drifting out to meet us over the water. We both felt tremendous elation at having completed the first and most difficult leg of our journey.

Plans for an early supper and peaceful night were shattered when we made fast alongside a motor fishing vessel, and an unmistakably English voice called out, 'Whisky or gin, old boy? We've got plenty of both.' So began our riotous association with Captain Bayliss and the crew of HMS *Rothesay*, who had come to Tangiers for a weekend's leave. Although I remember few details of the evening, I know that it was 0330 before we eventually turned in.

Next day we had a glorious run through the Straits of Gibraltar, with hot sun blazing down and a force-four wind dead astern. Arriving at 2230, we found the harbour packed with over forty of the warships which had been on the exercise.

Our original intention had been to stay for no more than eight or nine days; but we became so overwhelmed by local hospitality that three weeks passed before we put to sea again. Also, we had a good deal of work to do on the yacht: some minor repairs were needed as a result of the storm, but she had got into a filthy state inside, and we had to empty the cabin, scrub it from top to bottom, and repaint it before we felt fit to continue.

I also devoted several hours to writing home – a long report, laboriously picked out with two fingers on a typewriter, which I sent (by arrangement) to the Orderly Room in Dukes Road, where Mr Wolland had it expertly retyped, and forwarded duplicated copies to my family. In particular, I related how we hired a car for one weekend and drove over the border into Spain, visiting Malaga and Granada. A less happy experience was a trip to La Linea, the border town, tersely recorded in the log by Julian:

> Very gory and provincial bull-fight in La Linea in the evening. Five out of six bulls retired exhausted from wounds and had to be despatched by an attendant. Matador in tears. Drank whole bottle of Tio Pepe during performance by way of an anaesthetic. Shocking dinner in La Linea afterwards.

Back in Gibraltar, I was jolted by a sudden challenge. In the middle of a party Commander Pat Driscoll of HMS *Rothesay* mentioned – in a faintly snide fashion – that he had not noticed me ascending the Rock before breakfast every morning, as was his own custom. What, he asked, was the SAS coming to? I replied that by 0600 I had already been up and down, and must have been too early for him. Perhaps, I suggested, he would care to meet me at 0500 the next morning? To my horror, he said he would be delighted. Thus at 0500, still in pitch darkness, a naval commander, lieutenant and midshipman met myself and Julian, whom I had dragged in to satisfy the honour of our own service. We reached the top before dawn, and were down again in time to enjoy a gargantuan breakfast aboard *Rothesay*. As I reported home, 'although we were outnumbered three-to-two, I think the army won the day, as one hundred per cent of the crew of *Cape Albacore* turned out, and only one per cent of *Rothesay*.'

On 20 April we could find no further excuses for delay, and set out again. After a Royal Naval launch had given us a tow out of the harbour, we picked up a good westerly wind in the Straits, and were soon on our way – only to hit an easterly swell, which produced an awkward motion and made us both sick again, lowering our spirits. Our next destination was Malta, which we hoped to reach in fourteen days; but we soon found that this was a wildly optimistic estimate, for we met an easterly wind and were then becalmed. Our lack of progress was demonstrated all too well by an incident on 23 April: at 0600 we threw an empty honey-pot over the side and took a dozen abortive shots at it with the revolver which we had brought for self-defence against pirates in the Red Sea. Eight hours later, as I was on watch, I noticed something in the water, and found to my chagrin that it was our target, which had spent all day floating round in a huge circle.

Worse followed. That night the east wind blew up into what the locals called a Levanter, and with the wind came cloud, rain, high humidity and oppressive heat. Rather than risk damage by bashing into the heavy seas, we hove to and waited, with a stream of ships passing by, several dangerously close. For day after day we were either becalmed or forced to make best use of small breezes which came from all points of the compass. This tested our patience severely, as we had to keep changing the sails: from twin jibs, when running, to main and Genoa, or sometimes to Genoa on its own. There was some compensation in the large numbers of migrating birds, particularly swallows, which passed over and frequently landed on board.

> These birds were often flying into the wind [I wrote home], and many collapse and die of exhaustion or drowning half way across. Others, more fortunate, find a convenient ship to rest on – and most appreciative guests they are. Julian had one settle on his shoulder, and I had one which spent a good few minutes preening himself on my knee. All these birds are quite wild, and the kind one may find anywhere in the English countryside, but such is the comradeship between all living things at sea that these same birds will safely and happily use a man for a perch.

Finding ourselves held up at the mercy of the wind, we kept changing our plans. At one stage we decided to by-pass Malta and make straight for Beirut; but then on 7 May we realized that our water and rations would not hold out that long, so instead we headed for Pantelleria, a small, mountainous island halfway between Sicily and the coast of Tunisia.

'The inhabitants are sleepy, lazy, poor, helpful, squalid, delightful,' I wrote home, 'and, in the case of the innumerable small boys who hang round the boat from dawn to dusk, thieves in the nicest possible yet most expensive way.' Charmed by this crowd of youthful villains, we fell in love with Pantelleria, even though it had little to offer. There was a medieval prison, half a dozen shops, and no proper water supply. The inhabitants of the town lived in shacks among the ruins caused by Allied bombing in the Second World War, when the island was an Italian base, and seemed to survive on a little fishing and wine-making.

Planning to stay for a couple of hours, we remained in the harbour for nearly three days, taking turns to explore the interior in the company of friendly natives. 'Pantelleria – enchanted island', Julian wrote in the log – and so we found it. We put to sea again on 12 May, but, as Julian recorded, the attempt proved abortive:

> The wind drops instantly, and we spend one of the most baffling and uncomfortable nights of the whole voyage. Violent squalls from five different directions. Between squalls come sudden eerie calms which leave us rolling hideously in quite a choppy sea. The southern (scirocco) wind is so hot that it makes us think the island is erupting. We slink back to Pantelleria soon after first light.

For the next three days we were storm-bound, as a north-westerly gale raged outside the harbour, and not until 17 May did the weather look more propitious. Then we tried again – and once more Julian recorded his frustration:

> Local fishing boats go out at crack of dawn. Sea is calm. We locate a venomous pong which has been plaguing us for some days – condensed milk festering under the fresh-water cans. We use our last money to pay for a pluck out of harbour at 1330 hrs. No sooner do we cast off than the wind drops dead. Light airs from all directions. Tears of exasperation.
>
> 1445 hrs. Don't know which way to go. Sky has been overcast all day. Bank of cumulus in ENE suggests Levanter. Almost berserk.

That evening a strong wind blew up from the north-west, and for the next twenty-four hours we fled before it under bare poles, or with only a trysail or storm jib up. But at least we were going in the right direction; and when that gale abated, we entered a halcyon period which lasted twelve whole days. The wind remained in the west or north-west, but never at more than Force Three, and for day after day we made between seventy-five and a hundred miles in perfect weather.

The farther east we went, the hotter it became, until we found it difficult to sleep by day, when the cabin temperature went up above 100°F. We therefore changed our routine, and each tried to get five hours' sleep at night, with a siesta during the day. Twice, when we were temporarily becalmed in the morning, we swam – and each dip was an experience never to be forgotten. We knew that to go swimming in 1700 fathoms of water, some seventy miles from land and with no other ships in sight, was not a project to be taken lightly. We therefore laid out a long rope astern, and made it a rule that we never both went into the sea at the same time; furthermore, the man on board remained poised to throw out a coiled line and a lifejacket, in case the swimmer was attacked by cramp. Each time, I found that I had to pluck up courage before diving into such an expanse of crystal-clear, deep-blue ocean; and once I was in, I seemed to be hit by a feeling of alone-ness, almost of panic, which I had to fight off. As soon as that passed, however, it was superseded by a sensation of well-being and freedom more glorious than I had ever experienced.

At noon on 1 June, with great excitement, we sighted the lighthouse at the entrance to the harbour at Port Said, and the dome of the Suez Canal Authority's magnificent building. The wind held up, and Cape Albacore entered the bay at a spanking five knots; then we dodged down a line of merchantmen until a couple of scruffily uniformed but friendly Egyptians shouted at us from a rowing boat and directed us to the Yacht Club moorings.

Our previous experience of the Canal Zone put us on our guard. We knew that Egyptians had no reason to like the British, especially after the Suez campaign (in which Julian had taken part), and we expected to be met with hostility. In fact people went out of their way to be helpful – but we soon learnt that the country had become a police state alive with Government agents and informers anxious to earn the odd piastre. Mail was censored and telephone lines tapped, and one had to be very careful about what one said in public.

Easily our most valuable contact was Derek Rosoman, a director of Stapledons, our agents. Not only did he help us complete all necessary paperwork in record time: he obtained the lowest prices everywhere, arranged a free tow down the Canal, and, as I put it in my latest letter home, 'turned the whole of Port Said, and Stapledons in particular, upside-down for our benefit,' giving us a tremendous lunch and dinner on our second day. Considering that the entire British population of the town amounted to fifteen, he was probably glad to see new faces; but by any reckoning he was exceedingly hospitable. He also brought me an enormous pile of mail, cleverly forwarded by Poppet Codrington, whom I had left in charge of postal arrangements at home.

In the intervals of shopping and being entertained ashore, there was the usual work to be done on the yacht – cleaning, scrubbing, painting, charging batteries, and so on. Early on Monday, 4 June, our launch appeared as promised and took us in tow on the tail of the morning convoy down the Canal. As our maximum speed was seven knots, the big ships, travelling at eight knots, gradually drew away from us, and under the hot, clear sun our journey proved most peaceful. For the first few miles the banks were lined by reeds, but these soon gave way to scrubby trees and bare desert, in which the heat haze constantly created mirages.

For big ships, the Canal was one way, but we were small enough to slip past oncoming convoys, and whenever we met a British ship there were vigorous exchanges of waving. We stopped for the night at Ismaelia, where we had a swim; in the morning the Greek pilot of our towing lighter came on board and insisted on taking the tiller, which enabled us to relax, reading, watching the other ships, and (in my case) thinking back to the time I had spent with the DLI at St Gabriel's Camp, just a few miles off our route.

At Suez, Stapledons had again made excellent arrangements

on our behalf: an agent met us, and we were given a very good berth. Thanks to the economies which Derek Rosoman had achieved, we felt able to afford a tourist visit to Cairo, some eighty miles to the west, and we set off in a Russian-built bus driven at lunatic speed by an Egyptian who kept his right foot down hard on the accelerator and his right hand down hard on the horn. Cairo struck Julian as 'beautiful and very romantic'. To me, who had last seen the city nine years earlier, it seemed that tremendous improvements had been made, not least in the clearance of slums and, in spite of my reservations about Nasser's methods, I had to admit that his regime had made startling progress.

Somehow we could not find the cheap hotel which Derek had recommended, so we ended up staying for two nights in the Semiramide, listed as 'Grande Luxe', but charming and old-fashioned, with a stylish, roof-garden restaurant. In the company of a good, honest guide called Mahdi I went round the bazaar and the Arab Quarter, where I watched copper-engravers and bone-carvers at work with tools which had scarcely changed in three or four millennia.

In the evening we went out to the Pyramids at Gizeh, where performances of *son et lumière* were being given. Luckily that day's show was in English, and it made a profound impression:

> As we sat down, we had the Great Pyramid of Cheops on our right, with that of his son Cephren to its left. In front of them crouched the Great Sphinx, with the body of a lion to symbolise strength and royalty, and the head of King Cephren and the head-dress of his Queen. Two other pyramids stretched back into the darkness, and as the lights came on, growing steadily brighter to a background of music, a sonorous voice boomed from the Sphinx, 'I have seen every dawn for these past five thousand years.' We were lucky enough to have a quarter-moon, which hung so beautifully over the two larger pyramids as to be almost artificial in appearance.

That night we slept like the dead in the unaccustomed luxury of sheets, and next morning had breakfast in bed at 1000. That sybaritic indulgence left us a bare two hours to see the Cairo Museum, which also seized my imagination: never had I seen

such a collection of treasures, among which the golden sar-
cophagus of Tutankhamen was only one dazzling highlight.
I reeled out of the museum with my head full of plans to study
Egyptology, and also to visit the Upper Nile.

Back in Suez, while I worked on the yacht, Julian gleaned all
possible information about navigation in the Red Sea, one of
the most treacherous stretches of our route, with its uncharted
reefs and unpredictable currents, and the added hazard that
refraction caused by heat often makes it difficult to take accurate
sights of sun and stars. By now we were both nervous about
our finances, which had run right down, and when an article
appeared in an Egyptian newspaper announcing that the yacht
Capo Albacoro belonged to 'an oil prince from the Hadhramaut',
I was moved to write home:

> All I can say is that if the average oil prince has anything
> like the overdraft which Julian and I will have after this
> trip, he can keep his oil, and I will settle for being a soldier.

Before we left Suez we took on ten extra gallons of water, and
made a resolution to ration ourselves to four pints a day each,
for all purposes, until we found we were ahead of schedule.
Then on 10 June we set out on our final leg – only to become
becalmed a day later, and to feel the stunning heat of the Red
Sea. The cabin temperature climbed to 130°F, and for much of
the day we faced the alternatives of sweltering in the humid
shade below or scorching in the sun on deck.

On 13 June, as we cleared the Gulf of Suez, we found we had
company in the form of an evil-looking shark, which seemed to
be keeping one eye on our naked (and no doubt succulent-
looking) limbs, and the other on the metal spinner twirling at
the end of the hundred-foot log line as it measured the distance
we were travelling. Two mornings later, during my watch, the
log gave a sudden, high-pitched whirr, and I turned just in time
to see £20-worth of equipment vanishing as the shark's
breakfast.

In the northern half of the Red Sea the wind seemed to die
away at night, and then rise gradually in the morning to a force
of five or six during the afternoon. Mostly it blew from the

north, which suited us fine, but as it was increasing each day, steep, choppy seas would build up, which gave the yacht an uncomfortable motion, and produced occasional freak waves. On the night of 14 June Julian had just taken over the watch when two such monsters hit us:

> The first had just broken and merely slopped over the stern. The second broke as we were on it. *Cape Albacore* first upended, then careered down the face of it, quickly broaching-to. Cockpit half-filled. Helmsman drenched. *Cape Albacore* lay farther over than she ever has before. Beer and broken bottles everywhere.

Below decks, everything had shot across the cabin, and the mess was indescribable. The bottles which had smashed were only part of the problem: those which had survived were so shaken about that, as I started to clear up, they began exploding, one by one, spewing beer and glass splinters all over the place. It was like being in the middle of a minefield, not knowing which bottle would go up next.

For seven more days we made steady progress. 'We are now as sunburned as one can be,' Julian wrote in the log, 'and we can sit out naked all day except when becalmed. It is then necessary to wear a shirt.' The northerly winds gradually died on us, and on 22 June we reached the point at which the southwesterly monsoon, blowing from the Cape of Good Hope to Arabia, began to predominate. Now, within a few days of our destination, we met some of the trickiest conditions of the voyage – for not only was the wind opposing us, but at the same time a fierce, three-knot current was sweeping us out of the Red Sea and through the Straits of Bab el Mandeb.

At first this current accelerated our progress, but as we bore down on Perim, the small volcanic island at the very bottom of the Red Sea, it almost brought disaster. Our charts showed that we could pass Perim either in the wide channel to the west, or in a narrow but deep channel to the east. After careful consideration we chose the eastern channel, between the island and the point of Arabia.

All went well until we were within three miles of Perim. Then the wind died, leaving us without motive power or steerage.

The barren, rocky shore of the island drew rapidly closer as the current swept us down towards it at nearly three knots. There was no question of kedging or anchoring, as the sea was many fathoms deep. Lacking any means of steering accurately, we decided that our safest course was to pass outside the island – but our sole means of altering direction was a single, ten-foot oar which we had brought along as an emergency mast. Frantically we freed it and, taking turns, rowed as we never had before, first on one side, then on the other, as the bows swung round.

Struggle as we might, we were still heading for the rocks, on which we could see waves exploding. Yard by yard we made progress to the west. It was midday, and the sun was at its fiercest. Each of us lost pounds in sweat as we laboured with that heavy oar, praying for wind as we panted. None came. For forty-five minutes we battled all-out to save our little boat from destruction. In the end we were so close that we could hear as well as see the breakers bursting on the shore – but God was with us, and to our unspeakable relief we slipped past Balfe Point, only seconds from shipwreck and ruin.

The rest of the voyage was an anti-climax. Aden lies only a hundred miles, or one good day's sail, east of Perim, but it took us four days of frustration to crawl that puny distance. Nevertheless, on the evening of 26 June, in a moment of high emotion, we saw the rugged outline of Shamsan rise over the horizon. This was what we had planned and dreamed about for eighteen months: our mission was about to be accomplished.

When we finally dropped anchor in the outer harbour at Aden around 0300 on 27 June, we had spent sixty-nine days at sea, covering 4200 miles, and each of us had put in eight hundred hours at the helm. Our success was due entirely to Julian's planning, navigation and seamanship. Our personal relationship had survived the stresses of the voyage extraordinarily well, and we had had plenty of fun and excitement. Occasionally Julian had sworn at me when I had done something stupid, but that had not worried me, and we had never had the semblance of an argument. Knowing that my life was in Julian's hands, and having a high regard for his ability at sea, I had never felt like squabbling about technical details, but had been content to implement whatever policy he called for.

Not that we had much time to compare notes, for Julian had already over-run his leave, and was obliged to take the next Comet back to London, at 1000 on the morning of the twenty-eighth. My own immediate problem was to restore my finances by selling the yacht, which I had already advertised, at the same price as I paid for her, in the United Kingdom and Aden. I felt fat and flabby from lack of exercise, but all the same triumphant. In a list of possible improvements attached to my last letter home, I suggested that we should have installed a refrigerator – an essential, which we had foolishly dismissed as a luxury when Falmouth lay under snow – and that we should have taken 'the largest, most expensive, most expansive and softest Dunlopillo cushion you could imagine', for the helmsman to sit on. 'Hard cockpit boards for eight hundred hours at the helm cause acute discomfort.' Finally, under the heading 'Was it worth it?', I wrote, 'Every penny and every backside-sore mile of it' – and that remains my verdict to this day.

CHAPTER 13

SECRET AGENT: ADEN

1962–63

For the first time in my life I was on loan service, attached to the headquarters of the Federal Regular Army. Apart from a few British officers, the FRA consisted entirely of Arabs; its base was Seedaseer Lines, in Khormaksar, on the isthmus in Aden itself, but its five battalions were stationed at various points up-country, charged with the all but impossible task of maintaining order among feuding tribesmen, and promoting British policy, which was to unite the various independent rulers in a single federation. When I arrived, at the end of June 1962, the political atmosphere was still stable, but only just: to the north, in the Yemen, Republican elements fostered by Nasser were already fomenting trouble against the Royalists, and Nasser in turn was backed by the Soviet Union. Once again – as in Korea and Malaya – I was caught up in the bitter struggle of a country linked by tradition to the West against Communist-inspired aggression.

Aden had been a British possession since 1839: for more than a century it had served us as a stepping-stone on the route to India and the Far East. Over the years we had built up a complicated network of treaties with tribal leaders, and out of these agreements developed the Western and Eastern Aden Protectorates. Yet in all our occupation we had behaved in deplorably self-centred fashion: concentrating on our own trade, we had done almost nothing for the local people. We had never built a tarmac road outside the town, and although we had set up a loose up-country administration, and some rather feeble attempts at schools, we had never brought the warring tribes together to create a unified state, or introduced significant improvements into their primitive way of life. The result was that the Arabs never developed any particular loyalty to us; and the only effective way we had of keeping the rulers on our side was by bribing them with arms, ammunition and money. British control of the hinterland was thus always fragile, and when the Communist-inspired challenge came down from the north, it began to crack up.

Thanks to the help of John Woodhouse, who was on the staff in Aden at the time, I settled in quickly. Seeing that I needed transport of my own, I bought another Lambretta, which was all I could afford after the extravagances of the voyage.[1] I lived in the Officers' Mess in Seedaseer Lines, where I had a room in one of the prefabricated buildings.

These had no air-conditioning, but, even in the sticky months of the summer when the monsoon was blowing, the heat never bothered me too badly, and an illusion of coolness was produced by the grass in our compound, which was watered religiously every day. In the mess I met some interesting new colleagues, but all British, for at that date the Arab officers had a mess of their own. Hardly had I arrived when I came across a lovely Anglo-Indian girl, the daughter of a warrant officer. Maybe the fact that I had recently spent three months on a boat affected my judgment, but she seemed stunningly attractive, and I fell for her. Probably it was just as well that she did not reciprocate my infatuation, for in those days marriages across the ranks were by no means encouraged – and in any case, at the age of twenty-eight, I did not want to tie myself down.

In Aden itself the British presence was still strong: a civilian High Commissioner, Sir Charles Johnston, presided, but the Headquarters, Middle East, was also based in the colony, and there was a substantial garrison of regular army units, supported by a Royal Air Force detachment on the airfield at Khormaksar. One of my first essentials was to learn Arabic, and I was soon sent off on a course at CALSAP, the Command Arabic Language School, Aden Protectorate. There the chief instructor was Leslie

---

1. I did eventually manage to sell *Cape Albacore* for £1550 to a South African called Clyde Meintjes, thus recouping a large part of our outlay.

McLaughlin, a brilliant teacher who made us all very enthusiastic. Hard work as it was – we had to learn about thirty words every night – I enjoyed the course; and because all our instruction was phonetic, I taught myself to write the script. Although my Arabic never became fluent, I learned enough to carry on simple conversations and – most important – to complete the formal exchanges of civilities which open any meeting in that part of the world.

The Commanding Officer of the FRA was then Brigadier James Lunt (who later became a major general and the author of several excellent books, among them *The Barren Rocks of Aden*, an account of his time in the Colony). An equable man, with academic leanings, he had built up a close affinity with Arabs, but was equally good at sorting out young British officers such as myself.

As a Junior Intelligence Officer (technically a G3), I worked directly to the G2, Lieutenant-Colonel Mike van Lessen, a splendid character, with giant moustache and greying hair, who was known as 'Himyaritic Harry' from his prodigious knowledge of, and fascination with, the ancient civilizations of Southern Arabia (Himyar was a traditional king of the Yemen). Mike was quite unable to delegate tasks to subordinates, and tried to do everything himself – with the result that I was not exactly overburdened; but he often disappeared on archaeological expeditions, leaving us alone – and later he handed over to Melise Wagstaff, an Engineer officer who was a stickler for accuracy and detail.

My job consisted largely of correlating intelligence reports from the battalions up-country and writing daily 'Intsums', or intelligence summaries. Every morning I would motor the fifteen miles to Al Ittihaad (The Federation), the office complex designed to house the Federal Government after the British had withdrawn, and at 9 a.m. I would attend the daily intelligence meeting, briefing people on FRA developments. The meeting would be chaired by George Henderson, the Senior Political Officer, and was usually informative and useful. In the corridors there was time for discussion with the other political officers such as Ralph Daly and Robin Young, and often those from the out-stations – Bill Heber-Percy, James Nash, Michael Crouch – would be there as well. As many of these men had worked as Colonial Officers in the Sudan, they were immensely knowledgeable.

The correlation of intelligence was essentially a desk job which, although interesting, did not present any great challenge. As always, my instinct was to escape from office routine and head out into the open spaces – the jagged, naked mountains and gravel deserts of the interior – and luckily I had good reason to do so, as I needed to visit the FRA battalions and see for myself the conditions in which they were operating. It was also essential that as Brigade Intelligence Officer I should get to know my Field Intelligence Officers, who worked independently throughout the Protectorate, as well as the Intelligence Officers in the FRA battalions. The FIOs were dedicated men – and none more so than Squadron Leader Williams, who lived with his wife (a nurse who ran a small medical centre) in a little stone house at a settlement called Mukairas, way out in the wilds, at considerable risk to both of them.

Even at that stage it was not safe to drive into the hinterland alone: there were shooting incidents every day between army units and the tribesmen, and supplies for the garrisons went up in well-organized convoys. As often as possible, I joined one of these. On the day the convoy was to travel, infantry would go out at dawn, or even during the night, to start picketing, and man the hills on either side of the road. By early morning they would have occupied selected peaks, and there they would sit, dominating the road and denying the high ground to the *adoo*. We in the convoy would clear our passage by radio or the use of flags, and drive through to our destination – often Dhala, some seventy miles due north of Aden, and 4000 feet above sea level. Sometimes the pickets would stay out all night to protect us on the way home next day. It was a tough life for the *gundi*, or native soldiers, running up and down those mountains of baking rock; but it was what they were used to, and what they were there for. Occasionally I went out with them, but usually my aim was to visit one of the battalions and spend a couple of days in their company. In this way I managed to travel a good deal, and built up a knowledge of the whole Protectorate.

The interior was a wild and primitive place. Even the rulers lived in tall, mud buildings with few windows – for protection from the heat – without any form of plumbing, let alone electricity. They had very little furniture, but sat on carpets and ate with their hands. Women lived in deep purdah, their heads and faces covered or at least (as in Dhala) painted all over. The men habitually chewed *qat*, a plant with leaves like those of privet which produces a stupefying effect and was regarded by the British – in their typical pursuit of efficiency – as the curse of Southern Arabia. Among these rugged mountain people, rifles were highly prized, not only for purposes of attack and defence, but also as status symbols. Whether or not it was wise, we, the British, kept tribesmen on our side by handing out weapons, with boxes of ammunition as additional sweeteners, and it was these arms that bought loyalty and support.

One memorable excursion took me to Dhala, where the Political Officer was James Nash. 'The people are a surly lot, and have a reputation for sticking daggers into Europeans,' I wrote home, 'and for generally causing them as much inconvenience as possible.' Together with our local intelligence officer, I went to visit a village on the Jebel Mifra, a fastness approachable only by stone steps several hundred years old, hewn out of rock. As we drew near the foot of the cliffs not long after dawn, I reported,

> we could see our final objective some miles away in the morning mist, like a large soup-plate suspended on the clouds. With rifles loaded and ready in case of ambush, we set off with two tribesmen in front as scouts. The women who were working in the fields ran away when they saw infidels approaching.
>
> One of our escorts insisted that we should have breakfast before attempting the final climb, and a villager brought out some boiled goat's milk and unleavened bread. Squatting on the stony ground, we all shared the large loaf, and took turns to dip our next mouthful into the bowl of milk. After this refreshment, we set off.
>
> The staircase wound up a chimney through otherwise unscaleable cliffs, and the steps had been worn smooth by the bare feet of centuries. The top of the mountain was a mass of green fields – a land of milk and honey compared with the barren wastes below. To our surprise and pleasure, we received a warm welcome from the Sheikh, and were invited into his mud house. The ground floor was taken up with cattle, and we were led up a winding medieval staircase to the top floor, where he had his best room.

Shoes had to be removed before entering, and everyone squatted on rugs. We started off with some highly-spiced brew which he called coffee, and conversation swung to the inevitable subject of the battles which the Sheikh had fought. We heard how he had fought against the British in 1958, and as a result had had to flee into the Yemen. Now he was very pro-British, as he had recently received a gift of rifles from the Administration.

As we left, he gave us a warm farewell, and in his stentorian voice shouted to the villagers 2,000 feet below to be sure of seeing us safely on the correct route home.

The tribesmen possessed a variety of ancient weapons, and once, after prodigious haggling over chipped glasses of mint tea, I managed to buy three matchlock muzzle-loaders, at least a hundred years old, for the equivalent of £1.25 apiece. Back in Aden, I thought we would try one out. We therefore took it into the Officers' Mess – why, I cannot imagine – rammed some powder down the barrel and applied a match to the lock. I wrote home:

A deathly hush. More powder down the barrel. Another match, and another disappointing silence. By this time our enthusiasm for a bang knew no bounds, and we decided to fire the thing properly. A heap of powder was stuffed into the priming hole, the gun laid on the table, and, with bags of confidence that nothing would happen, we applied a further match.

'Spectacular' best describes the events which followed. Little did we know that the Bedu had also had trouble making the gun fire, and had left it loaded with a ball of lead and six rounds' supply of powder. Our powder trail started off with an encouraging fizz, shortly followed by a gigantic roar. The gun shot off the table, dented the rear wall of the room with its butt, and loosed off clouds of black smoke, which nearly choked two very frightened officers. When the smoke cleared, we found that all the charges had fired, and a lead ball had disappeared through the wall of the Mess into the garden. Further investigation failed to produce any bodies, so we adjourned to the bar for a spot of liquid fortitude.

When stuck in Aden, I found the physical challenge I was looking for in playing squash – the open courts were like ovens, and excellent for taking off surplus weight – and in running up and down Shamsan, the extinct volcano which towers 1800 feet above the town. I would ride my scooter to Steamer Point, leave it there, and set out for the summit: the ground was extremely steep, and much of it was covered with loose rock. The combined ascent and descent took about ninety minutes, and I soon incited a couple of colleagues to accompany me. In time I became so addicted to the mountain that I conceived the notion of staging a race to the summit, which I named the Shamsan Scramble. The idea caught the imagination of local people, and when the event took place for the first time, in May 1963, it attracted over fifty entrants, including three women. As I remarked in a letter home, the top 'was like the Empire State Building after the lifts had packed up'. The race was won by a seventeen-year-old Arab boy, who was wiry as a spider and incredibly fit.

A few days after the race, bad news arrived. A helicopter on SAS operations in Borneo had crashed into the jungle, killing all its occupants. Among the dead were Harry Thompson, and 22nd SAS's second-in-command, Ron Norman. The accident swung my mind back on to SAS affairs – not that it ever forgot them for long – and left me with a feeling of personal loss. In spite of his temper, I had always liked Harry, and hoped that if he commanded 22nd SAS, as seemed likely, I might serve as a squadron commander under him. Already I was angling to return to the SAS for my next posting, some time in 1964.

Things took a more cheerful turn when one day there appeared in Aden a young architect from New Zealand, David Armstrong, who was hitch-hiking round the world. Recognizing a kindred spirit, I suggested to him that he might join me in an experiment to see if we could survive a weekend on a desert island, living on what we could catch. He agreed immediately – and so one Friday we set off, allowing ourselves a minimum of equipment: a knife, some primitive fish-hooks, a length of piping, and two large tin cans. The spot we chose on which to cast ourselves away was an island along the coast west of Aden. In fact it was an island only at high tide: at low water it was joined to the mainland by a causeway, but we behaved as if we were marooned in mid-ocean.

We reached it at last light on the Friday, and found that it was very small – only about one hundred yards by two hundred

– and consisted mostly of sand, with a few big rocks sticking up out of it. Having found a shelter of sorts in the lee of a rock, we turned our attention to the turtles which were coming ashore to lay their eggs in the sand. We soon captured one and tied her up, with the aim of killing and eating her; but first we needed a fire, not only to cook our meat, but also to distil sea water in our cans. Although there was plenty of dry driftwood lying about, we found that igniting it was no easy matter. Every schoolboy knows that castaways start fires by rubbing two pieces of wood together: in practice, however, it is extremely difficult to produce enough friction. David and I rubbed pieces of wood together until four in the morning, with the turtle eyeing us balefully all the while. In the end we gave up and went to sleep, without having had anything to eat or – a greater privation – to drink.

Soon after dawn we were on the move again, scouting for shellfish. Again we tried to make a fire, and as we were struggling, up rowed an Arab in a small boat. The sight of two Brits furiously rubbing sticks together seemed to leave him speechless, and he went off without saying a word; but evidently he took pity on these lunatics, because he returned an hour later to present us with a box of matches, a flask of hot, sweet tea and some fish. By then we had begun to doubt whether we would last the weekend, so we threw our principles to the winds and accepted the gifts with gratitude.

The tea went down like nectar, and our spirits rose as we got a good blaze going. Then came another setback: our primitive still began to function quite well, but when we tried to drink the distilled water, we found that it was contaminated with petrol. Clearly our tube had been used for siphoning fuel. Meanwhile our turtle was still casting us reproachful glances, no doubt apprehensive about what the next stage of her career might be; but by then we had grown rather fond of her, and in any case we were not hungry, partly because we had eaten the fish brought by the Arab, and partly because we were so short of liquid – a state which diminishes appetite. We therefore untied our captive, and she staggered back into the sea.

Thus ended an interesting but only moderately successful

experiment. All we had learnt was that survival, in the pure sense of the term, is a taxing exercise in itself, which leaves little time or energy for any more constructive activity. Nor did I have much luck with my final attempt to salvage something from the wreck. Once again I was Food Member in the mess, and took back a few turtle eggs with me, thinking that they would make an unusual savoury at the end of dinner. They were certainly different, but they turned out to have three serious drawbacks: first, they tasted fishy; second, they were full of grit; and third, the whites, instead of setting when cooked, turned slimy – so we ended our meal with hot, fishy slime laced with grit. (It was hardly surprising that, at the next mess meeting, my term as Food Member came to an abrupt end.)

In spite of these disappointments, David became a good friend. A compulsive wanderer, and a dedicated sailor, he hung around Aden for a few months before setting out on his travels once more. In the end he ran out of money, and the Foreign Office began threatening that they would confiscate his passport and deport him if he did not make arrangements to leave Aden promptly. Short of funds though I was, I lent him £30 – enough for him to take passage home to New Zealand in some merchant-man – and told him not to bother to pay me back until he could afford it, even if this took several years. Two years later, in August 1964, a letter from him reached me in Borneo: it contained a cheque for £35 (the extra £5 representing interest) and the news that he was earning enough money to be attending college in his spare time and reading for a degree in English. We have kept in touch intermittently ever since.

In Aden, survival remained much on my mind. Here was a chance to practise SAS techniques of escape and evasion, survival and resistance to interrogation in a new environment. Early in 1963 I somehow obtained authority to run a combat survival course on behalf of Headquarters, Middle East. Officers from the army, navy and air force put in for it, or were drafted to take part, and candidates arrived from far and wide – from Aden itself, from Bahrein and East Africa.

In making my dispositions, I enlisted the help of two former SAS sergeants, and we devised a tough programme, flying out twenty specialists from the Joint Services' Interrogation Wing

to grill captives. I created a scenario in which participants would
be on the run in enemy territory, and would have to make for
a spot on the south coast, opposite the island on which David
and I had marooned ourselves.

We began with seven days' instruction, in class room and
nearby desert, during which we taught participants to live off
the land, to navigate with primitive equipment, and to live and
move in enemy-occupied territory. Among other skills, they
learnt how to kill and butcher goats and sheep, how to escape
from prisoner-of-war camps, and how to contact friendly agents.
After this gentle introduction, we turned them loose in the
desert for six days and nights, with instructions to make for the
final rendezvous on the coast, seventy-five miles to the south-
west. Each man was accompanied by a Marine Commando,
since by no means all the local Arabs were well disposed towards
us, and single men might have been in danger.

Once on the run, hunted by enemy troops, our men were
allowed to move at night only. Their rations were meagre, and
they received only two and a half pints of water in every twenty-
four hours. Every time they reached a check-point, they were
given a medical examination, and three officers were retired on
medical grounds, as were five of the Marine Commando escorts.
One pair were fired on by hostile Bedouin, but another were
befriended by Arabs who gave them water, milk, goat cheese
and information about the dispositions of the enemy. I myself
dodged about from one check-point to another, keeping a general eye on progress.

During their cross-desert trek, several participants had become
temporarily lost and covered a hundred miles or more before
reaching the rendezvous, only to find that they had to swim out
to the deserted island, each with his dinner in the form of a
pound of potatoes and a live goat slung over the back of his
neck. There – according to the scenario – they were on safe
territory – and most of them, rather than face killing their goat,
lit fires and boiled their potatoes in sea water.

The exercise culminated in a simulated clandestine pick-up at
night by RAF launch. Everyone had to swim quarter of a mile
out to sea and be dragged aboard. As I reported in a letter home,
the voyage back to Aden was hardly luxurious:

Myself *(left)* aged four and my
brother Michael with my mother
at The Homestead, in Kent, the
first home I remember.

My father as a Surgeon
Lieutenant Commander at the
beginning of the Second World
War.

Portrait of a rebel: my school-leaving photograph at Harrow.

The one nanny who could manage us, Christine Turnbull, with my brothers David and Michael, myself and Rupert Nicholas. The folding .410, my first gun, was a prize possession.

Legacy of a night out at Harrow: Eton's motto writ large.

Potential officers' platoon, Strensall, York, 1952: myself as a 17-year-old private soldier *(top centre)* with, *clockwise from top right*, Tom Luckock, Ted Easton, Tony Pheby and Brian Oatway Harris.

Devastation by shell-fire: the DLI front-line position in Korea, 1953.

A long way to fall: camel racing with the DLI in Egypt, 1954.

Right and below left: SAS selection course, 1956. Briefing Major Dare Newell, architect of the post-war Regiment, and route-planning in the Welsh mountains.

Emerging cold and disorientated from interrogation on a combat-survival exercise, as a 30-year-old Squadron Commander.

Above: My first SAS command, Malaya, 1957. Key members of 6 Troop included 'Lofty' Allen *(top centre)*, Jock Baird, my signaller *(top right)*, Bill Mundell *(on my left)*, Lawrence Smith *(on my right)*.

Left: Hunting terrorists in deep jungle, Malaya, 1957.

Below: Jerry Mulcahy severely injured after our operational parachute jump into the Telok Anson swamp, Malaya, 1957.

Above: Slow boat to Aden, 1963: our yacht *Cape Albacore (inset)* is towed through the Suez Canal.

Above left: Oman, 1958. 'Tanky' Smith in action with his .30 Browning machine gun during the cave raid on Jebel Akhdar.

Above: Johnny Watts, with myself behind, on the top of the Jebel Akhdar, after our dawn attack, 1 December 1958.

Left: After victory on the Jebel Akhdar, I demonstrate the 3.5-inch rocket-launcher used in the cave raid to Said bin Tariq, later Prime Minister of Oman.

Above: Dawn in Aden, 1964: myself *(left)* back from an SAS patrol with my signaller and mentor, Geordie Low *(right)*.

Right: Exhaustion: myself after three days and nights in rebel territory, Aden, 1964.

Below: A daylight hide-out in the mountains.

Left: Rebel partners: *Firqat* guerrillas in the Salala mountains, 1971.

Below: Castaways: myself and David Armstrong on our desert island, with the contaminated still, Aden, 1963.

Right: Before the battle, Mirbat, 1972: the BATT house in the foreground, with the fort visible behind.

> The sea was very rough, the launch very small, and all of us very smelly. They had to batten us down in the hold next to the engine room. The journey took nine hours. We were overcrowded, the hold leaked, and many were sick.

The surviving goats, meanwhile, had been driven back over the causeway at low tide, loaded into a lorry and taken to Aden. The driver was a small, fair-haired man who arrived at the Operations Room covered from head to foot in dust, hatless, and with a pair of goggles pushed up on to the top of his head. Marching into the tidy, air-conditioned room, he said to the Operations Officer, Dick Trant, 'Excuse me, sir. I've got a load of goats out there. What d'you want done with 'em?' Dick, who had a very short fuse, thought the man was trying to take the mickey out of him, and erupted.

Those who came through the course were considerably surprised, not to say shocked, by their experience.[1] Most were amused, but also a little bemused, as they had never known anything like it. I think the authorities were slightly stunned as well – and I was not asked to repeat the experiment; but in self-justification I could point out that we had stretched people's horizons without killing or seriously injuring any of them, and I was delighted when the Commander-in-Chief, Middle East, sent for me and congratulated me on the way things had gone.

Still trying to escape the office, I occasionally managed to arrange a temporary attachment to one of the FRA battalions. Luckily for me, James Lunt realized that I was not happy sitting at a desk, and was generous about allowing me out.

With my work in the office and these frequent excursions, it may sound as though I had plenty to do; yet my instinct was to pack my days to the limit with extra projects, among them free-fall parachuting. With some difficulty, I obtained permission from Middle East Headquarters, and began jumping from Army Air Corps Austers, for which we had to develop a special

---

1. Our leaflet on 'Primitive Medicine' recommended (among other remedies) cow's manure as suitable for poulticing boils and abscesses. 'This may appear to you revolting, and not what the doctor ordered, but the effect it has on boils and abscesses may change your mind very quickly.' On wounds it said: 'Do not worry if the wound becomes fly-blown and maggots appear. Although this will be uncomfortable, maggots will dispose of septic areas and leave the wound completely clean.'

technique to extricate ourselves from the passenger seat. I loved free-falling as a high-risk sport, but I still also saw it as a means of infiltrating patrols deep into enemy territory, way ahead of conventional troops, to produce intelligence which could be sent back by radio. Whenever I had a couple of hours to spare, I would pack my parachutes on the tarmac at Khormaksar and make two or three jumps into the desert near the airfield.

The months seemed to roll away, and by the summer of 1963 I was beginning to feel oppressed by the approach of a particular personal horror – the Staff College exam, which loomed like a thunder-cloud on my horizon. Much as I disliked the idea of spending time in the academic atmosphere of Camberley, I had been persuaded that the only realistic way of advancing my career would be to go through the college; so I had arranged to sit the exam – in Aden – in the winter of 1963, and slogged away at the homework needed to tackle the papers. (After one trial paper, the examiner remarked: 'Your spelling is too original to be of much value.') I believe that all along I was subconsciously inhibited by the knowledge that, if I passed, I should have to defer my return to the SAS. Nevertheless, at the same time I decided that I must learn to type properly: I had made a start during my secretarial course in Shrewsbury, all those years earlier, but I had never mastered the skill properly, and now set out to achieve acceptable speeds and accuracy.

As if all this was not enough to keep me occupied, I was gradually drawn into another activity far more exciting than any of my official duties: I became an undercover agent.

The man who introduced me to this new role was Tony Boyle, a tall, thin, dark airman then working as ADC and Private Secretary to the High Commissioner. The son of Marshal of the Royal Air Force Sir Dermot Boyle, Tony had flown fast jet fighters in Scotland and Germany, and come out to Aden for an obligatory ground tour in the middle of his RAF career. Part of his job in Aden was to organize hospitality at Government House, and one day early in 1963 who should arrive to stay as a guest of the High Commissioner but David Stirling. Tony knew, of course, that Stirling was the founder of the SAS, and soon saw that he and Sir Charles Johnston were old friends. One night after the two had dined together alone at Government House, Johnston excused himself and went to bed, leaving Tony to drink whisky with Stirling on the terrace.

Presently Stirling started to talk about his idea for sending support to the Royalist forces who were waging a guerrilla war of resistance against the Republicans in the Yemen, and asked Tony if he would help people as they passed through Aden. So began an extraordinary, covert operation which lasted for five years, substantially debilitated the armed forces of Egypt, and had a profound effect on events throughout the Middle East.

The Royalist Government had been overthrown by an Egyptian-inspired revolution in the capital, Sana'a, on 27 September 1962: deposed, but not defeated, the Imam had fled from his palace dressed in women's clothes, and had established himself with his loyal forces in the mountains. As Stirling pointed out, it had not proved easy for the Republicans to defeat him, and now, if he were boosted by expert outside help, he might survive indefinitely. Because the operation had not been officially sanctioned by the British Government, the SAS itself could not take part. Yet here was an ideal opportunity for former members of the Regiment to exercise their skills in a mercenary role – and who better to direct them than the one-time Commanding Officer of 21st SAS, Jim Johnson?

The operation began in characteristically relaxed fashion when the Royalist Foreign Minister of the Yemen, Ahmed al-Shami, invited Jim round for a drink in London, together with Billy Maclean, the Member of Parliament for Inverness, who had fought with SOE in Albania during the Second World War. Asked if he thought he could help, Jim gave a cautiously optimistic reply, and inquired if funds were available. The answer was, 'Certainly.' Al-Shami at once signed a cheque for £5000, but because he could not write English, Jim had to make it out – and he did so in favour of the Hyde Park Hotel (whose Chairman, Brian Franks, one of the architects of the post-war SAS, was then the Regiment's Colonel Commandant). At the hotel Jim sent for Salvatore, the Manager, and asked him to cash the cheque. 'All right,' he said, 'but what do you want all that money for?'

'Let's say to give a dance for my daughter.'

'But it can't cost that much.'

'OK, then. I want to open an account.'

So he did, and the money was kept in cash, in one of the hotel's deposit boxes.

Jim went to work recruiting in England and France, and the first team – three Britons and three Frenchmen, all Arabic speakers – was soon put together. The initial plan was that they should fly out to Aden, go on to Beihan, and be smuggled over the border into Yemen, with the aim of destroying the Egyptian military aircraft lined up on the tarmac at Sana'a airstrip. The leader of the party was the wartime SAS veteran Johnny Cooper.

Word of what was brewing inevitably reached Whitehall, and the day before the team was due to leave the United Kingdom, Duncan Sandys, the Commonwealth Secretary, rang Stirling and told him to stop.[1] Stirling rang Jim and said, 'I'm sorry, but it's all off.' Jim was so angry that, although he agreed to stand the men down, he changed his mind early that night and began telephoning airlines until he found an Alitalia flight which was leaving for Libya in the early hours of the morning. At once he booked tickets, drove the team to Heathrow with their heavy kit and shoved them on board the aircraft. In the morning, when the Duty Officer at the Commonwealth Office rang Stirling and said, 'You haven't done anything stupid, have you?' Stirling was able to reply with a clear conscience, 'Certainly not'.

So the operation was launched, and in spite of formidable difficulties men, arms, ammunition, money and medical supplies began to flow through Aden for despatch up-country. Their natural route into the Yemen was through Beihan, where the Sharif was a staunch ally of Britain, and prepared to post strangers on their way without asking awkward questions. To cross the border, they would join a camel train at night, and they might have to remain in the saddle for eight or ten hours, since the camel men would not let them set foot on the ground until they were well clear of the frontier: Arabs have relatively

---

1. Sandys himself was still keen that the operation should proceed, but he had been unnerved by rumours that he was the 'headless man' who had appeared naked in a photograph with the Duchess of Argyll: the scandal was already threatening his position, and he feared that any further exposure would lead to his political downfall.

small feet, and a single European-sized print would have given the game away.

At first it was Tony Boyle who fielded the mercenaries in Aden and sent them on: he evolved an efficient system whereby a Dakota would be parked on the airstrip close to the spot where the twice-weekly Comet from London came to a halt, and passengers and their heavy freight would transfer straight to it, without passing through customs. In time, however, Jim Johnson felt that he needed an army officer to handle the traffic, and so he asked Tony to recruit me.

By our own assessment, the international repercussions of our enterprise were widespread. The Americans, who had recognized the Republican regime in the Yemen, were embarrassed by the fact that Britons were fostering the Royalists. The French unofficially took an active part, though with gradually diminishing enthusiasm, routing aid through their African enclave Djibouti. The Israelis were keen to further any operation which debilitated Egypt, and gave covert support, as did the Iranians. The Saudi Arabians financed the operation throughout, providing facilities in Jeddah and elsewhere. As for Nasser – he became incoherent with rage at the way a handful of foreign mercenaries was tying down large numbers of his troops. He knew quite well who the ringleaders were, and once sent Jim Johnson a message saying that if he cared to come to Egypt, he would have a free holiday in government premises for seven years. Sana'a Radio's incessant propaganda promised rewards for the capture, alive or dead, of named individuals: £5000 for the head of Major John Cooper, and so on.

Meanwhile Jim and a small headquarter team were directing affairs from various offices in London, under various covers, among them locust control schemes and the distribution of television films. In 1963, when I became involved, their lair was in the basement of Jim's office at 21a Sloane Street, and his sheet-anchor there was Fiona Fraser, the ravishing daughter of Lord Lovat.

With this extra commitment, which grew inexorably, my life became busier than ever. Often I would meet someone off the London Comet, make what arrangements I could to ease his passage through customs, and – to avoid being seen in contact

– pass him a type-written note asking him to book in at a certain hotel, where I would meet him for lunch next day. Then I would send him up to Beihan, either by a Dakota of Aden Air, or by Land Rover, and he would slip through the Yemeni frontier at night. These clandestine movements led to many ridiculous clashes with my routine intelligence work: my up-country agents – who had cover-names like Dallas and Tip – would send word that mysterious strangers had appeared in the rest-house at Beihan, and next day I would solemnly include these reports – of my own people's movements – in my Intsum.

For communication with London, we used the normal post and civilian cable network, disguising our activities by means of simple codes. A little red 'Universal Telegraphic Phrasebook' gave hundreds of cipher-words which helped keep messages short – INFAG, for instance, meant 'leaving on the first', RAVEA 500 'have remitted £500 as requested' – but such messages could be read by anybody, and to make them more obscure we introduced code words of our own: BLACKBIRD for aeroplane, CHOPS for money, HAPPY for anti-tank, and so on. In time we all became slightly obsessed with our own amateurish attempts at secrecy. Once, when I reported that my grandmother was dying – which she was – the team in London spent hours trying to decipher the message's hidden meaning. Another time Tony Boyle (by then back in England) sent a message 'IN SWAY OVER WEEKEND', and everyone in Aden became tremendously excited, thinking that a parachute drop of arms and equipment was imminent. Word went all the way up the line into the Yemen, and when nothing happened, we were acutely disappointed. So were the Egyptians, whose intelligence service had intercepted the message and alerted the Yemeni defences to look out for parachutists. All Tony had meant was that he would be spending the weekend with his parents at Sway, the village where they lived in the New Forest.

With traffic building up fast, I became anxious that people would cotton on to what we were doing, and when I heard that the immigration authorities had been told to take a special interest in travellers heading for Beihan, I suggested ways of improving security: people on their way out should break their journey somewhere in Africa, so that they did not appear to have come from the United Kingdom, and they should arrive not only with a good cover story, but also fully equipped, so that I did not have to take them shopping in Aden – a task which attracted unwelcome attention.

Because there was a limit on what individuals could carry in the way of arms, ammunition, explosives, radio sets and money, we were constantly trying to devise new methods of delivering supplies in bulk. Parachute drops were frequently proposed, if rarely used, but the French did fly in several plane-loads to the airstrip at Beihan. We also developed plans for bringing a dhow in to the coast of Wahidi, east of Aden, but this ambitious scheme never came to fruition.

The pressure on me increased sharply in September, when Tony's tour of duty ended. He had begun to suffer severe head-aches, and an x-ray suggested that he might have a tumour on the brain. Luckily this diagnosis proved wrong, and the trouble turned out to be migraine; but it was bad enough to prevent him flying fast jets any more, and he resigned from the air force. This was a great loss to the RAF, as he clearly had a distinguished career ahead of him; yet it was a considerable gain to us, since he promptly joined Jim Johnson's team in London, and several times returned to Aden during the course of the operation.

His departure coincided with a swift build-up of activity, and by October even I, with my appetite for hard work, was stretched to my limits. On 6 October I wrote to Tony, 'I am in danger of having to give up the army altogether, as it gets in the way!' and I warned Jim:

> I am doing in the region of six hours a day on this. This is fine, and I can keep up the present pressure, but cannot increase it. More people in the Yemen will step it up considerably, therefore please think about some kind of relief. If the work really increases, we shall have to think of having someone full-time in Aden.

Up in the Yemen Johnny Cooper was starting to achieve results, and sending back reports of successful ambushes and mine-layings: 'Egyptian lorry blown up. Seven dead.' But he was also demanding more and more money. 'Send chops,' was his constant refrain – causing me to cable London:

30,000 MTD [Maria Theresa silver dollars] required for monthly pay and expenses. Grave difficulties. Action impossible without it. Immense possibilities on Sana'a if more money arrives.

By then we had established an efficient radio network, with a station at Nuqub, in Beihan, working forward into the Yemen and backwards to Aden, and another in Aden itself, which could communicate directly with London. The network was manned by two SAS veterans from the Second World War, one of whom arrived in Aden with suitcases so overloaded that they burst open as he staggered through customs.

At the end of October, with my own time running out, and the wretched Staff College exam still looming, I enlisted the help of a colleague in the FRA. My aim was that he should take over from me when I left in January, and he and his wife began to share some of my clandestine load. By then I was getting up at 4.30 a.m., or 5 at the latest, trying to work for the exam (which became less and less credible as the weeks went by), doing paperwork for the Yemen operation, and then going for a run before breakfast.

In the third week of November David Stirling again visited Aden, and I met him for the first time. Many people could not stand him, and found him so overbearing that they could not work with him; but to me he was, and will always remain, a great man and a hero, as large in spirit as he was in stature.

I found him extremely exhilarating. His personality was so strong that he had a magnetic effect on other people; he was also generous, hospitable and articulate, and he put over his own ideas with such force that it was difficult to argue with him. Even if some of the ideas did not seem very sound, he had a knack of making them appear brilliant. He also had a strong sense of humour, although a slightly wry and brutal one, in that he would make fun of an uncomfortable situation. After the war he had rather lost interest in the SAS, growing absorbed in the problems of Africa; his aim there was to improve the standing and influence of the black population by means of education, and he foresaw the immense social changes which were coming, decades before they arrived. Now, however, the operation in the Yemen had rekindled his enthusiasm for irregular warfare: revelling in intrigue, he was full of ideas for the discomfiture of Nasser and the Republicans.

My first meeting with him was rendered unforgettable by its timing. It took place at Government House on 22 November 1963, and as we sat talking after dinner in the dark on the terrace, we heard over the radio the dire news that President Kennedy had been assassinated. (I learned later that, one day earlier, Kennedy had telephoned the British Prime Minister, Sir Alec Douglas-Home, and asked for his personal assurance that the British mercenaries would be withdrawn from the Yemen. Home said that as far as he knew we were not involved, but that he would make inquiries — and the next day Kennedy went to Dallas.)

My own nemesis was hard upon me. Over the next few days I sat the Staff College exam . . . and failed ignominiously. Not only had I taken on far too many other projects: I had also been in the wrong frame of mind, not really wanting, at the bottom of my heart, to spend the next year sitting at a desk in Camberley. Had I passed, I should have had to reschedule my future; as it was, failure opened the way for me to return to the SAS early in January.

By the end of 1963 the security situation in Aden was deteriorating fast, and terrorism began to take hold as various political groups sought to increase their influence before the British pulled out. An organized campaign of violence developed in Crater, and curfews were imposed. The intensity of local feeling stood revealed to the world on 10 December, when a grenade was thrown at the new High Commissioner, Sir Kennedy Trevaskis, as he stood on the airfield, about to take off with a delegation for talks in London. With matchless courage George Henderson flung himself between the grenade and Sir Kennedy, taking the full force of the explosion. He died in hospital ten days later, but not before he had been awarded a bar to the George Medal which he had won six years earlier, also for gallantry. News of the award was telegraphed out to Aden, so that he knew of it before he died.

With terrorism spreading, and the expatriate community

driven in on itself more and more, our clandestine operations became increasingly difficult. On 22 December I wrote to Fiona:

> Aden is infinitesimally small, and everybody knows every-one else. It's rather the same situation as in a small provin-cial town in the UK, except that with Arabs news gets around more. Also, the Arabs who man the cable office are, like all Arabs, very conscious politically, and prick up their ears at anything to do with the Yemen.
>
> All my outgoing mail is handled by soldiers in the unit, and of course they keep their eyes open to events. The story going around now is that I am due to get married any day! The reason given is the vast number of tapes and letters I've been sending you so carefully sealed!

One further difficulty I now experienced was that men began to come back from the Yemen heavily tanned and bearded. It made perfect sense to grow a beard up-country, because it saved time and trouble shaving, and protected the wearer's face from sunburn; but in the claustrophobic surroundings of Aden a beard stood out horribly, and at once proclaimed where its owner had come from. 'I'm afraid it embarrasses me to be seen out with what are obviously shady characters, to say the least,' I told London. 'Don't forget, we are respected citizens, not clandestine cut-throats, like you lot.'

As the year ended, I had a mad rush to pack up and leave, having received an order posting me back to 22 SAS. John Woodhouse's instruction was to fly straight to Brunei and carry out a reconnaissance, so that I would know what conditions 'A' Squadron could expect when it went out there later in 1964. I was delighted to do this, but it meant that, while I was dismant-ling my own operation and handing over, I also had to pack all my possessions for despatch to the United Kingdom.

Never a great one for elaborate farewells, I slipped away from Aden quietly in the first week of January, having had a most stimulating tour. All along I had taken it for granted that, if news of what I was doing had broken, I should be left on my own: I never expected anyone in authority to stand up for me. As always, I did the job because I enjoyed it, not because it might somehow promote my career. On the contrary, if anything had gone wrong in Aden, it might have finished my army career for good. I never received any payment for my extra work: I did it for the excitement and interest it provided, and also because I knew that the operation was fostering British interests: we were backing the Royalists in the Yemen without Britain being seen to be involved. If the mercenaries had been working against the interests of the United Kingdom, I should never have supported them; but as they were taking on some of the most obnoxious of the Queen's enemies of the day, my sympathies were with them entirely.

CHAPTER 14

DEATH IN THE MOUNTAINS

1964

Early in January I flew to Brunei, and spent ten useful days there on reconnaissance. Back in England, I snatched a few days' leave. I had been abroad for two years – not the four widely predicted by Aunt Joyce – and was pleased to find my mother happily settled with the Lytes. (It was my paternal grandmother who had died: Granny Lawley, though by now blind and bed-ridden, was still living with Joyce at Old Place.) Then I rejoined 22nd SAS at Hereford as commander of 'A' Squadron. That morning when we flopped down in triumph on the top of the Jebel Akhdar in January 1959, I had confided to Tony Deane-Drummond that my highest ambition was to become a squadron commander – and now, at the age of thirty, I had achieved it. As John Woodhouse – one of my heroes – had recently taken command of the Regiment, I felt confident that the future would bring plenty of action.

There was not long to wait, for plans changed, and before the Squadron went out to the Far East, it was diverted to another operation in Arabia. Arriving in Hereford, I found plans well advanced for 'A' Squadron to fly to Aden for a desert exercise; and, since I knew the Protectorate well, it was natural that I should go out on a reconnaissance. Back in my old haunts, I discovered that the smuggling of arms and men into the Yemen was going great guns: Johnny Cooper and his men were causing the Republicans serious trouble, and already some 40,000 Egyptian troops had been drafted into the Yemen in attempts to suppress the Royalist resistance. In Aden, however, the situation had deteriorated: infiltration from the north had increased, and in the Colony itself rival nationalist political groups were jockeying for power with ever-increasing violence. Up-country, dissident tribesmen had become so aggressive that a major operation was about to be launched against them by a combined group known as 'Radfan Force' (later shortened to 'Radforce'), consisting of two battalions of the FRA, strengthened by 45 Commando Royal Marines, a company of the Third Battalion of the Parachute Regiment, an armoured car unit, an artillery battery and a detachment of Royal Engineers.

Here, surely, was an operation in which the SAS might play a useful part – yet there seemed to be no mention of Special Forces in the plans. I went to see the Commander-in-Chief, Lieutenant-General Sir Charles Harington, and suggested that we should not wait for our projected exercise, but should upgrade it into a live operation, and call the SAS deployment forward. I pointed out that although Radforce was well equipped in other respects, it lacked any deep-penetration troops, who could go in behind enemy lines to secure dropping zones for paratroops and report enemy movements and locations, thus providing information for air-strikes and artillery. Such tasks, I said, would be ideal for the SAS. Should we not ask for them to come out? 'Good idea,' said Harington, 'just what we need,' – and he gave me authority to call 'A' Squadron's deployment forward.

I sat down and composed a signal to John Woodhouse – STAND 'A' SQUADRON BY FOR MAJOR OPERATION. DETAILS FOLLOW – and in my excitement I gave it the highest possible priority – 'Top Secret Operational Immediate Exclusive'. Little did I realize what havoc this would create – but it was not long before the error of my ways was borne in on me by a characteristic rocket from the boss. 'I am sure you do not realize what is involved in TOP SECRET OP IMMEDIATE EXCLUSIVE SIGNALS', wrote Woodhouse, 'so I will explain.'

> The signal goes to a UK Command Headquarters – in our case Chester, this being the lowest level equipped for Top Secret cipher. The one Signals duty Land Rover then has to be sent from there on a three-hour journey to Hereford. Before this can be done, I have to be fetched from whatever part of the country I am in (London, as it happened) because

you ensured that no one else could receive the signal. All
this had to be done in this case, only to find that there was
no degree of urgency whatever!

Lesson learned, I hope!

Expostulate though he might, Woodhouse as always was on the
lookout for a promising operation: he agreed to my proposal
and stood the Squadron to, while I flew home to make preparations. As the deployment was top secret, the men were not
allowed to tell their families their true destination: instead, they
said they were off for a quick-recall exercise on Salisbury Plain.
Since sudden departures were part of SAS life, nobody ques-
tioned this explanation.

The order to move was given on 20 April, and two days later
the Squadron flew to Aden. By then things were moving so fast
that we had no time to acclimatize: within eighteen hours we
were sixty miles north of Aden at our forward base in the village
of Thumier, which consisted of a few mud huts, now augmented
by military tents, in a stretch of flat, bare desert framed all round
by the high mountains of the Radfan. The place had been chosen
because it was a natural site for an airstrip – which was built in
due course – and for the time being it became a hive of military
activity.

Our own task was to move out into the mountains at night,
penetrate deep into rebel territory and find out what the enemy
were doing. In particular, our job was to locate suitable dropping
zones for the Parachute Regiment. I was lucky enough to have
two outstanding officers in my Squadron, both captains: Robin
Edwards and Ray England. Robin was a Cornishman, from Padstow: big, dark and broad-shouldered, he softened his otherwise
rugged appearance with a winning smile. Even in the Regiment
he was something of a legend, for as a boy he had contracted
polio, but had fought the disease off with such spirit that he
passed his SAS selection course, as fit as anyone. Although a
formidable soldier, he was an exceptionally kind man, full of
common sense – the sort of person with whom you could discuss
any problem. He and I had known each other for some time
and become close friends.

Ray England was very different, but equally effective. Lean, dark and hyper-efficient, he was exceedingly tough and full of unorthodox ideas. Later he went into operational research and led a crusade to develop better boots (in the SAS the search for the perfect boot is never-ending). Such was his zeal in this respect that he became known as 'Boots' England. Another field which he pioneered was that of the use of Christian names: not only did he address his men by their first names, he also encouraged them to call him Ray. This, as I have said, was a practice of which I did not altogether approve, as it could lead to problems of discipline; but Ray was one of the few who had the strength of personality to carry it off.

I was well served in having such excellent troop leaders; yet I myself now began to experience the problems – one might even say penalties – which beset a commander of rising seniority. As always, my instinct was to lead from the front: to go out on patrol, and find out for myself what conditions were like at the sharp end. Yet I realized that even though, when I did that, I might function efficiently as a patrol commander, I was not able to give other patrols the help and guidance which should be coming from a higher level. As Squadron Commander, my job was to know what conditions were like forward, but at the same time to have the sixth sense and experience to discern when a patrol commander needed back-up, and quickly to do something about it – whether to call down air or artillery support, send in reinforcements, or evacuate the unit. My true role, in short, was to stay at base, controlling movements and manipulating resources – tasks which could not be carried out if I were pinned down in the mountains at the end of a radio set.

I lived with a permanent conscience over this dilemma. I always wanted to go out, and felt I ought to, because I hated sending other people into danger while I sat back in relative comfort and safety. Somehow I had to strike the right balance between, on the one hand, seizing opportunities for gaining first-hand knowledge, so that I could make judgments based on my own experience, and on the other hand staying behind to see that my patrols had their requirements met. What made things easier was that, whenever I talked to soldiers or other officers about the problem, they were clear in their minds about where I ought to be, so that I never got sideways glances or recrimination if I did not go forward.

Another tremendous help was the arrival of 22nd SAS's new Second-in-Command, Lieutenant-Colonel Mike Wingate Gray, who joined us from the Black Watch. He later confided that he found it difficult, coming, at the advanced age of forty-one, into the close-knit family of the SAS, which had different values and mental attitude from the rest of the army; but his presence was a godsend to me, because he was well able to take charge of our rear base. Although he scarcely knew the SAS, he had been through most of the Second World War, in North Africa, Sicily, Italy and north-west Europe, and his operational experience, coupled with genial common sense, won everyone's respect.

With him in control at our tented camp at Thumier, I did feel able to go out – and the patrols which we mounted in the Radfan were even more demanding than our operations on the Jebel Akhdar. The main problems were heat and lack of water: at the end of April, daytime temperatures were rising to 120°F, and we had to carry all our water with us, our aim being to stay out for four or five days.

Only first-class soldiers could have achieved what ours did: self-discipline was of paramount importance, because we were plagued by thirst, and had to exercise fierce control over the desire to drink – otherwise our water would have been gone in a few hours, and the patrol would have had to be aborted. Soon it became clear that different people needed water in different ways. I myself found it best to march for most of the night without drinking, in spite of the craving for water; then, when we had halted and I had stopped sweating, I would sip very slowly, so that the liquid could be absorbed by my body, rather than go straight out in evaporation. Another man, however, might find that he could not carry on without drinking on the move. We had to accept that people varied, and, as usual in the SAS, we laid down no hard and fast rules: it was up to every individual to manage his own water intake. The most we could carry was four pints per day per man, which was not enough: as time went by, we became progressively dehydrated. Besides budgeting every drop of water, we also had to eat large numbers of salt tablets, without which we would have gone down with heat exhaustion, hallucinations and related problems.[1] Even with every precaution taken, we finished patrols in a state of utter exhaustion: the photograph on Page X gives some idea of how we felt when we came in.

Food was less of a problem, as we did not seem to need very much; but we selected what we took with care: small tins of baked beans, steak-and-kidney pudding, biscuits high in calories. We ate relatively little, living on our reserves until we were back in camp, and then feeding ourselves up with extra rations. During a patrol there was no question of washing or shaving, so that one came back in a filthy state.

Our method was to move out at night, go as far forward as we could under cover of darkness, and then lie up beneath camouflage nets among the rocks in a spot which commanded a good view. Luckily the tribesmen seemed to dislike fighting or moving about at night, so that we could move with relative freedom. But it was essential to be in position before first light, and in a *good* position, because once dawn broke, we could not move any more without being seen – for one of the extraordinary things about Arabia is the way in which, if you stop for five minutes, people rise up out of the desert, even though there appears to be no human habitation for miles around. As we had found out in Oman, it was simply not worth being spotted: if the *adoo* saw us, they would begin sniping from a distance, summon reinforcements and try to close in for a pitched battle. Once, as we moved out towards a destination two nights' march away, we were obliged to hole up for the day in a deserted Arab hut – and a dire mistake it proved. A filthier, more vermin-ridden hovel I have never seen: the place was alive with lice and fleas, and by the time dark fell, releasing us, we were all infested.

In any lying-up position, two men would be awake and on lookout with binoculars during daylight hours; but as soon as they saw something happening, they would wake up the patrol commander. Being in charge was thus extremely tiring: the day-time heat was so ferocious as to make sleeping difficult, and whenever one did drop off, the chances were that one would

1. Contemporary wisdom claims that replacing salt in this way is not very effective, as tablets do not dissolve quickly; but they were all we had.

be woken again in short order. It was like being the captain of a ship, in that one needed to be told everything that was going on.

On every patrol I was given sterling support by my signaller, Geordie Low – a slight little man, with a freckled and wizened face, very amenable, but incredibly tough, and, although so small, able to carry a full bergen as far and fast as anyone. In technical terms he was first class, and taught me a great deal about signalling; yet, almost as important, he was also a marvellous companion, totally frank, and ready to tell me in outspoken terms if he thought I was making a hash of something. He had an amazing ability to disagree with me, but then, if I persisted in taking my own course of action, accepting my decision. Considering how far apart we were in rank, our relationship was remarkably close – and our understanding enabled him to help me in more ways than were apparent to outsiders.

For years I had known that I was colour-blind, and now I realized that my hearing was not as good as it had been. Almost certainly it had been damaged by excessive firing of weapons; whatever the reason, the fact remained that I was leading patrols in a hostile environment with my faculties dangerously diminished. To make good this deficiency, Geordie and I devised a series of silent signals with which he would alert me. If a flare went up, for instance, one tap on my right shoulder meant that it was red, two that it was green. A single tap on the left shoulder meant that Geordie had heard something, and that we should stop to listen.

Our early patrols showed us that the enemy were scattered over the mountains in some numbers, and that they were sharp-eyed and alert. After only a week or so, we were asked to clear and mark out a dropping zone for the Parachute Regiment on a feature called Cap-Badge, to the north of a long valley, the Wadi Taym, which struck up into the mountains east of Thumier; and it was our efforts to do this, beyond the range of our artillery, which led to a grave setback.

The man I selected to lead the patrol was Robin Edwards. From our maps, and from the intelligence which we had built up over the past few days, we chose what looked like a good position for him to lie up in and observe rebel movement in the area of the DZ. We could see that he was going to have a long night-march, but we discussed it carefully together and decided that it was feasible. John Woodhouse, who came to Thumier that day – 29 April, my thirtieth birthday – heard our plans and approved them.

At last light the eight men were lifted by helicopter to a point five thousand yards inside enemy territory, but they had scarcely started their march before the signaller, Trooper Nick Warburton, was hit by a severe stomach upset: he had felt fit when they left, and the trouble was apparently brought on by the meal he had eaten before departure. Although he kept going, he inevitably slowed the patrol down. Back in the tent which served as our operations room at Thumier, I knew precisely what was happening, because every time they had to stop, Robin came through on the radio and brought me up to date. The sets were working well that night, and we had good, clear voice communication. By 0200 it had become clear that Robin was not going to reach his objective before daybreak. After discussing alternatives, we agreed that the patrol should find some other high ground, spread out well in a defensive position, put up their scrim camouflage nets, and hope to sit the day out, before going on the next night. This sounded a reasonable plan, but I knew he would have difficulty finding a good position, for in the dark it is hard to judge how the country will look by day. What appears to be good, isolated high ground, well away from other commanding hills, suddenly in daylight becomes much lower and more closely overlooked than you hoped.

This happened to Robin. The eminence he selected turned out to be uncomfortably near neighbouring hills, yet his patrol had no option but to settle down and hope for the best. In fact the worst occurred. At 1100 a single goatherd appeared from nowhere and wandered towards their position. They had three options: first, to let him see them – whereupon he would run off and rouse his companions into action; second, to overpower him silently; third, to kill him with a single shot, hoping that nobody would pin-point the source of the report. The first option was clearly a non-starter, and Robin, knowing what eagle eyes mountain Arabs have, felt that the second was the same: a scrimmage out in the open would surely be seen by someone up in the rocks overlooking them. The third option seemed the best, and when a confrontation became inevitable, the patrol took it.

All this was reported back to us on the radio. Aware that Robin was not happy with his position, and knowing also that he was out of artillery range because he was on the back of a hill, I had alerted the RAF in Aden and requested support from the Hunter fighter-bombers of 43 and 208 Squadrons. Now I asked them to stand-to for immediate action.

Sure enough, the single shot immediately brought out the local dissidents, who hurried up to vantage-points and searched the ground for intruders. In the end they spotted the SAS positions and began sniping at them. Ever since my Korean days I had made it a rule with my soldiers that they should be parsimonious with their ammunition, shooting only when necessary, and when they had a good target. Now the patrol put this precept into practice, sniping back whenever they spotted movement among the rocks, but generally holding their fire.

When radio reports made it clear that the numbers of rebels were increasing, I called in the Hunters. Cap-Badge was only eight minutes' flying time from Aden, and the first pair of aircraft were quickly overhead, diving in with rockets and cannon-fire. Fuel limitations meant that each pair could spend only fifteen or twenty minutes over the target, but during that time they wheeled and dived relentlessly, until another pair could take over. In all, during the day, the Hunter pilots fired one hundred and twenty-seven rockets and over 7000 rounds of ammunition. (Each SAS man, in contrast, fired an average of thirty rounds, only a quarter of what he carried.) I believe that without the air support the Arabs would have closed in and annihilated the patrol, for the tribesmen outnumbered the SAS by seven or eight to one; as it was, the Hunters kept them at bay until evening.

All day in Thumier rescue schemes were mooted. Several individuals volunteered to go in, and the commander of a helicopter flight offered to try to extract the patrol by air. Mike told him he would certainly be shot at – which he was: he made a gallant attempt, but came back with bullet-holes in the petrol tank and rear rotor of his aircraft. A battery of the Royal Horse Artillery brought down fire on the approaches to the position, in an attempt to deter more *adoo* from congregating, but in general

Mike had to calm people down and veto ideas which would have almost certainly entailed loss of life.

Then, at about 1745, in the critical twilight period as dark came down, the Hunters had to stop flying. The Arabs would realize that the aircraft would have to go home, and I felt sure they were planning their attack for that moment.

Robin sensed this too. As the light failed, and snipers moved in ever closer, dodging from rock to rock, he decided that the only thing to do was for the patrol to slip out, using fire and movement to cover each other. Nick Warburton sent a message to say that they were about to move down into the nearest wadi, to start the journey home – and then the radio went dead.

So began one of the most ghastly nights of my life. It was clear that something had gone seriously wrong. The best we could hope for was that the radio had failed – but that seemed unlikely, as it had been functioning perfectly all day. We were very much afraid that the patrol had been over-run, and all its members killed or captured. Together with Mike Wingate Gray and Lawrence Smith, my Sergeant Major, I sat in the operations tent talking through every possibility. The worst thing was that, in the dark, we could do absolutely nothing to help. For hour after hour we tried to raise the patrol on the radio, but no answer came. In the end, at about 0300, I went and lay on a camp bed in an alcove, with orders that I was to be woken instantly if any message came through. Racked as I was by anxiety, I was also exhausted, and fell asleep, until someone roused me at 0500.

Still there was no news; but then, soon after dawn, a message came through that British soldiers had been sighted five miles away down the wadi. Full of sudden hope, we leapt into a Land Rover and raced to the spot, to find Trooper Geordie Tasker – a great big, red-headed, excellent fighting man – together with Corporal Paddy Baker, who was limping from a serious wound in the leg, and one other.

We were overjoyed to find that at least some of our men were alive; but the story they told was grim. When Robin decided to break out, everyone had got ready, and at the last moment he had turned to Nick Warburton, telling him to let us know they were on their way – only to find that the signaller was dead, killed by a shot through the head. Then Robin himself got up, and as the patrol moved out in formation down the hill, he was immediately picked off and killed. The rest of the men reached the cover of the wadi, hotly pursued by Arabs, who were determined to cut them off. Paddy Baker, wounded though he was, took control, and directed a masterly rearguard action, several times leaving a couple of men behind to ambush followers, while the main body pressed on – a difficult operation at night, in country which you do not know (he was later awarded the Military Medal). So skilfully did the men move that after a couple more clashes they broke clean with the enemy; and although they themselves were split into two groups, they all trickled back to base, minus the two dead.

The disaster had a profound effect on me. To lose two men from a small unit would have been bad enough. To lose one of my closest friends was worse. But worst of all was the feeling that the whole thing was my fault. I blamed myself bitterly for not having spent more time identifying better alternative lying-up positions before the patrol set out. I knew that even a good one might not have saved the day, but at least I would have known that I had done the right thing.

I was in that most difficult of all positions for a commander: full of personal remorse, and yet obliged to press on with the war. Needing to gain control of myself, I walked off into the desert and sat on a rock alone. A few minutes' solitude and self-examination helped clear my mind. This was no moment for self-pity: on the contrary, it was more important than ever to be robust and resilient. So I went back to the tent and prepared to carry on.

The incident brought out a weakness endemic in the SAS. Because it is such a small unit, and its members share the stresses and dangers of campaigns at such close quarters, they inevitably grow very close to each other – far more so than in other regiments – and when losses do occur, they hit all the harder. Nevertheless, soldiers are resilient and, if properly led, bounce back quickly after a reverse. Thus in the Radfan, although the survivors of the patrol were exhausted by their ordeal, I knew that the worst thing to do would be to let them sit about and reflect on their misfortunes. Rather, as soon as they had recovered, we sent them out on another patrol.

The loss of two men put Mike and me in a quandary. As far as their families knew, they were still on Salisbury Plain, and somehow we had to let the next-of-kin know what had happened as quickly and humanely as possible. But before we could make the necessary arrangements, we heard that the bodies had been decapitated and the heads taken to Taiz, a rebel stronghold some fifty miles inside the Yemen, where they had been exhibited on posts. This was bad enough, yet worse followed: on the evening of 3 May, Major General J. H. Cubbon, the General Officer Commanding Land Forces, Middle East, called a Press conference in Aden and blew the whole story – not merely confirming the two deaths, but giving away the fact that the SAS were involved in the campaign. The news caused uproar in the United Kingdom, not least because the Americans for some reason denied its veracity, thereby adding confusion to outrage. On the ground, we knew that the story of decapitation was all too true, because a patrol went out at night and recovered the bodies, which were later buried in Aden with full military honours. Questions were asked in the House of Commons and in the Lords, and Cubbon was widely criticized for giving the event unnecessary publicity. I daresay he thought that the story was bound to break anyway, and that it would be better coming from him than from anyone else – but he was generally considered to have made a fool of himself.

I myself wrote letters of condolence to the parents of the dead men. I knew how important it is for people who have lost loved ones to learn exactly what happened; so I wrote as best I could, and also resolved to go down and see Robin's parents in Cornwall when I reached home. On 10 May I sent a report to John Woodhouse, who by then was in Borneo, and in his reply he addressed the point with typical decisiveness:

> It is no use telling wives that a squadron is on training if it is on operations. We never did this previously, and I did not realise it had been done in this case. Someone will be killed, and you cannot delay the news of this in any overt military operations. As SAS were in uniform in Aden, it was pointless not to tell the wives this. This is the lesson – not that Cubbon told the Press.

Later in May Radforce was disbanded, and control of operations passed to Headquarters 39 Brigade, under a new force commander, Brigadier C. H. ('Monkey') Blacker.[1] The SAS continued to patrol vigorously until the end of the month: I myself led several more patrols, and every time we went out into enemy territory, we inevitably carried in our minds all-too-vivid memories of what had happened to our comrades.

I am glad to say that our training stood us in good stead, and we suffered no more casualties. All the same, we finished our tour with the feeling that this had not been an ideal operation. As Mike Wingate Gray remarked in a letter to Woodhouse, written on 11 May, he thought that paratroops could do what we had been doing:

> We are only operating in a super-infantry role of short-range penetration, and tough, well-trained troops could do it equally well. We are only using part of our skills here.

In spite of the limitations, Middle East Headquarters told Mike that the intelligence which we produced was 'the best, indeed the only' intelligence they had ever had on the region. Also during this period Ray England developed a profitable affinity with the Army Air Corps (which he later joined), and pioneered the business of arming light aircraft effectively. Until then an armed helicopter had been simply a helicopter with a man sitting in the open doorway, holding a light machine gun, with which he sprayed hostile elements below; now Ray incited the Corps to fit their aircraft with weapons of every kind.

After the Jebel Akhdar campaign 22nd SAS had shrunk to two squadrons; but soon, as senior officers appreciated the organization's potential, it climbed back to four, including 'G' (for Guards') Squadron, formed when Major General John Nelson was commanding London District, and the Household Division decided to take on sponsorship of one squadron. Even

---

1. A short, quick-moving, energetic cavalryman, Blacker became a General and was knighted in 1969. In 1966 he kindly supported Mike Wingate Gray's recommendation which secured me a place at the Staff College, but later, when he was Adjutant General, he had the sense to resist suggestions that I should become his Military Assistant.

with this extra manpower, the Regiment was under intense pressure, for counter-terrorist operations in Borneo had proved extremely demanding, and we in 'A' Squadron were due to relieve 'D' Squadron there in the summer of 1964. Thus when we pulled out of Aden at the end of May, we knew we were in for a rapid turn-round in England.

In the short leave which followed, my life took an unexpected but decisive turn. Going down to stay with the Beaks at Ramridge in Hampshire, I found that they had organized a drinks party before lunch on a Sunday. What they did not tell me was that, thinking it time I was manoeuvred in the direction of marriage, they had invited a few young people, and telephoned some friendly neighbours, Basil and Margaret Goode, asking them to bring over their two unmarried daughters, Pamela, who was nineteen, and Bridget, who was twenty-six. Pamela was away, so that only Bridget came; but my first sight of this stunning, freckle-faced red-head destroyed my long-standing policy of woman-avoidance at a stroke. As it happened she was in poor form, suffering from a bad cold which had spread into an eye-infection, and she had come to the party only under duress (as indeed had I).

I knew nothing about her, except that her father was a retired army officer, and that she was working as a secretary at a merchant bank in London. Yet nothing could dim my enthusiasm. So excited was I that immediately after lunch I rushed upstairs and shaved off my revolting gingery moustache in the hope that it would increase my chances when the Goodes returned that same evening to look over the house, which was on the market.

Bridget for her part (as I discovered later) thought little of me. I struck her as ill at ease in company, with a habit of looking at my feet and rubbing my hands together, reluctant to be sociable with anybody. The fact that I was in the SAS did not impress her at all: she knew nothing of this clandestine outfit, and anyway at that stage had little interest in the army, as her father's latter career had been mainly on the technical and development side. As for my moustache – she did not even notice that I had one, still less that I shaved it off during the day. Undeterred, I laid plans to see her again as soon as possible, and invited her to have dinner with me the following Saturday.

Before then, however, I had the painful task of going to see Robin Edwards's parents and telling them how he had died. Because they lived so far away in Cornwall, I arranged to stay with them for a night, and as I drove westwards in my MGB, my mind churned in a whirl of conflicting thoughts and emotions. Death, life, despair, hope: sadness about Robin and anxiety about how his parents would react to my visit battled with excitement and elation at the idea of Bridget. The fact that only a few days were left before my squadron set out for Borneo stepped up the emotional pressure immeasurably.

Having wound my way through the lanes of Devon and Cornwall to Padstow, I knocked on the door of the house in some trepidation. I need not have worried. The Edwardses were marvellously warm, and greeted me as if I had been another son. Much as I wanted to tell them the truth, I was nervous about bringing up gory details in front of Robin's mother, and hoped that I could talk to his father and brother alone. The family had anticipated this, and they settled me on a sofa with my back to the door in the living room, while both men sat facing me. So I told them how the tragedy had come about; they asked many questions, and our conversation must have lasted an hour and a half. All that time I was concentrating intently: only when we came to an end did I notice a slight sound behind me and turn round, to find that Mrs Edwards had been standing in the open doorway, listening to every word. Both parents were extraordinarily brave, and the calm courage with which they heard me made an impression which has lasted all my life.

It came to me then, as never before, that when someone dies the tragedy is not so much for him, or her, as for the other people who have to go on with their lives. With one particular and important strand in a family's life broken, the rest of them can only look back on the person lost. In the Services, the danger is that after an initial period of concern friends and relatives feel they have done enough and leave the next of kin alone – whereas what bereaved people really need is long-term help and companionship.

The stoicism of the Edwards family left me heartened, and by the weekend I had done some useful research in another direction. I had found out that Bridget's father, Colonel Basil Goode, had been in the Loyals, but that he was an infantryman with a technical bent, who had concentrated on the development of small arms and in particular of the 105mm tank gun. I had also discovered that Bridget herself had attended agricultural college at Seale-Hayne and achieved a National Diploma in Dairying.

Our dinner duly took place at a restaurant in Winchester, and, little as I knew of her, I felt certain that she was the partner I had unconsciously been looking for. The knowledge which I had gained during the week enabled me to carry on a decidedly unromantic conversation about farming, and in particular about how we had both kept pigs at home (one of hers was called Ermintrude). The evening went reasonably well – although I had a nasty feeling that an army officer talking pigs cut a poor dash in comparison with Bridget's sophisticated London friends. Despite this, when I arranged to drive her back to London I felt emboldened enough to ask if she would marry me. Her answer – as she herself later put it – was 'a flea in the ear', and I really could not blame her. I had known her for just over a week, and seen her four times, only once alone. My own haste could perhaps be excused by the fact that I was about to take off for Borneo; but I was left with the feeling that, even if I might have played my cards more skilfully, I was nevertheless in with a chance.

CHAPTER 15

BORNEO

1964–65

Again we were fighting in the jungle, and again our enemies were Communist-inspired terrorists. The theatre was the nine-hundred-mile frontier that separates the north-western states of Borneo – Sarawak and Sabah, both former British colonies – from the major portion of the island, known as Kalimantan. As in Aden, Britain had traditional links going back many years with the threatened territories, and also with Brunei, the small but wealthy sultanate on the north-west coast, between the two, which was as keen as either of them to preserve its independence. Once again the attempts at subversion were being directed by an outside force, in this case President Sokarno of Indonesia, whose aim in his policy of confrontation was to subvert and eventually take over the new-born Federation of Malaysia, created in 1963.

By then Kalimantan belonged to Indonesia, and when insurgents began to cross the border, the SAS was called in to help defend airfields, or retake them if they were captured; soon, however, its role was switched to that of patrolling the frontier and repelling infiltrators, who had begun coming across the border in armed bands up to fifty strong.

A more daunting task would be hard to imagine – yet it was one to which the SAS was ideally suited. Patrolling in deep jungle, against well-armed and organized terrorists, our soldiers had to exercise all the skills in which they had been trained. Extreme physical endurance, coupled with the ability to live in the jungle, read its signs and outwit native opposition, was only the first of their requirements: they had also to be expert signallers, medical practitioners ready to deal with a wide range of ailments, and above all skilled linguists − for, as in Malaya, the success of our campaign depended largely on communicating with the jungle people so that we gained their confidence and friendship: in other words, won their hearts and minds.

The role of 'A' Squadron, when we arrived in June 1964, was to take over from 'D' Squadron, who had had a gruelling tour, six months long. The debilitated state in which we found them convinced me that six months was too long: henceforth, four-month tours became the norm. The men of 'D' Squadron had not spent all that time on a single stint in the jungle, as we had in Malaya. Far from it − they had been in and out countless times, for John Woodhouse had devised a new policy known as 'Shoot and Scoot', whereby any patrol which bumped the Indos (as we knew them) would fire first and rapidly withdraw. Nevertheless, the soldiers were thoroughly run down, not only by weeks of short rations but also by the mental strain of having to remain alert for weeks on end. The essence of SAS operations is that they must be directed from the highest command level in the theatre, wherever it may be: only in this way can best use be made of the Regiment's unique skills. Nowadays this truth is widely accepted, but it was poorly appreciated thirty years ago. Many people, not understanding our role, still regarded us with suspicion, and some with jealousy, because we always had the best and latest equipment. Critics felt that we had little to contribute to large-scale campaigns.

As soon as I arrived in Brunei, I therefore went to see the Director of Operations, Major-General Walter Walker, at his headquarters on Labuan Island, off the coast of Sabah, just north of Brunei. A remarkable Gurkha officer, Walker was tall, spare, dark-haired and energetic, with a tongue as sharp as his mind, but always prepared to hear what one had to say. At that date he was one of the few senior officers who did understand the SAS: having seen how effectively our people could operate, he had become a stalwart supporter, and consistently battled with the system to obtain everything we needed. He it was who made the famous remark, towards the end of the campaign, that in Borneo one SAS squadron was worth ten infantry battalions, because the intelligence which we provided enabled him to make full use of his other forces.

It was also my job to liaise closely with the commander of the infantry brigade which was the main striking force in the theatre, so that the best possible use could be made of SAS skills within the overall plan of operations. Here too I was lucky, in that Brigadier Harry Tuzo also gave us unequivocal backing.

Our own headquarters were in the Haunted House, a large villa loaned by the Sultan of Brunei, and so called because it was supposed to contain the ghost of a girl murdered during the Second World War by the Japanese equivalent of the Gestapo, who had used the place as their base. To us the ghost was a decided asset, for although it never appeared to any of our own people, it kept locals away, and so was excellent for security. In fact the Haunted House suited us in every way, as it had plenty of space: Operations Room, communications equipment, stores, transport, accommodation for people coming in off a patrol – all fitted in easily.

Within forty-eight hours of arriving, the first of our men were in the jungle. For me, one immediate problem was to control the anger aroused by the murder of Trooper Paddy Condon, who in March had been ambushed, wounded, captured by the Indos and done to death. Condon was an 'A' Squadron man, who had volunteered to join 'D' Squadron when they had sent out an urgent call for a signaller; and the knowledge that one of our own men had been tortured and killed of course made our people furious. Given the close relationships which exist within the SAS, such anger was inevitable; but although anger is useful at times, if it is kept in hand, I knew that it could become dangerous if it ran out of control.

At that stage the Indos were sending patrols across the border, with the aim of forming bases on our side. From these they planned to subvert the rural people, and, later, to cause unrest in more populated districts. Our task was to push them back, and at the same time to win the confidence of the Ibans, the Muruts and the up-country tribes. Our aim, as always, was to fight not for territory but for information, on ground of our own choosing and with forces of our own denomination. But because the Indonesians were moving in huge groups, forty or fifty strong, and our patrols consisted of only three or four men, our policy in any clash remained to shoot and scoot. In an ambush, it is the first few rounds which count: as soon as surprise is lost, a slogging match breaks out, and the strongest side wins; but if you can be really accurate in the first contact, and make sure that it takes place on your own terms, you can impose heavy casualties, and still slip away without casualties of your own.[1]

In the hearts-and-minds campaign, our main targets were the Ibans, traditional head-hunters who reverted enthusiastically to ancient practices whenever they saw a chance. They lived in bamboo long-houses raised on stilts, tilled patches of land around their villages, and pursued jungle game tirelessly. To make ourselves part of their lives and win their trust was a sensitive business. In the early days it was too dangerous for a patrol to sleep in a settlement, because we had to presume that some of the villages might still be on the Indos' side. A patrol would therefore arrive and spend time with the Ibans, getting to know them and treating their sick, before it disappeared back into the jungle. The visit would have to be short – not more than half an hour – so that nobody with treacherous inclinations could run a message to the nearest enemy and enable them to ambush us. At the same time, we had to make the Ibans confident that we could protect them if the Indos reappeared in strength after we had gone – and to this end we devised a system known as 'Step-Up'. In Brunei a platoon of Gurkhas was on stand-by day and night, ready to fly into any trouble-spot at zero notice, and we deliberately exploited the magic of our radio sets to impress the Ibans. 'Right,' we would tell them. 'All we have to do is send a message up into the sky, and help will come very quickly. Just watch.' In twenty minutes or so helicopters full of armed Gurkhas would be landing in the settlement, and everybody was tremendously heartened.

By such means we gradually won the Ibans round – and

---

1. The four-man patrol is the basic unit of any SAS formation, the idea being that it contains men with different specialist skills – in signalling, language and medicine – and that if one of them is incapacitated, two can carry him to safety while the third guards the party's retreat. In the jungle it was tempting to experiment with still smaller patrols, of three or even two men, since they caused even less disturbance; but if a man was badly wounded, his evacuation posed severe problems.

nobody had greater success than Sergeant 'Gypsy' Smith, whose easy, quiet personality made him particularly good at establishing relationships with the natives. A great man for gadgets, he once spent five days building a primitive hydro-electric generator in the village of Talinbakus. Using pieces of signals equipment and a specially ordered bicycle dynamo and lamp, he astonished everyone by lighting up the headman's house with the first electricity ever seen on the frontier.

As in Malaya, we found that the natives themselves were far the best source of intelligence: no matter how skilfully we incomers might move around, we could never have the same feel as the locals for spotting people who were out of place or did not fit in. Just as in an English village the parishioners immediately notice a newcomer, so in the jungle, which was sparsely inhabited, it was the tribesmen who picked up the first traces of novelty – a strange footprint, a broken branch: we depended on them to be our eyes and ears all along the frontier.

One hazard of the hearts-and-minds campaign was that we were frequently obliged to eat with the villagers. Almost always the main item on the menu was boiled pig, which we knew was full of worms, and it had to be washed down by a fiery rice wine called *tapai*. Several of our men became infested with tapeworms, but to have refused food or drink would have undone half our good work.

Among our strongest supporters were the Kalabits, a tribe who lived on a plateau three thousand feet above sea-level, and who, over the past eighteen months, had come to worship the SAS, not least because our medics had treated so many of them. In a letter to my family I wrote:

Many of our soldiers have been asked to take a Kalabit wife. Most of them speak the language to a greater or lesser degree, and they are individually well known in the villages.

I stayed in a small village called Lang Mo. The patrol medic, an experienced man, had a three-hour round every morning, and carried out everything from injections and stitching cuts to delivering babies and pulling out teeth. One day we went to a village further down the river. Here there was tremendous excitement as we arrived, and everyone turned out to meet us. The first event was for me to be introduced as a friend of the patrol's, and this was very necessary, as we could see the shrunken skulls of many unfortunates who have crossed the tribe in years gone by. These heads are all lined up on the rafters just outside the main door of the village, and give visitors many an ugly grin. We have on the whole succeeded in stamping out this unpleasant habit [of head-hunting], but it's in their blood and traditions. Only the other day there was a dispute between two communities, and one of them went off and came back with two heads from the other.

In this village there was a woman very ill in childbirth. The medic was able to deliver the child safely, but the woman died. This caused much sadness, and they spent the night wailing – a terrible noise. We fed the child and got it going on life's way, and then asked the husband who was going to look after it. However, they have no one to look after children when the mother dies, and they would not adopt our method of bottle-feeding it. This was too big a step for them. The result is that they suffocate the child and bury it with the mother, and this is what they did in this case.

Describing another foray into the jungle, I remarked that if we made a mistake shooting the rapids on the river, 'God or the Devil is likely to be our next companion.' I was pleased to record that during the fourteen days of the patrol I had lost ten pounds, and that the jungle, though much the same as that in Malaya, was even more sparsely populated, so that we had moved for days on end without coming across any habitation:

I've never seen so many leeches. I once pulled off twenty-five in five minutes, and then had to give up, as I could not keep up with the rate at which I was picking them up. Leech competitions are great fun. You collect some competitors and each put five shillings in the kitty. You then choose a thirsty-looking leech – all about the same size – and on the word 'Go' put it on any part of yourself. You then leave it, and the first person to have his leech drop off full of blood is the winner. Better than a transfusion!

Such reports make it clear that I did from time to time manage to escape the routine of headquarter life and make off into the jungle; but, as in the Radfan, I had problems resolving the conflicting pressures on me as Squadron Commander. Patrols in Borneo were uncomfortable, dangerous and demanding, and I felt that I had a duty to know what conditions were like, particularly towards the end of our first tour, when, having made it almost impossible for the Indos to operate on our side of the frontier, we began to go on the offensive and work up the concept of cross-border patrols. These were top secret, and clearly they involved even higher risks. More than ever I was anxious that I should know the form myself: otherwise I might ask people to do things which were impossible, and put them in unnecessary danger.

My constant urge, then, was to join patrols; but I also knew that my job was to remain at base and direct operations – a responsibility of which I was frequently reminded by John Woodhouse, who in October 1964 wrote with his usual succinctness:

> I have no objection to you going once on a 'special op.' [i.e., a cross-border patrol], but it is quite wrong for you to do it more than once. Not necessary, and would be considered hogging the limelight or far worse gong-hunting, however pure your motives really are. Troop operations are for troop commanders, not you or me. Squadron ops for you, not me. Don't read this to mean that I am not going to visit your Squadron. That is different! A bore, I know.

I was not helped, in this respect, by the fact that I had Lawrence Smith as my Sergeant Major. A tremendous man, on whose experience and judgment I could rely completely, he also had a knack of vanishing into the jungle at the first whiff of an opportunity. I could not forbid him to go, because it would not have been fair to keep an aggressive, front-line leader permanently sitting around in headquarters; but whenever he did disappear, I was effectively pinned down, as I insisted that one or other of us, with our extensive experience, should be at base to deal with emergencies.

In those days the spirit and ideas of John Woodhouse influenced us all strongly. Not only did he visit us whenever he could: he also wrote frequently – and never did he express his view of

SAS ethics more clearly than in a rebuke to one of my colleagues:

> I understand that relations between you and some of your troop have been strained. I assume that you are still heart-and-mind dedicated to making a success of your SAS career. On that assumption, and my conviction that you have the intelligence and imagination and basic knowledge necessary to command SAS troops, I am going to give you advice which, if you can follow it, will lead to your success.
>
> My personal knowledge of you is based on the short time we spent together in Malaya. I will use an example from that to begin my advice. At the end of a not very tiring day we stopped on a ridge some distance from water. You sent the two soldiers to get it. In the SAS as an officer, particularly in your first year or two, you have got to prove your enthusiasm, your superiority in physical endurance, and your SAS skills, to your men.
>
> If you had gone for the water, this enthusiasm to take on more than your share of the burdens would not have passed unnoticed by the soldiers. In the SAS you will never get the devoted support of your troops until you have proved to them by your personal example that you will never spare yourself physically or in any other way.
>
> Next, it is your duty (which should also be your natural wish) to do the best possible for your men ... You will never succeed unless you like soldiers. If you find that soldiers in general irritate you, then frankly you are in the wrong regiment, for in none will you be in closer and more frequent contact with them.
>
> Lastly you must subdue any embarrassment and swallow your pride and tell your Troop that you recognise that things are not as they should be, and tell them briefly that you accept there can only be one person at fault if this is the case – yourself. If you can do this, and do as I advise you, you will not find them unresponsive.
>
> I am very keen for you to succeed, so try to accept what I have written.

One of Woodhouse's strengths was his realization that the judgment of personalities was subjective, and always needed a double check. People in the Regiment had elephantine memories, and never forgot any lapse which was thought to have impaired operational efficiency: it was said that if you had once been convicted of making a dangerous noise by rattling your mess tins on the side of a *bukit*, you were saddled with a reputation for incompetence which you could never shake off. Woodhouse, however, saw the value of moving people around, and giving them a chance in a new environment.

To live up to his standards was a constant challenge, in headquarters as much as in the jungle. It was important that all SAS activity had a clear purpose: we could not risk people's lives purely for the sake of patrolling, and we therefore planned patrols with the utmost care, dividing the jungle into separate areas and fitting every operation into a matrix, so that our intelligence-gathering covered the frontier with maximum efficiency, and there was no risk of one patrol straying into another's territory. I personally briefed every patrol commander on his mission before he left, and debriefed him when he returned.

No matter how much care we took, we kept suffering casualties. During my two tours with 'A' Squadron we lost twenty-five per cent of its fighting troops killed or wounded. In purely numerical terms, this meant relatively few men – about fifteen out of sixty; but as a proportion, it was exceptionally high. We were dogged by the fear that if we lost a lot of men quickly, we would not be able to replace them, because there was no pool from which trained men could be drawn. Writing home after we had had a man killed – the fourth in only three months – I reflected on the peculiar pull and loyalty which the SAS exerted:

> I had a charming letter from his mother, whom I wrote to. She said how sad it was, but that he had been devoted to the SAS and would not have been happy anywhere else in the army. Nor would he have fitted in. She finished up by thanking the Squadron and me for all the help we had given her, and hoped some of us would visit her when we got home. It is very humbling when people can be so generous in such a sad loss.
>
> All the parents of the men killed this year have taken the same line. I suppose it is a reflection on the *esprit de corps* that the SAS builds up among its members, and some part of it spreads to the families. Most of the officers and men here do not really fit in in normal units of the army, and that's why they're here in the SAS, which is not like anything else in the Services. All the men are as if in a select

club, and have a very tight and jealously-guarded exclusive-
ness attached to their membership. Once SAS, always SAS.
I must say, I for one don't feel I'm in the army, but only in
the SAS.

Engrossed as I was in the jungle war, I was also waging an active
campaign on the home front. On my way out to Borneo I had
paused in Singapore to send Bridget a length of blue-and-gold
brocaded silk. Later I found that at first this had embarrassed
her, but that in due course she had it made into a striking
evening dress. Now my strategy was simple: to maintain a steady
bombardment of letters, by which (I hoped) her indifference or
resistance – from that distance I could not tell which it was –
would in the end be worn down. The fact that she scarcely
answered did discourage me to a certain degree, but not enough
to make me lay off. 'Things are going quite satisfactorily,
woman-wise,' I wrote to my family in August 1964. 'Letters are
very much a form of remote-control, but for the time being all
is well, on the basis of not too quick, not too slow.'

Unknown to me, another factor was working in my favour.
Bridget's family, feeling it was time she got married, had started
to agitate gently on my behalf, urging her to reply to my letters
and take more interest. So, brick by brick, the wall began to
crumble, and I sensed a breakthrough when, at last yielding to
persistent requests from Borneo and pressure at home, she
allowed her sister Pamela to take some photographs of her, and
sent me one small print, which I treasure to this day.

When our first tour ended in October, I headed home in a
fever of anticipation, not even sure that she would be prepared
to see me; but I was winged on my way by a generous personal
signal from the Director of Operations, Walter Walker, praising
the contribution of the Squadron and sending 'thanks for a job
most splendidly done'.

While still in Borneo I had taken advice from Poppet Codrington on how to make the best impression on Bridget when I
reached London. 'Get her some flowers,' Poppet had said – and
so, determined to move things on apace, I armed myself with a
bunch and went round to the little house on the corner of
Cheval Place, off the Brompton Road, which Bridget was sharing

with two girl-friends. When she opened the door, I thrust the flowers awkwardly into her hands, and was rewarded with a warm embrace and a supper of grilled lamb chops, which I praised lavishly.

Whether or not it was the flowers that did the trick, our relationship blossomed at extraordinary speed. So close had we suddenly become that, next day, I took Bridget round to meet the Codringtons in Tite Street, and that weekend we went down to stay with David Lyon and his first wife Nicola at their home in Berkshire. The knowledge that I would have to return to Borneo in May charged proceedings with enormous urgency. Within a few more days we were engaged, and we set the date of our wedding as 13 February 1965. When Bridget's parents sent out the invitations with the letters 'MC' after my name, many of her parents' generation imagined that she was about to marry someone much older, who had won the medal during the Second World War.

Inevitably, the imminence of a wedding caused ructions in my family. Granny Lawley was by then too frail to leave home, but Joyce made a terrific, predictable fuss, her main aim being to prevent my mother attending the ceremony. Kitty would let the family down, she announced. She could not possibly come to the church, or to the reception. Apart from anything else, she had nothing suitable to wear. Until the last minute Joyce prevaricated about her own movements, endlessly discussing alternative ways of travelling to London, and speaking frequently of hire-cars.

Bridget's mother handled all this brilliantly, soothing Joyce with calming reassurances. Bridget herself, visiting Old Place for the first time, was astonished to find the dark and apparently ancient house crammed with paper: every step on both staircases was stacked at the sides with old correspondence, newspapers and magazines, for Joyce had become a compulsive hoarder, unable to throw anything away.

Officially, my Squadron was back at Hereford, and the men were busy catching up on their training courses; but I found that I needed to devote a good deal of time to personal administration. One early decision was that Bridget and I would buy a house of our own, and hold on to it as long as we could, no matter where I might be posted, even if it meant that we would be separated from time to time. We were determined that, if we had children, they should grow up in a firm base, rather than constantly move about and have to keep making new friends, as many Service families do. After a frantic search we found a house which suited us perfectly. A typical Herefordshire cottage, rendered and painted white, it stood alone on a tiny crossroads, and had been nicely done up by the previous owners, the Woottons, who had also kept the large garden in immaculate order. The price, £5700, was on the high side, but reflected the house's pleasantly isolated position.

We were married at Holy Trinity, Brompton (Bridget's parish church) on a cold and blowy February day – the thirteenth was a Saturday. Partly because everything had happened so fast, the occasion seemed particularly fresh and magical to both of us. My mother came to the service and caused no embarrassment to anyone; Joyce, at the last minute, declined to attend. The reception was held at the Army & Navy Club in Pall Mall, and afterwards we flew off to Gibraltar, where we hired a car and crossed the straits on a ferry for our honeymoon in Morocco. There we had an idyllic time, spoilt only – in Bridget's eyes – by the fact that I felt obliged to report whenever we were near a British consulate, in case some crisis had blown up and I was wanted for duty.

Back in England in the middle of March, we were at once caught up in a tragedy, for two SAS men, Corporal Richardson and Trooper O'Toole, were drowned off the Welsh coast in a canoeing exercise. Hardly had we come home when we had to attend their funeral – and the sight of me in Service Dress uniform, with medals, had a profound effect on Bridget: then, and forever afterwards, she associated the uniform with death. Furthermore, she suddenly realized that she had an obligation to look after the wives of people in the Regiment. O'Toole had been unmarried, but Richardson left a widow – an intelligent girl of high calibre, and Bridget, who is basically very shy, was faced with the difficult and delicate task of comforting her.

Because there had been a delay in completing the purchase of our cottage, we had to spend six weeks in a small modern house on an estate near Hereford racecourse. With big plate-glass windows front and back, and only a glass partition between the rooms, the place was like a fish-bowl, and we were delighted to escape to our older and more solid house in the country. There we discovered, to our joy, that Bridget was pregnant, and I, determined to create a proper home, set to in the garden, hopefully planting vegetables, even though I knew I would be away when most of them grew to fruition.

All too soon 'A' Squadron's second Borneo tour came round, and in May I was off again, leaving my young wife in a state of acute loneliness. I do not think either of us had realized how bad this would be; but for Bridget it was a dire and depressing transformation, from being an independent girl in London, going to a busy office every day, and surrounded by friends, to becoming a dependent wife, pregnant, and stuck out in the country, in a house where the baker delivered bread three times a week, but otherwise she scarcely met a human being unless she walked to the shop in the village.

She did have other wives for company in Hereford, some twelve miles away – among them Sybil Wingate Gray, whose husband Mike had just taken over from John Woodhouse as Commanding Officer, and Buffy Slim, wife of John Slim, now Second-in-Command. Both were extremely good to her: they brought her into army life, and became stalwart friends. All the same, she did not enjoy those few months. One factor which I think helped her survive was my habit of being very frank with her about what I was doing. In general, SAS men are encouraged to tell their wives as little as possible about their movements, and many tell them nothing at all; but I quickly saw that Bridget had the rare ability to keep her mouth shut, and I felt I could share everything with her, whether the details were to do with military affairs or our own finances.

Back in Borneo, we heard details of one of the most extraordinary feats of survival known even to the SAS. On 25 February, while Bridget and I had been on honeymoon, a cross-border patrol from 'D' Squadron had run into an ambush, and two men had been seriously wounded: Trooper Ian Thomson had been shot through the left thigh, high up, and Sergeant Eddie Lillico (known as 'Geordie') through the pelvis, the exiting bullet carrying away a three-inch chunk of his right buttock. Through superhuman courage, presence of mind and self-control, both men had survived and been rescued. Thomson's feat, in crawling back towards the border, was itself an epic performance, but Lillico's was barely credible. Having spent a night curled up under foliage in the jungle, barely able to move, dozy from morphia and loss of blood, he had come round to find a follow-up party of Indonesians within a few yards of him, and when an RAF rescue helicopter came prowling overhead, hunting for him, he forbore to switch on his SARBE search-and-rescue homing beacon, because he knew that if he brought the aircraft in, it would offer the enemy an easy target. Then he waited for the Indos to move off, and by a herculean effort dragged himself on arms and elbows more than two hundred yards, until he was right on the border ridge. There, at last light, Flying Officer David Collinson, RAF, made his nineteenth search-pass, picked up the message from Lillico's beacon, and by inspired flying brought his helicopter in low enough to winch him out. Lillico later received the Military Medal, and if ever a man's conduct vindicated our high claims for the quality of people in the SAS, it was his.

In Brunei again, we found many changes in key personnel. Walter Walker had finished his tour without the recognition that he deserved, returning to the United Kingdom with a Distinguished Service Order, but not the knighthood with which a less outspoken officer in his position would surely have been rewarded. He had defended Malaysian Borneo with rare vigour, managing the difficult political side of his command no less skilfully than the military operation; but the exceptional directness with which he championed his forces – not least his beloved Gurkhas – had made him unpopular in high places. In his determination to secure what we needed, he had never hesitated to confront his superiors head-on. Helicopters were a prime example: he saw that without more helicopters we could not fight the war properly, and when the system would not provide enough aircraft, he attacked Whitehall and Headquarters, Far East, like a tiger, even going so far as to make a public protest – and in the end he got what he wanted, though ultimately at his own expense.

His successor as Director of Operations, George Lea, was of course no stranger to us: he had commanded 22nd SAS during

my time in Malaya, and now we were delighted to see him
again. Because of the success of the Special Forces' operations,
and the demand for more troops of the same kind, a half-
squadron of the New Zealand SAS had arrived in April, and 1
Squadron of the Australian SAS in May. A small SAS theatre
headquarters had been set up on Labuan Island, and from now
on either Mike Wingate Gray, the Commanding Officer, or his
Second-in-Command, John Slim, was present all the time. At a
lower level, my policy of attending SAS selection courses as an
observer, and deliberately choosing the most promising candidates for my Squadron, now began to pay off. Three new Troop
Commanders arrived on the same day – and three better men
would have been hard to find. In the course of their distinguished careers Mike Wilkes and John Foley both became Generals, and Malcolm McGillivray, after admirable service in the
SAS, proved too independent a spirit to be fettered by the army,
leaving to seek his fortune in Scotland.

Returning to the jungle, we found that 'D' Squadron had
begun cross-border operations in earnest, and it was our task to
carry them on. In this we were backed at the highest level by
Denis Healey, who had become the Labour Minister of Defence
in October, and who – rather surprisingly, for a Socialist politician – had a realistic grasp of military matters, understood the
cost-effectiveness of the SAS, and gave us his full support. This
demanded no mean courage on his part, for although we greatly
hoped that nobody would discover what we were doing, it was
an important personal and political decision for him.

In the event, we kept our movements so secret that the Indonesians never really knew what we were doing, and they never
managed to prove anything, for we took every care to leave no
trace of our presence on their territory. Ray England, in particular, showed amazing ingenuity, disguising the tell-tale tread of
our boots and devising special bags which caught empty cartridge cases as they spewed out of machine guns.

These patrols offered another instance of how the SAS was
(and is) prepared to change tactics as the situation demands.
Instead of small parties of three or four men, we now needed
powerfully armed forces of full troop strength – sixteen men –
to take on the large bands of Indos likely to be found across the

border. Preparations for every patrol were immensely thorough. A week or so before the men departed I would have them in for a briefing; then, nearer the day, they would rehearse their standard operating procedures in front of me. Especially if they were planning to set an ambush, I would take them through every detail, so that we at base would be thoroughly in their minds, and that much better able to help if they ran into trouble. For instance, we would rehearse their action on capture, and what they might or might not say under interrogation. We would check that each man was carrying his escape money in two different places, so that if one lot were found, he would still not lack the means to buy his way out.

The actual packing of bergens was a lengthy process: every ounce counted, and it was vital to stow things in roughly the order in which they would be needed. To me the weight of bergens was critical: a soldier carrying too big a load is inclined to crash along head-down, backside up, without paying proper attention to his surroundings – the classic way to blunder into an ambush. I therefore limited the weight of bergens to sixty pounds, and began to have them weighed at the last minute, on the airstrip, before the patrol went in by helicopter. Anyone overweight had to remove something – and once word of this rule went round, excess loads became a thing of the past.

The patrol would be landed as close to its objective as was compatible with maintaining security: the shorter the distance which people had to walk to the frontier, the better. The border itself was unmarked but easily recognized, for it followed a pronounced ridge, beyond which everything was enemy territory. At first we were not allowed to penetrate more than three thousand yards; even so, to minimize the number of trips in and out, patrols went in for three weeks at a time, and this meant that rations had to be scaled down from 4000 calories a day to barely 2000 – a regime on which men could survive for a limited period, but one which steadily diminished their physical reserves. As time went by we managed to build up caches of food, either buried in the ground or stored in special containers in trees, with cryptic signs leading to them; but in that saturated environment it was difficult to make food keep for long, and the wild pigs had phenomenal powers of excavation.

Most patrols had a specific objective: to ambush a river or track, to capture a prisoner, to photograph particular places. When we discovered that the enemy were communicating by telephone, I sent out Mike Wilkes with a patrol to tap the line. This was no easy task, as the cable was slung on trees beside a path used by Indonesians, and concentration on fixing up tape recorders diminished the soldiers' ability to detect people approaching. Nevertheless, they secured a useful intercept, and our Intelligence people kept quiet about how the information had been obtained.

By June 1965 we had established a regimental headquarters in Kuching, the capital of Sarawak, on the coast some four hundred miles south-west of Brunei. Our base there – similar in many ways to the Haunted House – was known as Pea Green House, or PGH for short. One day I was sitting on the verandah, dressed only in a pair of drawers cellular and flip-flops as I read the newspapers, when a car drove up below. There was somebody standing near me, and I casually asked, 'Who's that?'

'It's the Director of Operations,' he replied.

'Christ!' I leapt to my feet. Clearly the General was going to hit the Ops Room in about thirty seconds, or however long it took him to climb the stairs. There was nothing I could do but receive him in my state of undress. Yet things were even worse than I thought: up the stairs with George Lea came the High Commissioner for Malaysia, Lord Head. Without flinching at my appearance, they made straight for me and shook hands.

'Sorry, sir,' I said. 'We weren't quite expecting you.'

Head was magnificent. A keen supporter of the SAS since its inception – and indeed, as a friend of David Stirling's, one of the founder members – he now made it seem that to be met by a half-naked junior officer in total disarray was an everyday occurrence. At the first opportunity I grabbed a pair of trousers and dragged them on, realizing to my horror that the visitors had come for a briefing. Quickly we sat them down while the Operations Staff rallied round, and I started the briefing still doing up my fly-buttons. Considering the circumstances, things went off fairly well, and as the VIPs departed, they seemed pleased. I, anything but pleased, discovered that the officer at Brigade Headquarters responsible for arranging visits had omitted us – the people who mattered most – from his distribution list. Later, when Head became Colonel Commandant of the SAS, we often joked about the incident, but at the time it was acutely embarrassing for me.

'Kuching is much more civilized than Brunei,' I told my mother on 10 June, but my standard complaint – that I could not go into the jungle as often as I wanted – remained the same. One consolation was that I travelled a great deal by helicopter, and saw much of the country from the air; but it was not the same as being on the ground.

With cross-border operations in full flow, I felt a greater need than ever to know what things were like at the front; and when Mike Wingate Gray came down to Kuching for a spell, I was able to join a patrol led by Sergeant Maurice Tudor. By then – September 1965 – we were allowed 10,000 yards across the border, and our aim was to ambush the River Ayer Hitam, which we knew the terrorists were using. Because the numbers of enemy going up and down the river were substantial, we went as a whole troop, sixteen strong, with myself and Geordie Low, my faithful signaller, tagging along at the back.

I was well aware that for the rest of the patrol the presence of outsiders was a bore. The members of 4 Troop all knew each other intimately, and functioned together with the smoothness of a well-oiled machine. The addition of new people was a potential irritant: we were not in the minds of the rest of them, and although in theory there should be no problems, we could not be certain how we would work together in a crisis. For Maurice, there was the additional aggravation of having an officer behind him, not interfering, but probably thinking critical thoughts about the way he was leading. For me, there was the irritation of not being in control, since I was merely a guest or passenger – of having different ideas about how things should be done, and of being obliged to suppress them.

In the event we managed to sublimate these potential difficulties. The stretch of the river for which we were aiming lay in flat ground: to reach the bank Maurice and his men had to work their way through a dried-out mangrove swamp, while I and Geordie stayed a few yards behind to secure their return route and guard their bergens. As we waited, Geordie opened up communications with Squadron Headquarters and began to tap out coded Morse messages – but not for long. The patrol had scarcely reached their ambush positions when, at 1.45 p.m., two long-boats slid into sight, each with a crew of eight soldiers. Never moving, the SAS men allowed the craft to come well into their chosen killing zone before they opened up. Two minutes later, every Indonesian was dead; one boat had sunk, and the other grounded.

From our back-stop position we heard the volley of intensive rifle and machine-gun fire burst out, and just as suddenly stop. Seconds later members of the patrol came hurtling back with the news that they had glimpsed two more long-boats, and that a follow-up operation was almost certainly under way. As we pulled out rapidly, incoming mortar bombs confirmed that the Indonesians were reacting angrily to their loss. (It is no fun being mortared in jungle, as bombs detonate in the tree-tops, and hurl shrapnel downwards.) We slipped away, heading back for the border, but on a roundabout route, and by nightfall we had thrown the enemy off our tracks.

Having gone that far, I was loath to return prematurely to my desk in Headquarters; and so, once we were well clear, Geordie Low and I slipped away on our own and disappeared into the jungle for a few more days. In tactical terms, our little patrol was of limited value, although it did give me first-hand under-standing of the pressure under which my soldiers were operating. I also had a chance to practise signalling, at which I was still inefficient, but determined to become competent so that, like everyone else in the Regiment, I should have a special skill.

Concerted action enabled us to deal the Indonesians a series of damaging blows. Intelligence provided by SAS patrols, exploited by a competent back-up force of Gurkhas and British infantry, enabled us to hit the insurgents in their sanctuary areas just over the border and deny them the security of bases to which they could easily retire. This combination of good intelligence and fast reaction, running in parallel with the hearts-and-minds campaign, played a major role in the ultimate victory of the Western forces.

Whenever I was stuck at base, whether in Brunei or Kuching, I developed the habit – which I have tried to maintain ever since – of writing to Bridget every day. There was plenty of opportunity, for we had to mount guard every night, and – this being the SAS – the Squadron Commander did his stint along with everyone else. Letter-writing was an ideal way to help pass the time, even if one was limited by considerations of security as to what one could say.

There was also plenty of time to worry – about Bridget, about our future, about money. Having always lived more or less free in the army, I realized belatedly that the combination of a house, a wife and a baby on the way had placed a severe strain on my finances. Again and again in my letters I agonized about amounts which now seem ludicrously small. When my mess bill rose to the dizzy height of £9 12s a month, I remarked, 'Terrible how it adds up. It's the booze that does it, I'm afraid.' I instructed Bridget to sell my MG, if possible for at least £700. She herself had a scarlet Mini, number HOT 515 and known as Red Hot, and I decided that we would have to manage with one car for the moment. Hearing that there were going to be defence cuts, I considered the idea of taking an early retirement pension; 'If we got the chance of, say, £6000, and £500 a year for life, it would need very serious consideration indeed to see whether I stayed in or not.' In July 1965 I wrote: 'Money rears its ugly head again. Despite a £31 travel claim and a massive local overseas allowance of £41, untaxed, I overspent by £45 again last month.' When Bridget complained mildly that I was keeping her short, I sent her a monthly bank statement so that she could see where all the money was going.

> My monthly pay at UK rates is £125, while our outgoings are: mortgage interest, £26, life policy £21, allowance to you £40, leaving me with £38 a month. We have to find everything out of that – car tax, insurance, rates, repairs, mess bill, etc. The fact is I'm afraid it just won't work, and with junior on the way it will work even less.
>
> We have to remember that the day I leave the SAS, I lose 30s a day in pay, or £540 a year due to loss of rank and para pay . . . You will note I've drawn only £5 16s in cash. We will survive OK till the end of my tour, but may then

seriously have to consider selling the house. You poor old thing! You should have married one of those rich London bankers after all. Life would be so much simpler.

Our tour came to a close at the end of October 1965. The war dragged on into another year, but in April 1966 the Indonesians began to sue for peace, and a settlement was reached in August. It warmed our hearts to hear Denis Healey tell the House of Commons that future chroniclers would record the campaign as 'one of the most efficient uses of military force in the history of the world'.

As we prepared to head for home, I felt that I had been extra-ordinarily privileged to hold a command with such strong political overtones. For much of each tour I had been the senior SAS officer in theatre, and as such I frequently had to deal with senior politicians, among them the High Commissioner Lord Head, the Conservative Defence Minister James Ramsden and his Labour successor Denis Healey. For an officer still only thirty-one, this was invaluable experience.

On a personal level, I was pleased and surprised to receive a Bar to my Military Cross; but this was only one of many awards won by 'A' Squadron during our time in Borneo. Lawrence Smith also won a richly deserved Military Cross for his part in directing a substantial battle – only the second MC won by a warrant officer since the Second World War – and Ray England and Corporal Jimmy Catterall won Mentions in Despatches. I saw my own award as reflecting the merit of the Squadron as a whole – and in any case I had no cause to feel complacent, for nothing could diminish my alarm at the idea of becoming a parent. 'I just can't see myself making stupid clucking noises, and generally being a good and indulgent father,' I wrote to Bridget. I warned her that I intended to push a pram only 'in a remote lane, provided there's no moon, and preferably after midnight, when there are fewer people about.'

CHAPTER 16

HOME FRONT

1965–69

I came home on leave to the cottage late in November 1965, to find Bridget heavily pregnant, with the baby due in the New Year. Our plan was that it should be born in the National Health Service ward at the County Hospital in Hereford, and we had every intention that I should be present at the birth; but at the last minute our hopes were frustrated, when the hospital authorities refused to allow me into the delivery room. This was sad for both of us, because Bridget's first birth was magically simple: she was left alone in the second-stage labour ward for so long, before the midwife reappeared, that the baby more or less arrived on its own – a beautiful, dark-haired girl, born on 2 January 1966, whom we called Nicola, after David Lyon's wife.

For a few precious weeks I lived at home, driving in to work at the barracks in Hereford every morning. After months of fruitless advertising, Bridget had managed to sell my beloved MG to one of my SAS Troop Commanders, John Foley (who later became Commander of British Forces, Hong Kong): when she knew that a potential buyer was coming to look at it, she had it specially tuned and took it out for a final run down a new stretch of dual-carriageway near Monmouth. The fact that it went sweetly up to 120mph no doubt helped sell it – but I mourned its absence, and had to make do for the time being with a drab grey van for transport to and from the camp. The soldiers were busy on courses, brushing up their individual skills, as always while in the United Kingdom, and there was plenty of administrative work on which to catch up. Then suddenly in March we were off again, back to Aden, for an unexpected three-month tour. This was tough on Bridget – and for the first time she really appreciated the bitter truth that in our life, whenever there was a clash between family and military interests, the Regiment would always come first.

The tour proved less interesting than we hoped, and only a pale shadow of our operations two years earlier. Again we were deployed up-country, astride the Dhala road, and our task was to intercept convoys of trucks trying to smuggle arms from the Yemen to the south. After our last experience in those precipitous and craggy hills, I did not want to risk lives unnecessarily, and our work consisted mostly of long periods of surveillance, during which we kept watch on the wadis which we knew the enemy were using.

My thoughts often turned to home and family, and when I wrote saying that we should christen our next daughter Phillida, Bridget became highly suspicious, supposing that somehow, as the British presence in Aden crumbled and disintegrated, I had met a stunning blonde with that name. In fact that was exactly what had happened – but the girl in question was only about four years old, the enchanting daughter of an expatriate friend, who was working out there.

Back home in June, I had hardly settled down when the Squadron was off once more, this time on a three-week exercise in the United Kingdom. Then Mike Wingate Gray asked me to write a report on the Borneo campaign, which was coming to a successful end, and as I laboured at this I realized to my dismay that my time with the SAS was almost up.

I was due to leave the Regiment in August, and my immediate future looked grim. Mike and Bridget together had persuaded me that I must go through Staff College, without which I would have very little chance of worthwhile further promotion; and, thanks to Mike's intercession, I had been awarded a place on the course starting that autumn, without having passed the entrance exam – one of the few people in history to have beaten the system in this respect. Mike argued that if an officer had been so continuously committed to operations that he had not had time to prepare adequately for the exam, he could be granted an exemption; and his advocacy, generously backed by that of the Divisional Commander, Major General Monkey Blacker, won me a place. As a preliminary to Staff College, I was due to take a three-month course at the Royal College of Military Science at Shrivenham, in Wiltshire.

I could not believe that I was leaving the SAS for good: like everyone else in the Regiment, I had become infected by its habits, principally that of working all-out, not because anyone was telling me to, but because I wanted to and enjoyed it. Like everyone else, I had struggled to maintain high standards. Nevertheless, try as I might, I occasionally lapsed, and once, not long before I left, I fell victim to the system of voluntary fines which John Woodhouse had instituted. If someone was late, or forgot an appointment, or lost some item of equipment, he would be fined, and the money would go towards the next squadron party. The higher the rank of the offender, the larger the fine – an unofficial but democratic system, which kept people on their toes. One morning in the summer of 1966 I went to fetch my van, to drive to work, only to discover that I had lost the key of the garage. By the time I had cut the padlock with a hacksaw, I was late for the 0800 muster parade; people decided that, as I was a major, the next party should be a particularly sustained and high-octane occasion, and I had to pay up £50 – a lot of money in those days.

Even when I left the Regiment, I clung to old habits, among them that of Nosey Parking. This began as a military discipline, but grew into something which permeated civilian life as well. In the SAS I made it a rule that all cars must be parked nose-to-the-road, so that in any operational situation the driver could make an instant get-away. Nosey Parking, with bonnet to wall or kerb, was an offence for which drivers automatically received a fine – and in a light-hearted way everyone informed on everyone else, to swell party funds. Much to Bridget's irritation, especially when we arrived somewhere late for dinner, and I fiddled about manoeuvring the car to suit my whims, I kept up the practice at home.

Shrivenham was ghastly. In purely physical terms the College was perfectly acceptable – the brick-built halls of residence offered reasonable accommodation, and the food was not bad – but the course itself was disastrous. It was supposed to give us an introduction to the impact of science on defence technology, and its concept was good; the trouble lay in the execution. The teaching was far too academic, and pitched way over the heads of officers who had no scientific bent or training.

Rather than abandon our cottage prematurely, Bridget stayed there with Nicola while I commuted back and forth. I would drive over to Shrivenham – about seventy miles – early on Monday morning, return home on Wednesday (a half-day), motor back to Wiltshire on Thursday, and home again on Friday night. Our aim, in which I feel sure we were right, was to create a stable environment for Nicola and whatever children might follow her.

When I went to the Staff College, however, we had to move and live at Camberley. We let the cottage fully furnished to a couple called Crawshaw, both doctors, who proved ideal tenants. Our quarter in Queen Elizabeth Road, Camberley (for which we had to pay rent), seemed a poor swap: an old-fashioned house, with reasonably sized rooms, but cold and unfriendly, with a coke-fired boiler, and a garden full of sour, sandy soil which grew hardly anything.

By the time my course began, in September 1966, I was ready to buckle down to a bit of learning; having rejected the opportunity at school, I thought it time I caught up. I decided to work as hard as possible, since I felt I owed it to the people who had gone out of their way to win me a place. Nevertheless, I found the going tough: too late, I saw how foolish I had been, and now began to pay for my earlier academic idleness. Even so, I saw that the course was first class, and it taught me a great deal. Much of the early curriculum was focused on staff duties: we learnt formal methods of writing administrative instructions, operation orders and so on; there was also a good deal of essay- and paper-writing, and this I found a substantial help in improving my powers of expression.[1] Outside, we stamped about the countryside on TEWTS – tactical exercises without troops – during which we would decide how to attack various features if we

---

1. Bridget used to correct and improve my essays – and it was standard practice for wives to help in this way, typing out finished copies and so on. One student who had his English severely criticized rejected the strictures on the grounds that the essay had been written by his wife, who had a 2:2 in English – whereupon the member of the Directing Staff responsible retorted: 'Well, it was corrected by *my* wife, and she's got a 2:1 in English!'

had real forces at our disposal. After fighting in numerous live campaigns, I found some of this rather tame – but I took comfort from the fact that I was learning every day.

If life on the work front tended to lack stimulation, that on the home front turned all too fraught. At the end of 1966 Bridget became pregnant again, but after less than three months we had a sudden scare when she threatened to miscarry. In a nightmare scene an ambulance with its siren wailing rushed both of us to the Cambridge Military Hospital at Aldershot. After treatment there, and a few days under observation, she returned to our quarter apparently all right, but almost immediately the trouble started again, and our army doctor told her that the only thing to do was to have a complete bed-rest for the next six weeks, not getting up under any circumstances. So began a period of the utmost discomfort for her and anxiety for both of us. Luckily my mother had improved so much by then that she came to stay, and she eased our predicament by cooking and generally helping to run the house, while Nicola went to stay with Bridget's mother.

Difficult as it was for us, this period helped my mother a good deal, since it kept her busy and made her feel needed. In 1965 the Lytes had moved up to Prestbury, near Cheltenham, and she had gone with them; but soon after that her increasing independence – which I had always encouraged – led her to seek accommodation in an hotel, and in November 1966 she had moved to the Milland Place Hotel, near Liphook in Sussex. By this stage, fifteen years after her accident, she had recovered to such an extent that strangers, meeting her for the first time, did not realize how ill she had been, and merely thought her rather vague.

After six weeks Bridget cautiously began getting up again, and the last months of the pregnancy passed normally, and in the early hours of 18 September 1967, a little bundle of trouble called Phillida, with a mop of coppery curls, came into the world fighting. I was once again excluded from the birth, because complications developed, but all three of us are eternally grateful to Colonel Brown, the obstetrician, for the baby's safe delivery. Our problems at home were compounded by the fact that Nicola – a bad sleeper from birth – still would not go through the night without waking up several times. The later the hour, the livelier and more demanding she became, and now, with a new baby keeping us on the move as well, we both grew zombified with exhaustion.

During this period I made the disturbing discovery that my hearing had deteriorated more than I thought. The doctor who gave me a check-up thought the trouble had been brought on by firing the new, high-velocity self-loading rifle, which came in at the end of the 1950s, when we were first in Oman. (At that date nobody appreciated how much damage this could cause, and we never thought of wearing ear-defenders while training.) Threatened with being down-graded medically, which would have effectively brought my army career to an end, I argued that an officer of my seniority did not need to have hearing as acute as men more junior, and that after so much money and time had been invested in my training, it would be better for the army to keep me on, even if I was slightly deaf, than to get rid of me. My appeal was accepted, on condition that I would take a special test every three years . . . and, whether by good luck or good management, I contrived to be abroad every time the date came round.

In October tension rose with the approach of the day on which we students would get our Black Bag postings – so called because the fateful documents were brought down from London in a black briefcase. These postings were crucial, as they determined the shape of our careers during the next all-important years. Anyone who got a fast-moving job immediately after Staff College could rely on a series of promotions in the years ahead – always provided that he succeeded at each job; if you were landed with a dreary initial appointment, you could be sure that the opposite was true.

Members of the Directing Staff had been suggesting to me that it was time I broke away from Special Forces and tried something different. They did this out of kindness, I know, meaning to help; yet I remained stubbornly devoted to the kind of work I knew and liked best. I realized that I would have to hold a staff post of some sort next, and that for the first time in my life a real desk job loomed; luckily I heard that in the newly formed Strategic Command Headquarters there was going to be a position for an advisor on Special Forces, and, ignoring conventional wisdom, I put in for that.

Our postings were kept deadly secret until at last they came out of the Black Bag; and when I opened my brown envelope, I found to my unbounded relief that I had got the job I wanted, as G 2, Special Forces, at Strategic Command. So, as my fellow-students fanned out all over the world – to Hong Kong, Malaya, Nigeria, Germany – I moved a short distance across country to Wilton, near Salisbury.

The next two years, late 1967 to 1969, were the quietest of my career to date. The newly formed Special Forces cell was directed by Brigadier Michael Blackman, a former SAS officer who had had an exceptionally gallant war.[1] Working under him at Wilton were two staff officers, myself and Karl Beale, from the Parachute Regiment, who later became Second-in-Command of 22nd SAS; our job was to advise the Commander-in-Chief on all matters concerning Special Forces. I skidded along the surface, more or less managing to survive, but it is probably significant that one of my clearest memories from that period is of Bridget's irritation when I passed on a rocket which I had received for wearing shirts ironed with insufficient precision. (She frequently heard me described as 'the scruffiest officer in the British army', and no less frequently told me to take more trouble with my appearance.)

As staff jobs go, that was by no means a bad one. One compensating factor was that the lack of pressure gave me a chance to settle down to married life – and at the age of thirty-three, it was high time that I did so. With our cottage still let, we moved to a quarter at Harnham, up the hill on the Blandford side of Salisbury. It was a lovely area in which to live, with open country all round and the centre of the city within walking distance, so that Bridget could go shopping with both babies in their pram.

For our first six months at Salisbury Phillida was a normally

1. Captured at Tobruk, he escaped from a prisoner-of-war camp in Italy and trekked three hundred miles down the Apennines, a substantial part of the way without boots, his only pair having disintegrated.

wakeful baby, but Nicola drove us almost to distraction by still refusing to settle at night: even when she did drop off, she would keep waking up at intervals, for no discernible reason. In our efforts to help her sleep we tried every remedy we could think of – a slightly narcotic cough mixture, brandy, and, in desperation, barbiturates prescribed by a doctor. These brought us a break for three nights, but then Bridget decided that it was simply not safe to give such a young child any more.

The problem was finally solved by a wise old country doctor, who explained that an intelligent baby has a lively brain but cannot think ahead: the trouble with Nicola, he said, was that she imagined night as a great big, black curtain coming down, and every evening she was worrying about how she could escape from it. The answer, he told us, was to fill her mind with ideas about what she would do next day: as she went to bed, we should talk about how she was going to play in the sandpit, where she would go for a walk, what she would have for lunch, and so on. We listened to this with some scepticism, but when we tried it, we found that it certainly helped. The doctor also said that Nicola, being bright, would benefit from nursery school, so we bundled her off just before she had turned three.

From Salisbury we went on our first family holiday, to Angle Bay, in Pembrokeshire. Haunted by memories of dreadful seaside vacations when I was a boy, I set out strongly opposed to the idea, but Bridget won me over, and the trip turned out such a success that the magnificent beach at Angle Bay became our bucket-and-spade centre over the next few years. Another attraction was the ramshackle hotel on Thorn Island, housed in a fort built during the Napoleonic wars, which laid on delicious lobster suppers.

At Salisbury I sought to modify my natural cack-handedness by enlisting for a course in carpentry. Incredible as it may sound, I had won a prize for carpentry at St Peter's Court, where I had constructed a pair of warped and lop-sided book-ends. (When I asked why I had been given the prize – the only one I won at school – I was told that it was 'for effort'.) Now I enrolled for evening classes run by the council in Salisbury, and excelled myself by building a collapsible Wendy-house – a splendid creation, with doors, windows and hatches which opened. This was so popular that it has moved around with us ever since, and will, I hope, one day be done up for our grandchildren.

I also took up bee-keeping – a hobby which I found absorbing. Having answered an advertisement in the local newspaper, I bought three hives with working colonies inside them, and after a hazardous car journey managed to set them up in a field at Wilton, just outside the camp's waste-disposal unit, where all the classified papers were burned. Although frequently stung, I taught myself how to look after the bees, and all went well until one day they attacked the wretched man who worked the incinerator – probably because the smoke had irritated them. I was summoned before the Camp Commandant, ordered to remove my hives from the area, and told to stop harassing the staff. Another disaster occurred when I brought some lifts home, extracted the honey and left the empty combs in the garage overnight. A small amount of honey dripped out onto the floor during the night; next morning the bees discovered it, and suddenly the air in front of the house was alive with them. Even when I took the lifts away, they continued to infest the area – and as one had to pass the garage to reach the house, access became decidedly hazardous. The postman would not deliver the mail any more, and nobody would visit us during the hours of daylight: for over a week the bees held us in siege.

In spite of this setback, I was determined to keep them, for I had learnt that bees are one of the few productive creatures which the owner can easily shift around. When we moved back to Herefordshire, I would be able to take them with me; and if, God forbid, the evil day came on which I had to work in Whitehall, I planned that they should live on the roof of the Ministry of Defence.

In the middle of 1968 our financial position, already precarious, deteriorated sharply when the Crawshaws announced that they were going to have to leave the cottage, as they had taken up appointments elsewhere. With no rent to cover our mortgage commitments, and no further tenants in prospect, we feared that we were going to have to sell the little house, of which we had both become very fond. Thank goodness, our nerve held, and we hung on to it. Then, at that low ebb, a new financial opportunity suddenly presented itself. Joan de Robeck, a life-long friend of Bridget's mother, owned a house in London which had been divided up into four flats. She herself had recently sold leases on all the flats and moved out into a residential hotel, but had retained the freehold of the building, which she now offered to us at a price of £1500.

In those days £1500 seemed a fortune, and we had no money to spare. Nevertheless, the investment would produce a return of ten per cent, and also, if we bought the freehold, we would be able to raise a 100 per cent mortgage to buy one of the flats, when it became available. Bridget felt that it would be madness to commit ourselves so heavily, at a time when we were already stretched to our limits; but I sensed that this was an opportunity which might never occur again, and after some sharp arguments persuaded her that we should go ahead. Thus we acquired the freehold of the building; and when one of the flats came on the market I wrote to a mortgage company asking for a loan. As I had said that I wanted to buy a flat for my daughter, they inevitably asked how old she was; and when I answered 'Three', they were not impressed. But with a loan of £5500 from a solicitor we bought the flat; we filled it with cheap ex-army furniture and let it to two young German bachelors for enough money to cover our mortgage payments. This turned out to be the best investment I have ever made. Not only did it give us and our children a base in London: in twenty-five years the value of the property, which I still own, has gone up twenty times.

Had my next posting been to some awkward place, we might well have had to sell the cottage; but as things turned out, we were able to hold on to it. About half-way through my two-year tour at Wilton I had begun looking around for possible jobs, and found that the post of Second-in-Command of 22nd SAS would become vacant at about the right moment. Needless to say, I fished for it, and by a miracle landed the one job which I really coveted. So, at the end of 1969, to our delight, we were able to return to our own house, and settle down there at least for the next couple of years.

CHAPTER 17

WITH THE FIRQATS

1970–72

When I returned to 22nd SAS my whole horizon brightened, not least because I was once again working under Johnny Watts. In the Jebel Akhdar campaign of 1959 he had commanded 'D' Squadron, to which I was posted; now he was again my immediate superior, and commanding the Regiment; but he had not changed in the slightest. Still irrepressibly enthusiastic, still as scruffy as ever, with a cigarette dangling permanently from one corner of his mouth, he was much loved by the soldiers, and a marvellous man to work for, in that he delegated responsibility fearlessly, never interfered with the work of a subordinate if things were going well, and was always looking for adventure.

Another feature which had not changed was our accommodation. The camp at Hereford was still known as Bradbury lines, and the Regiment lived in wooden huts, connected together in groups called spiders, which had been built in the 1930s and condemned at the outbreak of the Second World War. Plans were afoot to replace them with modern concrete buildings, but for the moment we occupied them happily. Never mind the fact that rats and rabbits took up residence beneath the floors, which were raised clear of the ground on bricks: the huts were warm and comfortable – when they did not catch fire – and the very idea of giving them up was anathema to many of the old hands. The main offices were in a block alongside the square: in the middle was the Commanding Officer's, flanked on one side by that of the Second-in-Command, and on the other by that of the Adjutant. Our windows looked out over the square to the Clock Tower, on which are inscribed the names of those who have lost their lives – a constant reminder of our duty in taking care of our men.

And yet, if physical conditions remained traditional, I soon discovered that in operational and ideological terms the SAS had entered a period of rapid change, and was struggling to adapt itself to a multi-national role. Its heart and mind, and many of its methods, still lay in the jungle, where it had fought with such success; but now that confrontation was over, the Regiment needed to find new theatres in which it could make a contribution, and in particular to identify and develop a role for itself in Europe, which still looked likely to be the major battlefield of the future. To speed development, the Director,[1] Brigadier Fergie Semple, had brought in an excellent man, Ray Nightingale, as Senior Intelligence Officer, and Johnny had consolidated his role into that of Operations Officer. Ray came from the King's Royal Rifle Corps, and no better man could have been chosen for this key position: working direct to the Commanding Officer, he wielded considerable power and influence.

At first my principal brief from Johnny Watts was to identify theatres, geographical and political, in which the SAS might be able to make a contribution; and one area which held particular promise was the Persian Gulf. Already we had small teams out there, but in March 1970 Johnny got wind of something bigger, and, travelling as 'Mr Smith', flew out for a quick reconnaissance. The Labour Government had recently announced its intention of withdrawing British armed forces from the Gulf, and numerous political organizations, armed with Soviet or Chinese Communist money and weapons, had begun jockeying to fill the power-vacuum which our departure would create.

Of special concern to us was Oman, where old Sultan Sayid bin Taimur was still clinging to power, and, against all the urging of his British advisors, keeping his country firmly in the Middle Ages with his ultra-reactionary policies. His son Qaboos, already thirty, had been educated at Sandhurst, commissioned into the Cameronians and sent on a tour of Britain to observe our civil institutions; but since his return to Oman he had been kept

1. The Director, SAS, commanded all the Regiments from Group Headquarters in London, and was the immediate superior of 22nd SAS's Commanding Officer.

under house arrest, unable to play any part in governing his country. Particularly at risk was the southern province of Dhofar, where rebellious tribesmen had established themselves in the mountains, and were making violent nocturnal raids on the coastal plain.

Johnny quickly saw that a great deal was at stake. The rebellious Dhofaris were being manipulated from long range by the Communist empires of Soviet Russia and China, whose aim was to subvert the whole of southern Arabia, and so gain control of the Straits of Hormuz at the entrance to the Gulf. If they succeeded, they would have a stranglehold on the supply of oil to the Western world. Here, surely, was a classic opportunity for the SAS to go in on the ground floor and shore up the regime in Oman before it crumbled and set off a domino effect of other states toppling to Communist control all up the Gulf.

Johnny's early overtures came to nothing, because the old Sultan would not agree to his idea of arming loyal Dhofaris and encouraging them to fight the dissidents. But then, on 23 July, Sayid bin Taimur was at last deposed in an all-but-bloodless coup, during which he shot himself in the foot with a pistol. After an ignominious exit from his palace, he was bundled on to an aircraft and flown to England, where he lived in luxurious seclusion for the last two years of his life.

His son Qaboos took control and set about the colossal job of modernizing his country. Soon a message arrived in Hereford asking if the SAS would provide bodyguards for the young Sultan. At once Johnny picked Sergeant Major Bob Slater and four others, all good Arabists, and sent them to Salala, where they guarded Qaboos for the next four months, literally sleeping across his door.

Whenever Johnny was abroad – as he frequently was – I held the fort at Hereford, running SAS affairs in his absence, and so getting an early look at the problems of commanding an organization with such far-flung interests. At home, Bridget and I settled into our cottage again. We had come back to find everything in perfect order; but as Bridget was pregnant for the third time, we saw that we would soon need more space. We therefore planned to extend the house, and in due course took in a former garage to form a large sitting room, with a fourth bedroom and new bathroom above. To our delight, our third baby turned out to be a boy, born (with me present at last) on 15 June 1970 at the Louise Margaret Hospital in Aldershot, to which we had returned because Bridget had had such excellent treatment there earlier for Phillida's arrival. As we wanted to give the boy a good old English name, we called him Edward, taking our inspiration – extraordinary as it now seems – from Edward Heath, who was elected Prime Minister in a stirring and unexpected victory over Harold Wilson four days later.

I did not have long in which to play the role of father. In the middle of August Johnny announced that he was going to send me out to the Gulf. 'You can sit in Sharjah for a bit and see if anything's happening,' he said. 'Scratch around, get your feet under the table, and if something crops up, make sure we're in it.'

It was tough on Bridget that I should disappear abroad at that moment, leaving her to look after three small children, the last only two months old. Yet this was the lot of most Service wives, who were (and are) frequently called on to make personal sacrifices in furthering their husbands' careers. From my own point of view it was wonderful to be bound for Arabia again. With me, as Operations Officer, came Neville Howard, a lively, dapper and – considering that he was from the Coldstream Guards – surprisingly short man, who was easily underestimated because of his size, but had a steely will, and later commanded 22nd SAS. As the British were already beginning to pull out of the Gulf, there was plenty of space in the camp at Sharjah, and we commandeered a hollow square of prefabricated buildings, inside which we could conduct our affairs without being over-looked.

Soon I was on my way down to Oman to see Hugh Oldham, a former DLI officer who had acted as military adviser to the old Sultan, and was still working for the new one. He told me that the place had scarcely changed since my last visit in 1959: there were still no roads, schools, or medical facilities, and agriculture on the once-fertile plain of Salala, between the mountains and the sea, had been devastated by the old Sultan's deliberate repression. The political problems in Dhofar were becoming serious, for the mountain rebels were receiving assistance from other Communist-backed insurgents in the southern part of the Yemen (now known as the People's Democratic Republic of Yemen, or PDRY), and threatening to overwhelm Sultan Qaboos's small armed forces. It was clear that he needed advice and assistance in suppressing the revolt.

I returned to Sharjah in a state of some excitement. Once again, my luck seemed to be in: wherever I went, I found trouble brewing. Just as in Aden, I was able to signal Johnny and say, 'Good prospects action. Send team,' and in September out came a small force of fifteen men under Keith Farnes, a tough and unorthodox officer from the Parachute Regiment, with a particular gift for getting on with his soldiers. His general directive was to start working out a policy for the defence of the Salala plain and the eventual defeat of the *jebali* rebels; and because, in political terms, this was a highly sensitive task, the infiltration of his team into the Oman was done with the utmost secrecy. They went to ground in the coastal town of Mirbat, with instructions to live with the local people and win their support, but not to move out of their immediate area.

Such was the beginning of the campaign which may go down in history as the most important and far-reaching ever fought by the SAS. Our involvement in Oman, lasting more than four years, rolled back and finally dissipated the tide of Communism which threatened to overwhelm southern Arabia. In shaping this campaign, the SAS should be credited with great military and political foresight; for myself, I was fortunate enough to be in the right place at the right moment, and helped set in motion a chain of events which had a powerfully beneficial effect on the region.

In Sharjah, we began to pick up whispers about potentially dangerous developments in the Musandam Peninsula, the rhino-horn of land which pokes up into the Straits of Hormuz, the very throat of the Persian Gulf. Through a contact in Dubai I learnt that a force of Iraqi trouble-makers was trying to subvert the Shihoo, a primitive tribe who roamed the barren mountain deserts in that neck of Arabia. Musandam was part of Oman, but the old Sultan had never paid it or its people any attention, and now there was a danger that alien forces might become established there. If that happened, they could at the least harass our military withdrawal, and at worst, if a Communist-backed regime gained control of the mouth of the Gulf, the consequences for the supply of oil to the Western world might be catastrophic.

Again I signalled Johnny Watts with the news that I had found a role for the SAS. In England Ray Nightingale put together a small force, but plans grew so fast that before the SAS contingent even reached the Middle East the Commander-in-Chief, Middle East, Major General Roly Gibbs (later CGS), asked his Commander of Land Forces, Brigadier Philip Ward, to mount a joint assault which became known as Operation Breakfast. While a combined force of SAS and the Trucial Oman Scouts made an air- and sea-borne landing on the coast, a troop from 'G' Squadron would free-fall at night into the Wadi Rawdah, a precipitous valley which came up from the sea and ended in a bowl with a floor four thousand feet above sea-level, guarded by sheer mountain walls seven thousand feet high. Here at last was an operational setting which demanded the use of free-fall entry – the possibility which I had foreseen when I first took up parachuting in 21st SAS. The idea was that if any of the enemy escaped the coastal invasion and made their way inland, they would be cut off by the parachutists, who would also tackle any dissidents already up-country.

By any standards this was a hazardous undertaking – the first time that the SAS had used free-falling on a live operation. But because surprise was essential, and there was a risk that helicopters would be shot up if they tried to land men in the mountains, the air-drop seemed the best option.

Leading 3 Troop was Mike Rose, another outstanding Coldstreamer who went on to command 22nd SAS and become a general.[1] This was my first experience of him in action, and a refreshing one it was. His career had been unusual in that, having been just too young for National Service, he went to Oxford and took a degree before enlisting in the army. A tall, slim man of quite exceptional energy, both mental and physical, he fired off ideas as other exuberant people fire off jokes. So lively was

---

1. He was knighted in the New Year Honours of 1994 and appointed Commander of the United Nations Forces in Bosnia.

he, in fact, that directing him was like trying to school a young racehorse, and I had the feeling that he was only half under control.

On the face of things, Operation Breakfast was not a success. The assault on the coast proved slightly farcical. As a result of cartographic error, our people swept in from the sea by heli-copter and rubber dinghy to land at a place called Jumla, only to find no sign of any Iraqis. Too late, they realized that we had confused Jumla with another village called Gumla, a few miles down the coast. There, in due course, they did find a house containing medical supplies and documents, which showed that the building had been used by the enemy; but the Iraqis them-selves had vanished.

The drop into the Wadi Rawdah was excellently planned by G Squadron, and I myself put in several training jumps with the men of 3 Troop. At the last minute I briefed them in detail before their plane took off from Sharjah at 0300 on 12 December. As its lights disappeared among the stars over the desert, I was left with that awful feeling, which by then I knew so well, of being unable to do anything more except wait to hear what happened.

The troop jumped from a height of 11,000 feet at 0400, and the operation was faultlessly executed, bar a single stroke of bad luck; one of the men, Lance Corporal Paul Reddy (always known as 'Rip'), was killed when his parachute failed to open. Nobody knew exactly what happened; but it seemed that Reddy, a light and tremendously fit man, had done his usual trick of cramming a few extras into his bergen at the last minute, 'just in case'. This time the extras consisted of thirteen loaded Bren-gun magazines, weighing several pounds apiece, and it appeared that the weight of his bergen had rendered him unstable, so that he began tumbling in the air and became entangled in his parachute lines.

His death was a severe blow: not only had we lost a good man, but a helicopter had to come in and collect his body next day, blowing the secrecy of the operation. Again, our people found traces of enemy occupation – marks of base-plates where mortars had been fired, and so on – but although the SAS had arrived unseen, and lay up for a day and a half in observation posts, they spotted no enemy movement. When they emerged from hiding and confronted the Shihoo, the tribesmen were surprised, but not as astounded as our people had hoped. Rumour claimed that these were stone-age people who had never set eyes on a white man: in fact they were fully familiar with occidental faces, as some of them worked on the oil rigs in the Gulf. Nevertheless they were still extremely primitive, and lived in an environment of almost inconceivable harshness. One man whom we found with terrible burn-marks on his stomach told us he had been given the standard treatment for a headache.

Yet even if Operation Breakfast produced no immediate or tangible result, its long-term effect was incalculable, for it awakened Oman's interest in its northern province. An SAS troop stayed in Musandam for a month, under Fred Fearnley, mapping the area, winning hearts and minds, and (for three memorable days) entertaining the Commander-in-Chief, Roly Gibbs, who suddenly announced that he would like to join a patrol. Before he went out into the desert, he was nervous that he might not be fit enough to keep up, and therefore put great effort into his preparations. Of course the soldiers would never have left him behind, and I did my best to reassure him; but he took his preparations seriously, and went off to the range several times to fire his weapon. Just before he left, he came to me and said proudly, 'I've got the weight of my bergen down to an absolute minimum. I've cut my toothbrush in half!'

Before we pulled out of Musandam, we brought in units of the Sultan's Armed Forces, who built an airstrip in the bottom of the wadi, and Qaboos began to pay serious attention to a part of the world which, by virtue of its topography, had immense strategic importance. The British withdrawal from the Gulf proceeded without any of the fighting or unrest which had made our departure from Aden so unpleasant, and a nation favourably disposed to the West still held the key to the Gulf.

Meanwhile in Dhofar things began to develop. As in Malaya and Borneo, our aim was to help local people help themselves: with luck we might be able to give them a start at rebuilding their country, but it was they who, in the end, would have to manage affairs. As soon as it became clear that we were going to be there for some time, Johnny Watts put forward a five-point plan for the renaissance: we would give priority to civil reorganization, agricultural and economic development, intelligence gathering, psychological warfare and military operations, in that order. The SAS detachment was given the innocuous name of the British Army Training Team, or BATT.

From the beginning the key element in our plans were the *firqats*, or bands of local fighting men: literally 'companies', the word came to mean any Dhofari units. Just as we had harnessed the skills of the aborigines in Malaya and the Ibans in Borneo, so now we began to recruit and train irregular soldiers loyal to the Sultan. Our aim was that they should defend the settlements on the plain, and also lure rebels down off the *jebel* by persuading former associates that under Qaboos normal life was better than scratching an existence as guerrillas in the hills, and by showing those who had suffered under Sayid bin Taimur that the cause for which they had been fighting no longer had any validity.

Only by training native soldiers could we build up a force large enough to defeat the rebels, for the British had no intention of sending out large numbers of their own troops: any major deployment would have been politically unacceptable. The *firqats* were excellent fighters, and our role was to harness their natural potential by shaping what had been wild, disorganized *jebali* into coherent formations and helping them plan operations properly.

In doing this we faced a dilemma. On the one hand we wanted these people – who fought well without shoes and with ancient rifles – to remain very much as they were, for they formed an essential part of the Omani community. At the same time the pressure was on to equip them with boots and modern weapons, which led to a softer life, destroyed their individuality and their ability to act as guerrillas, and in general made them less inclined to go out and fight. The more kit we gave them, the more orthodox and less effective they became. Besides, the traditional civilization of the *firqats* acted as a draw to the rebels in the hills, many of whom secretly longed to come down and join them. We thus had to set the right balance, and this took a long time.

To set up what became known as Operation Storm, I flew down from Sharjah to Salala, the capital of Dhofar, on the south coast. There I met some of the *firqat* leaders and sketched out the start of our campaign. Having established that the operation was viable, I came back to the United Kingdom to brief the Director of Military Operations and the Vice-Chief of the General Staff, Major General Monkey Blacker, on the progress we were making. One point on which I insisted was that we must have a tented field hospital, with a full team of surgeons, anaesthetists and nurses: without proper medical support, I said, we could not sustain Operation Storm and have soldiers risking their lives in a country where conditions were so primitive. Since no other medical facilities existed, casualties would have had to face a two-hour flight before receiving treatment – a quite unaccept-able situation. The DMO began to mutter that the army was short of field surgical teams, and would have trouble providing one. Whereupon Monkey Blacker exclaimed, 'I don't care how difficult it is. We're not having soldiers on operations without an FST. Let's get on with it and find one.' Which of course they did.

As the operation built up, we moved our headquarters from Sharjah to Salala. At first we kept the lowest possible profile – and our self-effacement proved effective: we were in Dhofar for more than two years before anyone from the outside world discovered that the SAS was working there. Partly it was the state of lawlessness which kept us close to base: in 1970 much of Southern Oman was bandit country, and to travel outside Salala was exceedingly dangerous. We also established footholds in two other coastal towns, Taqa and Mirbat, but we had only a handful of men in each, and if the locals had turned against them, they could easily have been wiped out.

For the next eighteen months Johnny Watts and I took it in turns to run affairs at Hereford and in the rest of the world, while the other flew out for a spell with the teams in Dhofar. It was a tiresome journey – thirteen or fourteen hours each way in a Hercules C–130, with a stop in Cyprus – and one of us did it every six weeks or so; but in our view it was essential to maintain close contact with the commanders at the front. Only by personal visits could we maintain a clear understanding of the military situation, which was changing from day to day, and gain the information necessary for long-term strategic planning.

We also needed to review the capabilities of every officer, and the strengths and weaknesses of the units in the field – for the conduct of people on live operations is often markedly different from their behaviour in peace time.

Communication between Oman and the United Kingdom was still primitive, and it was impossible to exchange ideas satisfactorily at a range of four thousand miles. We did have a direct radio link, open twenty-four hours a day, which was exceptional at that time, but all messages had to be encoded and sent in Morse, so that long conversations were impossible. We generally relied on a full sitrep (situation report) every evening, and a shorter update in the morning – although if a battle was in progress, reports would come in continuously. In spite of this link, the squadron commanders on the ground frequently had to take major decisions without consultation, so that a great deal depended on the directives which Johnny and I had given them.

The young Sultan gave us all the help he could: a man of striking good looks and regal presence, he was skilled at making contact with his subjects, and lost no time in stopping the archaic practices which his father had maintained. But at first his country was desperately poor and backward. Although Oman had oil, no field had yet been opened up, and Qaboos went through a challenging period as he tried to win the backing of a large nation without having the resources for rapid development. Lack of support and direction had run his armed forces down into a low state, and he needed time to rebuild them. He also had to create an air force from scratch, and to set up a transport and supply organization.

The basic idea of Operation Storm was to give him time. Our aim was never to become the stand-alone heroes of Oman; rather, it was to provide Qaboos with a breathing space in which to gain control of his country before it was over-run. For this reason he welcomed our work warmly, especially in the field of agriculture. The Salala plain, once (and now again) exceedingly fertile, had been ruined by his father's repressive policies: wells had been filled in, and the beautiful old *falajs*, or water-conduits, smashed. In due course we brought in an Engineer team to find water, drill new wells and put irrigation systems back into action. Under Major Geoffrey Durrant (later Director of the Army

Veterinary Corps) we set up demonstration farms and imported
Hereford bulls to improve the local cattle: the cows, however,
were so small that the bulls tended to crush them when mating,
so we had to build special mounting-platforms to take some of
the weight. In general, we tried to teach the people to get better
value out of the crops and animals which they had, rather than
seeking to change their habits. One of our simplest and most
successful innovations was teaching them to make hay during
the prolific growing season. Until then they had always killed
off their bull calves in the summer, because they knew that after
the monsoon rains had dried up, there would not be enough
grass to feed them: now, the ability to store grass was in itself
a revolution.

The SAS commitment grew steadily, as Ray Nightingale
brought in a large Intelligence Section, manned by the Intelligence Corps, to meet the unquenchable thirst for information.
At the same time, we concentrated on a propaganda campaign,
and built up our psyops unit under Corporal John Ward, who
had come from 21st SAS with a string of A-Levels behind him,
and now took on the job of broadcasting, producing leaflets,
bringing out a local newspaper, and so on.

We also became more and more involved in fighting – which
at first we had been specifically forbidden to do, for fear that
we would suffer casualties, and that if news of them leaked out,
political pressure would cause our entire operation to be called
off. To make progress, and to give the *firqats* the idea, we began
aggressive patrolling at night, very much as we had on the Jebel
Akhdar a dozen years earlier. Soon we laid to rest one of the
favourite myths which had been assiduously promoted by the
defence forces of the day – that during the summer monsoon,
when winds off the sea brought in mist and rain, it was impossible to operate on top of the mountain, four thousand feet above
sea-level. The rocks became so slippery, it was alleged, that you
could not stand up on them; the blackfly were so virulent that
nobody could live with them. This nonsense needed challenging,
and our soldiers soon put paid to it by leading some of the *firqats*
up the mountain during the monsoon, with no trouble at all.
Conditions in these hills were quite different from on the Jebel
Akhdar, for here the monsoon rains, sweeping in from the

Indian Ocean, produced thick scrub six or seven feet high, particularly in the wadis, and this gave the rebels useful cover.

Later, becoming more ambitious, Brigadier John Graham, Commander of the Sultan's Armed Forces (SAF), organized construction of the Hornbeam Line, a thirty-five-mile barrier of wire and mines designed to cut the routes along which the enemy were bringing in supplies by animal train from the west. The SAF then manned strategic points on the high ground along it, while the SAS led *firqat* patrols to intercept *adoo* supply and reinforcement operations.

By the end of 1971 one whole squadron was deployed in Dhofar, and at periods of handover, when one tour ended and another began, two entire squadrons, or over half the Regiment's strength, were in the theatre. Whenever I went out, I would discuss the campaign at length with the Squadron Commander, and if possible join a patrol, tagging along at the back like an ordinary trooper. But this, though good fun, took up a lot of time and energy, and represented only a tiny part of my job as a whole.

In Hereford, holding the fort during Johnny's frequent absences, I became more aware than ever of the vital role played by our padre. Any padre is useful to a commanding officer, as he can keep his finger on the pulse of a unit in a way which the CO himself finds impossible; but at that date the SAS was lucky enough to have an outstanding man, the Reverend Walter Evans (known to all ranks as 'Evans Above'). This small, unobtrusive Welshman was endowed with a quiet wit, wisdom and humanity which enriched our lives immeasurably: he had the gift of being able to talk to anyone, and, without seeming to pry, of discovering people's innermost thoughts. He was thus invaluable to myself and Johnny, in that he could gauge morale far more accurately than we could; and whereas a soldier might give me a superficial 'Fine, sir,' when I asked him how things were, he would open his heart to the padre. Walter was particularly good at going round and talking to the families, and he was in his element at Sergeants' Mess parties, not minding that the language grew rougher as the evening wore on. As he remarked afterwards: 'Out it would all come – *in vino veritas*.' Inspired by

Walter's example, for the rest of my career I always made a point of consulting my senior padre, to gain an unbiased opinion on the state of morale from outside the chain of command.

In November 1970 Johnny Watts flew Walter out to Oman to conduct a Remembrance Day service in the desert. He took a tape-recorder with a couple of hymns, and began the service at 0730. Just as he finished, a young officer came up and said, 'I'm so sorry, padre. I forgot to tell my troop. Would you do it again?' So he did – and immediately afterwards the mail arrived. The officer opened a letter and cried out, 'Good God. I've been posted back to my regiment in UK.' Whereupon a voice piped up from the back: 'Padre, I never knew prayers could be answered so soon!'

Yet where Walter really came into his own was on combat survival courses, when he gave talks on faith in captivity. These were supremely moving, and although they did not usually elicit many questions, he found that two or three men waited behind at the end to talk to him; the friendships which he formed ran so deep that they persisted for twenty years or more, long after he had left the Regiment. He was a star, and we valued him more than we could say.

After a while I decided that procedures in our headquarters needed streamlining. In particular, I declared war on the tide of paper flowing from one office to another, by the simple expedient of banning typewriters, except in the central pool. I reasoned that if people had to write everything out by hand, it would diminish their verbiage – and in this I was soon proved right. But the ban led to a serious clash with the officer commanding 'G' Squadron.

This man tended to query every order which I issued as Second-in-Command, and he contested the one about typewriters. That, however, was only a pretext for starting a real row about who was running the Regiment: when he in effect challenged my authority to act as Commanding Officer in Johnny's absence, I decided that this was intolerable, and, without being authorized to do so, suspended him from duty. I then rang Fergie Semple, the Brigadier, and was blown up for exceeding my powers; but by then I was so angry that I laid my career on the line.

'I'm sorry,' I said, 'but I just can't work with him. One of us has got to go. If it's not him, it's me.'

Next I rang Dare Newell, who had already retired but was still regarded as a father figure by the Regiment. He commiserated with me, backed me up and said that he would put in a word at Group Headquarters; yet my rage persisted, and to burn it off I drove fast to Brecon and climbed Pen-y-Fan in a perfect fury – my usual remedy at such moments. Soon Dare's advocacy won the day and my *bête noire* was sent packing, having upset many people besides myself. Even if I had not made a decisive move, I do not think he would have lasted long, for mutual trust is essential among soldiers with their lives at risk. I even remembered that in Korea where a fellow platoon commander had lost the confidence of his men they had shot and wounded him when on patrol to ensure his removal.

So, at the end of 1971, I was leading an exceptionally busy life, full of travel and responsibility, and enjoying it hugely. Then came a sudden jolt. In December Johnny was out in Dhofar, directing offensive operations, when he got a signal from the Ministry of Defence telling him that he was being posted to the Staff College at Camberley in twelve days' time. This meant that his tour as Commanding Officer was cut short, and that I – the only person directly in line to succeed him – was pitchforked into command. For some time I had been hoping that I might take over from him; but I had never expected that the change would come so soon. As it was, I took over in January 1972, at the age of thirty-seven.

CHAPTER 18

COMMANDER 22ND SAS

1972–74

As I had deputized for Johnny so often during the past eighteen months, the change was less traumatic than it might have been, and I was fortunate in having, as Director, Brigadier John Simpson, who took over from Fergie Semple early in 1972. A large and ebullient Gordon Highlander, with a robust sense of humour and an unquenchable enthusiasm for sailing, John had worked with the SAS in Borneo and understood our methods thoroughly.[1] Moreover, while giving me first-class support in high places, he was prepared to let me operate on a loose rein.

Physically, all I had to do was move one room sideways, into the CO's office. Nevertheless, I had a great deal to learn. I began to see that commanding 22nd SAS was like having one's fingers in a whole variety of pies, all of which were cooking simultaneously. Dhofar was our biggest pie by far, but there were plenty of others that needed attention: during 1972 and 1973 we had officers and men in twenty-three different countries, ranging from the Far East to South America, many engaged on highly sensitive projects; and because I could not give all of them detailed attention all the time, it followed that one essential

---

1. He described his recruitment as Director in the following terms: 'One day I was cornered by Johnny Watts, Tony Jeapes, Ray Nightingale and Tanky Smith (who was then RSM), and the following exchange took place:
   Tony: "This conversation's never taken place, and if you ever mention it, it'll be the worse for you."
   Johnny: "Would you like to command the SAS?"
   Myself: "Don't be so bloody stupid. A: I'm forty-three, and would never pass the selection course, and B: I can't parachute because I've got a dicky knee."
   Tony: "You've passed."

of command was intelligent delegation. This style of command served me in good stead for the rest of my career, because I think – under all my surface energy – I am fundamentally a bit lazy, and happy to leave detail to other people. In self-justification, I may point out that nobody can hope to run every small unit of a large organization, be it military or commercial: the leader must stand back and avoid becoming bogged down in minutiae, otherwise he (or she) will be exhausted, and fail to get the best out of subordinates. Another vital factor is the selection of personnel. You must choose people whose chemistry suits you – people with whom you can work, and who feel easy working with you. Further, you must have complete professional confidence in them, and not worry that they may not be up to their jobs; if you do start to worry, you must get rid of them, and quickly. With the right people, you can have misunderstandings and disagreements, and yet carry on, secure in the knowledge that things will come right in the long run.

I considered it important to make my personality felt, and my directions understood, right through the ranks of the SAS. It would have been all too easy to give directions to my Squadron Commanders in Dhofar, and to have left the rest to them; but if I had, my own wishes and personality would not have come through. For this reason I continued flying out to Oman as often as I could.

Operation Storm was still, in many ways, war by remote control. Yet full responsibility for what the SAS were doing in Dhofar still rested with me – and never was I more conscious of the fact than when a massed force of rebels attacked the BATT base on the outskirts of the town of Mirbat in the early hours of 19 July 1972.

The Battle of Mirbat has gone down in SAS annals as a famous victory – and so it was. The story has been told in detail, notably by Tony Jeapes in his graphic book *SAS Operation Oman*, so here I will only outline the action. What we had failed to appreciate was that for some time the rebels had been planning a major attack: the core of their force came all the way from the Yemen in the west, rounding up recruits as it advanced along the *jebel* and preventing people going down into the towns, so that no word of the plan would leak out. The fact that the *adoo* were able to collect more than three hundred men, and bring them into position above Mirbat without our getting wind of the attack, was a remarkable achievement. It may be that they thought the BATT outpost was only a medical unit, and did not realize there were a considerable number of SAS only thirty miles away, in our base at Salala; in any event, so confident were they of victory that they prepared Press releases, to be broadcast over Aden Radio, claiming that the raid was a complete success, and their agents sent these out without waiting to find out what had happened.

In command of the eight-man BATT was Captain Mike Kealy, a small, fair-haired man of twenty-three, quiet and self-effacing, who did not stand out in a crowd except perhaps because of his keen blue eyes. His base was a mud-walled house with machine guns mounted on the roof, just to the north of the town; and nearly half a mile to the north-east of that stood his other main bulwark, the tall, square mud fort, manned by some thirty members of the Dhofar gendarmerie and local tribesmen. Dug into a pit beside the fort was a 25-pounder gun, manned by Corporal Labalaba, a Fijian (and one of the SAS's best-loved characters) and an Omani soldier, Walid Khalfan, who has since had a distinguished career in his country's army.

The attack began with heavy shelling and machine-gun fire at 0530, just as dawn was breaking: a life-and-death battle raged for the next four hours, as wave after wave of enemy closed in with rifles and machine guns, pressing forward through the encircling wire to within thirty yards of the defenders. At the height of the action, when the gun pit by the fort temporarily fell silent, Mike Kealy and Trooper Tobin raced across seven hundred yards of open ground to go to the aid of the crew. They found Labalaba with his jaw blown off, still trying to fire the 25-pounder at point-blank range over open sights, and other men badly wounded. Hardly had they reached the pit when Labalaba was shot dead. Tobin was mortally wounded, but continued to fight off the enemy, as did Kealy.

Their superhuman courage – and that of all the defenders – enabled the garrison to hold out, but only just. Because of monsoon cloud down almost to rooftop height, it was impossible for the Sultan's Air Force to answer Kealy's urgent call for air support at once; but then, in a show of rare skill and courage, pilots brought their Strikemaster jets in at ground level to hit the *adoo* with bombs and machine-gun fire: so low did they fly that the aircraft returned to base bearing bullet-holes inflicted from above. The other factor which saved the garrison was the last-minute arrival of reinforcements from 'G' Squadron, which providentially was in Salala, about to take over from 'A', and now came in by helicopter just in time to frustrate the rebel attempt to enter the town.

To call Mirbat a close-run thing would be a masterpiece of understatement. The defenders' casualties were miraculously low: only two SAS men dead – Labalaba and Tobin – but had not reinforcements arrived at the critical moment, the position would almost certainly have been over-run, and many, if not all, of the gains we had made in Dhofar would have been thrown away. The Omani forces brought in thirty-eight *adoo* bodies and exhibited them in Salala – both as a demonstration of the Government's success, and as a warning to others that it was not worthwhile joining the rebel organization. But the total number of enemy dead was more like eighty: for the *jebali* it was a shattering reverse, and it marked the turning-point of the war. Thereafter the rebels fell to feuding with each other, and never posed as great a threat to the Sultan again.

In England we got the first radio reports from Salala very early in the morning, and could not tell from minute to minute what was happening. Yet now the importance of our training became paramount. While the fighting raged, there was nothing I could do to help; but such influence as I had on events was already functioning. If I had failed to set high enough standards of train- ing, or if the understanding between the Squadron Commander and his Troop Commander had not been sufficiently clear, the flaws would have been found out. But because everybody knew what they were doing, and because Mike Kealy knew that he would be supported by every means available, he was deter- mined to hold out. It was a classic example of how, under the SAS command system, delegation, trust and understanding at all levels pay off in a crisis.

When I myself went out to Mirbat soon after the battle, and spent a night in the BATT house, I realized all the more clearly that Kealy's own conduct had been beyond praise. I should have liked to recommend him for the Victoria Cross, but this was politically impossible, for a VC would have attracted far too much attention and publicized our presence in Oman to an unacceptable degree. In the event he was awarded the Distinguished Service Order – only the second or third man to win the DSO as a captain since the Second World War.[1] Corporal Bob Bradshaw was awarded a Military Medal, Trooper Tobin a posthumous Military Medal, and Trooper Labalaba a posthumous Mention in Despatches – although no announcement of any of the medals was made until four years after the event, for security reasons.

After Mirbat, Operation Storm moved into a different phase. Now that the Sultan's Armed Forces had been built up into an effective, self-contained means of defence, properly trained and equipped, the SAS was able to step back into a supporting role; other nations, including Iran and Jordan, also sent troops, and as the war moved westwards, pushing the *adoo* back towards the frontier of the Yemen, we concentrated on rehabilitating the *firqats* on their own territory up the mountain, helping to rebuild their villages and set agriculture in motion again.

Even with much of the Regiment committed to Operation Storm, the rest continued their normal programme of training, and in the autumn of 1972 we all went down to the south of France for an escape-and-evasion exercise. Everyone available took part, including my Second-in-Command, a quietly competent man called Richard Pirie. The exercise itself went well, but immediately after it Richard, driving into town at midnight, ran off the road and was killed.

At Hereford there was no officer in camp to undertake the grim task of breaking the news to Richard's wife, Caroline. So it fell on Bridget – and when she heard what had happened, such was the shock that for the first time in her life she fainted. Caroline, a close friend and contemporary, had already lost her first husband, killed in a climbing accident, and had been left

1. Kealy died tragically of hypothermia during an SAS exercise on the Brecon Beacons in 1979, while I was Director, SAS. The suggestion that he was murdered by agents of a disaffected Arab sheikh, made by Sir Ranulph Fiennes in his book *The Feathermen*, was preposterous.

with a baby daughter (another Nicola). Now she had been widowed a second time, again with a young child (Mark), and it seemed altogether too much.

Afterwards our own Nicola, then six, kept recounting how Mummy 'went to sleep on the floor'. Coming round, Bridget nerved herself to go down to Caroline's quarter, and telephoned for a baby-sitter to look after our own children. Then the padre – not Walter Evans, but his successor – rang to suggest that he should meet her near the house, to lend moral support. Bridget agreed and set out, only to find that the padre had lost his nerve and brought his wife along with him – a dreadful mistake. When all three of them appeared on Caroline's doorstep, she knew at once what had happened, and sent the padre and his wife away with scarcely a word. Bridget, realizing that Caroline needed to be alone, and that she was in control, having already telephoned her family, left soon afterwards. The incident gives some idea of the strain under which SAS wives and families have to live.

I myself was away a great deal, and it was Bridget who held our home and family together during those fraught years. The saga of how we bought a larger house typified the difficulties caused by my continual absences. When I became Commanding Officer, we could have moved into the house which went with the job: an attractive building, it had plenty of space, but was cold and draughty, and needed a lot of work to make it comfortable. Luckily we found another couple who were prepared to live in it, and for the time being we ourselves remained in our cottage, even though it was too small for formal entertaining. Then in 1973 we decided to look for a larger house to accommodate our growing family.

After various disappointments Bridget found somewhere which she thought would do: a traditional farmhouse, with a handsome façade and a fine view to the west. The place was in a sorry state, the back garden given over to a pig-run, and a jumble of broken-down outbuildings behind. The owner described himself as an antique-dealer, but the house was full of junk, with a few suits of armour, covered in cobwebs, in the corners. The rooms were filthy, and pervaded by a smell of decay. Nevertheless, as Bridget walked through the front door, she immediately had a feeling that this was it: she had the vision to see beyond the squalor and recognize that this could make a lovely home.

Needless to say, I was in Dhofar at the critical moment, and we had to exchange messages encoded and transmitted in Morse. Trusting Bridget's judgment, and in any case recognizing that I had no good grounds for objecting from such a distance, I sent a signal authorizing her to go ahead, and by the time I reached England, after a terrible journey, the deal had been done. I went straight to inspect this great new house, and my first sight of it – on a foggy November evening – appalled me. Everything seemed to be amiss, and next day an architect confirmed my fears: he pointed out that the elegant front faced the wrong way, and that the whole building was irredeemably awkward. Bridget dug in her toes, insisting that it needed only to be cleared of junk, cleaned from top to bottom, and repainted – and as usual she was right. We bought it, and never regretted the purchase. Our timing was exceedingly fortunate, too. Property prices were rocketing, and the value of our cottage was rising by £1000 a month. I played the market dangerously, hung on for as long as I dared, delayed the completion date on the new house, and eventually sold at a high price, a month before the major crash in prices.

Another pie into which the SAS first plunged a finger during my time as Commanding Officer was that of counter-terrorism. As international terrorism spread during the early 1970s, and the hijacking of aircraft became fashionable, we discerned a challenging new role for ourselves, and in the spring of 1972 I asked Andy Massey, who had recently joined the Regiment as a captain, to write me a paper on how the SAS might combat terrorism in the United Kingdom. He produced an admirable concept, outlining the kind of force we might create; we sent a copy to Group Headquarters in London, and they forwarded it to the Ministry of Defence, where it was quietly shelved. At that time it was clear Government policy that the military should have no part in dealing with unrest in the United Kingdom. Police primacy was absolute – and this was hardly surprising, as the Government was more concerned about industrial unrest than any other kind, and did not want the army involved in activities like the suppression of strikes.

But then, in September 1972, came the massacre at the Munich Olympics, when Black September Arab guerrillas burst into the Israeli team's lodgings, murdered two of them and took nine more hostage, demanding the release of two hundred Palestinians detained in Israeli gaols. The ensuing negotiations, hopelessly botched, ended in a shoot-out at Furstenfeld military airport in which four Arabs, one German policeman and all nine hostages were killed. The event awoke every government in Europe to the way things were going: suddenly a country had been invaded by foreign terrorists, heavily armed and deliberately imported from outside to foster their own political aims. In Britain we had no force able to deal with such an emergency – for the police were not equipped to take on soldiers armed with automatic weapons.

The massacre occurred on Tuesday, 5 September. That Friday evening, as I was about to leave for home, I got a call from the Director of Military Operations, Major General Bill Scotter, who said he had been asked by the Prime Minister what the army could do in response to terrorism. Our paper on the subject had quickly been dragged out, and Scotter wanted to know how long it would take to create the force which Andy Massey had proposed.

My immediate question was, 'How much money can we have?' – and on one of the few occasions in my life I heard the glad answer, 'Money's no problem – as much as you like.' Without really thinking, I said off the top of my head, 'Well, provided we can get adequate transport, we'll have a force ready for you in five weeks.'

The form of transport we had in mind was a brand-new, four-wheel-drive vehicle called a Range Rover, which had appeared on the market a year earlier. This seemed exactly what we needed – as capacious and rugged as its parent the Land Rover, but faster, and not too military in appearance. The trouble was that there was a long waiting-list of potential customers, and the Government had to authorize priority for us to winkle out three early models. These turned out potentially good, but not tough enough to carry the loads we needed to transport; so we had their suspension beefed-up, and fitted them with roll-bars, for our experience showed that early models had a dangerous propensity for turning turtle when driven hard.

Under the code-name Operation Pagoda we began to create the counter-terrorist team. I decided that the only way to achieve the necessary standard would be to dedicate people to the new task, and train them specially. This we proceeded to do: we selected the men, put them into training, and assigned them their own block in the camp. There they lived together, with their vehicles loaded, ready to scramble at any hour of the day or night. Our aim was to instil so much precision and drill into them that in emergencies the chances of emotion and fear influencing their judgment would be reduced to a minimum: nobody can entirely escape the excitement and stress of a crisis, but at least people can be trained to react in the most methodical way possible.

In five weeks a team of sorts was in being. Of course the SAS were not satisfied – they never are – and as time went on we refined methods, skills and equipment to a high degree; but at least we had an organization which could combat terrorists on our own ground.

Creating the team was one challenge, selling it to the police quite another. It was vital to us that the police should understand the capabilities and limitations of our new force, but their initial reactions were lukewarm. They looked on the SAS as a gung-ho bunch of desperadoes, and did not want us anywhere near them in a civil commotion, as they thought that our presence might only inflame a disturbance and turn it into a great military shoot-out. We therefore had to persuade them that we were capable of acting with surgical precision and control – and to this end we invited senior officers down to Hereford for a briefing on the Pagoda team. We explained that we were well aware of the police's constitutional primacy, and when we said that we actively wanted their advice, they came round to the idea of cooperation.[1] We in return took advice from them on

1. Before the Services can be deployed in support of the police within the United Kingdom, the senior police officer present at any incident must request the Home Secretary for their involvement, and he in turn must clear the use of the military with Cabinet colleagues.

what capabilities they themselves lacked, and began to devise ways of working with them. There were a thousand and one details to be tied up: we had to be able to communicate with the police efficiently by radio, and, at the ordinary human level, to get to know our opposite numbers.

Since that modest start, our meetings with senior police officers, and our training with their forces, have proved immensely fruitful. Harmony and friendship are essential in coalition operations of this kind: they ensure that police trust the SAS and send for them at an early stage of any operation, rather than waiting and bringing them in cold when the position has begun to deteriorate. Ever since the inception of the Counter-Terrorist force, realistic joint exercises involving both ourselves and the police have been staged to test procedures. At the start the most acute terrorist threat was perceived to be at Heathrow Airport. Exercises were conducted at the highest level, often being directed from the Cabinet Office Briefing Room, the subterranean command centre in Whitehall, where a Junior Minister would be in charge, and representatives of various security organizations present.

In all this we led the world, one jump ahead of any other nation. Today many countries have counter-terrorist teams, but they are all based on the pioneer work done by Andy Massey. Our set-up is now second to none − not even to that of the Americans, who have far more money to spend; for behind all the specialist weapons, assault equipment, technical devices and so on are the SAS. They are a living embodiment of the individualism of the British − a group of soldiers with the essential ability to work as a closely coordinated team, and yet able instantly to take the initiative, each man for himself, should the need arise.

Running the SAS, I realized how fortunate I was to be in charge of such a compact unit. The organization was so small that I could get to know every member of it, and also influence policy in a way which would be impossible for a commanding officer in the infantry or the armoured corps. This gave me a fine opportunity to use my imagination and bring in reforms. It seemed vital that everyone, officers particularly, should be searching for change all the time − and indeed one of the Regiment's strengths lay in its habit of looking ahead, adjusting techniques to meet future demands (the creation of the Pagoda team was a perfect illustration). Another source of strength was that the officers, and a substantial proportion of the soldiers, were not allowed to remain in the Regiment permanently, but had to return to their parent units between tours, with the result that nobody became introverted or brooded exclusively upon our own affairs. This constant interchange helped SAS people understand the rest of the Services, and vice-versa.

One area in which I thought we did need innovation was that of selection, especially of officers. I wanted to switch some of the emphasis away from purely physical ordeals and place more weight on tests of personality and character. I was concerned that purely physical standards were becoming impossibly high; the number of candidates who passed was growing ever smaller as the directing staff, with the best intentions, kept cranking up their demands. Difficult as it is to judge the moment at which to relax pressure slightly, I decided that the time had come. We had inadvertently begun looking for trained SAS soldiers, rather than for men with the potential to be developed, and we were running the risk of missing men who might turn out to be brilliant on operations, but did not shine in what was essentially a proving environment.

This is where the personal judgment and experience of a Commanding Officer can play an important role. As always, I myself took a close interest in selection, making sure to attend the officers' course, and often joining one or two of the candidates on their cross-country marches.

Another modest innovation was my order that everyone passing the selection course should buy and read a copy of Lord Moran's *The Anatomy of Courage*. The author was personal physician to Sir Winston Churchill, and his little book, published in 1945, was a curious mixture: first-hand descriptions based on his own experiences as a medical officer in the trenches during the First World War alternated with passages of philosophical speculation about the nature of courage. Yet if the result was uneven, I found it of absorbing interest. Moran had original ideas on subjects such as discipline, freedom of speech, cowardice and fear: he argued that courage, like capital, can be spent, and so needs careful husbandry, and that fear also can be positively managed. I myself found him inspiring on the subject of leadership in war, and many of my people derived substantial benefits from reading his book.

It was also my policy, as Commanding Officer, to keep members of the Regiment on their toes by staging secret exercises against them. Everyone had to be reminded that we were perpetually under threat, and should never feel that we were off duty. I found it valuable, therefore, to test reflexes by privily briefing one lot of people to carry out a raid on another lot, and see what happened – and on one memorable occasion I set up just such an attack on myself.

Since I was supposed to be keeping alert, and the Regiment was meant to be concerned about my security, I issued the Counter-Terrorist team with the challenge of kidnapping me. Nothing happened for a while, and I daresay I was lulled into a false sense of security. Then one lunchtime I went out behind the camp for my usual run, which I had foolishly allowed to become a bit of a routine, and suddenly I was leapt on by several men, gagged, bound, thrown into the back of a van and driven off. I suppose I should have been worried, but I was not, for although I cursed myself for having fallen into a trap, I thought I knew what was going on – though it did cross my mind that the kidnap could be real. Having been driven round Hereford for a while, I was taken out of the van, stripped to my underpants, and nailed up inside a large wooden crate. This was not particularly amusing, and not a very elegant fate for a lieutenant-colonel in command of a regiment – but, as I hoped, the villains soon telephoned the Officers' Mess and revealed where I was, so that people came along and let me out. The incident proved effective in making us all concentrate on personal security.

One of my most memorable encounters, which typified SAS spirit, occurred in the summer of 1973, when Staff Sergeant Houston of the Royal Signals, who had been badly wounded in Oman, reached hospital in London. John Simpson and I went to see him, and found him in a bad way: a battle accident with a mortar had cost him one eye and half his right arm, and he was clearly in severe pain. Because the field surgical team in Dhofar had given him only one chance in ten of surviving, I had had his family brought to London to say goodbye. Yet when John and I reached his bedside, all he was prepared to talk about were his chances of staying in the SAS: for twenty minutes we seriously discussed how the Director could make out a case to the Ministry of Defence for keeping a one-eyed, one-armed signaller in the Regiment. His final words to John were: 'Right, boss. You can also tell the bastards that I always thought this might happen, so I've trained myself over the years to do everything with my left hand as well. And in any case, I'm senior enough now that if something does need two hands, I can tell some other bugger to do it.'

As we left the ward, we did not have much to say to each other. In due course John made out a submission to the Ministry – but six weeks later the man was out of hospital and caught going for a run with fifty pounds of bricks in his bergen. Four months later, while still on sick leave, he went on a parachute exercise in Canada. He served on in the SAS for a number of years, before leaving to become a teacher.

In the summer of 1974, with the end of my tour in sight, I ceased to make innovations and aimed instead for a period of stability before handing over to my successor, Tony Jeapes. I knew that he would want to take a critical look at the whole organization and impose his own stamp on it, so for my last few months I thought it best to keep things running as they were. One evening, talking to Bridget, I was foolish enough to say, 'Well, thank God for that. We seem to have had a pretty good tour, and nothing's gone disastrously wrong.'

I should have known better. Next morning I found myself threatened by a scandal which could have destroyed not only my own reputation, but that of the SAS as well. We discovered that in Oman members of the Regiment had been drawn into practices which involved misappropriation of *firqat* funds. Details of what happened are no longer important; suffice it to say that sums of money had been taken in back-handers by our people, over a long period.

The problem suddenly facing me was how to deal with the irregularities. If we launched a major investigation and disciplinary exercise, we would inevitably bring the affair to the surface and cause a rupture in diplomatic relations with Oman, destroying the credit we had laboriously built up over the past three years. If we tried to contain the affair at a lower level, there was a danger that details would leak out later, and the fact that we had not reported it in the first place would compound our own felonies. Either way, scandal would give ammunition to the critics who were gunning for the SAS and hoping for our demise.

To me this was a disaster of the greatest magnitude – a setback which ruined any sense of achievement which I might otherwise have felt. I was forced to ask myself how much of the blame lay with me: had the improprieties resulted from my own lack of judgment, knowledge and involvement at lower command levels? Had my direction and planning been at fault?

There were, it is true, extenuating circumstances. Corruption was endemic on the *jebel*, where there were no proper accounts, and money was regarded in much looser terms than in England. Again, it was not the Queen's money, but *firqat* funds, which had been misappropriated. Further, at an early stage in Operation Storm I had seen the need to control money more tightly, and I had twice asked for staff to do the job; but manpower was scarce at the time, and nobody had wanted to go to the expense of sending out an officer from the Royal Army Pay Corps.

Yet when the scandal threatened to break, none of these considerations seemed to count for much. After I had discussed the matter fully with John Simpson, we decided to take it straight to the Colonel Commandant of the SAS, Viscount Head. Formerly Secretary of State for Defence and High Commissioner for Malaysia, Head had once (it will be remembered) surprised me in my underpants at Pea Green House in Kuching, and taken the incident in good part. Now he was precisely the kind of senior statesman the SAS needed in a crisis. Together with Simpson and Dare Newell, I explained what had happened. Simpson later recalled that this was the only occasion on which he had ever seen Head look seriously worried; after hearing us, the Colonel Commandant sent us away and thought the matter over for two days. Then he agreed to shoulder responsibility, and advised us to sort the trouble out within the Regiment, rather than in any way that might make it public.

So the matter was brought under control. Having consulted the Squadron Leaders, senior non-commissioned officers and my successor as Commanding Officer, I set up a board of inquiry within the SAS, which collected all the information available. The results were, largely speaking, imprecise; but money was paid back, one officer was transferred elsewhere, several other people were summarily dealt with by me, and over Christmas 1974 John Simpson came down to Hereford to deliver what he described as 'a blistering rocket' to the whole Regiment.

I was by no means alone in taking a serious view of the affair, which threatened the very existence of the Regiment. In an internal report, compiled for our eyes only, Dare Newell wrote that 'the possible repercussions of the "Storm" scandal are such that they could, in certain circumstances, bring about the dissolution of the SAS'. He emphasized 'the necessity of driving home to all ranks the enormity of their actions', and the need 'to ensure moral standards are raised to an acceptable level'. In one telling paragraph he warned:

> The situation, therefore, is such that, in order to save the SAS, not only has the Commander placed his career in serious jeopardy, but a senior statesman has risked opprobrium on our behalf. I feel that all regular officers and warrant officers at least should be made aware of what has been done for them.

Dare's conclusion was that the misappropriation of funds had been made possible by lack of proper control and supervision in Oman. In spite of this generous interpretation of events, I was left feeling deeply disturbed. The affair came as a reminder that the SAS are prone to the same weaknesses as people in any other sector of society, and need careful handling if they are not to cross the narrow gap between, on the one hand, doing a brilliant job at the cutting-edge of an operation, and, on the other, allowing themselves to be sucked down into actions which at first seem no more than a slight stretching of the rules. Never again did I assume that a job was finished until I had actually handed over to my successor.

I found some compensation in the fact that I was awarded the Distinguished Service Order for my part in launching and running Operation Storm; the citation was secret, and although I had it read out to me at the time, it was not until many years later that I was able to see it myself. Gratifying as that was, I should dearly have liked to hand over 22nd SAS to Tony Jeapes[1] without the smell of corruption hanging over it. Yet I knew that he was a first-class man, and I had every confidence in his ability to sort things out.

1. Later a Major General, he commanded South-West District.

CHAPTER 19

DESKBOUND

1974–76

When my tour with 22nd SAS ended, the authorities had some trouble deciding what to do with me: I had spent so much of my career with Special Forces that many people considered me unfit for any other form of service. When John Simpson recommended that I should command an armoured brigade, the Military Secretary (who decides senior appointments) told him not to be ridiculous; yet it was a serious suggestion – and, as things turned out, an oddly prophetic one, for in the Gulf War of 1990–91, as Commander of the British Forces, I did indeed have two armoured brigades under me. Thwarted in that direction, John recommended that I should go as Military Assistant to Monkey Blacker, by then the Adjutant General. Blacker, who had always supported me, said verbally that he thought this would be an excellent idea; John was therefore slightly surprised to receive a letter, couched in terms that he described as 'almost vitriolic', and probably written by one of the General's staff, demanding to know how anyone could possibly recommend me for that job, as I had no experience whatever outside Special Forces.

In the end – also through John's advocacy – I was sent to the Staff College at Camberley as an instructor in what was known as the Overseas Team, dealing with counter-insurgency. I was delighted to find that the Commandant was Hugh Beach: an exceedingly clever but modest man, much loved for his equanimity, for the high quality of the intellectual input which he injected into the Staff College course, and for his skill at developing other people's ideas in a sympathetic way.

To be back at Camberley gave me an uneasy sense of *déjà vu*, but this time I was at least working in my own field, which I knew well, and I was part of an excellent team. When I arrived the leader was Lieutenant-Colonel John Macmillan (later a lieutenant-general, and GOC Scotland), whose keen analytical mind and exceptional grasp of English wrought wonders on my own tortured prose. We also had John Walters (now General Sir John Walters), and a lively Australian officer, Peter Badman.

Soon I decided that our work dealt mainly with revolutionary warfare, and I put up a suggestion, which Hugh Beach adopted, that our unit should be renamed the Revolutionary Warfare Team. This was evidently too strong for my successors, and after I had left, the name was changed again to the Counter-Revolutionary Warfare Team. Our main task was to devise and run exercises in which imaginary terrorist and guerrilla attacks were about to take place, or had already done so. In a typical scenario, different groups of students, each in its own room with a battery of telephones, would represent the terrorists, the army and the control room from which counter-measures were being organized. The exercise was exceedingly complex, but this was what made it realistic – even to the extent of some students acting as journalists, who came along to interview the other participants and write reports.

Other exercises were set farther afield. 'Seven Maids', for instance, notionally took place in Oman – a country which I happened to know rather well, and about which I could present much realistic detail. Another scenario dealt with Chinese unrest in Hong Kong, and the response of the security forces in dealing with it.

Life in the mess followed a traditional military pattern, and one evening, to liven up a dinner night, I arranged with the waiters to fill two decanters not with port but with blackcurrant cordial, slightly watered to make it an acceptable colour. At the correct moment the decanters were reverently placed on the table and circulated clockwise, everybody filling his glass in preparation for the loyal toast; then the presiding officer rose to his feet and called, 'Gentlemen, the Queen!' We all stood and drank – and faces were a study. As people sat down, they were swallowing and licking their lips in the most extravagant fashion, and looking thunderstruck; but nobody wanted to be the first to condemn the port. Then suddenly someone shouted, 'Bloody Ribena!' and the secret was out. The decanters were taken away and washed thoroughly before being brought back filled as people expected them to be – whereupon I admitted responsibility, and by skilful argument managed to avoid having to buy the entire company a round of drinks.

To keep our family base stable, Bridget remained in our own house, with the children now going to day-school, and during the week I lived at the Staff College, commuting home at weekends. Possession of a few acres of land and some tumbledown buildings at last gave an outlet to my latent enthusiasm for farming. The buildings badly needed refurbishment, but because I could not afford to do them up on my army pay, I went into pig-rearing as a means of generating extra income. Instead of starting in a small way, and learning as I went along, I ignored Bridget's advice and plunged in on a grand scale, and so made some grand mistakes. For instance, we began buying in weaners – pigs about eight weeks old – which are likely to be carrying disease, and in spite of our efforts to isolate each new batch, one lorry-load of forty arrived with atrophic rhinitis (an inflammation of the nostrils). In my absence at Staff College, Bridget spotted the disorder and quite rightly refused to accept delivery of them, whereupon she had a monumental row with the suppliers, before vets confirmed her diagnosis, and the pigs were taken away.

In learning this new trade, we were enormously helped by kind neighbours: Phil and Paul, local farmers, taught us how to dock tails and castrate piglets; John and Sandra helped Bridget with the heavy work of feeding and mucking out during the week, and several times another marvellous couple, Basil and Ruth, came to our aid in moments of crisis. As our herd of fattening pigs built up to five hundred head, we found out what a tricky operation this was: profit margins were so small that, to make any return at all, we had to play the market with the utmost care. Every Friday evening when I arrived home I would ring up a local dealer who knew every twist of the trade, and find out prices. Then we would have to decide whether to sell a consignment, or whether to keep them on for another week, with the twin risk that demand might drop and the pigs might become too heavy to fetch the best price.

Over a period of three years we acquired a good knowledge of pig-management, and also learnt much about running a business – marketing, cash-flow, and so on. But we also created an enormous amount of worry for ourselves, for we generally lost money, and I would wake up in the middle of the night sweating at the thought of having £16,000 worth of animals out there in the yard, uninsured and quite possibly about to go down with some unspeakable disease. During one hot summer nobody wanted to eat pork, with the result that the market collapsed; yet Bridget, John and Sandra had no option but to go on pushing huge pigs into the dealer's lorry, knowing that each one would lose us £5. To help with the marketing, I began selling pig-meat to friends at the Staff College, and I also grew potatoes, which I would take back with me on Sunday evening, dumping pre-ordered sacks in people's offices on Monday morning.

By far the saddest episode in my time at the Staff College was the illness and death of my mother. The appearance of grand-children had given her a great fillip and a new purpose in life. So complete was her recovery by then that she achieved her ambition of renewing her original driving licence and acquiring a car; to outsiders, she seemed a perfectly normal sixty-year-old, with a rather poor memory. The children loved having 'Granny Doggy' to stay: she was endlessly patient about playing games with them, and for us adults her presence created an agreeable aura of calm in the bustle which always seemed to fill the house.

Then she got cancer. After all the deprivation which she had suffered, after half her life had been ruined, it seemed incredibly hard that she should die a lingering and painful death – but so it was ordained. By then my brother Michael had married Su Hipwell, a lovely, vivacious girl, who could almost (but not quite) control him, and bore him two fine sons, Simon and James. When my mother fell ill, Su angelically took her into their house at Tidworth and looked after her. For some months my mother could be moved across the road to the Military Hospital for treatment; but then, as the disease took hold, she became an in-patient for her final few weeks. I have never forgotten how she looked when I last saw her in intensive care: she was almost unconscious with the drugs which controlled her pain, and terribly thin and wizened. I could see her dying before my eyes.

I explained to her a financial plan which we had devised at the last minute, whereby, before she died, we should make over a substantial slice of her assets into a trust fund for the education of our children, and so save death duties. Although her affairs had been in the hands of the Court of Protection for many years, and she had not been in control of her own capital, she was thoroughly practical, and both understood and approved what I was doing: in her view the family came first, and she could think of no better use for the money than to help give her grandchildren a good education. So we managed to create a trust fund just in time. Soon afterwards she died, aged sixty-six, and we buried her in the churchyard at Tidworth. I could not escape the feeling that she had suffered unfairly: she had grown up with the advantage of comfortable means, for sure, but she had never done anything to abuse her privileges. Her cheerful and outgoing nature had contributed to the gaiety of life, and her first marriage, however short and interrupted by my father's Service postings, had been happy and fruitful – only for her to be struck down by a series of cruel blows.

We were still grieving for her when another tragedy hit the family. Su, who had nursed my mother so selflessly, herself was diagnosed as having a cancerous tumour on the brain. In spite of two ghastly operations, and constant chemotherapy, she remained astonishingly cheerful and courageous, and in the summer of 1978 we all had an extraordinary holiday together at a villa just south of Bilbão. Michael had been posted as Naval Attaché to the British Embassy in Madrid, and Su had not been able to accompany him because she was so ill; but she insisted on coming out to this house which Michael had rented, and we had the most intense holiday of our lives, at the same time tragic and hilarious, with our emotions heightened by impending catastrophe. At the end of it Su went home, and Michael followed her back to their house at Tidworth; there he nursed her until she died in his arms, just before Christmas. She was buried in the same grave as my mother, and we planted two trees in the churchyard, one to commemorate each of them. Her sons, aged eight and ten, were staying with us at the end, so that it fell to Bridget to tell them that their mother had died; but Michael managed to come down for Christmas Day. After that he shaped his life and sacrificed his career in the Navy for their sake, always influencing his postings so that he would have a chance to look after the boys and bring them up.

As always when the end of a tour approached, the question of my next posting began to loom large. Then one day the Ministry of Defence telephoned to ask if I would be prepared to go out to Khartoum, to run the British Army training team there. If I would, said the caller, I would be on loan service, and I would be promoted to full colonel.

Well! Personally, I could think of nothing better, but I knew that most service families would regard Khartoum as hell on earth, and I suspected that Bridget would be horrified by the idea of going to live in the Sudan with three youngish children. So, for a few hours, I sat at my desk in a state of high excitement, trying to work out the tactical presentation of this opportunity to the home front. When I rang home that evening, I put together a fantastic story of promotion and prospects for me, excitement, travel and education for the children. Bridget's initial response was exactly what I had expected: that the idea was crazy, and that on no account should we disrupt the children's school plans by taking them off to so outlandish a place.

We had three days in which to decide – and I flatter myself that by then I had become quite crafty at playing domestic poker. But Bridget behaved in characteristically positive fashion, and came round to back the idea of Khartoum with enthusiasm at least as great as mine, and with far greater practical understanding of how to crack the problems involved.

Once we had taken the decision to go, we had six months in which to prepare ourselves – and some intricate planning was needed. We had to close down our pig-breeding enterprise, dispose of the animals, let the house and sort out arrangements for the children's schools and holidays. One cardinal element in our plans was that we should drive out part or all of the way in a vehicle of our own, for we would need one in the Sudan, and we had heard that any car shipped into the country unsupervised was stripped of everything removable long before it reached its destination. Through a friend, Ben Harvey-Bathurst, we therefore bought a long-wheel-base Land Rover: a former test vehicle, almost entirely rebuilt, with a reconditioned engine, it was in effect a new car, although slightly odd looking, with a van-type back and small windows rather high up in the sides. Thanks to the generosity of the Rover company, we got it for the absurdly low price of £1250, and it proved a star performer, never giving the slightest trouble.

After trying many permutations, we perfected our plans as follows: I would fly out to Khartoum on my own to take over the job in January 1977. Bridget would fly out with the children to join me for the Easter holidays. Then she would take the family home in time to put Nicola into boarding school for her first term. In July I myself would fly home, and we would all drive out together on a great overland trip in the Land Rover, motoring as far as Aswan in Egypt, take the ferry to Wadi Halfa, just inside the Sudan, and then put the vehicle on the train – however primitive it might be – to Khartoum.

This was the official programme. Yet from the start I harboured a secret hope that we would also drive the last section of the route, the five-hundred-odd miles across the Nubian Desert, which stretches southwards from Wadi Halfa to Khartoum. I knew that the most sensible thing to do would be to put the Land Rover on the train; but the challenge of crossing the sands under our own power was one that I found difficult to resist.

Our wedding at Holy Trinity, Brompton, 13 February, 1965.

Below: Our first child, Nicola, was born on 2 January, 1966.

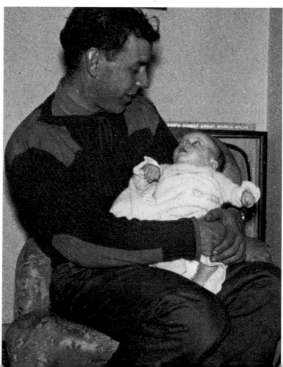

Men for all seasons: training the counter-terrorist squad, formed after the Munich Olympics massacre in 1972.

6 May 1980: out of sight of the public at the back of the Iranian Embassy, the SAS prepare to abseil down the building.

One man suffered severe burns when he became entangled in his ropes.

Above: Bridget and me outside Britannia House, Port Stanley, with our Igloo greenhouse in the background.

Right: Rough passage: joining a Royal Navy guardship of the Falklands, 1985.

Below: Farewell to the Falklands: boarding a TriStar, with the steps lined by buglers of the Light Infantry, July 1985.

Below: Testing the water: the GOC Wales pioneers the route for the Cambrian Patrol, 1986.

At Buckingham Palace having received the KCB in 1988 with the whole family, *(left to right)* Edward, Bridget, Phillida, myself and Nicola

THE GULF WAR

Above: Brigadier Patrick Cordingley outlines his battle plan, November, 1990.

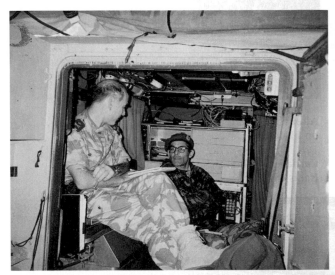

Right: Being briefed before the land battle by Major General Rupert Smith in his command vehicle, February, 1991.

Below: Discussing the battle plans with Major General Rupert Smith *(on my right)*, and Brigadier Tim Sulivan *(on my left)*.

After the Safwan ceasefire talks, General Norman Schwarzkopf with Prince Khalid on his left.

Carnage at Mitla: military and civilian looted vehicles destroyed from the air as Iraqis tried to flee.

Magic Carpet at work: the ticker-
tape Victory Parade in New York,
10 June, 1991, was a great
tribute from the American people
to the coalition servicemen who
took part in the Gulf War.

Home at last, May 1991: the gift
of a Methuselah from Moët &
Chandon put extra fizz into our
family reunion.

CHAPTER 20

ON THE NILE

1977–79

Khartoum is built on the confluence of the Blue and White Niles, and the difference between the two rivers is plain to see. The water in the Blue Nile, which has come down out of the Ethiopian highlands, is relatively clear, and bluish-grey, while that of the White Nile is brown and milky with silt: where the two torrents meet, a sharp dividing line is preserved for some distance before the waters mingle.

Arriving on my own, I took over both job and house from my predecessor, Colonel George Rochfort-Rae, a genial fellow who welcomed me with a hand-over party to which he invited a large number of guests, mainly Sudanese. Besides the Arab-style house, with its high wall enclosing a garden compound, in the European quarter near the airfield, he bequeathed me a wizened old cook called Osman and a mongrel called Barry. When sober, Osman was a first-class chef, and produced delicious meals; but he had a weakness for the bottle, and although I tried to keep all drink under lock and key, he would occasionally get at it – and then I had to fend for myself until he sobered up again. Barry looked like an outsize, spindly beagle, brown and white, with extra-long legs. He had been handed to George by the French Ambassador, and it was clear that at some stage in his life he had been ill-treated, for he had a phobia about being handled. For most of the time he seemed relaxed and friendly, and, if he knew you, he would even let you touch him; but the moment you tried to take hold of him or restrain him, he would spring away or bite you.

This extreme nervousness made the administration of his

annual anti-rabies injection a nightmare; yet it was in a way an advantage, for he was highly alert, and made an effective guard-dog. With law and order largely broken down, and Khartoum plagued by burglars, it was reassuring to have him loose in the compound at night. Later he was joined by a tortoise called Tarzan, who came to us as a baby but grew at an amazing speed.

My first few days in the Sudan were enough to show me that the country was in a parlous state. Long dalliance with the Soviet Union had left wreckage everywhere, and the scrapyards were full of obsolete Russian military equipment. Starvation in outlying areas had driven a mass of refugees into a shanty town on the outskirts of Khartoum – hence the ever-increasing burglaries. Roads in the city were so badly potholed that journeys took three or four times as long as they should have, because drivers had to weave from side to side in search of a clear route. Raw sewage ran out into the gutters, the electricity supply failed repeatedly, and the telephone system worked only intermittently.

When I arrived, in mid-winter, the daytime temperature was fairly comfortable, but as spring came round the thermometer soared, and by the height of summer it was often showing 140°F or more. Such heat was really formidable and draining; and whenever the desert wind called the *haboob* blew – which it sometimes did for days on end – it would fill the air with dust so thick that you could scarcely see five yards. Everything became coated with a dense brown film, and then, if rain fell, it would come down like brown sleet.

In spite of these natural hazards, I quickly began to enjoy myself. I found the Sudanese generous and kind individually, but fundamentally idle. My job was to run the British Army training team, and at the same time to act as Chief Instructor at the Staff College, which had about eighty students. I decided at once that the best way of operating would be to share my office with my Sudanese opposite number, Fadhlala Burma Nasser (he and his wife were hospitable and highly intelligent, and became good friends). Our arrangement worked well, as it meant that we swapped ideas – and this, in my view, is the point of loan service: that the British should not impose their own methods and try to run foreign armies along British lines, but rather that they should help train local people in a manner that suits the temperament and methods of the country.

Apart from Fadhlala, the officer with whom I had most to do was Major General Abdul Majid, Chief of Operations in the Sudanese Army.[1] I was lucky to be dealing with him, because he was hard-working and got things done in spite of the system – so much so that his nickname among the British was 'Black Magic'. The only trouble was that his efficiency gave him a fearsome reputation among his own people, who were much in awe of him.

I soon developed a routine to suit the climate: up at 0545 for a run followed by a shower, and into the office at 0645. We would work until 0900, giving lectures and running exercises similar to those at Camberley, and then have an enormous mess breakfast of eggs, beef sausages, liver, bread and coffee. Our second working session lasted until 1400, and that would be it for the day. The students at the College were a microcosm of Sudanese society. Most were northerners, and Muslim, of Arab extraction, but there was also a smattering of Christian souther-ners, of African descent, who tended to be soot-black. The most noticeable of all were the Dinkas, who were often immensely tall – seven foot or more. Efforts were being made to increase the proportion of southerners, but there was always a degree of frostiness between the two, and in terms of intellect, ability and education the northerners were miles ahead.

Our British team was small – only eight in all – and I got to know them all extremely well. One couple, Terry and Maureen Finney, were old friends from Hereford, for Terry, a linguist fluent in eight languages, including Swahili, Arabic and Greek, had instructed the SAS, and now was teaching military history and tactics at the Military Academy. Other good friends included Keith Mackintosh, who advised at the armoured school, and his

1. Later he was promoted Chief of Staff, and at the end of 1979 he came on a visit to Britain soon after Margaret Thatcher had been elected Prime Minister. I was accompanying him back to Heathrow in a car when he turned to me and said, 'Peter, I just don't know what your country's coming to. Your Head of State, the Queen, is a woman, and that's bad enough. But now look what's happened – a new Prime Minister, head of the Government, also a woman!'

wife Judith, Bugs and Janet Hughes, and Lieutenant-Colonel
Roger and Joan Jones: later we were joined by Tom Mickley
and his wife Veronica. Tom, who became my Chief Clerk, was
a brilliantly inventive Warrant Officer from the Royal Pioneer
Corps, who could turn his hand to any mechanical problem,
whether on land or on water – an invaluable gift in a country
where equipment was constantly breaking down. Other indispensable allies were Colonel 'Dicky' Bird, the Defence Attaché,
who was famous for routing a burglar by brandishing his sword,
and his wife Ruth, a great cracker of dry jokes. From the
Ambassador down, the staff of the British Embassy were
extremely good to us, and we were allowed to shop in the Commissariat Stores – a valued privilege, as there was nowhere else
in the city where one could buy family essentials such as baked
beans or marmalade, and even the Commissariat often ran out.

The struggle to survive, and to obtain the essentials of life,
was so unremitting that members of the expatriate community
depended on each other for help. Whenever the power failed,
for instance, you were faced with an awkward decision about
the deep-freeze: should you leave it shut in the hope that the
current would come on again within a few hours? Or should
you whisk the precious (and often irreplaceable) contents across
town to the house of a friend in an area where electricity was
still flowing? The city was often full of Europeans frantically
ferrying food in all directions.

In spite of the physical limitations, I found Khartoum a fascinating place, for it is steeped in history – the siege of the city, the
death of General Gordon, Kitchener's operations on the Nile,
and above all the battle of Omdurman, in which the young
Winston Churchill took part.[1] Gordon's palace still stands, as
Government headquarters, and the battlefield of Omdurman
has scarcely changed: the little hillocks and wadis described by

1. General Charles Gordon was Governor-General of the Sudan from 1873 to 1880,
and was sent back there in 1884 to suppress a revolt by the followers of Mahommed
Ahmed, the religious leader known as the Mahdi. Besieged in Khartoum, Gordon
inspired the native garrison to hold out with the utmost tenacity, but in January
1885 the town fell, and he was killed, two days before a relief expedition under Lord
Kitchener reached him. The Mahdi's successor, the Khalifa, ruled the Sudan for thirteen
years until, in 1898, Kitchener led a joint Anglo-Egyptian expedition against him and
shattered his power at the battles of Atbara and Omdurman.

Churchill in *The River War* are still there in the flat desert, and one can walk over the ground on which the 21st Lancers delivered the last full-scale cavalry charge of modern warfare.

The arrival of Bridget and the family for the Easter holidays cheered life up enormously. We were naturally worried about how the children would react to the heat, especially Phillida (then nine) and Edward (seven), both of whom were red-headed and freckled. The house had no air-conditioning, and only primitive fans for cooling; but in the event the children were so excited by the novelty of everything that they hardly noticed the temperature. Bridget was horrified by domestic conditions, and particularly by the kitchen – a windowless outhouse with a flat roof on which the sun beat relentlessly, heating the room like an oven.

With her usual determination, she made the best of things, and we gravitated more and more to the point on the Blue Nile where Kitchener's paddle-driven gunboat *Malik* was moored and maintained as the headquarters of the local sailing club, still with a Maxim machine gun mounted forward. In spite of fears about bilharzia – which was certainly present in the White Nile – we were soon happily swimming and trying to water-ski in the Blue Nile. We also sailed in the club's Nile Class steel boats – although the season was short, for at the height of summer the *haboob* made sailing too unpleasant. Another favourite resort was the Sudan Club, where we could swim whenever the pool's filter system was working, play squash and enjoy simple meals in the company of other expatriates.

After what seemed an extraordinarily short time Bridget and the children were gone again, back to England for the summer term at school, and I was on my own, being looked after by Osman and a houseboy. Gradually my expectations focused on our great overland trip planned to start in July, and soon I too found myself back in England, taking early mid-tour leave and making final arrangements for our departure. We had had our Land Rover fitted with seats in the back and a big luggage-rack on the roof, and we kitted it out to a high specification, with jerricans of water and extra fuel, and spare tyres.

I had long since decided that the children were not going to sit mindlessly in the back of the vehicle for five weeks, crying out every few miles, 'Are we nearly there, Mummy?' To make them concentrate on the trip I told them that there would be a prize of £5 for the person who kept the best log of the journey. Differences in age clearly made this an unfair competition from the start, but to the children £5 was big money and a powerful incentive. They were all keenly aware of the value of money, for at the early age of about six we had introduced them to a simple banking system, whereby they received their twenty-five pence a week pocket money not as cash but as a credit to their accounts; when they wanted to buy something, Bridget would lend them the money, and they would enter a debit in the appropriate column. If they ran up a debt, they had to pay it off. In this way they learned about money, and the importance of managing it properly.

And so, with the children seriously over-excited, and equipped with a scrapbook apiece, we set off for Dover on the first leg of our marathon. My special device for minimizing boredom was a then new-fangled cassette-tape player, and strains of *The Sound of Music* floated endlessly from the back seat, interspersed by arguments about whether that tape should be played again immediately, or whether we should have *My Fair Lady* instead.

The Finneys, who had managed to complete the journey twice, had briefed us on the hazards in and beyond Egypt, the chief of which was food-poisoning. Bridget had therefore taken enormous trouble selecting a supply of tinned and dehydrated food on which we could live independently of local supplies, and the vehicle was loaded to capacity with tins and packets, as well as with vitamin pills, to compensate for the lack of fresh ingredients. We also had full camping kit, with calor-gas burners for cooking.

Our drive down through Europe went well, and the journey was marred only by a freak accident to Edward. While staying with friends in Switzerland, I kicked a football which hit him on the side of the face and somehow trapped a nerve, causing one cheek to swell up and his mouth to become lopsided. The problem seemed to be so serious that at one point we feared we might have to return to England; but luckily our host was a leading physician, and his prompt treatment put the trouble right.

As the days passed, the children's log-books proved their worth, whiling away many an hour, and often we had to delay our start in the morning while one of the authors brought entries up to date. From Venice we took a ferry, via the Corinth Canal and Piraeus, to Alexandria, where we arrived in the blazing heat of August. There on the quay we waited interminably to go through customs, entertained by the gully-gully men with their disappearing snakes and chickens, while Bridget fed us sardines and cold baked beans – all she could reach – and in the end it was timely help from a member of the staff of Westland Aircraft, who knew which palms to grease, which saved us. Major General John Strawson – then head of Westland's Egyptian office – had kindly arranged this assistance; furthermore, although he himself was away, the same member of his staff, together with his driver, gave us a lead from Alexandria south to Cairo and through the capital to the fashionable suburb of Heliopolis on the eastern outskirts of the city. There Strawson had put his villa at our disposal, so that we were comfortable and well looked after.

In Heliopolis we made plans for our journey up the Nile. The first necessity was to secure tickets for the ferry which sailed up Lake Nasser from Aswan to Wadi Halfa, and the second to book a place on the train across the Nubian Desert, from the Egyptian border to Khartoum. (The lake is in fact a stretch of the Nile, created by the building of the Aswan High Dam, which engulfed the once-beautiful colonial town of Wadi Halfa.) The Finneys had warned me on no account to leave Cairo until we had tickets for the ferry: otherwise, they said, we should never get a place. But booking proved impossible, for unprecedented rains in the Sudanese desert had caused a flash flood and washed away a major stretch of the railway line: until the railway reopened, we were told, no tickets could be sold for the boat. After several days of fruitless argument I decided that we must press on, as we were already behind schedule, and I did not want to return to duty late.

We therefore drove on south, stopping for one night at El Minah and for three wonderful days at Luxor, where we visited the Valley of the Kings on donkey-back and saw all the sights, blessedly free of other tourists, who had been driven off by the August heat. To eke out our finances we stayed in a low-grade hotel, and Bridget insisted that we must refuse all meals except breakfast: to obtain fresh food, I went out one afternoon while the children were having their rest and bartered with an Arab for two scrawny chickens, which I brought back and smuggled past the hotel porter alive in a sack. With the children still asleep I wrung their necks and plucked them, and Bridget promptly put them in our pressure-cooker, over our gas burner on the windowsill. That chicken stew was pronounced delicious by all ranks.

So far our journey had been relatively straightforward, but the next stages degenerated into nightmare. We found Aswan in a state of chaos, packed with thousands of people held up by cancellation of the ferry-service and unable to return to their homes upriver. Somehow we got tickets on the first boat, only to find that, with five minutes' warning, we were going to be separated from the Land Rover – and all our supplies – for the next three days, because vehicles were being loaded on to a separate barge to make room for extra passengers.

Knowing that even the first-class lavatories would be unin-habitable, Bridget whipped out what she regarded as essentials for the voyage: a child's pot, a bucket, water, sterilizing tablets, basic food and a means of cooking. Grabbing all this, and the children, we struggled aboard, and discovered that our accom-modation was third-class, in the bowels of the ship. To reach it, we had to pass the on-board slaughterhouse, and our cabin turned out to be like a mortuary, with no windows of any kind. The heat and smell down there were indescribable, and I rapidly decided that we could not spend several days in such a hell-hole.

When I explained our predicament to a sympathetic Sudanese official and fellow-passenger, he at once said, 'You can't possibly live down there. I'll sort it out for you,' – and by some miracle he did. Suddenly we were being shown on to an ancient barge which had been strapped alongside the main ferry to accommo-date the overflow of passengers. To gain access to it we had to clamber over the side rails of both vessels, which had been lashed together. The deck was already solid with Sudanese and Egyptian families camping out in the open; we picked our way through them to two narrow second-class cabins, side by side. Each had a porthole which opened on to the seething deck, and two bunks – nothing else, but they were a thousand times better than the dungeon down below, and at least gave us a measure of privacy.

There we were based – not, as it turned out, for the two and a half days scheduled, but for four, as unforeseen events delayed us. One was the breakdown of an engine, which meant that we travelled at a reduced speed, and the other the death of a passenger, who expired from heat and overcrowding. While the man was being buried with full Muslim ceremony at Abu Simbel, the ferry remained anchored offshore, offering a splendid view of the temple, with its great stone figures gazing out over the water; on board, meanwhile, a woman gave birth to a baby. After that we chugged slowly on up the lake in barely tolerable conditions. For breakfast we ate bread and omelettes in the ferry's dining room (except on the last morning, when the food ran out). For the rest of the time Bridget fed us from her reserves – and when the few crude buildings of the new Wadi Halfa at last came in sight, our relief knew no bounds.

Not that things on shore were much better. In stupefying heat we had to queue for customs and immigration, and the one hotel was so sordid that we decided to camp in the open, on the sand. By then the train service to Khartoum had been restored, but such a backlog had accumulated that we were faced with a three-week wait before we could get a place for the Land Rover. Clearly this was impossible, and we had no alternative but to drive across the desert.

At this stage I have to confess that family memory is not united about the episode which follows. Bridget, putting the safety of the children first, had assumed from the outset that we would take the train – and she points out that if I had been seriously intending to drive across the desert, I would have included basic essentials like shovels and sand-ladders in our kit. I, secretly longing for adventure, had hoped all along that we would do the desert drive – and when she suggested that I should try to pull rank at the booking office, by saying I was the senior British officer in the Sudan, returning for duty, I declined. At this she flew into a rage – which, as she later admitted, was a mistake when the temperature was 140°F.

Throughout a second whole day we waited for our documents, and found that the authorities would let us drive only if we went in convoy with at least one other vehicle. We therefore teamed up with two German couples who were similarly delayed by the wait for documents; their papers came through in the afternoon, and when they found they could not start because *our* documents were not ready, one of the women also threw a tantrum. When our own clearance eventually surfaced at 1100 on the third day, I was all for waiting until evening, when the worst of the heat would have passed, but the Germans were desperate, and we agreed to go at once.

So we set off across the Nubian Desert. There was no road, and the recent heavy rain had washed out all tracks, even those of camels. No animal or vehicle had crossed since the flood, so we navigated partly by compass, partly by keeping parallel with the ancient railway, which ran on our left. The terrain varied: much of it was flat, but patches of gravel and soft sand made for poor going, and we could do no more than fifteen or twenty miles per hour. Although the Land Rover was perfectly stable, it was also packed, and hot as Hades.

At least it kept going, which was more than the Germans' vehicle could manage. We were scarcely out of sight of Wadi Halfa when their ancient Jeep became overheated, and we were all forced to stop. Parking alongside, we slung an awning between the two vehicles to give some shade – and it was then that we realized that Phillida was about to go down with heatstroke. For some time she had been fretful, and Bridget had been telling her to pull herself together; but now suddenly we saw that she was seriously ill. Her face had turned the colour of a beetroot, and there was something odd about the attitude of her arms, which seemed to be stiffening.

We feared that if we did not immediately cool her down, she might die. Luckily we had plenty of water, so we wrapped her from head to foot in soaked towels – and soon, as her temperature came down, her colour returned to normal. We also made her drink our one remaining bottle of Schweppes tonic water, hoping that the quinine in it might reduce her fever, and it certainly seemed to help.

After that scare, we vowed never to drive in the heat of the day. Instead, we pressed on in the evening and into the night, stopping to camp at about midnight, when the moon went down, and going on again at 4.30 a.m. It was a punishing routine for us, and worse for the children: on some stages, in soft sand, without sand-ladders, we managed barely five miles per hour, even with all of us except the driver pushing, and our precious supply of water was so hot that we scarcely had to heat it to brew up tea. We stopped for a day in one of the tiny railway halts – most of them unmanned – which were dotted across the desert like beads on a string, and refilled our containers with foul-looking water, which we sterilized with tablets. Once, as we rested in the shade of some buildings, a railwayman gave Bridget what she described as the best present of her life – a fresh lime, which enabled us to drink hot lime juice, and was immensely refreshing, rather than hot, chlorinated water, which was disgusting. For food, we lived almost exclusively on spaghetti Bolognese, which she made from tins of minced meat and tomatoes, and pasta cooked on our gas burner, the whole flavoured with dried herbs and spices.

For Phillida, the low point of the trip came when she realized that she had lost her beloved rag-doll Sunflower – named after her halo of yellow wool hair – whom she had made at school, and who had become her special companion. Sunflower had spent the first few thousand miles of the journey sitting on her lap; then, somewhere in the desert, she had gone missing. The expedition came to a standstill while we emptied the vehicle and searched it from end to end; but no sign of Sunflower did we find, and we were forced to the lugubrious conclusion that she had gone missing on active service in the desert. Phillida was terribly upset, and there was nothing we could do to comfort her.[1]

At long last we reached Atbara, a garrison town on the Nile,

1. Months later in Khartoum we had occasion to unscrew the spare wheel of the Land Rover from its bulkhead, and there we found the doll, jammed down in the space between. The joy of her owner was unconfined, and we held a special Sunflower party to celebrate her resurrection.

where we were warmly welcomed at the army camp. A shower and a meal put us in good heart for the last stretch of several hours – on a track, now – and so we rolled into our destination, several days behind schedule.

In Khartoum we immediately faced another crisis, in that we found we had all but lost our house. During my absence the landlord had tried to call in the lease, and the Sudanese army, who leased the place at a very low rent, had only just managed to hang on to it. At one point the owner had begun to throw out all our possessions into the street, and only a swift intervention by Roger Jones, backed by the Sudanese army, had stopped him.

It was clear that we were going to have to move, but to find somewhere suitable was by no means easy, and we stayed put for the time being while we hunted for new accommodation. Because house agents did not exist, we had to pick up gossip and follow elusive trails. Had I, a European, gone looking round on my own, I would have been comprehensively ripped-off; but luckily a kind Sudanese, Colonel Hassan from the Staff College, came with me and did the bargaining.

After a prolonged search we found a house in Omdurman, on the west bank of the White Nile and, as it turned out, the move suited us well. Our first house had been in the European quarter, but in Omdurman we were among Sudanese, in a romantic area near the Khalifa's palace (now a museum) and the Mahdi's tomb. The house was of reasonable size, owned by a delightful retired judge, a former Sudanese Attorney General, who lived next door. Attractive and modern as it was, the house was rudimentary: there were no skirting boards round the base of the walls, so that lizards were constantly running in and out, as were spiders and beetles. The bathroom was reasonable, except that frogs came up and regarded humans beadily from the bowl of the lavatory, and every morning we would find the soap freshly gnawed by rats – not a comforting sight in a country riddled with rabies. The kitchen had one cold tap and a concrete draining board so ill-fitting that the water ran off it on to your feet. There was an ancient, though serviceable, calor-gas stove, but not a single shelf or cupboard, and no means of heating water. As there were neither curtains, nor any fittings for them,

Bridget had to go out and buy lengths of water-pipe for rails.

From our flat roof, on which we had breakfast at weekends and sometimes held parties, we could just see the Nile. Once for a party I bought two live sheep and had them killed and skinned in the Staff College during the morning; they were then cooked in clay ovens by Sudanese friends, who brought them along to our house whole. We were delighted to find that some of the Sudanese women accepted our invitation, along with their husbands: this, in local terms, was a real honour, and although we found it hard to communicate, we greatly enjoyed having them.

Supplies of food were erratic, and in spite of monthly orders sent up from Kenya, particular commodities often ran out (flour and rice were difficult to keep, as they became infested with weevils, unless you had space to store them in a deep-freeze). On one occasion we were all down to our last few ounces of flour and sugar when a senior RAF officer, Air Vice-Marshal Joe Gilbert, then in command of 38 Group, passed through on his way to Nairobi in a C-130 Hercules.[1] When he came to our house for a barbecue, and heard how short we were, he promised to see what he could do; and a few days later he returned from Kenya bringing us hundredweight sacks of flour and sugar, and a huge basket of fruit. Suddenly we were the most popular expatriates in Khartoum, handing out largesse to all, including our Sudanese neighbours.

Living in Omdurman posed a difficult strategic problem. Because the Sudan was in a state of chronic political instability, we half-expected a coup at any moment, and we knew that in any civil commotion both sides would fight for the bridge over the White Nile, a key feature of the city. On our side was the radio station (already pock-marked by bullets from the most recent revolution), and on the other, some twenty minutes' drive away, the airport, the embassy quarter and so on. This meant not only that, in the event of an uprising, we might be cut off on the wrong side of the river, but also that whenever we went out to dinner in Khartoum we could not risk leaving the children at home, even with a reliable sitter, but had to

1. Now Air Chief Marshal Sir Joseph Gilbert, he became Deputy Commander-in-Chief, Allied Forces Central Europe, before retiring in 1989.

bundle them up in sleeping bags and take them with us.

In the Easter holidays our main recreation was sailing. We would pile the family into one of the eighteen-foot boats, join a flotilla of two or three others, and sail upstream until we found a sandy island; there we would have a barbecue and camp overnight before drifting back downstream. The children adored these expeditions, and on one of them Edward excelled himself by capturing a goat. 'Bugs' Hughes (who later commanded the team) had challenged him to find one, and very soon afterwards Edward reappeared carrying a kid, which we had to return hastily to its mother and its irate owner.

As there were no competent secondary schools in Khartoum, we had to maintain our arrangements in England, and the children's journeys to and fro demanded careful organization. We therefore selected St Clotilde's at Lechlade, a Catholic convent school which included a large number of Church of England children, and this proved a huge success. For Edward, I hankered after Wellesley House, which had absorbed my own old school, St Peter's Court, at Broadstairs; but Bridget rightly insisted that it was ridiculous to think of sending a boy to a school nearly two hundred miles from our base in the west, when there were equally good establishments nearer home. In the end we compromised on Cheam, near Newbury, which was close to Bridget's parents. The heroine in all our school arrangements during our time in the Sudan – and later in the Falkland Islands – was Bridget's mother, who selflessly ferried the children between London Airport and their various destinations every time a term began or ended.

During our second summer we went for a holiday in Kenya, organized for us by a friend who was working in Nairobi. Most of the family flew down from Khartoum, but Edward came straight from London after his first term at Cheam, just after his eighth birthday – a very small figure emerging from an immense Jumbo. Arriving in Nairobi by air, we were overwhelmed by the order and cleanliness, an amazing change after the squalor of Khartoum. The roads in the capital were smoothly asphalted, with scarcely a pothole; flowerbeds blazed everywhere, and in the market we found fruit and vegetables galore. In a hired Nuffield Trust Land Rover we drove down to the coast, where we had a glorious week in a bungalow on the beach at Malindi. Then, together with our friend and his family, we drove round some of the game parks, finishing up in the Masai Mara, where we arrived in the middle of the annual wildebeest migration. This was an astonishing spectacle: the animals were advancing across country in a column, ten or twelve beasts abreast, and the line reached back into the distance as far as the eye could see. As they came to the Mara river, they plunged straight in and, although most reached the far side safely, many were dragged to their death by crocodiles. Thanks to good local contacts, we were able to camp out in the wilds, where we could hear the animals snuffling round our tents in the dark.

Back in Khartoum, full of the wonders of our holiday, we found most of the city out of petrol, and monumental queues, often twelve hours long, trailing back from the few pumps still open. This meant that we had to make maximum use of our two bicycles – one an adult's, the other a child's – as no other transport was available.

Because the compensation which we British were receiving for putting up with conditions in Khartoum in no way made up for the deprivations we were suffering, I set myself the task of seeing that our allowances were raised to a level at which they accurately reflected the quality of our life. This meant increasing our loan-service pay, and obtaining basic comforts such as hot water systems, curtains and decent furniture in our homes. Thus I launched into a long-range battle with the Ministry of Defence, knowing full well that the engagement might last for months, if not years.

So it turned out: the people in Whitehall stalled and prevaricated endlessly. I kept getting unsympathetic letters signed 'Miss E. O. Wren', and this creature, whoever she was, became the target of our frustration and resentment. Miss Wren was regularly blasted and damned in most ungentlemanly language, and someone drew a picture of her for the notice-board, portraying her as a rotund, middle-aged civil servant who passed her time fobbing off requests with disobliging answers.

People coming out to visit us began to hear about Miss Wren, and somehow word of our fantasy must have reached London, for suddenly I received a personal letter signed by the lady herself. It was an extremely nice letter – indeed, a charming one – which said, more or less: 'As I hear you have a drawing of me on the wall in your office, I thought you might like some photographs with which to compare it.' With the letter came some snaps of a stunningly attractive girl, about twenty-five, wearing a bikini. Our hate campaign collapsed like a house of cards. At once Miss Wren became something of a cult heroine – although suspicious minds raised the possibility that the photographs might not be of her at all, but of her niece or a friend.

In any case, we took some snaps of our own, and made up a dossier portraying rat-holes in the walls, flooded drains, broken furniture and collapsed water-systems, which we forwarded to the Ministry of Defence, with a final plea, through our new-found ally, for allowances to be reviewed. The evidence seemed to shock the Ministry into action: people there at last realized that we were not exaggerating, and our allowances were sub-stantially increased and back-dated, and new furniture was despatched.

With the struggle to exist so continuous, it may sound as though I had no time for work. Far from it – the routine of the training team proceeded satisfactorily, if without much excitement, and we broke new ground by teaching the locals techniques for dealing with hijacked aircraft. Having discussed international terrorism at some length with Abdul Majib, I persuaded him that we should bring out an SAS team to train some Sudanese, and we devised a major exercise on one corner of the airfield, using an old Dakota as the hijacked aircraft. To make things realistic, we put some hostages on board, among them several wives and the Finneys' daughter Victoria, and I took trouble to explain to Majid the need for negotiation: if necessary, I said, you must be prepared to talk to the terrorists for days on end. His response was exactly what one would expect in that part of the world: 'Why not just go in and shoot them?' In the end the aircraft was stormed by the Sudanese, who did very well when sufficiently chivvied.

Throughout our time in Khartoum we were struck by the friendliness of ordinary people: strangers kept offering to do things for us – to carry our laden shopping bags home from the *souk*, or lend us oil lamps during power cuts – and in spite of the precarious nature of the regime, it was always safe for Bridget to walk about the streets unaccompanied. When the time came for us to leave, our Sudanese army friends insisted on throwing a huge party for us: they hired a paddle steamer, loaded it with refreshments, installed a band, and off we went down the Nile for the day. Considering that a colonel earned about as much as a British corporal, it was an outstandingly generous gesture.

So ended two years which were highly educational, not only for the children, but for myself and Bridget too. As my tour came to an end, we sold most of our possessions, including the Land Rover, which, being in good order, commanded a high price. For the past few months we had not been able to use it, because of the petrol famine: it had stood in the yard with two gallons in the tank, in case there had been a coup, or we had had to rush a child to hospital. Yet the shortage of fuel seemed no deterrent to would-be purchasers. To catch buyers' eyes, I placed an advertisement on the board in the Sudan Club: 'Two bicycles for sale, £7000, plus Land Rover thrown in free', and I soon sold the vehicle to a local merchant for the full amount – which then had the same value as sterling. When he asked how I would like him to pay, I said, 'In cash, please,' fearing that a cheque might bounce; and next morning – even though it was Friday, the Arab day off – he appeared with seven thousand one-pound notes wrapped in brown paper. Having laboriously counted them, and found the total correct, we racked our brains to think of a safe place in which to hide them until the banks reopened; and in the end we hung the parcel inside the cistern of the lavatory, with an audience of inquisitive frogs watching from the bowl.

In the matter of my career, providence smiled on me yet again. I had been hoping for some time that I would be in the running for the post of Director of the SAS Group, and when this became vacant, there was nobody else available with the necessary experience. Thus at the end of 1978 I came home to take up one of the most fascinating commands in the British army.

CHAPTER 21

DIRECTOR, SAS

1978–82

Even after a two-year absence abroad, I found it relatively simple to settle back into SAS harness, because I knew so many of the people involved. Once again I took over from Johnny Watts, who went off to command the Sultan of Oman's armed forces. The commander of 22nd SAS at the time of my rejoining was Mike Wilkes, and his successor was Mike Rose, both of whom I had known for years. Nevertheless, I had a great deal to learn, for command at the level of Director was substantially different from that on lower rungs of the ladder.

As the SAS had expanded both its numbers and the spread of its activities, and as the Regiment had become more widely accepted in the Regular Army, so the need had grown for Special Forces to be represented in London. Our operations had become sensitive at a very high level: as they often carried international political impact, the headquarters in London had become correspondingly more important. One vital advantage of being in the capital was that we had immediate access to the Ministry of Defence – and indeed kept a representative permanently stationed there. By this means we generally managed to pick up the first hints of impending trouble, for such whispers generally started in the MOD.

It would be tedious to recall every one of the numerous operations that took place during my tour as Director; but I hope that some idea of the scope of the post will emerge if I concentrate on three main themes: the problems of working in Northern Ireland, counter-terrorism and the siege of the Iranian Embassy, and the Falklands War.

By the time I took over, at the end of 1978, the SAS had been deployed in Northern Ireland. At the beginning of 1976 they had been sent in by the Prime Minister, Harold Wilson, who committed them without warning in a deliberate blaze of publicity. There had been a few minor problems – as when some men strayed over the border into the Republic – and every time something went wrong, the IRA sought to make capital out of the incident, working up a campaign of black propaganda against the Regiment.

Shortly before I assumed command there had occurred what became known as the Dunloy incident. Our soldiers had found a weapons cache in a grave, and had staked the site out, lying up for several days and nights hidden in a wet ditch at the edge of the churchyard. One night a man appeared, lifted the top of the grave and took out a semi-automatic weapon, which he pointed in the direction of the watchers. They, thinking that he had seen them and was about to shoot, opened fire and killed him.

Clearly the dead man had been a member of the IRA; but he was only sixteen, and probably a low-grade operator. The IRA opened up a vociferous propaganda barrage, producing pictures taken seven or eight years earlier, when the youth was singing in a choir, and presenting us as having killed a choirboy. When a pathologist examined the body and pronounced that the man had been shot from the back, rather than the front, strong doubts were cast on the soldiers' version of events.

Two facts were immediately clear to me. The first was that the soldiers never wavered in the details of their story, and the second that they would be out of their depth trying to defend themselves in a court of law against a case brought by clever, highly paid lawyers seeking to secure their conviction. I myself was convinced of the men's innocence. It was not just a question of wanting to believe them because they were my men: I believed them with all my heart, and I therefore determined to give them unstinting support.

First I charged one of the squadron commanders with the task of seeing them through the courts – a job which he carried out with outstanding efficiency. Then I approached the Adjutant General, General Sir Robert Ford, who said that we could have as many defending counsel as we needed, at the Army's expense. Since the case was to be heard in Northern Ireland, we selected the best Northern Ireland counsel, and briefed them thoroughly. At first they were doubtful, supposing that our defence might be no more than a military exercise in damage limitation; but once they had talked to the two accused, they changed their minds.

It was clear that a great deal would hang on the forensic evidence; and so – again with support from the Ministry of Defence – I was authorized to commission a second examination of the body, this time by Dr James Cameron, a well-known pathologist who had often worked for the Metropolitan Police. He showed that the dead man had been shot through the head from the front, and that as he fell two more bullets had entered his back, making a downward track towards his left hip.

In due course the case came up in court and ran for a week. Cameron's evidence, supported by photographs, had a strong influence, and the defendants were cleared, although the judge expressed reservations. The soldiers' ordeal offers an excellent illustration of what troops in Northern Ireland have to go through while doing their duty. A tremendous responsibility rested on the shoulders of those two men watching night after night in the churchyard. If they had not opened fire, they themselves might have been shot, and if the man had escaped, they could have been blamed for failing to capture a terrorist or prevent further incidents. When they did open fire, they were accused of murder.

The next salvo in the IRA's black propaganda attack came early in 1979, in the form of a story that an SAS sergeant had raped the wife of a doctor in Northern Ireland. The aim, as always, was to portray the Regiment as ill-disciplined and out of control, a liability to all concerned. For a while the story remained a fairly minor one, but then in the third week of March the *Daily Telegraph* ran a prominent news item, and followed it, on Saturday 17 March, with an editorial which demanded an official inquiry by Roy Mason, the Northern Ireland Minister. Immediate action was needed to prevent any further escalation of the rumours.

I was incensed. Already confident that the story was a fabrication, I made inquiries which confirmed my belief. We had never had anyone in the area named, and nobody answering the description given of the sergeant had been in Northern Ireland. I decided that an authoritative refutation was necessary; but I knew that if I made one, as Director, SAS, nobody would pay any attention. Some heavier gun was needed. I promptly telephoned the Colonel Commandant of the SAS, Brian Franks, seeking his help exactly as John Simpson and I had sought that of Anthony Head in 1974. Franks, who had been in the wartime SAS, responded with equal alacrity and agreed to issue a Press release under his own name.

By the time I got through to him at his cottage in East Anglia, it was already Sunday morning, and our riposte would be no use unless we issued it that day. I therefore suggested that I should travel up, brief him thoroughly and work out a statement with him. He agreed, with the proviso that he must look after the guests whom he had invited to lunch. The weather happened to be foul, with snow lying, more on the way, low cloud, mist and rain. The only way to reach Franks in time was by helicopter, so I arranged for an aircraft to pick me up off a field near our house, and away we went on a flight that turned out to be hairy, to say the least. Even with an experienced pilot, we could hardly pick our route through the fog, which was hanging almost down to ground level; for much of the way we had to follow the motorways, on which we could see cars' headlights, and on which, we knew, we would meet no sharp gradients.

So we felt our way to East Anglia, and landed in Franks's garden in time for lunch. After the meal he and I sat down to thrash out a suitable text, which – there being no such device as a facsimile machine in those days – his son took to London and delivered to Reuters early that evening. At that date it was unheard of for the SAS to go public, and we felt sure that a Press release from the Colonel Commandant, denying all knowledge of the alleged sergeant, would attract wide attention. Sure enough, the item came up prominently on the television news at both nine and ten o'clock, and at midnight – by which time I was back home – I got a startled call from the Director of Public

Relations at the MOD, demanding an explanation. Next morning the story hit the headlines in every national newspaper and died a natural death.

Ever since its inception in 1972, the counter-terrorist team had been training hard and standing by for emergencies. Many other countries had followed our lead and set up similar units of their own, notably the Americans, whose Delta Force was formed by an admirable Special Forces officer, Colonel 'Charging' Charlie Beckwith. A tremendous worker, and a great personality, Charlie was one of nature's enthusiasts: as his colleagues remarked, when he arrived in the world, he broke the mould. He spent some time serving with us in the SAS, and generally seemed to have everything going for him. Yet he also harboured a streak of bad luck which appeared to dog him in whatever he did.

Early in 1980 he invited me out to the United States to witness the validation of his own newly formed counter-terrorist team, which had spent the best part of a year training. I watched a major exercise, which covered immense distances and culminated in the storming of an aircraft. I found Delta Force highly professional, and admired the way they went about their business – but then, with the exercise barely over, Charlie came up to me, and, without further explanation but with a great sense of urgency, said, 'Look, I'm sorry, but we've got to go,' – whereupon the whole lot of them disappeared, leaving us to find our own way home from the remote military airfield.

Later we realized that President Jimmy Carter had, at that moment, issued orders for the team to stand by for Eagle Claw, the operation to rescue fifty-three American hostages from the United States' Embassy in Teheran. The plan was an ambitious one, as the distances involved were vast. Briefly, the idea was to fly in elements of Delta Force to Desert One, an airfield two hundred miles south-east of Teheran, and to lift the rescue team in from there to its target by helicopter.

Charlie was in command of the assault party, and once again his bad genie intervened: through no fault of his, the attempt, on the night of 24–25 April 1980, ended in fiasco, with eight Americans dead and several helicopters destroyed. Yet I am convinced that the plan was sound, and could have worked: I say this with some authority, for immediately afterwards the Americans invited me and a colleague to Special Forces' Headquarters in the United States for a debriefing session, during which they went through every phase of the operation. What ruined it, I am sure, was the fact that the military commanders were not their own bosses: as in Korea, they were not allowed to take major decisions on the spot, but were obliged to refer them back to the White House. Carter retained tight control, and kept interfering, with the result that everyone was looking over his shoulder. It was a classic illustration of the fact that a supreme commander – civilian or military – must delegate authority if he is to get the best out of his people.

The Desert One disaster made all counter-terrorist forces re-examine their procedures; and when, on the morning of 30 May 1980, armed Arab terrorists seized the Iranian Embassy in London, our own team at Hereford was, as always, on standby. At that moment, however, it was about to deploy on an exercise devised by the Home Office and the police in Northumbria: reports were coming in of a fictitious terrorist incident in the far north-east, and reaction was imminent.

In London, the first senior police officer on the scene at 16 Princes Gate was Deputy Assistant Commissioner John Dellow, who immediately took charge of the emergency.[1] After a close look at the terrace building, front and back, he set up a temporary command post in his own vehicle and began organizing his forces to cordon off the area. One of his earliest moves was to send for the police terrorist dogs, which are kept at Heathrow Airport: he thought they might be useful if the gunmen attempted a mass breakout.

It so happened that one of the dog-handlers who heard the radio call was Dusty Gray, a former SAS corporal, whom I had known for years. Tall, distinguished-looking, with a moustache as big as his sense of humour, Dusty was a typical old hand from Malaya, and now his immediate reaction was to alert 22nd SAS's base in Hereford. Suddenly, among reports of the aircraft hijack

1. Later Sir John Dellow, CBE, he was Deputy Commissioner, Metropolitan Police, 1987–91.

in Northumbria, there arrived this quite different message about dogs.

Mike Rose, the Commanding Officer, at once suspected that the Home Office was boxing clever, trying to confuse him with contradictory information. 'Look here, Dusty,' he said. 'Are you pulling my leg?'

'On the contrary, boss,' Dusty protested. 'We're on our way to Princes Gate. You're definitely going to be needed.'

In a flash Rose was on to me at SAS Group Headquarters in London, asking us to obtain confirmation from the Ministry of Defence that a major incident was brewing. When Whitehall failed to produce any definite reaction, Rose did not wait, but despatched his team immediately: away they went, outstripping bureaucratic obstruction and evading the Press, to pitch up for the time being at a hideaway in Beaconsfield, within easy reach of the capital. Rose himself flew by helicopter to RAF Northolt, on the western fringes of London, and there borrowed the Station Commander's car to drive into town. Arriving at Princes' Gate in civilian clothes, he introduced himself to Dellow and made a quick reconnaissance.

At SAS Group Headquarters I and my Chief of Staff, Bruce Niven, were probing hard for information, and for official permission to deploy our team. Presently we learnt that the terrorists had taken prisoner at least twenty hostages, including a police constable, Trevor Lock, who had been on duty outside the door of the Embassy. Some of the captives were members of the Embassy staff, others visitors. In a protest against the regime of Ayatollah Khomeini, the terrorists were seeking recognition of the Iranian province of Khuzistan, which they also called 'Arabistan'. In particular, they were demanding the release of ninety-one political prisoners held in Iran, recognition of the 'national rights of the Iranians', an 'end to the liquidation campaign and daily mass exterminations', and an aircraft to take them and their prisoners out of the country once their demonstration was over.

As soon as I heard the news, I began angling for a place in the Cabinet Office Briefing Room, and within hours I was there, sitting next to the Director of Military Operations, Major General Derek Boorman, in the first of a series of highly charged meetings which occupied the next six days. In an undistinguished rectangular room without windows, up to twenty-five people sat round a long table, with nothing to distract them except a battery of television sets mounted above head level and, on one end-wall, a digital clock with small flaps, one of which tumbled down with a snap every time a minute ticked by.

The company at the table included representatives from the Foreign Office, the Ministry of Defence, the Security and Intelligence services, and public utilities such as the gas board, water board and the British Airports Authority. The Chairman was the Home Secretary, the Rt Hon. William (now Lord) Whitelaw. Until then, I must admit, I had always regarded Willie Whitelaw as no more than a jovial, avuncular figure. Now I had reason to change my opinion. From the start he handled those difficult meetings with calm, incisive authority, which reminded everyone present that during the Second World War he had served with distinction as an officer in the Scots Guards. Never autocratic, he let people have their say, yet always brought a discussion to an end with a firm decision, leaving nothing in the air.

The Prime Minister, Margaret Thatcher, did not attend our sessions, preferring to delegate authority to the Home Secretary; but her spirit and ideas were very much present, and right at the beginning she made three ground rules clear: first, the terrorists were to remain subject to the laws of the United Kingdom; second, they were not to be allowed to leave the country; and third, the police were to negotiate with them for as long as might be necessary – months, even – to achieve a peaceful solution. Hearing this, I felt certain that the siege would end in bloodshed. The Government was not going to give way, nor – I was convinced – were the gunmen: my experience of Arabs told me that once the terrorists had taken that line, they could not and would not surrender, because to climb down would entail too great a loss of face. So, at the outset, it seemed that sooner or later there would be a confrontation and a shoot-out. Furthermore, the police were not equipped to deal with what amounted to a military force of half a dozen fanatics armed with automatic weapons, hand-grenades and possibly explosives: therefore, sooner or later, the SAS would have to be involved.

Nevertheless, the decision to let the SAS loose in the streets of London was not one to be taken lightly: clearly there was a risk, if a large-scale shoot-out occurred, that a considerable number of people might be killed. There was never any question of the SAS going in unless the terrorists resorted to violence first; but after extensive discussions in the COBR, Whitelaw decided that an assault on the Embassy would be justified if two or more of the hostages were killed. One death, he ruled, could occur as the result of an accident, and negotiations might carry on after it; but if a second hostage were murdered, and more were threatened, that would be sufficient cause for an attack.

The chain of command was complex but clearly defined. As always in the United Kingdom, police primacy remained absolute: the army could act only if the Home Secretary authorized it to do so. The senior police officer concerned was the Commissioner, Sir David McNee, but in practice he delegated operational command to his man on the spot, John Dellow, who was first class in every way: quick-witted, calm, resourceful, and an able administrator.

On the army side, the Home Secretary was being advised by the Director of Military Operations and by myself. Had other army units been brought in, the DMO would have liaised between them and the Home Secretary; but since only the SAS were involved, I acted as the direct link between the military and Whitehall. My role was to give the Home Secretary the best possible advice on the advantages and disadvantages of sending the SAS in, and to explain the risks involved in any assault. Just as McNee had his operational commander in the form of John Dellow, so I had mine in Mike Rose, who was responsible to me for drawing up the military plans and keeping me advised of them.

The politicians felt it essential that the siege should be accepted by the public as a major incident which justified the kind of build-up already in progress. A degree of public presentation was therefore necessary, and soon it became clear that much time and energy would have to be devoted to managing the media. At the site John Dellow corralled reporters and television teams into a small area about a hundred yards west of the Embassy which became known as 'Pressville'. Obviously it was vital that the terrorists should see as little as possible of the counter-measures being taken around them, and the last thing we wanted was that they should watch our preparations on television. Intensive surveillance by the police suggested that there were three television sets inside the Embassy; measures for jamming them were considered, but in the end dropped, partly because of technical difficulties. Dellow also considered blocking the television crews' view with high screens abutting on to houses neighbouring the Embassy, and indeed had screens made; but in the end they were never put up, for fear that the sight of them would give away to the terrorists the fact that an assault was imminent. In any case, the media men hired hydraulic bucket-hoists (known locally as 'cherry-pickers') to raise their cameramen above obstructions.[1]

The besieging forces quickly moved into position. The police first considered establishing their forward control room in the Royal School of Needlework at 25 Princes Gate, a few doors to the west of the Embassy, and the ladies in charge there gallantly gave up their ground floor to an invasion of detectives and con-stables. But the place was cluttered with priceless artefacts – ancient tapestries, regimental colours in for repair, peers' coronation robes; worse, there was an absolute ban on smoking in the building. Dellow did not think that his men could endure such a deprivation for days on end, and was forced to look for somewhere else.

Next door, at number 24, nearer to what the police were already calling 'the Stronghold', he found a Montessori Nursery School. This was quickly evacuated, and the furniture, being tiny, was easily removed. The only conditions laid on the police were that they should take care with the miniature lavatories in the basement, feed the hamster which was left in residence, and not molest a duck which was nesting on a windowsill. As communications equipment and generators poured in, Dellow established his control room in the attic, under the eaves. One priority task was to establish a clear link with the terrorists, so

---

1. Ironically enough, after a five-day vigil one crew descended from their eyrie for a tea-break just before the assault at last went in, so that they missed the action altogether.

a green field telephone was passed in through the window, on which they could talk to the police negotiators. The man who did most of the talking – the gunmen's leader and spokesman – identified himself as 'Salim'.

Needing a Farsi interpreter urgently, Dellow ran into an unexpected problem: the only one available was a young woman, and it was police policy not to use women in dealings with Muslim men. Yet now they had no alternative: the girl joined them, and proved a decided asset. Not only was she quick at translating: Salim seemed to believe that through his telephone conversations he was establishing a special relationship with her. The police also brought in a psychiatrist, who continually analysed the terrorists' state of mind.

Mike Rose, meanwhile, had found an ideal Forward Holding Area for his unit designated Red Team. This was the Royal College of General Practitioners at numbers 14 and 15, next door to the Stronghold on the other side. During the afternoon he had reconnoitred a concealed route into the building, through some flats at the back of Princes Gate, across a garden and along the communal basement passage which ran the length of the terrace. At 0330 on 1 May an SAS officer and twenty-four men slipped in unobserved.

Within an hour they had put together a makeshift plan, which they could launch at ten minutes' notice if the terrorists began to shoot their victims; but this was a relatively crude scheme, whereby they would smash through the windows of the top floor and fight their way downwards with firearms and CS gas, in the hope that they could rescue at least some of the hostages before all were massacred. Inevitably it would lead to high casualties; the longer and better objective was to formulate a more considered plan, which would take account of all the intelligence that could be gleaned about dispositions within the Stronghold.

Intelligence-gathering thus became our priority – and the Embassy posed a formidable problem. Built on six floors, four of them above ground, it contained more than fifty rooms. By good fortune we already had some knowledge of it, for during the reign of the Shah, when Iran was a friendly nation, an SAS party had surveyed the building at the Iranians' request, and made recommendations for improving its security. Now the Red Team needed to learn its every detail. Old plans were produced and memorized. During the first night police carpenters built a scale model of the first and second floors, with all doors opening in the correct direction. On the morning of Day Two – 1 May – the Pioneer Company of the Irish Guards began building a life-sized replica of the Embassy, floor by floor, out of timber and hessian, in a hangar at Regent's Park Barracks, off Albany Street, which became the SAS's main base for the duration of the siege. We also brought in people who had been in the Embassy recently, so that we could take account of recent changes, the positioning of large pieces of furniture, and so on.

The house next door to the Stronghold, number 17, posed special problems. Being the Ethiopian Embassy, it was in effect foreign territory; but such was the crisis that arrangements had to be made to gain access to it. The Stronghold itself, built in 1851, the year of the Great Exhibition, was of true Victorian solidity, with party walls of granite, twenty-two inches thick on one side, nineteen on the other. Even so, it was vital that the terrorists should not hear any sounds caused by activity within number 17, and a call therefore went out for ambient noise to be increased. In the COBR the request produced a striking illustration of what can be achieved if everyone is prepared to cooperate. The senior representative of the gas board immediately arranged for a repair crew to begin working on a non-existent main in Princes Gate, just along from the Embassy, and within minutes a gang was drilling away there. This produced a splendid amount of noise, but soon proved counter-productive: the disturbance put the terrorists' nerves so much on edge that the police had to call the gas men off. Then Mike Rose suggested that aircraft coming in to land at Heathrow should be re-routed so that they passed over the southern boundary of Hyde Park at low level. Again, a suggestion which in normal times would have led to protracted bureaucratic wrangling was translated into action within minutes. Down came a stream of aircraft, almost to roof-top height, with a useful increase in noise and vibration. In spite of it, the terrorists heard sounds in the walls and became suspicious.

The longer the siege dragged on, the more time our soldiers

had to perfect their assault plan. The essence of it was speed
and surprise: the aim was to attack every floor of the building
simultaneously, and to break in so fast on all levels that the
gunmen would not have time to execute anyone. Success
depended on every SAS man knowing his task precisely: the
soldiers had to be able to pick out the terrorists, recognize every
hostage (from memorizing photographs), and keep within
pre-set boundaries so that there was no risk of shooting each
other.

Central to the plan, in every sense of the phrase, was a light-
well in the middle of the building, which terminated in a glass
dome at the top of the second floor, with clear space above it.
At first we discussed the possibility of men abseiling straight
down the well, through the dome. Then a better idea emerged
– that of making up a pair of special stun-charges, and lowering
them on to the dome, so that as the assault went in, a very
loud explosion in the centre of the building would distract and
confuse the inmates.

At 0330 on Day Three – Friday 2 May – a second SAS team,
designated Blue, slipped into the Forward Holding Area and
relieved their colleagues, who had been on continuous standby
for almost twenty-four hours. The Red Team were smuggled
away in vans to Regent's Park Barracks, where they got some
sleep and began rehearsing assault moves in the wood-and-
hessian model of the Embassy. Although there had been intensive speculation in the media that the SAS would be called in,
nobody had yet spotted any of our people, and reporters were
still vainly watching the barracks at Hereford for signs of a mass
pull out.

Towards evening on Day Three the terrorists began to modify
their demands: ceasing to insist on the release of political prisoners in Iran, they concentrated instead on the idea of securing
a bus which would take them to an airport, and an aircraft to
fly them and their captives to the Middle East. At once Mike
Rose considered alternatives to an assault on the Stronghold: it
might be possible to overpower the gunmen either on board a
bus, or as they were going out to it, or as they transferred to an
aircraft.

As the strain took its toll on the hostages, they started to suffer from various ailments, and the terrorists released sick individuals one at a time. With each came more information about conditions inside the Embassy. We learned that there were six gunmen, and that they were armed with at least two hand-grenades apiece, as well as with hand-guns and automatic weapons; but we still could not tell whether or not they had the means to blow up the building, as they claimed. Sickness was one area which Dellow thought he might be able to exploit: he consulted a doctor to see if the food being sent into the Embassy could be treated with some preparation that would make the inhabitants ill, but after discussion dropped the idea as impracticable.

In the COBR our marathon sessions continued, as every possible line of action was talked through; but, whenever I could, I slipped away to Princes Gate to get the feel of conditions at the front. Because I wore civilian clothes, and at that stage had never appeared on television, I could come and go without attracting attention. As usual, Mike Rose was irrepressibly optimistic, and I was glad to find that he had established an excellent working relationship with John Dellow: they had set up a coordinated intelligence cell, and were holding joint briefing sessions every six hours.

In the middle of this frenetic activity I was caught up in a minor crisis of my own. As we had been working closely with the Germans on counter-terrorist measures, we invited their expert Ulrich Wegener to come over and have a look at the way we were handling the siege. It was he who had set up the German counter-terrorist unit, GSG–9, and led the raid to free the hostages held on a Lufthansa aircraft hijacked to Mogadishu; and now he showed a lively interest in our preparations. Having spent the night in my flat, and being about to return to Germany, he casually said, 'Oh, by the way: I'm carrying a pistol. What shall I do about it at the airport?'

There was I, in the middle of the hottest emergency seen in London for many a year, harbouring a foreigner armed with an undeclared weapon. I rang my friends in the Metropolitan Police and explained what had happened. Their reaction could not have been more helpful: they cut through the red tape, sent four men round in a van, escorted Wegener to the airport and saw him on to the aeroplane, all without a murmur.

That evening, Sunday, Mike Rose and Hector Gullan, the major in command of the assault team, came round to my flat for supper, and ran through their plans one last time. While Bridget cooked spaghetti, they spread out large-scale drawings of the Embassy on the floor, and we examined every detail. It was a typical SAS occasion: not a formal briefing, but an opportunity for people who knew each other extremely well to exchange ideas and further refine what was already a clearly thought out operation.

On the morning of Day Six – Bank Holiday Monday, 5 May – yet another meeting took place in the COBR. People felt that negotiations would continue for a while yet: the latest idea was to bring in the Iraqi Ambassador to mediate with the terrorists. Willie Whitelaw was due to drive out to Dorneywood, the official residence of the Home Secretary near Slough, to preside at a lunch which had been arranged for some time. Now he suggested that he should cancel the appointment; but after some discussion, and because the position in the Embassy seemed stable, he was persuaded to go as planned.

When the COBR meeting broke up, late in the morning, I went down to the control room in Princes Gate. There it became clear that events were about to accelerate. All morning the terrorists had been giving out new deadlines for action, and at 1230 PC Lock revealed over the negotiators' telephone that they had grown extremely edgy. Salim, the leader, came on to say that they proposed to kill one of the hostages. Shortly afterwards Lock reported that they were tying somebody up downstairs. At 1240 Salim announced a new deadline of two hours, with a threat that one hostage would be killed every half hour thereafter.

At 1250 Abbas Lavasani, the Embassy's chief Press Officer, came on the line pleading for action. If hostages were going to be killed, he had volunteered to be the first to die, and now his martyrdom seemed imminent. At 1255, as I sat talking to Dellow and Rose, two shots suddenly crashed out.

Had Salim shot someone – or was it bluff? Through Lock, the police tried to find out what had happened, but the constable did not know. Mike Rose believed from the sound of the shots that someone *had* been killed. So did Dellow. Whatever had happened, the terrorists were clearly close to breaking point, and I set off post-haste back to the COBR.

Whitelaw did the same. At Dorneywood he and his party were about to sit down to lunch when news of the shooting arrived. He saw no option but to abandon his guests and head back to London flat-out in his 4·2 litre Jaguar. Never, he confided as he arrived, had he had a more exhilarating journey. With police outriders clearing the road ahead of him, his driver Jack Liddiard covered the twenty miles from Slough to Whitehall in nineteen minutes; as they hurtled over Hammersmith Flyover, Whitelaw glanced down at the speedometer and saw that they were doing 120mph.

Our discussions assumed a new urgency. If one of the hostages *had* been executed, the murder moved things sharply forward, and a military operation looked probable. For the next two hours, together with Whitelaw and Boorman, I went through every detail of the options and risks involved. I explained that, with the progressive refinement of our plan, the risks had steadily diminished, but nevertheless were still high. I said that even if things went well, we must expect forty per cent of the people in the building to become casualties. Anything less than that would be a very good outcome. At the end I reiterated that the decision to go in would be a political one, even though it led to the use of military force.

Whitelaw then turned to me and said: 'Peter, I want you to understand two things. The first is that, if and when the operation is launched, I will not interfere in any way; the second is that if it goes wrong, I will take the responsibility afterwards.' The fact that the Home Secretary spoke up like that, in front of everyone else, impressed me a great deal: here was that rare being, a politician who was not trying to protect his own career, but was prepared to shoulder responsibility.

He then asked me to put our troops on standby, to go in at short notice. I instructed Mike Rose, who told Dellow that he would need two hours to get ready for the deliberate assault. At 1550 Dellow asked him to set preparations in motion. At 1630 I again visited the site, to make certain that my assessments were accurate. As always, I felt it essential to see what things were like on the spot, so that I could describe the scene with authority to people who had not witnessed it at first hand. In the Forward Holding Area I talked to members of the assault team, and found the atmosphere typical of the SAS immediately before an operation: there was no sense of over-excitement or tension; rather, an air of professionalism and quiet confidence prevailed. These men had been superbly trained, and they had so often practised the kind of task they were about to carry out that it had become almost an everyday event. This is not to say that they lacked courage or imagination: on the contrary, they knew full well that the terrorists were heavily armed, and that the building could be wired with explosives, and might go up as they broke in. They simply accepted the risks and carried on.

At 1700 – sooner than expected – Mike reported to Dellow that he was all set: at any time from then on his team could go in at ten minutes' notice. At 1705 PC Lock managed to report menacing snatches of conversation – 'We'll do something before sunset . . . Kill two, or three, or four . . . Kill all by 10 p.m. . . .' – and said that furniture was being moved to barricade doors and windows. At 1750 he again came on the telephone, and the police tried to use force jargon to test the veracity of what the terrorists had been saying. The negotiator suggested, for instance, that Salim was 'getting moody' – Metropolitan slang for stepping out of line. Any London policeman should have realized that he was asking if the terrorist leader was telling lies, but Lock was under such stress that he missed the implication.

At 1820 the police played one of their final cards: they had brought yet another mediator in the form of the Imam from the mosque in Regent's Park, and now they put him on the line to Salim. A conversation began, but while it was still in progress, three more shots went off inside the building. Then Salim announced that a hostage had been killed: 'Another in half an hour. All the hostages together.' Soon afterwards the front door opened, and a body was flung out into the street. An immediate autopsy showed that the man – Lavasani – had been dead for more than an hour, and could not have been a victim of the most recent gunfire. Thus it seemed highly probable that a second hostage *had* been murdered, and that the minimum conditions for a military assault were in place. (In fact nobody else had been killed. The shots were fired as a bluff – but, as it turned out, a fatal one for Salim.)

Receiving the information in the COBR, Whitelaw tried to telephone the Prime Minister, to obtain her approval for sending in the SAS. She was on her way from Chequers to London, and the first attempt to reach her failed because her car was in a valley. At the second attempt the call went through and she gave her consent. Whitelaw then said to me, 'Right, you can send them in.' While he passed authority to Sir David McNee, with the proviso that the timing of the attack was a matter for the police commander at the scene, I told Mike Rose that he could accept Dellow's authority and put the plan into action.

Mike had very properly insisted that he must have written authority for the assault (in case someone should later claim that he had exceeded his brief), and Dellow was on the point of signing the document a couple of minutes before seven o'clock when another telephone call suggested that the hostages might after all be released. A delay ensued while the interpreter tried to work out what had been said; but the message was so muddled that no sense could be made of it, and Dellow signed the authority at 1907. So, although he himself retained overall command, control of the military assault passed to Rose.

The SAS needed ten minutes to make final preparations and move into position; for that time, the police had to keep the terrorists in play and prevent them killing anyone else. In this final emergency Dellow ordered the negotiators to drop their normal tactics: until then they had never promised anything which they could not deliver. Now they began to talk as though a coach to Heathrow Airport was actually available, and to discuss exactly where it should pull up outside. They also pretended that the Iraqi Ambassador was about to arrive. Taking turns, two policemen, known to the terrorists as Ray and Dave, spun out every facet of the proposed arrangements.

Inside the Embassy tension was running dangerously high. Several times in mid-conversation Salim slammed down his receiver, and several times the admirable Trevor Lock came on the line, seeking reassurance that no assault was going to be made on the building.

TREVOR: He's insisted that I come down and speak to you and tell you directly that if anything is done re attack, all hostages will be killed.

RAY: Trevor, what we're doing ... we're trying to make arrangements for the Iraqi Ambassador and the airport. You know, this is what we've got to accept now, Trevor.

TREVOR: Yes, sir. But it's got to be done urgently.

RAY: We're doing it now.

TREVOR: They're worried about the fact that you're going to attack the Embassy in the meantime.

RAY: Trevor, what I'm trying to do is get him on the phone to agree arrangements, Trevor.

TREVOR: Stand by. [Pause] That is an assurance to me, isn't it, sir?

RAY: Of course.

TREVOR: You're not going to attack ...

RAY: Look, I want to speak to him about the airport, Trevor, that's all.

SALIM: Hello.

RAY: Now look, Salim. It's between eight fifteen and eight thirty that the aircraft will leave. Now the coach, we hope, will be there in about twenty minutes. Now don't get worried.

SALIM: OK. Don't put it exactly ...

RAY: No, no. I'm going to put it at the end of the road. It will have curtains, but we will leave the curtains open until you tell us to close them. OK. Now I'm going to go back upstairs to say that you agreed to the Iraqi Ambassador coming. I will give you back to Dave, because he may have something else to say. Hold on, Salim.

SALIM: Talk to Trevor.

TREVOR: For my own peace of mind, and the other hostages, can you assure me that there will be no attack, and everything is being done as you said to Salim?

DAVE: All we're trying to organize, Trevor, is the coach and the aircraft, and the movement of the Iraqi Ambassador. Now in order to do that I want to do that as calmly, as safely as possible. I need to speak to Salim. So if you can tell him that if it's necessary ...

TREVOR: I'm sorry to interrupt you, sir. Salim wants to talk to you.

DAVE: Good.

SALIM: And the driver will be Mr Trevor.

DAVE: Well, let me discuss these things, because it's important we get these right, Salim.

SALIM: Mr Trevor, he will lead the coach to the airport.
DAVE: If we have one coach, is that going to be enough?
Because Mr Trevor will only be able to drive one coach,
won't he?
SALIM: Ya, it's one enough. Twenty-five people - twenty-
nine people, sorry.
DAVE: About twenty-nine seats. Now, whereabouts shall
we put the coach first? Shall we put it . . . ?
SALIM: Opposite of the door.
DAVE: Well, opposite of the door is a very vague phrase. If
you're looking out of the window . . .

As this masterly prevarication proceeded, some of the SAS men
were sidling along the roof, laying out their abseil ropes and
lowering the stun-charges down the light-well. More were
creeping along the basement alleyways, front and rear. All were
dressed in black from head to foot, hooded and wearing gas-
masks. Snipers concealed in vantage-points opposite the front
and back of the building redoubled their vigilance.

In the COBR, tension rose inexorably. Until then the room
had always been filled by a buzz of discussion, as ideas were put
up, knocked about and adopted or discarded. Now there was
nothing more that anyone could do or say. The SAS were going
in, to resolve the situation or fail. The talk died away until no
sound remained except that of the digital clock on the end wall.
Snap! went the little flap as it fell, marking the passage of every
minute. *Snap . . . Snap . . .*

Had we realized that television camera crews were about to
cover the assault live – at least from the front of the building –
we could have switched on our sets and watched one of the
most astonishing spectacles ever seen on the small screen, as the
broadcasting companies broke into their scheduled programmes.
But somehow this idea never occurred to us, and during the
countdown I was the only person left in touch with Princes
Gate. Through my headphones I could hear Hector Gullan giving
his orders, and the men talking to each other as they moved
into position. From the open doorway of the communications
room, I kept up a running commentary: 'They're on the roof
. . . They're laying out their ropes . . . They've got the charges
down the light-well . . . They're ready . . .' Then I heard the

code-word 'Hyde Park', telling the abseilers to hitch themselves to their ropes. At last came 'London Bridge', the signal to drop, and Hector calling, '*Go! Go! Go!*'

Right to the final moments the police negotiators kept talking. Salim, ever more jumpy, had got wind of the attack. 'We are listening to some suspicion – er – movements,' he cried. Dave reassured him that he had nothing to worry about, but he repeated, 'There is suspicion, OK. Just a minute. I'll come back again. I'm going to check.' Those were his last words to the police. Seconds later a heavy explosion rocked the building, and the bluff was at an end.

I heard the detonation through my headphones – or rather, I heard two. I knew at once that something had gone wrong. The explosions – the stun charges in the light-well, and the windows being blown in – should have been synchronized, but they had become separated by a few seconds. Or had the whole building gone up? It was a bad moment. I went back into the Briefing Room and said, 'I'm afraid there have been two explosions. It may be that our people have failed to coordinate, or the terrorists may have blown up the Embassy, and our soldiers with it.'

Nobody moved or said a word. Then over my headphones I heard shots, shouts, screams and our soldiers calling to each other. 'It's all right,' I said. 'The assault's going ahead.' Then: 'At least one hostage is dead . . . but the majority are alive. The terrorists don't seem to be doing too well . . . Now the building's on fire . . . but the hostages are out on the lawn . . .' When I heard somebody in the Embassy call out, 'PC Lock is alive and well and a credit to the Metropolitan Police,' I said, 'Home Secretary, I'm very pleased to be able to tell you that the assault has been largely successful. Some soldiers have been injured, but not seriously. One more hostage has been killed, and others may be hurt. But five of the terrorists are dead, and the sixth has been captured.'

Tension snapped. Papers flew in the air. Everyone leapt up, shouting and laughing. A roar of talk broke out. Bottles of whisky appeared from some secret cupboard, and we all had a much-needed drink.

Within minutes Whitelaw and I were on our way to Princes

Gate, where Mike Rose had already handed control back to John Dellow. By the time we arrived, and congratulated both of them, the Embassy was fully ablaze, and fire-crews, who had been standing by for days, were tackling the flames. The assault team had been spirited away, back to Regent's Park Barracks, where Margaret Thatcher, accompanied by Denis, joined them for an impromptu party. Again there was a terrific release of tension, as the men relaxed for the first time in five days, and found themselves chatting over a few beers with an immensely grateful Prime Minister.

There she heard for the first time the details of what had happened. Suspecting that the terrorists had moved the hostages round at the last minute – as indeed they had – the SAS had hit every floor of the building simultaneously. But not everything had gone according to plan. In the event, only one of the stun charges lowered down the light-well had exploded, and the other had failed to detonate. Also, the charge had gone off a few seconds prematurely. A more serious snag had developed when a staff-sergeant abseiling from the roof became entangled in his ropes, and was left hanging in mid air, being scorched by flames escaping through a blown-out window every time he swung in towards the wall. Eventually he was cut down, but not before he had sustained serious burns.

The rest of the assault went perfectly. A single shot by a sniper in Hyde Park accounted for one of the terrorists as he leant out of a front window, and four were killed by precision marksmanship inside the building, just in time: they murdered one more of their prisoners, but that was all they could manage. The surviving hostages were thrown down the stairs like human packages, from man to man, and bundled out into the back garden. The sixth gunman tried to pose as one of them, but was detected and overpowered (he is now serving a life sentence in gaol). The reason the building caught fire so quickly was that the terrorists had spread newspaper under the windows, beneath the curtains, and at the last minute sprinkled them with lighter fuel: although it turned out that their threats of having laid explosives were bluff, their incendiary devices proved quite effective.

For the soldiers who had taken part in the raid, the aftermath was inevitably something of a let-down. First, that same evening, they had to seal their weapons in bags, label them, and surrender them to the police, who kept them until a coroner's inquiry could be held. Next morning detectives flew to Hereford, where they spent thirty-six hours taking statements from members of the team, and making an exhaustive record of where and when every shot had been fired. (For the soldiers, this process was rendered less disturbing than it might have been by the fact that they had regularly practised it with the police on exercises in earlier years.) Later, at the inquest, and at the trial of the surviving terrorist, there were arguments about whether or not excessive force had been used and people came up with the sort of rubbish which they produce when they have time to think about an event academically. On the day there was no time for the luxury of reflection: Mike Rose's brief was to rescue the hostages alive, and he and his team did it brilliantly. Nevertheless, at the inquest we were concerned that if the evidence failed to justify what we had done, our people could hit trouble.

In the event this did not happen, but the possibility that it could emphasized an important point: just because a Minister authorizes a soldier to do something, that man may not break the law. A Minister has no right to set aside the law; nor does the Brigadier or the Commanding Officer of the SAS. In fighting terrorism, we repeatedly put our soldiers into very difficult positions: on the one hand they are being told to combat terrorism in the streets, but on the other they are still subject to the law of the land, and may not shoot anyone except under precisely defined circumstances. If we had gone into the Iranian Embassy earlier before the terrorists killed anyone, and provoked the deaths of hostages by starting a battle, we should have been in grave trouble.

The immediate effect of the siege on the Regiment was extraordinary. Letters and cards of congratulation poured in from all over the world. Hundreds of people, aged apparently from five to ninety, wanted to join up immediately. Recruiting for 21st SAS lifted so sharply that applicants were parading outside the gates in Kings Road, all apparently convinced that a balaclava helmet and a Heckler & Koch sub-machine gun would be handed to them over the counter, so that they could go off and conduct embassy-style sieges of their own. These people had to be disillusioned, and the Commanding Officer of the day, Keith Farnes, had a good way of doing it: he put them all on the running track and doubled them round until they dropped. Only those who showed exceptional stamina were considered for further selection.

More seriously, this operation, carried out with surgical precision in the heart of the capital, transformed the SAS's reputation overnight, and demolished the negative effects of the propaganda campaign with which the IRA had been trying to denigrate us. For months I had wanted to show that the SAS were not shady, behind-the-scenes operators, but first-class soldiers – and suddenly this fact had been demonstrated to the world in the most convincing way. All at once the real value of the SAS to the country – in filling a gap in the struggle against terrorism – was manifest.

Requests for professional advice poured in from many countries. In British political circles a certain degree of smugness developed over the way in which our success contrasted with the failure of the Americans in Operation Eagle Claw. Yet in the Regiment we never felt that we had any cause to be complacent, for, having been thoroughly briefed on the problems of the American rescue attempt, we knew that ours did not compare with them in any way. Going to war on the edge of Hyde Park was totally different from secretly deploying a large force into a foreign country thousands of miles from home. Our main concern had been to keep out of the way of the Press, not to avoid any armed enemy. As Mike Rose put it, 'All we had to do was catch a number 9 bus down High Street Kensington.' Besides, in contrast with the Americans, we were blessed with leaders who understood the vital importance of delegation. Instead of insisting that important decisions be referred back to them, Margaret Thatcher and Willie Whitelaw left their subordinates to achieve the goals they had set.

For myself, it was highly frustrating to have to remain in Whitehall when action at last began – yet it would have been quite wrong for me to be in Princes Gate at that moment. My job, I knew, was to see that everyone in the COBR was properly briefed, to offer advice when they wanted it, and if necessary to keep them off the backs of the front-line commanders. It was essential that, as head of the SAS, I should stand back, have confidence in my subordinates, and let them do the job which I had given them.

When the crisis came, events fully justified our claim that our counter-terrorist team was the finest in the world. Furthermore, we saw the effect of all the leadership and direction which Johnny Watts and I had exercised over the past months. I had complete confidence in Mike Rose: I understood him and trusted him. The same was true *vice versa*, and on through every rank. It was this harmony of purpose and understanding, operating at every level in the Regiment, which enabled us to win the battle of Princes Gate.

One of the hazards of being Director was that the job entailed an immense amount of travel, much of it in aeroplanes. Prolonged sitting in aircraft seats began to exacerbate the back injury which I had sustained while parachuting in Wales some years earlier, and when I set off for New Zealand in the spring of 1981, to talk to the New Zealand SAS and Ministry of Defence about security matters, particularly in connection with the siege, the long journey brought matters to crisis pitch.

Deciding to make full use of the trip, I called in on the way at Brunei, where we had a training team. I survived the visit, but in very considerable discomfort, on which pain-killers had little effect. When I reached New Zealand, the pain had become intolerable, and I had no option but to report to a doctor immediately. I was sent for X-rays to a hospital in Wellington, and there, thank heaven, I fell into the skilled hands of Wyn Beasley, a leading orthopaedic surgeon, who forbade me to travel any farther until I had had treatment. After trying a week's traction in vain, he agreed to perform a laminectomy, to remove those accretions on my backbone which were trapping spinal nerves.

If a laminectomy goes wrong, it can leave you paralysed, but I had full confidence in Wyn, and he did a perfect job. I awoke feeling numb and stiff, but soon I was on my feet again and enjoying the social life of the ward. The nurses were wonderfully cheerful, and saving, every one of them, to go to Europe. What impressed me most was that they had no intention of remaining there: they wanted to have a look round and see what the place was like, but after that they were determined to come home.

Even though I knew hardly anyone in New Zealand, I had a constant stream of visitors bringing me fruit, magazines and so on, and I was made to feel thoroughly at home. One of my most regular callers was the Chief of the General Staff, General Poananga: it was he who introduced me to kiwi fruit, which he later retired to grow commercially. Several former SAS men came in, among them John Mace, who had served with me in Malaya in the 1950s.

My fellow patients included a chirpy bulldozer driver who had had an accident out in the sticks, a Royal New Zealand Air Force corporal who was in catering, but had smashed himself up, and a sixteen-year-old boy whose spinal cord had been crushed when he was trapped between the garage wall and the car with which he had been tinkering. After eight or nine operations, he was still far from cured, but had all the pretty nurses crowding round his bed to talk to him.

Thanks to the skill of Wyn Beasley, I was able to brief New Zealand ministers, who came to my bedside – so that my mission was in the end more or less accomplished – and after three weeks I set out for home. The return journey was a testing experience, and the worst part of it was the drive in a staff car from the airport to home. There, I was not at all pleased to find that Bridget, against my explicit instructions, had acquired an eight-week-old lurcher puppy called Kesty, which had been pressed on her by our neighbours Martin and Elizabeth. A dog was the last thing I wanted – or thought I wanted – but in due course I was won round and became enormously fond of her.

My recovery was accelerated by a spell of therapy at Headley Court, a Service establishment specializing in rehabilitation. Having arrived feeling a bit sorry for myself, I soon snapped out of that when I saw how much worse off than me most of the other inmates were. Three weeks of remedial exercises, designed specifically for my condition, wrought a huge improvement, and I was able to return to work – although eighteen months passed before I was back to full fitness again.

*   *   *

December 1981 brought the death of my poor Aunt Joyce, at the age of seventy-five. When my grandmother died, and Old Place was sold, she had moved to Bognor and lived in two flats converted into one, both crammed to the doorways with furniture, china, books, pictures and the memorabilia of ages. The rooms were so packed that one could hardly move through them, and there she lived, hemmed in by her possessions and increasingly crippled by arthritis, but wonderfully looked after by the elderly yet devoted Mrs Puttenham, who had come with her from Old Place.

With the death first of her mother and then of her sister, the principal threats or challenges to Joyce had been removed, and towards the end of her life she softened noticeably. We did all we could to give her company by going on beach holidays and taking the children to see her, which she much enjoyed, and by putting in short visits whenever possible. Having been maddened by her for years, I had now forgiven her, and indeed felt sorry for her. I realized that she was a tragic victim of the First World War: she had seen the youth of the country destroyed, lost two potential husbands, and been left bitter and frustrated by her lot. I am glad to say that at the end she was reasonably content, and even if the mean streak in her persisted, she was kind to us and our children.

She spent her last few months in a nursing home, and was buried at Pagham, in the church where she herself had worshipped. I found that at one stage she had indeed cut me out of her will, but that she had reinstated me later, and now she left her money to myself, Michael and David equally. Coming at a time when we were all extended by school fees, the legacies helped a great deal, and with some of the money we arranged to increase the pension which she had arranged for Mrs Puttenham. We also sold most of Joyce's furniture. When the Senior Director of Phillips, the auctioneers, came down to look at it, he was astonished: never in his life had he seen such an accumulation packed into so small a space.

The seizure of the Falkland Islands by Argentina in April 1982 burst on us suddenly. I think everyone in Britain was taken by surprise, not least the Foreign Office. Nevertheless, the moment we heard that South Georgia had been occupied, we – the SAS – took urgent steps to make sure that we had a role in any conflict that might develop.

I was at work in our London Headquarters when the news broke. At once I sent my new Chief of Staff, Neville Howard, into the MOD to find out what was happening. Like a ferret diving down a rabbit-hole, he disappeared for hours. Meanwhile in Hereford Mike Rose was leaping up and down in his anxiety to proceed at once to the South Atlantic – but before I could give him any positive directions, a curious call came through on the telephone.

'SAS, Switzerland,' said a man with a thick German accent.

'Really?' I said. 'That's interesting. We haven't got any SAS in Switzerland.'

'No, no. This is the Ski Association of Switzerland. We are working since some time on a promotion scheme with Scandinavian Air Services. All SAS, *nicht wahr*? We think you should come here and join in a ski race, which we would sponsor. Please find time to look into this and come up with some ideas.'

I sent the man packing fairly promptly; but to this day I am not sure what the call was about. It may have been someone trying to distract us or pull our legs – and if it was, they did the job quite realistically. Yet it was not a good moment for jokes.

What with Ferret Howard harassing the Ministry, and Mike Rose champing at his bit in Hereford, our expectations of action rose sharply. All other plans were dropped as we concentrated on the problem of how to reach the Falklands before any other British troops. Emissaries sped round to the embassies of countries such as New Zealand which might offer us a jumping-off point.

We also activated our contacts with American Special Forces. These were already close – the result of long-term collaboration and many exchanges – and now they paid off handsomely. At the scent of battle our American colleagues were raring to join in the action, but, being prevented from doing so by political considerations, lent us some of their best equipment, including the Stinger, a hand-held, ground-to-air missile system which was just coming into use. It so happened that we already had an experienced non-commissioned officer in the United States,

Corporal Paddy O'Connor; he was rapidly diverted to Delta Force, where he took a crash course on the Stinger, and within days he was on his way back to the United Kingdom with a consignment of missiles and launchers. Similar generosity led the Americans to send over several of their newest radio sets: we already had two in this country, and the system proved a war-winner, as it enabled men on shipboard or on shore in the South Atlantic to talk to Hereford or London in perfectly clear speech and with total security.[1]

As the British military machine geared itself up, a sense of tremendous urgency galvanized people at every level, both inside and outside the armed forces: the managers of shipyards, depots and stores were all swept up in the general excitement. Since no contingency plan existed for dealing with a situation of this kind, everything had to be improvised at zero notice. Suddenly we were all working frantically long hours – in bed at 0200 if we were lucky, and up again at 0600. Realizing that any attempt to recapture the Falklands would be first and foremost a naval operation, I myself went to Fleet Headquarters at Northwood to see Admiral Sir John Fieldhouse, Commander-in-Chief of the Fleet, a marvellously straightforward Yorkshireman whose razor-sharp mind was masked to some extent by his benign exterior, and who had the invaluable gift of remaining calm even under intense pressure.[2] He received me most civilly, and seemed enthusiastic about the possibilities for action by the SAS which I suggested – principally that we should infiltrate reconnaissance patrols ahead of any invasion force, so that they could give our people an accurate idea of how the Argentines had deployed their occupying forces.

Our most pressing need was for intelligence about conditions in the Falklands. In particular, we needed to know about the texture of the landscape at that time of year – and when I heard

1. In due course O'Connor parachuted into the South Atlantic, together with a consignment of Stinger missiles and launchers, and was picked up by one of the Task Force ships on its way south. Alas, he was killed in the disastrous helicopter crash (see below) before his new-found expertise could be transmitted to many of his colleagues.
2. He later became Chief of the Defence Staff, and was created Lord Fieldhouse in 1991.

that Sir Cosmo Haskard, a former Governor of the Islands, was in London, I hastened to call on him. He gave us some of the best information we collected; he also told us that his son was at Sandhurst, training to join the Gurkhas, so we immediately sprang him from there and took him to Hereford. Having been brought up for six years in the Falklands, with a country background, he too was able to give us vital help.

In the general chaos of mobilization Mike Rose managed to jump the gun, very much as he had at the start of the Iranian Embassy siege. Without any official permission, he took 'D' Squadron to Brize Norton and got them on board an aircraft; before anyone in authority realized where they were, they had arrived at Ascension Island, four thousand miles down into the South Atlantic and half-way to their target. Soon I too was on my way there, having secured a seat in an aircraft carrying Fieldhouse and other senior officers.

Ascension presented an amazing spectacle. The island itself is strange enough – a wilderness of rust-red ash cones rising from deserts of tumbled lava – but by then it was humming with activity such as it had never seen before. A small armada of warships and transports lay off the coast to the west, and above them helicopters swarmed as they cross-decked men and stores, and ferried others to and from the land. On shore, equipment was piling up everywhere, and much fitness training was in progress. I saw Mike Rose and 'D' Squadron, and Mike and I together lobbied Brigadier Julian Thompson, CO of 3 Commando Brigade: he was an old friend, and needed no persuading that Special Forces were of high potential value, but I wanted him to be fully aware that we were around and hoping to be employed.

Back in the United Kingdom, my role was to liaise and advise at the highest level, for some of our proposed operations were highly sensitive, and needed not merely military approval but political backing from the top. Our plan to infiltrate reconnaissance teams, for instance, carried a high risk: if anything went wrong and people were captured, the whole British game would be given away, for it would be clear that an invasion was being mounted. I thus had to convince both John Nott, the Defence Minister, and Admiral of the Fleet Sir Terence Lewin, Chief of the Defence Staff – and through them the Inner Cabinet and the Prime Minister – that the risk was acceptable, and that the SAS could make a significant contribution to the plan for recovering the islands. To maintain the closest possible liaison, we established an SAS cell in Fleet Headquarters at Northwood, and there our people took part in the central planning of operations. We also maintained a cell in the Central Staff at the MOD – and of course, just because a war was brewing up in the South Atlantic, our other commitments did not come to a sudden end. The counter-terrorist team, for instance, remained on standby, as usual, and the Regiment continued operations in many more distant theatres.

Working at or near the hub of events, I quickly appreciated the colossal contribution to the campaign made by the Prime Minister. Once Margaret Thatcher had taken the decision to recover the islands, she let nothing stand in its way: once she had committed her forces, she made certain that they had the best of everything the country could provide. Equally important, she herself stood back and let her Service commanders take the necessary military decisions, delegating authority in a way that gave her commanders the highest confidence.

This is not the place to tell the whole story of the war. Suffice it to recall a few points of special interest. At the outset of the campaign we narrowly escaped a catastrophe in South Georgia, where we launched Operation Paraquat, an attempt to recover the island, but hopelessly underestimated the severity of the weather on the Fortuna Glacier. Only the inspired flying of Lieutenant Commander Ian Stanley (who won the DSO) in a Wessex III helicopter rescued the reconnaissance party, after two other helicopters had crashed. Three days later a combined force of Royal Marines, SAS and SBS fought their way into the former whaling base of Grytviken and recaptured South Georgia in the first victory of the war – a major propaganda coup.

The reconnaissance patrols of 'G' Squadron also performed admirably in what was by any reckoning a hazardous operation. From the beginning of May, three weeks before the main assault, helicopters flew them blind into remote spots in the Falkland hills, and there they lay up in thoroughly unpleasant conditions, watching tracks, depots, troop deployments and aircraft movements, and determining which sites would be most suitable for the landing. It was a measure of their skill and discipline that none of the patrols was found or captured. After the war criticisms were made that the intelligence which they produced was never passed on far enough down the chain to be of practical use; I think this was true, but the fault lay with the system, not with the men on the ground.

On the night of 14 May forty-five men of 'D' Squadron carried out a perfectly executed attack on the airstrip on Pebble Island, off the north coast of West Falkland. Lifted in by helicopter, they destroyed six Pucara and four Turbo-Mentor aircraft, and one Skyvan transport. Still more important, they denied the Argentines further use of the airfield. The defenders, taken completely by surprise, managed to inflict only one minor injury.

By far our worst setback occurred on 19 May, when the Squadron was cross-decked by helicopter from HMS *Hermes* to HMS *Intrepid* – a distance of only about half a mile. On the last flight of the day, the Sea King, carrying three crew and twenty-seven passengers, plunged into the sea and sank almost at once, with the loss of twenty-two lives. Not all, but the majority, were badged SAS, and the tragedy was one of the most severe ever suffered by the Regiment.

News of it reached me, like a nightmare, at 0200 in my London flat. Accentuated by the hour, this was a savage blow: I did not immediately have the names of the men who had been killed, but it was a certain fact that I had known many of them, and to a small regiment this was an immense loss. Next day Mike Rose's wife Angela, together with one of his fellow officers, worked with extraordinary speed and skill to contact close friends of the families who had been bereaved, and briefed them so that the next of kin would all be told at the same time during the afternoon. Used as we were to breaking bad news, we were not geared up to handling casualties on such a scale, and the disaster put a severe strain on the regimental system. Bridget, who felt the tragedy as deeply as I did, thought it would be wrong to plunge in immediately, but later made a point of visiting all the families in the area.

Another tragedy, though on a smaller scale, again left me deeply saddened. On 10 June the Argentines at last spotted an

SAS patrol at Port Howard, on West Falkland, overlooking the Falkland Sound. The commander, Captain John Hamilton – who had led the raid on Pebble Island – tried to shoot his way out, and gave covering fire for his companion. He himself was killed, and the second man captured. Hamilton was awarded a posthumous Military Cross, but we were much saddened by the loss of an outstanding man at the eleventh hour of the war.

For once our own command structure was not altogether satisfactory. I remained in charge of strategic planning and decisions made in the United Kingdom, and Mike Rose, who established his headquarters on board HMS *Fearless*, controlled tactical operations at the other end. When we were both on Ascension, he, being the determined, strong character he is, had insisted on going south with 'D' Squadron and taking a small regimental headquarters with him. My view was that, with the bulk of the Regiment still in the UK, and plenty of able junior commanders forward, he should have stayed behind to direct affairs at, and from, Hereford. Against my better judgment, I let his enthusiasm sway me, and allowed him to go. On reflection, I believe I was wrong to do so – but to this day he and I cannot agree on the issue.

At the sharp end, the deployment worked very well; our communications allowed Mike to talk to Hereford and London with the greatest clarity – and it was extraordinary to be able to discuss things in detail with someone 8000 miles away. But at home the arrangement led to problems. In Mike's absence, the Second-in-Command of 22nd SAS, Ian Crooke, assumed control, and although in himself he was admirable, he did not have the same authority as the Commanding Officer. Whenever he was faced with a difficult decision, he had to refer it to Mike, which inevitably wasted time; also, I found that I myself was having to spend longer in Hereford than I should have.

Matters came to a head when, in the middle of the war, we decided to deploy another whole squadron. I was dismayed to find that the attitude of this unit seemed luke-warm. I was also puzzled, because I had never known such a lack of enthusiasm: throughout my career the SAS had invariably reacted like hounds to a fox the moment they scented conflict. The trouble, I found, lay in the squadron commander, who himself did not believe in the proposed operation. To my mind there was only one thing to be done, and that was to remove him immediately. Clearly this was a regimental matter, and the decision should have been taken by the Commanding Officer; but as he was not present, I had to act myself. At midnight one night I dismissed the man from his post, and in his place appointed Ian Crooke, a first-class practical leader. By morning the attitude of the squadron had changed entirely, and they were ready to go. The episode demonstrated the impact that one man can have, for better or for worse, on a body of servicemen. With Crooke now overseas as well, I placed Neville Howard in temporary command at Hereford.

To remove an officer from his command in the middle of a war is not an action which anyone would take lightly. I was not worried about the impact on the individual: tough as it was on him, I had to do what I thought was right for all the people whose lives were going to be at stake. The more worrying question was, how would the squadron fare under a new leader? In the event, the war was all but over by the time the second squadron reached the theatre, so that the change of commander made little difference. Mike Rose afterwards maintained that if he himself had been at Hereford, he could have controlled the errant officer and brought him into line. 'Maybe,' I told him. 'But that's the whole point. You weren't there when you were needed.' With two whole squadrons – the bulk of the Regiment – in the South Atlantic, there was a far stronger case for having the Regimental Headquarters in the battle-zone; so in the end the argument between Mike and myself came down to a matter of timing.

He was certainly in the right place at the end of the war. With the help of a Spanish-speaking colleague, he spent much time and energy persuading the Argentines to surrender, and he was present when the ceasefire was signed at Government House, Port Stanley, on the evening of 14 June.

Although the Falklands War lasted only a few weeks, clearing up after it continued for much of the rest of my time as Director. Sustained operational activity left me less time for family affairs than I should have liked, and in my frequent absences the burden of dealing with the children, both at home and at school, fell mainly on Bridget. At St Clot's (as we knew it) Nicola did very well, but Phillida found it less easy to settle. Once her dyslexia had been diagnosed, she took her academic work seriously; yet her rebellious spirit found school discipline hard to take, and her ebullience led to constant clashes with the staff. In due course we realized that life would be easier all round if we made her a weekly boarder, so we brought her home at weekends. In spite of her difficulties, Phillida left St Clot's with ten O-levels, as did Nicola, and both girls retain fond memories of the school.

At home I taught Edward to read a map and use a compass, to navigate his way across country, and generally to look after himself out of doors. We began in the lanes and fields round our house, then progressed to the Welsh mountains. Whenever anyone went into the hills, I made it a cardinal rule that they should be equipped with the basic means of survival – a bergen containing a sleeping bag and a sweater, a groundsheet and a bottle of water. The need for these was usefully rammed home one day when we walked over Pen-y-Fan and came on a boy who had collapsed in the middle of a youth expedition: his companions were doing quite well, giving him hot tea and keeping him warm, but his condition made everyone ponder the hazards of being out in high country.

Thinking back to how much I had enjoyed the Shropshire cricket matches when I was a boy, together with some neighbours we organized a game for our sons and their friends, and then, becoming more ambitious, I laid on a survival course with the help of my old SAS colleague Lofty Wiseman, probably the greatest living expert in the subject. Edward invited a dozen of his school friends, all about ten, and I required each parent to sign a disclaimer, agreeing to accept the risks involved. We took the boys out into the woods at Eastnor Castle, the estate belonging to my friend Ben Hervey-Bathurst. The first evening we gave each of them a rabbit, dead but not gutted, with a pile of potatoes, some onions and a box of matches. We showed them how to create a shelter out of a groundsheet, and how to gut and skin a rabbit; but most of them were too squeamish or too excited to tackle their prey, so that they went hungry for the evening. One boy came up and asked, 'When do we have to go to bed?'

'No particular time,' I told him. 'Whenever you like. But you're going to have to be up at six in the morning.'

Lofty and I bashaed down on a ledge which gave us a good view of the camp and brewed ourselves a sumptuous curry, the smell of which wafted down over the ravenous boys below. The unwise ones went rampaging round the woods until nearly midnight, with the result that they were not very lively when we pulled them out of their sleeping bags by the hair at 0600; but by then they were starving, and they got down to skinning and cooking like savages. That day and the next were filled by a busy programme of activities, skilfully arranged by Lofty: trapping, snaring, fishing, searching the hedges for edible fruits and leaves. We finished with a barbecue, and the course was voted a wild success. Years later I met several young men who counted the survival course among the most memorable experiences of their childhood. Phillida, I know, was aggrieved not to have been included, but I decided firmly that these were boys' activities – and I don't think she has ever forgiven me for my chauvinist outlook.

In 1982, when Edward was twelve, there came the great day when I turned him and his friend Alexander (son of our neighbours) loose on a day's hike in the mountains. I think I was more anxious than they were, and I slunk along one hill behind them, keeping out of sight below the ridges, until I had made sure they were heading in the right direction. Later I let them camp out alone for two nights, with a long march between.

The next year, 1983, I organized something similar: Edward's Field Day, a variety of events and activities which we staged in an SAS training area. Feeling slightly worried that someone might get hurt, I tried to arrange insurance cover through Lloyds, only to find that no broker would touch the proposal – so once again I asked all parents to sign certificates saying that they were happy for their sons to attend. Rifle-shooting, clay pigeons, swimming, fly-casting, map-reading, fire-lighting, a run over the assault course and abseiling from a tower made for an action-packed day, which again ended in a barbecue.

During this period we had once more taken up farming, and

in this I was enormously helped by the arrival on the scene of a young man whose family had a small-holding nearby. In an informal rather than a legal sense, Simon entered into a share-farm arrangement, whereby he managed our fields and the animals being reared in our buildings, in return for a percentage of whatever profits we made. To have an energetic and practical man on the scene was thoroughly reassuring, especially when I was away – as I was going to be for much of my year at the Royal College of Defence Studies in London.

CHAPTER 22

DEEP SOUTH

1984–85

If I pass swiftly over my course at the Royal College of Defence Studies, from September 1982 to December 1983, it is not because my time there was in any way a disappointment. On the contrary, I found it stimulating and beneficial: it gave me a chance to stand back and look at my profession from a distance, in company with able, up-and-coming people from all over the world. I formed an ideal partnership with John Michel, a senior civil servant from the Ministry of Aviation, and together we wrote a thesis on leadership in industry, comparing it with leadership in the Services. There were numerous opportunities for travel, and I was lucky enough to visit India and Pakistan, as well as centres of British industry in the United Kingdom, NATO headquarters in Brussels and other institutions in Europe. Perhaps the most valuable legacy of the course was the number of high-level contacts which it provided: many of the friends made then have since become political, business or Service leaders in their own countries.

One highlight of the course was my venture into high finance. Together with John Stalker, Assistant Chief Constable of Manchester police force, and Captain Peter Goddard of the Royal Navy, I offered students and staff shares at £100 each for us to manage and invest in high-risk companies on the Stock Exchange. Participants were asked to sign certificates exonerating the organizers from blame if the shares went down, rather than up – but by sheer luck we had hit a moment at which the Stock Exchange was rising sharply, week after week. One disastrous morning, when we were meant to be touring the

Royal Naval submarine base at Faslane, on the Clyde, I woke
up to hear on the 7 o'clock news that a company in which I
had just invested heavily appeared to be about to go bankrupt.
Instead of looking at submarines, I spent the next few hours on
the telephone to London, trying to unscramble our investment
– with limited success. Fortunately, most of our shares did well,
and at the end of the course we reimbursed all entrants in our
scheme with £140.

Looking ahead, as always, I saw that the appointment of Military Commissioner and Commander of British Forces in the
Falkland Islands would come up for renewal in the summer of
1984: I therefore began lobbying with the Military Secretary,
and to my delight I heard in the summer of 1983 that this was
indeed to be my next job. From that moment, my sights were
set on the far south.

For once Bridget and I had adequate warning of my new job,
and time in which to prepare for it, especially as I came due for
a spell of what is known in the army as 'gardening leave'. This
five-month gap I spent happily at home, running the farm,
catching up on family business, and laying plans for my next
command.

The appointment posed a considerable challenge. Barely two
years after the end of the war, the islands were still an operational theatre, and I would be responsible for defending them
against Argentine aggression. Also, this would be my first triservice post, with the responsibility of commanding between
twenty-five and thirty ships, and the same number of aircraft,
besides a substantial army contingent – altogether some 5000
service men and women.

Because the job would encompass such a variety of activities,
I did everything I could to brief myself in advance, seeking advice
from the Ministry of Defence, the Foreign Office, the Ministry
of Agriculture, the Royal Veterinary College and other official
bodies. In London Bridget and I met Lord Shackleton, son of
the polar explorer and an expert on the Falklands, who had
carried out an economic survey of the islands in 1976, recommending (among other innovations) the construction of an
airfield with the capacity to take long-range jets. An immediately
impressive man, lively and enthusiastic, he arranged with the

Highlands and Islands Development Board for us to tour the Outer Hebrides, particularly Benbecula, South Uist and Barra, where we studied sheep farming in an environment not unlike that of the Falklands, and examined the interaction of military and civil communities (Benbecula is the base for an artillery range.)

We also met Captain Nick Barker, commander of the survey vessel HMS *Endurance*, who talked so magically of the far south as to banish any doubts we had about venturing down there. Another valuable contact was with Laing, Mowlem and Amey Roadstone (known for short as LMA), the consortium which had already begun building the new airport at Mount Pleasant, south-west of Port Stanley. Ewen Southby-Tailyour, a former Royal Marine officer and distinguished long-distance sailor, gave us numerous good tips. Many other people with Falklands experience helped us, and we read all the books on which we could lay our hands. From one or two hints, and several direct warnings, I gathered that relationships between the various interests on the islands were by no means easy – to which my reaction was that the more I heard before I left, the better.

In March 1984, when our preparations were in full swing, an unusual assignment temporarily diverted my attention. The Queen was due to make a state visit to Jordan, and because of the high level of terrorist activity in the Middle East, there was natural concern about her security. At short notice I was asked by the Chief of the General Staff, General Sir John Stanier, to go out to Jordan on behalf of the Prime Minister and make a personal assessment of the risks involved. This I was delighted to do, as the task enabled me to revisit places such as Petra and Aqaba which I had last seen thirty years earlier; I also renewed my acquaintance with King Hussein, who received me most hospitably at his office in Amman.

In my report to the Cabinet I concluded that the Jordanians were well able to protect the Queen, and recommended that the visit should go ahead. Then at the last moment a bomb went off outside the hotel in Amman where the international Press were gathering; in England, the Prime Minister called an emergency meeting of the Inner Cabinet, to which I was summoned, and the pros and cons of the visit were again debated. Eventually it was decided that the Queen should proceed as planned; the visit took place without trouble, and contributed substantially to international relations. My own career as a Queen's messenger was short-lived but fascinating, especially as it gave me a close-up view of Mrs Thatcher in action.

Back at home, I continued making plans for the Falklands. As a major general, I received a substantial baggage allowance – far greater than I needed for my personal effects in an operational theatre – so we made a bulk purchase of six Yamaha trail-motorbikes (four for ourselves, and two for Colonel Robert Corbett, my Chief of Staff) and had them forwarded to Stanley. We also bought a hemispherical Igloo greenhouse, which was well designed to stand up to fierce winds, and would enable us to grow some vegetables. I myself planned to fly all the way out, but because the air-bridge between Ascension and the Falklands was so overloaded, Bridget and the children, following at the end of the summer term, would have to cover the second half of the journey by sea.

On 16 June I flew to Ascension in an RAF VC-10, an eight-hour trip, and comfortable enough; but the second leg was a different story – thirteen hours on a canvas seat in the thundering belly of a Hercules, with the nagging anxiety that if the aircraft suffered serious mechanical failure, or if refuelling failed, it might have to divert to the mainland of South America, or even turn back. The best parts of the trip were those for which I was invited by the RAF crew to the flight deck to watch our aircraft refuel from tankers (which it did twice). Each mid-air rendezvous made a thrilling spectacle, as the pilot brought his lumbering transport close up under the tail of the tanker and slid his probe into the basket trailing on the end of the hose, so that the two aircraft were linked by an umbilical cord for fifteen minutes as 30,000lbs of fuel were pumped across.

The flight gave me time to think ahead. I was uncomfortably aware that although Mrs Thatcher was totally committed to maintaining the security of the islands, the Services were under pressure to save money by scaling down their forces. It was clear that much would depend on my relationship with Sir Rex Hunt, the Civil Commissioner. While still in London I had heard that things had not gone well between him and my predecessor, Major General Keith Spacie: a gulf had opened up between the civilian and military elements, and it seemed to me essential to bring the two sides together again.

Until the war, Rex had been Governor of the Falklands, in sole charge; but after the conflict two Commissioners had been appointed, of equal rank. In terms of protocol, the Civil Commissioner was half a step ahead, because he was the Queen's representative; yet in terms of getting anything done, he was miles behind, because the only resources on hand were military. Although Rex was nominally responsible for running the islands and restoring them to normal, it was the Military Commissioner who was defending them, and who alone had the capability of carrying out major works of improvement and renovation. The servicemen, totalling 5000, outnumbered the 1800 islanders by nearly three to one.

Rex's reputation reached out far beyond the Falklands. A former RAF pilot and a colonial administrator of wide experience, he had long since formed the habit of putting his own people first and Whitehall second. This, of course, by no means endeared him to officials in London; but he loved the islanders, and worked selflessly for them, and was exactly the man they needed at that moment – an outsized personality, and a leader with the magnetism to lift his people out of the morass created by the Argentine invasion.

We landed on the old airfield outside Port Stanley on a brilliant, still day, to find the ground covered with snow – a memorably beautiful sight. I was met by Keith Spacie, and as we drove out to British Forces' Headquarters at Lookout Camp, a school building that had never been used because of its faulty construction, on the outskirts of the town, he immediately began to brief me about the units and activities which we passed. As he was due to return to the United Kingdom on the same aircraft, he had only a few hours in which to hand over.

That evening at Government House Rex Hunt gave a cocktail party, at which I met him, his wife Mavis, and my senior officers. Among these was my Chief of Staff, Robert Corbett, a tall, upright Irish Guardsman, as likeable as he was efficient, but also a ruthless disciplinarian; there was also Captain Martin Bird, the

Senior Naval Officer, Falkland Islands (SNOFI, for short), who was round-faced and cheerful and immediately gave me confidence in his ability. It took me less than five minutes to see that I could work happily with Rex. I liked him and Mavis straight away, and within a few hours he and I had sketched out a basis for fruitful collaboration. I took the line that, as the Queen's representative, he was senior to me, and I therefore asked him if he would escort me round some of the outlying settlements, to introduce me to the people there. This he said he would be delighted to do – the trouble being that he had no means of transport. The Ministry of Defence had developed a disgraceful attitude towards him: because he was a civilian, official policy laid down that, if he wanted to travel about the islands, he must go under his own steam. This struck me as intolerable – a typical, parsimonious rule created by desk-bound bureaucrats 8000 miles away, who had no idea how things worked in the field. I insisted that, whenever it suited both of us, Rex should fly in my helicopter. When he accompanied me, I had my general's stars removed from the outside of the aircraft and replaced by the royal insignia, so that it should be clear to any islanders on whom we descended that the Queen's representative was their principal visitor. Civilians and Service personnel alike were immensely glad to see him, and I believe the mere fact that we went about together created a more constructive relationship between the islanders and the garrison. Thanks to Rex's support, I gained a high degree of credibility and support, which would otherwise have taken me months to win.

Rex and I also decided that whenever a troopship came down from Ascension carrying replacements for the garrison, we would go out together to greet the newcomers, rather than have them met by the Military Commissioner alone, as had been happening. Onshore, we combined in much the same way on public duties – once with disastrous results. To open a new refuelling bunker, built by the Royal Engineers, we laid on a small ceremony which by chance was filmed by a visiting television team from BBC Pebble Mill. The idea was that I should act as pump attendant and fill up Rex's famous red London taxi. When it appeared, and Rex stepped out resplendent in a full-length Astrakhan coat with matching hat – a get-up which would have turned heads in London – the cameras were already whirring. So with a flourish I plunged the nozzle of the hose into the top of the taxi's tank, not realizing that Don Bonner, the driver, had only just filled it to the brim. The result was that fuel spurted out all over Rex's head, face and coat: although he took the mishap in good part, he had to go straight to hospital for treatment, and the coat went to London, courtesy of the RAF, for cleaning. The television crew good-naturedly destroyed the film, rather than embarrass us by showing the incident in public.

I soon discovered that although on formal occasions Rex behaved with the dignity that one would expect from a leader of his stature, he was quite different when off duty at his home, Government House. There he and Mavis cheerfully entertained people of all ranks, mixed up together, and Rex took pleasure in showing off his sideboard and table mats, still riddled with bullet holes from the time when the house was occupied by the Argentines.

There were plenty of bullet holes, also, in my own official residence, Britannia House, a large, prefabricated, single-storey, wooden villa brought in and erected by the Argentines not long before the war. The ostensible purpose of the ranch-style build-ing had been to house the local head of LADE, the airline serving the mainland; but as services were minimal, the dwelling was far more elaborate than any manager could have needed, and was clearly designed for the Governor or some other senior official when the Argentines took the Falklands over. After the British victory, the building had become an officers' mess, before being put at the disposal of the Commander, British Forces. I was amused to find that it had a most elaborate bathroom, with a heart-shaped bath and a Jacuzzi; but it was a comfortable house – even if it creaked in the wind – and well equipped, with good furniture sent out from the United Kingdom. Its main drawback was that the tin roof had been so well perforated by gunfire and shrapnel that, in spite of attempts to patch it up, rain poured through, and during my first dinner party drips fell on to the smart mahogany table in such quantities that we had to get up and re-position ourselves in a drier part of the room.

The islands as a whole were in a poor way. The water system

had broken down; the diesel generators producing electricity
were worn out, unable to take the load thrust on them, and old
vehicles, huts, equipment and ammunition had been dumped
all over the place. Also, the islands were in a state of continual
alert, for the Argentinians were endlessly probing the edges of
the FIPZ, or Falkland Islands Protection Zone, and the likelihood
of a surprise attack seemed high. We did not anticipate any
large-scale assault aimed at recapturing the islands: rather, we
expected a night landing and perhaps an attempt to knock out
one of the hill-top radar sites vital to our defence. To increase
the efficiency of our intelligence gathering, I reverted to the
tactics which the SAS had refined in the jungles of Malaya, and
enlisted the help of the local population, who knew the place
best: everyone was exhorted to watch the coast and report
immediately if they saw anything or anyone unusual.

One symptom of the general tension was the fact that Phantom or Harrier fighter-bombers were airborne most of the day,
and during my first session at the Legislative Council (known
as LegCo), of which I was an *ex officio* member, there took place
a revealing incident. After being heartily welcomed, I made a
short speech which included the phrase, 'While we, the Services,
are here, your peace is safe.' Hardly had I uttered the words
when an aircraft went over so close to the roof that the whole
building rattled, and for a few moments proceedings were forced
to a halt by the all-obliterating roar. I half expected someone to
complain that the RAF were flying dangerously low, and that I
did not have control of my forces, but far from it: the noise had
scarcely died away when up chirped Bill Luxton – a farmer
descended from one of the original Royal Marine settlers, and
a fourth-generation islander – with the cheerful announcement:
'The sound of freedom!' To him and all the islanders, that roar
meant security.

My first weeks vanished in a whirl of briefings and visits to
outlying stations, most of which could be reached quickly only
by helicopter. I was impressed by the state of the forces' morale,
and particularly by the quality of the Royal Signals corporals
commanding the relay stations, in which four- or six-man teams
were living on mountain tops in the most demanding conditions,
often half buried in snow and fog-bound for days on end.

Nevertheless, I was annoyed to find that the military, far from making any attempt to fraternize with the civilian community, were busy cutting themselves off behind barbed wire. This – as I have discovered in many different countries – is thoroughly bad practice, as it has an inhibiting mental effect: anyone living inside barbed wire ceases to feel safe when he is outside his protective cordon, and he soon has to make a severe mental effort before he can leave base at all. When I found people erecting wire round my headquarters, I immediately stopped them and had the barriers removed.

No day had enough hours in it for all the urgent tasks facing me. My paramount need, as I saw it, was to establish myself as a true triservice commander. Of course I knew my own Service best, but it seemed essential that, far from showing any favouritism, I should display at least as much concern for the affairs of the Royal Navy and Royal Air Force as I did for those of the army, and use all three Services to the best of their individual abilities, yet as a combined force. Instinct told me that even at this level of command it was essential to appear frequently in person: otherwise I would become nothing more than a signature on routine orders. In practical terms, this meant visiting as many air-bases, radar-stations, ships and military installations as possible, and getting to know the maximum number of people in the shortest possible time – the urgency being increased by the fact that a normal Falklands tour lasted only four months, so that, with the exception of a few senior officers, the entire military population changed three times every year.

Visits to warships were one of my early priorities. So far in my career I had had little experience of the Royal Navy, but now I found that the officers and sailors were tremendously proud of their ships, and gave me a rousing welcome on board. Having flown out in a helicopter, I would be winched down on to the deck – a lively business if wind and sea were high. I remember particularly a first-class lunch on the frigate HMS *Andromeda*, one of my three major warships, whose Captain, Commander Michael Moore, gave me a chance to talk to his Lower Deck and Petty Officers' Mess. 'Great fun,' I noted afterwards, 'though the ice took some breaking. Discipline on HM ships is very rigid and clear-cut, with no room for relaxation, as officers and crew are on top of each other all the time.'

On land, members of the garrison were living in very poor accommodation, most of it consisting of Portakabins. Along the shore there were Scandinavian accommodation ships known as Coastels which looked not unlike more Portakabins stacked into floating blocks. These were both noisy and unhealthy – for the floors clanged like sardine tins when people moved about, and cold and influenza viruses were sucked into the air-conditioning systems so that they were spread efficiently round all the inhabitants. The ablution blocks of the Portakabin accommodation were separate, and people had to cross unlit, broken ground to reach them; in high winds, the doors were wrenched out of one's hand. Fortunately the obvious threat from Argentina kept morale high, but the fact that the servicemen's lives were all work and no play gave me cause for concern, and I set about developing three rest and recuperation centres, which were really forms of adventure-training camps. These at least gave service men and women a break from their arduous work.

When I arrived, the men had almost nothing in the way of recreation, and in a life as hard as theirs, two factors assumed critical importance. These were food and mail. In due course we managed to secure extra rations – one and a quarter per man per day – and they were certainly needed by men working out of doors in the winter. The mail, however, remained unpredictable, as it came down from Ascension on the air-bridge, and all too often bad weather or mechanical failure interrupted the service. I devised a system whereby, whenever this happened, news of the setback went out immediately over local radio, so that everyone knew what was happening. In this, as in any other activity, lack of information gave rise to rumours – and in an existence as tense as that, rumour is a dangerous enemy. One bit of gossip will light a fire: an idea blazes through the garrison, and morale takes a quite unnecessary dip just because some fiction has slipped into the system.

The only means of preventing such swings was to keep everybody well briefed, so that they could identify rumours for what they were, and reject them – and in this role of supplying good information, the Falkland Islands Broadcasting Service (FIBS), together with the Services' Sound and Vision Corporation, played a vital part. So tight-fisted were the authorities in London that I had a long, hard fight even to retain free blueys – the airmail letters on which all servicemen depend. Time and again the MOD threatened to begin charging for them, and time and again I insisted that the system remain the same.

The watchword of my time on the islands was 'normalization', which meant a gradual return to civilian life and peacetime accounting, and a progressive reduction of expenditure on defence. Such rationalization was obviously needed, but we, who had to make it work, took a very different view of the process from people in Whitehall. Of all the aggravations that made my job more difficult, haggling over money was easily the worst, and warfare raged perpetually between the civilian side of the Ministry of Defence, who persisted in trying to cut costs with no feeling for the realities of life down there, and the military side, who were trying to keep the islands secure, repair the ravages of the war, and prepare the Falklanders for resuming normal, peacetime control.

For me, the Ministry's meanness and insensitivity were personified in the form of the Command Secretary, who seemed unable to appreciate the fact that Service personnel were living a tough life and deserved all the creature-comforts with which the system could provide them. Instead of adapting to local conditions, he tried to apply civilian financial rules with an inflexibility and rigour quite inappropriate in the circumstances.

Official parsimony ranged from matters of high strategic importance to the most trivial details. Early in my tour, for instance, the MOD threatened to withdraw our garrison from South Georgia: since the island was nearly five days away from the Falklands by ship, and has no airfield, I made it clear that, if the garrison were removed, I could not continue to be responsible for South Georgia's defence. Later the MOD, in a drive to save costs, abruptly announced a thirty per cent cut in the RAF's fuel, which drastically reduced the fast jet pilots' level of operational readiness. On a lower level, the Command Secretary suddenly proposed to charge £2 apiece for the photographs which servicemen about to go home needed for their rail cards in the United Kingdom. (Until then the snapshots had been

provided free.) Even though the amount was relatively small, it
was introduced arbitrarily, and caused an eruption of annoy-
ance, especially as the cost of getting a photograph from a booth
in the United Kingdom was fifty pence. After protracted negotiations we managed to reduce the charge to fifty pence, but it
remained a serious irritation, out of all proportion to any financial gain to the MOD.

On a personal level, I was incensed when the Ministry
increased my rent on Britannia House by £1 a day, and insisted
that I should pay for Edward to come out for his third school
holidays, as if he had been travelling on a comfortable civilian
flight to Australia or New Zealand. I noted furiously: 'How on
earth can they expect me to do my job if they keep putting up
my costs in what is after all a seven-day-a-week operational
theatre?'

I quickly saw that the islanders themselves were still in a state
of shock. After a war, the inhabitants of a country cannot just
pick up the threads of their lives and carry on as before, the
moment the invaders have gone: as after a major operation or
bereavement, shock lingers, and the community does not return
to its normal behaviour for several years. When I arrived, in
June 1984, the Falklanders had long been pilloried by the British
Press as churlish, unhelpful and in no way grateful for the colossal effort which had been made on their behalf. In fact the
opposite was true: they were enormously grateful, and fiercely
loyal to Britain – which was not surprising, as almost all of them
are of British stock. Some were inclined to be dour, as islanders
often are, but their collective personality was nothing like as
difficult as the media portrayed it, and indeed many showed
exceptional generosity in extending hospitality to servicemen.
Tony Pole-Evans, who had lived on Saunders Island since 1938
– and had not taken a holiday since 1948 – invited thirty servicemen to tea in his house every month; another islander had
over 1500 names of servicemen in his visitors' book, all entertained free of charge. These were not exceptions, but rather
examples of normal behaviour throughout the islands.

A second agreeable discovery was that Falklands' weather is
not nearly as bad as it is usually presented. Port Stanley, lying
in the same latitude as London, gets more sun and less rain than

the British capital, and the air, being free from any form of pollution, is brilliantly clear. The main meteorological hazard is the incidence of high winds, usually in summer, but these are generally predictable, building up at about 1000 and dying away at 1600, so that in the brief summer, balmy evenings and out-door barbecues are the order of the day. The temperature seldom drops below −5°C even in the depths of winter. Because the wind often comes straight from the South Pole, and there is no Gulf Stream, the sea is very cold. The air is chilled, and on clear summer days this produces a serious risk of sunburn; but the weather is also highly changeable, and when the winds whirl round the compass, as they often do, one can experience all four seasons in a single day, with sudden snow in mid-summer if a blast comes in from the Pole.

One inescapable fact of life was that there were practically no roads. If a civilian wanted to make a cross-island journey, he had four alternatives: he could ride a horse; he could take a commercial flight in a light aircraft of FIGAS (Falkland Islands Government Air Service) and land on a grass strip; he could go by sea, if and when a ship was able to sail and set him down somewhere near his destination; or he could go by Land Rover over the endless peat moors – in which case, he might average four or five miles an hour, and find himself continually bogged. My Range Rover carried high-lift bumper-jacks and boards, on which the vehicle could be hoisted out of a soft patch and pushed across to one side, in the hope that the wheels would land on something firmer.

For me, one major novelty was the need to deal direct with the media. In the SAS my training and inclination had been to keep out of the limelight – and indeed, in the armed forces as a whole there was a rule that nobody talked to the Press without permission from the Ministry of Defence. Here in the Falklands, however, it was essential that the Commander of British Forces should give interviews, for no journalist felt he had got his money's worth unless his visit included a talk with the military boss. Besides, I was anxious to change the unfortunate image which had gained currency, and to put over the message that the Islanders were by no means as curmudgeonly as earlier reports had portrayed.

At first I was extremely cautious. Before any interview I laid down criteria as to what areas I would or would not discuss, and I asked for lists of questions and subjects in advance. Then I made sure that I had a witness present throughout, and kept a tape-recorder running so that the reporter knew he would be discredited if he departed from what had been said. I found it useful to start asking questions myself – a ploy which often disconcerted newsmen and put them on the defensive.

The theme of our lives was change, change, change. Every day there would be some new development, reorganization, new policy, new people arriving. Such was the pressure that one or two people were killed every month, and fresh crises continually blew up. A Royal Army Ordnance Corps man, dropped by helicopter on a mountain top to check stocks of petrol, was forgotten and left out for forty-eight hours, but survived, because he had obeyed instructions to take a sleeping bag with him. During a routine check of a Rapier installation, a corporal omitted part of the control sequence, and a missile took off. Two men blew themselves up by trying to transfer fuel to a lighted cooker.

One day the new tanker RFA *Olwen*, on her way down from Ascension, was hit by a freak wave which killed two merchant seamen and seriously hurt four others. The injured men needed urgent treatment, but the tanker was still so far out that we had to use another ship as a stepping-stone on which rescue helicopters could refuel. Then the next of kin of one of the dead asked that his body should be buried at sea, so when *Olwyn* had approached within range, senior members of the command group flew out for a funeral service on the afterdeck. In my view there could be no finer way for a sailor to be buried. The ship was barely maintaining her position in half a gale, with waves breaking alongside, and seabirds wheeled and dived screaming overhead. When the ship's company had gathered round in their best uniforms, the service was taken by a naval chaplain with a large red beard, his prayers half whipped away by the wind. At the end the body was committed to the deep, and the wreaths thrown after it floated out over the everlasting sea.

In another incident the pilot of a Phantom used some rocks

called the Needles as a practice target for cannon-fire. Somebody complained, and the ensuing row brought into sharp relief the whole question of wildlife. I am afraid that in a war wildlife does not enjoy a very high priority; but that was no excuse, once the conflict was over, for disturbing the magnificent birds and sea-creatures which throng the shores of the Falklands. I saw that part of my job was to help preserve the penguins, seals, sea-lions, elephant-seals, albatrosses and other species: to this end, it had been made a major offence for the military to harass any form of wildlife, and I did what I could to ensure that my people realized how privileged they were to spend time in this unique environment, where wild creatures feared man so little that they allowed us to walk among them on the shore.

One ever-present threat was fire. A fact little understood in the United Kingdom is that the Falklands are often very dry, and gunfire during training could easily set heathland alight. When that happened, the fire would spread down into the peat, and if it became established, it could burn for months. On one occasion this happened not far upwind of a vast dump containing thousands of tons of ammunition left over from the war. Convoys of trucks went in with water in an attempt to douse the smouldering front, but they became bogged, and only major excavations by bulldozers, which cut trenches ahead of the fire, eventually brought it under control.

By far the biggest single project in hand was the construction of Mount Pleasant Airport – known to all as 'MPA' – some twenty-five miles south-west of Stanley. To build an international airfield with a 9000-foot runway in the middle of a peat-bog, on an island with no roads, no local labour, very little suitable rock, no machinery or equipment and (above all) no docks – this was a truly prodigious feat, a triumph of engineering skill and will-power over an exceedingly difficult environment. The operation began with what amounted to a military assault landing: a ship came in as close as it could and lowered a ramp, down which a bulldozer crawled into the sea. Coming ashore, the digger began to hack its way through the peat, and other machines filled in behind it with aggregate from the ship, until a road had been created to the airport site some five miles inland.

To serve as a dock, the builders brought down an old steamship and ran it aground to form a pier, on to which they could cross-deck their incoming supplies. In this hulk lived the manager of the project, Bill Bloomfield, and his wife Enid, who took to her peculiar existence with extraordinary aplomb, the sole woman in a workforce which rose to a peak strength of 2000. Bill was a remarkable man by any standards: about sixty years old, he was shy and quiet, but a brilliant engineer who had travelled the world and – most important of all – a born leader. For his work on the airfield he received the CBE, richly deserved. No matter how dreadful the weather, he was out on the site every day, encouraging his men, and invariably wearing a white woolly hat which made him easy to pick out. He had a natural rapport with people of every kind, and he repeatedly demonstrated the truth of the claim that the place from which to lead is not an office desk, but the sharp end.

His men were specially brought in from the United Kingdom, many of them seasoned Irish navvies, accustomed to working a sixty-hour week and drinking their nights away; yet even they, tough as they were, had not bargained for the isolation, the lack of normal facilities and communications. Many broke down and collapsed in tears from a combination of home-sickness and depression, and had to be sent home. People were also repatriated if they persistently misbehaved, but to stop shirkers deliberately taking advantage of this practice, anyone who was evacuated had £400 docked from his pay as a contribution to the air-fare, and lost his bonus, which could be considerable.

To obtain solid footings for the runway, the builders had to excavate between two and twelve feet of peat – and the runway, of course, was only part of the project. The first requirement was accommodation for the workforce, and later came vast hangars, store-sheds, ammunition stores, fuel bunkers, living quarters for the garrison, offices and so on, until there was a complex of permanent buildings as big as a small town. Even to build the road between the airport and Stanley was a major undertaking: in places more than twenty feet of peat had to be dug out and removed before foundations could be laid.

Busy as I was, I looked forward eagerly to the arrival of the family, and on 28 July Bridget and the children hove up aboard

Uganda, the principal passenger vessel on the run from Ascension. Together with Rex and Mavis, I went out to greet them on my official launch, and to welcome the new draft of servicemen. 'Coffee and brown sugar and rum in the Captain's cabin,' I noted, 'and everyone full of praise for the children.' Nicola was then eighteen, and, having just left school, was anxiously awaiting the results of her A-levels; Phillida was almost sixteen and Edward fourteen.

That same day also saw the arrival of the Minister for the Armed Forces, John Stanley, on an official visit. He earned much credit for bringing with him a whole Stilton cheese, but then went down in our estimation by changing his plans a dozen times a day. His vacillations upset many of the servicemen, not least the First Battalion, Coldstream Guards, who had laid on an elaborate lunch at Goose Green, only to hear at the last moment that he was unable to stay with them long enough to eat it. Although he made a real effort to understand our problems, he seemed to be in a state of continual nervous tension, and therefore very insecure. A particularly difficult scene took place at the military hospital, where the officer in charge kept telling him, in front of myself and Rex, that the operating facilities were unacceptable. This put me in an impossible position: the medical officer had never complained to me before, and I could not comment on what he told Stanley.

Stanley's quick tour epitomized the difficulties which visitors caused us. Important people were constantly coming out from the United Kingdom, all with the best intentions, but also with no idea of the strain that their arrival threw on people already stretched to their limits. When someone asked Martin Bird what he thought was the Services' greatest problem in the Falklands, he replied without hesitation, 'Visiting ministers!'

Bridget quickly settled into Britannia House and made it more like home; but she was irked by the numerous restrictions which the MOD bureaucrats placed on her mobility. In their wisdom the Powers had decreed that Service wives were not allowed to drive, as no insurance could be arranged for them. For a while Susie Corbett had beaten this rule by driving one of the Mercedes jeeps left behind by the Argentines, but even this was decreed irregular. Why insurance could be arranged for the wives of islanders, but not for those of the garrison, was never made clear; yet in all my fourteen months in the islands I never managed to crack the problem.

Bridget was not entirely house-bound, as my driver could give her lifts in my official Range Rover, but this was frequently not available, and anyway she hated the formality of being driven. Also, as one of only four Service wives on the islands, she was forbidden to fly in military helicopters. Time and again some important visitor came to stay with us and went off by helicopter to tour the islands, returning wide-eyed with stories of how he had fished for sea-trout or been overrun by regiments of penguins – whereas for months Bridget herself never left the environs of Stanley.

For her, the final straw was the first of a series of command-post exercises (CPXs), designed to test systems and procedures in the event of another Argentine invasion. For three days Britannia House became an officers' mess, with all the windows blacked out and Bridget virtually confined to our own bedroom wing. Finding out that these exercises were going to be held regularly, and that in the event of a real invasion-threat she and other Service wives would be evacuated, she laid plans to evacuate herself and Susie Corbett, rather than be held prisoner in her own home.

In this scheme they enlisted the support of some new friends, Ian and Maria Strange. An outstanding conservationist and artist who had gone out from England many years earlier to run a mink farm, Ian had designed many of the stamps which put the Falklands and South Georgia on the philatelic map. Although he was rather shy and reserved, I engaged him to give regular talks on wildlife to the servicemen, and Bridget and I became fascinated by his accounts of his private kingdom, New Island, off West Falkland, which he had not been able to visit since before the invasion.

With a second CPX threatening, Bridget said, 'All right, evacuate me to New Island for the duration,' and this was what we did. Together with the Stranges, Susie and another friend, she flew out and spent what she described as 'three amazing days and nights' on the otherwise uninhabited island. The Stranges themselves opened up their house, and everyone helped them roll drums of oil up the shore to get the heating going; the visitors lived in some huts which Ian had built for tourists, and spent much of their time being entertained by the penguins, which were nesting by the thousand in rookeries along the coast. Ian gave an expert commentary on the birds' habits, and occasionally he reached into a hole to bring out a rare prion, confirming from the ring which he had placed on its leg two years earlier that the same bird had returned to the same burrow. The expedition was voted a spectacular success, not least because it broke the senseless embargo on Service wives flying, so long as they did not deviate from military routes.

Being part-time farmers ourselves, Bridget and I were fascinated by local methods of managing sheep, and a visit to Chartres, the farm belonging to Bill and Pat Luxton, was a revelation. Their land, on West Falkland, stretched for fifty or sixty miles; to bring in the sheep for shearing they would ride for three days, setting out on one lot of horses, and changing every now and then to others which were wandering about half-wild. Like all Falklanders, the Luxtons farmed almost entirely for wool, for which the sheep were bred: although they kept a few carcasses for themselves, ninety-nine per cent of the meat was valueless, since there was no market for it within reach.

At one point, when we saw a sheep on its back, obviously ill, our reaction was to try to put it right, but Bill was not interested, and said that the only sensible course was to kill it. He explained that his management was based upon the survival of the fittest. He had so many sheep, spread over such a huge area, that it was simply not practicable to treat them: if one was going to die, it died – and indeed in the end many of them did die of old age, having lived for up to ten years, whereas sheep in Britain are usually allowed only six or seven. The same principle was applied to lambing. The ewes received no help, but were left to their own devices. During the round-ups, ram lambs were castrated, but not culled for meat, as they are elsewhere. Many people find this a cruel regime, but in fact it is more natural than any system practised in England, since both sexes have a chance to live a full-term life.

The children's summer holidays sped past. Our trail motorbikes proved something of a disappointment: the family learned to handle them on a stretch of disused road, and did go out for picnics on them; but across country the going was so bad that we all found the machines rather a handful, and the summer season, when the peat dried out enough for travel, was all too short. A greater success was the Igloo greenhouse, which not only proved comfortable for sitting in on windy days, but also grew welcome salad crops, which Bridget raised in ammunition boxes filled with a mixture of local soil and imported compost. Her finest horticultural moment came when she was able to out-ploy the high-powered caterers on the Mount Pleasant airfield, who imported much of their food from South Africa, and always had wonderful fresh fruit and vegetables, which we seldom saw. One day they had laid on a banquet for senior executives of LMA, down on a visit, only to find at the last moment that they had no parsley. After an urgent telephone call, our chef sent some across, fresh from the greenhouse – and so grateful were the professionals that in return they gave us several whole fillets of beef.

Nicola got a temporary job as news-reader on the Forces Broadcasting Service, taking to the air as 'Nicola Knight'. 'Good but a bit squeaky,' I recorded after her debut on 14 August. Soon after that she received the welcome news that she had passed her A-levels in Politics, History and French, with grades just good enough to secure her a place at Durham University in the autumn. Phillida had an active time, staying with islander friends on the West Falklands, rounding up sheep, and together with Nicola spent five days on an army adventure-training course at Hill Cove. Edward worked for a week as an unpaid hand on one of the Falkland Island Patrol Vessels – small, flat-bottomed boats with a crew of about twenty which formed the inner cordon of our defence, patrolling close inshore to intercept any craft which might try to land a raiding party. He found it a tough assignment, as the weather was bad and waves constantly burst right over the ship, making him wretchedly sick. A more enjoyable attachment was to the Coldstream Guards, with whom he took part in a full four-day patrol, including night navigation.

Military affairs remained tense. The further my tour progressed, the more keenly aware I became of the critical importance of

Rules of Engagement, or ROE – the carefully laid-down code of practice which governs the response of armed forces to a threat or actual attack from an enemy. The Navy were in no doubt that under the rules obtaining they were allowed to, and would, kill any intruder who crossed into the FIPZ. Moreover, they would do so without asking permission from Fleet Headquarters in the United Kingdom. This seemed a good basis on which to be working, but I realized that I did not know enough about ROE, and took steps to learn more.

ROE are the means by which a Government controls its military forces: they lay down the extent to which captains of ships, pilots of aircraft or land commanders may retaliate against aggressors, and their purpose is to prevent conflict starting or escalating without due cause. The trouble is that politicians and the military inevitably have different views of the risks involved: the military want greater freedom of action than politicians are prepared to give them. If rules are too loose, the Services may open fire when faced with a situation which they believe they cannot contain; and if restrictions are too tight, they will lose ships or aircraft because they have not been allowed to open fire soon enough. Commanders know all too well how quickly a situation can deteriorate, and thus feel the need to have reserve ROE, which they can invoke if things suddenly look bad. The subject is complicated and difficult, but I was glad to be made to grapple with it.

Another vexed question was the employment of women. At the start of my tour the MOD were reluctant to send any women down to the Falklands; I struck a blow for good sense by importing as my personal assistant Liz Faeron, who had worked for me when I was Director, SAS; yet soon sheer necessity swept preconceptions aside. The RAF became so short of radar operators that they had no option but to post women to us; for as long as they could, the die-hards held out, claiming that it was impossible for women to come, because there were no separate lavatories or washing facilities. In the face of necessity, however, all such ridiculous objections evaporated: shift systems were devised so that both sexes could use the same facilities, and the RAF finished with women commanding some of the hill-stations, most successfully. Resistance to using women had dogged the whole of my Service life – and when I heard the argument about lavatories, I knew that the die-hards were at the end of their tether.

My longest-running battle was my campaign to preserve the garrison at a realistic level. One of a theatre commander's most important tasks is to make sure that his forces are adequate for the job given him by his political masters: he has to do as he is told; but if his forces are cut, he cannot be expected to provide the same level of protection as before – and it was difficult to make this stark fact register in Whitehall, or to paint a clear picture of the risks involved in any reduction. This led to inevitable differences of assessment between Whitehall and myself.

Luckily I had a first-class man representing me in London: Air Vice Marshal John Sutton, an experienced airman who was then Assistant Chief of Defence Staff in charge of Commitments.[1] As the senior officer in the MOD managing the Falklands, he took an enormous weight off my shoulders by dealing day-to-day with all the small worries and arguments generated in Whitehall, and also by fighting my case for the retention of realistic force-levels. He and I were in communication several times every week, but during the second half of September he flew out to the Falklands to obtain a first-hand grasp of the situation.

Ever since arriving on station I had planned to visit my outlying garrison in South Georgia, and in November I conceived an ambitious scheme for making a parachute drop into the sea off Grytviken, the former whaling station. Even I knew that my back would not stand up to a jump on to land, but I reckoned that it was good enough for a descent into water, and argued that to arrive in this fashion would save valuable time, besides creating a businesslike impression. Unfortunately a doctor who had been my orthopaedic adviser when I first damaged my back joined forces with Bridget to veto the idea, and the result was that my first sight of South Georgia was from an RAF Nimrod reconnaissance aircraft, which was making a survey down to the South Sandwich Islands, in the far south-east.

1. He later became an Air Marshal, was knighted in 1986, and since 1990 has been Lieutenant Governor and Commander-in-Chief, Jersey.

Because there were seats to spare, I took Rex Hunt along so that he too could visit one of the further reaches of his parish, and could brief me during the journey; the Nimrod did not have enough fuel to descend to low level over South Georgia on its way out, so as we passed, on 2 December, we sent the following radio signal:

> Civil Commissioner Sir Rex Hunt together with Military Commissioner Major General Peter de la Billière overhead Grytviken in RAF Nimrod of 201 Squadron send good wishes and greetings to garrison commander and military garrison of 1 Royal Greenjackets, also to British Antarctic Survey team on Bird Island.

We had fuel for only one low pass over the South Sandwich Islands, yet that was unforgettable. In the warmth of summer the ice-packs were breaking up, but the islands themselves rose out of the sea like giant white pyramids covered in snow.

Two days later, on 6 December, the Navy began an exercise designed to practise rapid reinforcement of the garrison on South Georgia. Seizing the chance, Bridget and I took passage in the Royal Fleet Auxiliary *Tidespring*, together with Bill and Enid Bloomfield, to give them a break. On the way we were cross-decked by helicopter to HMS *Minerva*, dangling beneath the aircraft on slings. The Captain, Mark Masterman, had invited us to spend a morning on board, and for a while Bridget steered the ship, amazed by the ease with which she responded to the movements of two small levers (gone are the days of the wheel).

During the three-day voyage I found myself thinking much of Sir Ernest Shackleton,[1] and when we arrived off Grytviken on 8 December, I noticed it was seventy years, almost to the day, since the explorer had reached that very spot in *Endurance* on his second expedition to the Antarctic. I recalled how the

---

1. On 5 January 1922, on his way to the Antarctic for the third time, Shackleton died on board his new ship, *Quest*, while she was moored in King Edward Cove, South Georgia. His body was embalmed and taken as far as Montevideo, en route for England, before instructions arrived from his widow directing that it should be buried on South Georgia. It was interred in the whalers' cemetery at Grytviken on 5 March 1922, and lies there to this day.

wooden ship had later been crushed in the ice, and how Shackleton led his party across six hundred miles of ice and ocean to
Elephant Island, whence some of them sailed seven hundred
miles back to South Georgia in an open boat and crossed the
uncharted mountains of the island – altogether an amazing feat
by an exceptional leader of men.

Gloriously fine, still weather greeted us, and the scenery
remained exactly as Shackleton described it – majestic and savage, a dazzling panorama of snow, ice, rock and sea. 'A rugged
and lovely place, full of romance and danger,' I noted in my
journal. But the old whaling stations of Grytviken, Leith Harbour
and Stromness were in a sorry state, with evidence of deliberate
destruction everywhere. The sight of such vandalism made
me furious – particularly as it seemed that much of it had
been carried out by British seamen – and I did what I could to
prevent further damage by having records made and photographs taken.

The excitement of our visit was increased by the fact that a
Russian Pavlov-class ship, with helicopters on deck, had arrived
off Grytviken just as our reinforcement exercise was about to
start. The captain was ostensibly in search of water, but the
timing of his appearance seemed too much of a coincidence,
and the Commanding Officer of the garrison dropped out of the
exercise to keep an eye on him. In spite of a hectic schedule, I
made time to visit Shackleton's grave, marked by a plain cross,
to inspect the wreck of the Argentine Sea King helicopter shot
down by the Royal Marines in 1982, and to climb the hill behind
Grytviken – an energetic foray which brought home to me the
extreme harshness of the environment, even in summer, and
confirmed what an impossible task the SAS had set themselves
in trying to land on the Fortuna glacier at the start of the war.
Of countless unforgettable sights, one of the most astonishing
was that of the seals and penguins in St Andrew's Bay. Somebody said that there were a million living creatures in view –
but the assembly was beyond any counting.

Over Christmas, I considered it vital that the garrison should
maintain its vigilance: the holiday was an obvious time for the
Argentines to put in a surprise attack, and I lost no opportunity
of reminding people that the Yom Kippur War of 1973 had

broken unexpectedly on the Sabbath. I decided that my own contribution to the festivities would be to visit as many units as possible, and, by careful planning, I managed to call in at sixty-five locations in only three days. At every stop I made sure that the service men and women were ready when I arrived, so that I could speak to each detachment with minimal delay. Besides warning them to be on the alert, I thanked them for the contributions they were making, and said how much their efforts counted, both to the Government of the islands and to me. (It may have been the excesses of my Christmas schedule which elicited from Bridget the famous remark that the only way she could see me was by making an appointment through my ADC.)

In the new year we took a short but memorable break. All the outlying islands are beautiful, but Carcass Island, in the far north-west, struck us as one of the loveliest. Owned by Rob and Lorraine McGill, it had no permanent human population, and was alive with wild creatures; but as well as the McGills' own home there were a couple of cottages which could be rented, and together with the Corbetts and their three boys we had a glorious holiday, each family taking one little house. At the height of the southern summer the weather was unbelievably fine: clear blue skies, no wind, and sun so hot that the children swam among the penguins in the edge of the icy sea. Walking through the tussock grass on the shore, we had to take care not to tread on the jackass penguins nesting in burrows, and not to position ourselves between the giant sea-lions and the water, for fear of attack if they found themselves barred from the ocean. We all felt a tremendous sense of isolation, which was increased by the McGills telling us that in the old days the inhabitants relied on white boards, exhibited by passing ships, to inform them that mail had arrived for them on the main island.

Soon after that the children had to return for their spring terms, but they came out again for their Easter holidays. This time Edward and Phillida were unlucky, in that their Hercules had to divert to Brazil, after a tanker had failed, but they eventually arrived none the worse, and rather thrilled by their adventure. Nicola landed a fulfilling temporary job in Stanley, helping prepare exhibits and plans for the new museum (among the exhibits were ration-packs handed out to Argentine officers and other ranks – the first much the same as ours, the second deplorably inadequate).

The event to which we all looked forward with a mixture of apprehension and excitement was the opening of the new airfield, scheduled for May 1985. Thanks to the efficiency and drive of Bill Bloomfield, work remained well up to schedule, but I could see that completion of the facility was going to cause major problems. Apart from anything else, it would give us another vast area to defend. The field was so large that it would take a hundred men to open it up every time an aircraft came in or left: a hundred men to switch on radars, work the refuelling equipment, staff the reception area, and so on. I also foresaw that once the road into Stanley opened, we would inevitably have clashes between servicemen and members of the 2000-strong workforce, who, unlike the garrison, were all concentrated in one spot. I wanted our people to be able to use the splendid new sports facilities at Mount Pleasant – for there were almost none anywhere else on the islands – but all these innovations were going to need careful negotiation.

Extraordinary as it now seems, protracted arguments raged about what the new airfield was to be called. Was it to be primarily a military base, or mainly a civil establishment, which I favoured? Who should have access to it? For some time the controversy dominated our lives, and in the end the Prime Minister herself intervened and decreed that Mount Pleasant would be a civilian airport, not an RAF station.

When the road was all but finished, Bill Bloomfield asked me and Rex Hunt to open it, and we devised a simple ceremony in which I flattened one last pile of rock with a bulldozer and Rex cut a symbolic tape. I made a hash of the bulldozing by pulling the wrong levers and almost ending in the ditch, but I sought to recover my ground by thanking the workforce for their outstanding contribution to the defence of the islands, and saying how proud the Services were to be working with them. 'Eighty weeks to touchdown' had been Bill Bloomfield's motto, and by an incredible feat he was about to achieve his target.

Somehow the idea came up that the most suitable public

figure to open the new field would be HRH Prince Andrew, who was then serving as a Royal Naval helicopter pilot on board the frigate HMS *Brazen*. We realized that there might be opposition both from Buckingham Palace, which had announced that he was not to carry out any public duties while on naval service, and from the Navy, who understandably did not want the routine of his ship upset. Rex Hunt and I therefore joined forces to put dual pressure on our mentors in the United Kingdom – he on the Foreign Office, I on the Ministry of Defence. We had learnt from experience that if the same request came through on both channels, it was likely to win sympathy – and so it turned out on this occasion. In due course we heard that the Queen was happy for Prince Andrew to perform the opening ceremony, and everybody was delighted.

The first time Bridget and I met the Prince was on *Brazen*, when her Captain, Commander Toby Frere (now Vice Admiral Sir Tobias Frere), invited us on board soon after the ship had arrived on the Falklands station: once formal introductions were over, we saw that the Prince was fully integrated into the ship's company, a normal member of the crew. (Wearing a thick, dark beard, he looked extraordinarily like his great-grandfather, King George V.) Then we invited him to a fork-supper in Britannia House – a crowded, enjoyable evening, made memorable by the fact that when he went to leave, his Land Rover's battery was flat, so that the party finished with him, myself and members of my staff all pushing the wretched vehicle downhill to give it a jump start.

In March I began making arrangements to visit settlements in the far west, at Port Stephens and on Weddell Island, and my plan was to use the survey vessel *Endurance* as my flagship. Then at the last minute she had to be diverted to rescue an injured member of a service expedition on Brabant Island, in the South Shetlands. In her absence, Toby Frere invited me to use *Brazen* instead, and nobly gave up his own cabin for Bridget and myself (authority having been delegated to me to waive the strict rule that women were not allowed on board HM warships).[1] So

---

1. Since then radical changes in naval regulations have allowed women to serve as members of the crew of HM warships.

Prince Andrew flew us aboard in the ship's Lynx helicopter, and we set off on a three-day patrol which was fascinating both for the contacts that we made with far-flung islanders, and for the insights that we obtained into life on a modern warship. 'Tremendous stress and responsibility on the shoulders of a captain,' I noted, but Bridget got a warm reception from all the sailors, who were eager to demonstrate their particular skills. One highlight of the voyage was our passage through the narrow channel leading to Port Stephens, which, with so large a ship, called for intricate manoeuvring. Safely in harbour, we invited Peter and Ann Robertson on board for dinner, and at the Weddell Settlement we got an exceptionally cordial welcome from Bob and Thelma Ferguson.

Back in Stanley, excitement built to fever-pitch on 1 May, the day planned for the first landing by a TriStar wide-bodied jet. Towards noon the entire LMA workforce gathered on the sides of the runway, and at last, eight hours out of Ascension and seventeen minutes behind schedule, a huge grey-and-white aircraft came dropping into view, flanked by a pair of escorting Phantoms.

'Historic day, in which UK and Falklands are brought closer together,' I wrote:

> Terrific emotion, with tough labourers in tears. The great Bill Bloomfield, who has led the workforce to this moment, was his usual quiet, self-effacing self, but even he was a little overwhelmed. A mighty cheer went up as the aircraft touched down, and once it was in the parking area the workmen swarmed round and gathered at the bottom of the steps in a crowd of hundreds, cheering the air hostesses.

That first touch-down was designed to test the new airport's systems, in preparation for the official opening ceremony two days later, on 12 May. Prince Andrew came in by helicopter on the eleventh, and began an intensive programme of engagements by laying a wreath at the Blue Beach cemetery. Later he laid the foundation stone of the new hospital in Stanley, which was to be named after him, and as dark was falling he walked through the town to open the school hostel, followed by a swarm of children. When I remarked to my Royal Air Force ADC,

Malcolm Jones, 'Now I know what it's like to be the Pied Piper,' Malcolm instantly replied, 'You mean we're all rats!' After a reception and a dinner party, the Prince spent the night at Government House.

On 12 May I recorded 'a great and successful day', on which many months of planning and hard work came to fruition. The assembly of people on the airfield was the largest the Falklands had ever known. Together with the Hunts, Bridget and I flew down from Stanley in a FIGAS Islander (a small turbo-prop aircraft). The Prince arrived by helicopter, and soon he, the Hunts, Bridget and myself were in the control tower, anxiously watching the sky to our right. Then we picked up the glare of the TriStar's landing lights, and a few seconds later it made a perfect touchdown, within less than a minute of its scheduled arrival time, as its two escorting Phantoms roared past and disappeared into the sky, reheats blazing. Rex and I then drove across the runway in his red taxi to greet our distinguished guests, led by Michael Heseltine, the Secretary of State for Defence, and his wife Anne. 'Speeches went on too long,' I noted afterwards – especially as the booming acoustics inside the huge hangar made them difficult to hear – but when the Prince unveiled a plaque and declared the airport open, there was a huge roar of applause and celebration. There followed a sumptuous lunch, laid on by LMA; but by then HMS *Brazen* had already set course for Florida, where her crew were to have a long-awaited run ashore after their tour in the far south, and Prince Andrew had to leave the festivities prematurely, leaping back into his Sea King and flying northwards to overtake his ship. With his natural, easy friendliness, his liveliness and ready sense of humour, he had endeared himself to everyone he met.

The fact that the new airfield was operational shifted the balance of the islands' defence. From now on, the MOD argued, it would be possible to augment the garrison within a few hours by flying in extra troops, should a major threat develop, and therefore the resident forces could be scaled down. It thus became harder than ever to justify force levels. Nevertheless, while the political situation remained unchanged, and the Argentines went on rebuilding their long-range attack capability, I remained firmly of the opinion that we must interpret their activities as a continuing threat.

With the journey made so much quicker and easier, it also became harder to ward off visits by VIPs and senior officers. At the beginning of June I noted: 'Chaos trying to sort out our entertainment programmes. We have had five ministers, four four-star officers – in total over twenty stars – inside six weeks.' None were less trouble, however, than the First Sea Lord, Admiral Sir John Fieldhouse, and his wife – one of the least pompous people on earth who, when I addressed her as 'Lady Fieldhouse', immediately announced that her name was Midge. When she complained that she and her husband rarely got any time to themselves, she sounded uncannily like Bridget, and she once brought down the house with her definition of an expert – 'ex', she said, meaning a has-been, and 'spurt' something under pressure.

On 5 June I received an absurd letter from an air commodore in the MOD stating in excitable terms that the new airport belonged to the Royal Air Force, and was to be controlled by the RAF alone. At this I telephoned John Sutton and demanded that the letter be withdrawn – which it was. It seemed incredible that senior officers in London could take such a blinkered view: they simply did not realize that although the airfield provided the essential means for rapid reinforcement in the event of an attack, it also released the islanders from their isolation, and was the gateway for development. Once our differences with Argentina were reconciled, the civilian role of the airport would obviously come to the fore.

The grimmest event of my last few weeks on the Falklands was a fatal air accident, in which a Hercules climbing away through cloud collided with a Royal Naval Sea King helicopter some sixty miles out to sea. The Hercules pilots brought their aircraft back to base with ten feet of one wing torn off – an incredible piece of flying – but the helicopter simply disintegrated, killing all four crew. Clearly there had been a misunderstanding, or at any rate a slow exchange of information, between the radar stations and the pilots; a Royal Naval enquiry was set up to determine how the disaster had occurred, and as a result several changes of procedure were introduced.

My tour was set to end on 19 July, but I began saying goodbyes nearly three weeks before that, and my last days on the islands vanished in a flurry of report-writing, valedictory visiting and 'gozome' or farewell parties. One of the first was what I described in my journal as 'the most heart-warming gozome' at the Look-out Camp mess:

> A superb dinner, with flowers flown out specially from Brize Norton, and all our best friends on the island invited. Clive Evans, my Chief of Staff, made a magnificent speech, and to cap it all we were given an original water-colour of a fur seal by Ian Strange. I was very touched, and could not have wished for a more moving or desirable present. It is quite beautiful, and we shall treasure it for life.

On 1 July Bridget was given a farewell dinner party by the Hunts, who offered her the rare privilege of choosing her fellow guests. All but three of the people present were islanders – reflecting how fond we had become of the Falklands and their people. Bridget left for home next day, seen off with champagne in the Portakabin VIP lounge at Mount Pleasant.

Next morning, 3 July, I attended my last session of LegCo, the Legislative Council. I had taken some trouble to prepare a speech, in which I proposed to tell the assembly that I would take home with me the impression of three key spirits: hope, without which there would be no future; determination, to overcome difficulties and try out new ideas; and confidence, in the future of the Falklands. Unfortunately, as I began to speak, the imminence of my departure suddenly broke over me like a wave: all at once I realized how sad I would be to leave these island people, who had won a special place in Bridget's and my hearts, and I was so overcome that I could not finish what I was trying to say.

Goodbyes continued to the very end, culminating in one dinner party with the Hunts, at which Rex made a generous speech, and another given by Air Commodore Clive Evans, who had taken over as my Chief of Staff, and his wife Terry. There I wore my dinner jacket for the first and last time during my tour. Departure day itself was full of surprises, not least from our chickens, which suddenly laid two eggs, the first in three months (we bequeathed them, and sold the greenhouse, to my successor, Air Vice Marshal Kip Kemball). An embarrassingly eulogistic signal arrived from the Chief of the Defence Staff, General Sir Edwin Bramall, praising my efforts to maintain harmony between the civilian and military communities, and saying that the high morale of the garrison was 'a source of inspiration' to the Chiefs of Staff.[1]

When I left the Headquarters, the staff lined the route and gave three cheers. At Government House the staff presented me with a Falkland Islands 1982 tie, and all the councillors, staff and wives came out to wave as my helicopter lifted off for Mount Pleasant. As we skimmed down the coast to the new airfield, a thousand memories came pouring back, and on the apron, to my amazement, I found long rows of soldiers, sailors, airmen and construction workers lining the route to the TriStar. Kip Kemball accompanied me, as did Lieutenant Simon Massey, my latest ADC, who came from the Royal Navy, and a Light Infantry bugler blew a fanfare as I walked up the steps; but the emotional pressure was so great that I could not speak to anyone. At the top of the steps I paused to wave; then I was inside, and somebody was saying that the whole scene seemed unreal, and not at all like me.

So ended one of the busiest and most rewarding tours of my life, in which two or three years' work had been crammed into one. My feeling about the islands remained (and remains) the same as always: that we should retain them indefinitely. For one thing, blood has been spilled in their recovery, and we have already written off half a billion pounds on them; after such expenditure, future maintenance costs will be relatively low. A second factor is the possibility that oil and other minerals will be developed round them. If this happens, the Falklands, far from being a drain, may prove a tremendously lucrative investment. The third factor is that if for any reason the Panama Canal is put out of action, the islands are strategically placed to control the long-haul routes to the west coast of the United States. Finally, and of greatest significance, the islanders themselves are

1. Now Field Marshal Lord Bramall, he became Lord Lieutenant of Greater London in 1986.

British to the core. For all these reasons, to abandon the Falklands now would be not only treachery to our people there, but
a grave financial and strategic miscalculation.

CHAPTER 23

WALES AND THE SOUTH-EAST

1985–90

Towards the end of our time in the Falklands I came to assume that I would serve for one more tour and then retire. I was fifty-one, steadfast in my determination to avoid any kind of staff appointment, and feeling that I had a pretty good career behind me. The question was, where would my last tour be? For a few weeks it had looked as though I might land a job as the Chief of Defence Staff's Military Adviser on Brunei, but this fell through – and probably it was just as well, since it would have meant living in the Far East, and travelling a great deal, which would have pleased me, but not my long-suffering wife. Instead, I went to Wales.

For Brunei, read Brecon. Having trained for years with the SAS in the Welsh mountains, I had come to regard them as a second home, and was delighted to be appointed General Officer Commanding Wales. I soon found, however, that relatively few soldiers are stationed in the principality. There are extensive training areas at Sennybridge, in the Brecon Beacons, and at Castlemartin, in Pembrokeshire, as well as an adventure school at Tywyn, on the west coast, and in those days the Royal Engineers' apprentices' college was still at Chepstow. Also, the Army Cadet Force is particularly strong, with many drill halls; but I found that I was commanding only about six hundred regular soldiers, besides five or six thousand territorials.

At the same time, I discovered that the people of Wales are proud of their military connections and their contribution to the British armed forces – and justifiably so, for they have some very fine regiments, and a distinguished record in battle. In terms of population Wales was producing a disproportionate number of soldiers for the British army, and we were relying heavily on being able to use Welsh training areas; yet we had hardly any regular soldiers based in the principality. I therefore launched a personal campaign to have at least one more major unit stationed on Welsh soil.

My headquarters was in the old garrison barracks outside Brecon – a forbidding fortress with stone walls twenty feet high and massive wooden doors. The twin entrance towers housed a command-post, communications centre and operations room for use in the event of nuclear war (there was also an alternative headquarters in a bunker dug deep into a hill, complete with its own hospital). Inside the barracks a parade ground was flanked by the Officers' Mess and administration blocks. My own office on the first floor looked out over the square, and was comfortable and well equipped: in typical army fashion, the facilities in Brecon were in stark contrast with those of the Falklands. Down there, stretched to our limits, we had been obliged to fight the MOD for every paper-clip; here, where life proceeded at a gentle pace, we had every amenity we could think of.

Our official residence, Penbryn, stood on the side of a hill a mile north of the town – a multi-gabled, tile-hung house dating from the 1930s, with the true awkwardness of that time built in. One of the house's best points was its view of Pen-y-Fan and the rest of the Brecon Beacons: looking out of the picture window in the dining room, we had a glorious prospect of mountains framed by trees, with no other building in sight.

For a few weeks I was so busy, rushing about my new command, that I hardly noticed my home surroundings. Then one day I realized that for the first time in my life I had mountains outside the front door, but was never doing more than gaze at them. I therefore worked out a route over Pen-y-Fan and its neighbouring summits which took two and a half hours to complete, and ran it once a week. Together with my ADC of the day and Kesty the lurcher, I would drive out to a pub called the Storey Arms, leave the car there, and run over the mountain: after a shower and breakfast, we would be at work by 1100, feeling extremely full of ourselves.

One important part of my job was to promote an effective

relationship between the military and the police, as part of our defence against terrorist activity. In fact there were few terrorist incidents in Wales, since the IRA looked on the principality as something of a safe area, to which they could repair if things became too hot for them elsewhere, and they preferred the place to stay quiet. All the same, it was essential for army and police to work closely together, and we regularly ran joint exercises to test emergency procedures in the event of a terrorist or nuclear attack.

On another level, it was my task to provide a link between the military and civilian communities: to foster understanding, we brought the military together with Lords Lieutenant, senior policemen, business leaders and other prominent people in a wide range of events. One particularly useful occasion was a day for the Welsh Members of Parliament, on which we gave a full briefing on the military in Wales.

The most important exercise of the year was the annual Cambrian Patrol, in which patrol groups of eight or ten men, led by sergeants or young officers, competed in tests of initiative and leadership over the mountains. It was already a demanding event, which my predecessor, Major General Peter Chiswell, had done much to sharpen up, but I decided to take it a step further. My aim was to place more emphasis on military skills, and at the same time to change the system of awards, so that instead of picking out only three patrols and declaring them winner, second and third, we gave every competitor the chance of winning a gold, silver or bronze medal. Until then, some units had put immense efforts into training their teams, but others had been discouraged by the fact that they had not had time to prepare, and declined to participate rather than not perform creditably. By introducing a system of medals, rather than holding a win-or-lose competition, I hoped to attract a larger entry, and thereby stimulate interest in, and improve standards of, patrolling throughout the army.

Particular innovations included tests in medicine, nuclear, biological and chemical warfare, signalling, map-reading, lake- and river-crossing and, at the end, a march-and-shoot competition. When people claimed that the lake across which we proposed to send teams was too wide, and the water too cold, I silenced them by swimming it myself, in company with my latest ADC, James Hall. The event became so popular that we had to extend it to five days and run it in three sections for regular soldiers, with a fourth for the Territorial Army.

Another organization in which I took a close interest was the Army Cadet Force, which lads and girls between thirteen and eighteen could join for adventure training and character building. The purpose of the ACF is not so much to turn cadets into soldiers as to prepare them for citizenship, and in this it succeeds admirably. It is true that most of the training has a military flavour – but shooting, map-reading, compass work and initiative tests are activities which almost all young people enjoy, and they are certainly more constructive than watching television or mooching around the streets at night. Believing strongly in the value of the ACF, I gave it a lot of time, and later was honoured when the organization asked me to become its president.

Being in Wales gave us a chance to see more of our children, and since we had plenty of space, we encouraged them to bring their friends to stay. All three were making good progress in their various ways. Nicola, having started reading for a general arts degree at Durham University, found that she wanted a more demanding course, and because her aim was to go into journalism, switched to politics and achieved a 2:1. Like her, Phillida left St Clotilde's with 10 O-levels, but failed to get into Canford, and instead joined the sixth form at Bromsgrove, in Worcestershire. This she found tough going, as the school had little understanding of boarders from far afield, and we were in the Falklands for her final year. In spite of this, she managed to achieve three A-levels, although her grades were not high enough to gain her admission to university. Her next step was to take a secretarial course at Queen's, in London, after which she did some temporary jobs. Then, while on holiday in the Italian lakes, she wrote home saying that she wanted to get a degree after all, and asking us to find brochures of suitable establishments. On her return, with the help of the local school's careers officer – who was exceptionally solicitous and efficient, even though we had no previous connection with him – she set to work to identify opportunities, and eventually, three days

before the academic term began, won a place at Ealing College
of Higher Education, reading psychology.

Edward, meanwhile, was enjoying Harrow. His instincts were
curiously similar to mine at the same age, but luckily his housemaster, Geoffrey Treasure, handled him brilliantly, giving him
a long rein and trusting him not to do anything too stupid. The
result was that he survived, achieving three respectable A-levels,
and won a place at Newcastle University, where he read history.

Thinking that Wales would be my last army appointment, and
being keen to develop a hobby which I could take up when I
retired, I turned once more to sailing. Several times in the past
– at school and later – I had dabbled in navigation, and now I
brushed up my knowledge with a postal course. At the back of
my mind was the idea that one day Bridget and I might take a
yacht on a long voyage – an echo of my trip to Aden – and we
went for several short sailing holidays. Because she was prone
to sea-sickness, and bored by the ocean, she enjoyed these trips
less than I did, but I hoped that her enthusiasm for sailing would
gradually grow.

She, for her part, had been nursing the idea of a year's travel
through India and the Far East, but this did not appeal much to
me, and our long-term plans stagnated. Then one day as we
were driving north to see Nicola at Durham, Bridget thrilled me
by proposing a compromise: we should travel through India to
the Far East, as she wanted, but then, perhaps in Singapore, we
should charter a yacht and sail on, maybe to New Zealand. This
seemed to me a terrific advance – but the longer my mind
worked on the idea, the more I came to feel that what I really
wanted to do was to sail the whole way from the UK to New
Zealand. Bridget described this as a hijacking of her original
proposal: whatever it was, it came to obsess me.

After two years in Wales I was on the verge of retiring when I
suddenly saw a chance of succeeding Johnny Watts as Commander of the Sultan of Oman's armed forces. This seemed an
ideal opportunity for me: I spoke some Arabic, knew Oman well,
and liked and respected its people. Within the British army I
was uniquely qualified for the job at that rank level; but when

I made inquiries with General Sir James Glover, the Commander-in-Chief UK Land Forces, I found that after Johnny's departure the post would cease to exist – or at least that it would pass to an Omani officer.

Yet my discussion with Jimmy Glover was far from fruitless, for he unexpectedly offered me another command – that of South-East District. Faced with this new opportunity, I abandoned ideas of retiring: the job would mean promotion to lieutenant general, more responsibility and greater potential for real military work – for South-East District is the exact opposite of Wales, in that it has the largest number of service men and women, of barracks, headquarters, training establishments and depots, of any district in the UK.

With the promotion came a knighthood, announced in the New Year honours for 1988. In going to Buckingham Palace to receive the award, I once again had to comply with the strict rule limiting the recipient to a maximum of three guests: this time, it was Phillida's turn to miss out, but she joined us at the Farmers' Club for a champagne lunch after the investiture. So, in January that year, we moved from Brecon to Aldershot and took up residence in the GOC's official home, Wellesley House, a solid, red-brick building erected in the 1930s. It was a much friendlier house than Penbryn, and easier to run. As in Wales, we were spoilt for staff, among them Corporal Iles, our outstanding chef, and an equally admirable House Sergeant, Sergeant Jones, who was quiet, equable and experienced at running social occasions for several hundred people. The garden included a grass tennis court, and helicopters could land on the garrison sports field just beyond our boundary.

My first need, on taking over, was to learn and understand the whole garrison, which, including civilians, amounted to 85,000 people. This meant a vigorous programme of visits, to meet Commanding Officers and their subordinates. (Since I had to write four hundred and fifty confidential reports every year, it was essential for me to gain some knowledge of the officers whose performance I was assessing.) The command was enormously diverse, encompassing many branches of the TA and Army Cadet Force besides regular units. In a typical week I would visit two or three barracks or depots, watch people training, listen to their problems, and initiate action to resolve their difficulties; also I would take the salute at parades, make speeches, and give talks on leadership and current affairs.

My packed programme entailed spending long hours on the road, and a car telephone became indispensable (I often used to defer calls in the office and make them when I was travelling). My first driver, Corporal Taylor, came with me from Wales: a taciturn Scotsman, he was totally reliable, and most experienced at his job. When he was posted to Scotland, I was sad to lose him but I had the good fortune to be sent Sergeant Alan Cain, a short, quiet and efficient man who had been trained in close-protection work. He excelled at finding his way and planning routes, which was all-important, as people naturally did not want me to arrive early for appointments, and we ourselves did not want to spend hours loitering along the way.

My personal security was always much on our minds. It was up to both of us to make sure that we were never being followed, and we took all sensible precautions: I went into work at different times, changed cars frequently and varied routes as much as possible. When travelling long distances, I always sat in front – partly because it was easier to talk and see out, and partly because it looked less pompous. I also wore a civilian jacket, and slipped my uniform on in a lay-by or behind a hedge shortly before we reached our destination.

As in Wales, my job meant that I had to attend countless parties, most of them laid on with the ostensible aim of keeping the army in touch with local society – Members of Parliament, mayors, local councillors, charity organizers and so on. Bridget and I would be out at some form of social engagement four or five nights a week, and on the few nights when we were at home we almost always had a drinks or dinner party. Scarcely ever did we get an evening to ourselves.

We were lucky enough to have Nicola living at home for nearly two years while she worked as a reporter on the *Aldershot News*, and the best party of our tour took place on 24 June 1989, when she was married in the garrison church to Andrew Ellis, whom she had met as a fellow-student at Durham. The weather played up to the occasion and gave us a blazing hot day. The church was so close to Wellesley House that although the bride went to her wedding in a stately limousine, she and Andrew walked back through the wicket gate to the reception, which was held in the garden, with the band of the Light Infantry playing beneath a mighty oak and four hundred guests spilling out of the marquee over the lawn. Altogether, it was a day for the family to remember.

Behind the routine training, which continued day-in, day-out, lay two operations of high importance: the build-up of the Joint Services skeleton headquarters, and the counter-terrorist campaign. To deal with the headquarters first: after the Falklands War it had been appreciated that Britain had no permanent triservice headquarters which could build on experience gained in the past, organize suitable training, and provide a nucleus for future operations. A skeleton headquarters had therefore been set up – and this, after my tour in the Falklands, was something in which I took the keenest interest. We built up a good triservice team, and their pioneer work attracted much attention in professional circles, especially overseas. Looking back, I believe that we succeeded in giving the concept of triservice operations more prominence, and although at the start of the Gulf War it had not achieved the stature I had hoped for, the whole conflict was nevertheless influenced by the training which had taken place and the procedures which had evolved under the auspices of the new headquarters.

I also held strong views on terrorism, which was thriving at the time, and on how the battle against it should be conducted.[1] When I arrived in Aldershot, millions of pounds were being spent on wiring-in camps and garrisons – a practice which, as I have said, I abhor. I delayed the erection of wire round my own headquarters for as long as possible, but I realized that while other military installations had become hard targets, my headquarters remained soft, and in the end I was obliged to give in.

---

1. The worst incident of those years occurred on 22 September 1989, when ten men were killed and twenty-two injured by an IRA bomb at the Royal Marines' School of Music at Deal, in Kent. Nobody had reported the terrorists occupying a house overlooking the barracks, although in fact they had been noticed. On the other hand, two terrorists were picked up reconnoitring a minister's house in Wiltshire.

This in itself was a victory for the terrorists. Our paramount necessity, as I saw it, was to carry the attack to the enemy by building up such an efficient intelligence organization that they would find it impossible to work effectively. Just like military operations, terrorist operations have to be preceded by reconnaissance, and it is during this preliminary phase that an alert community can often identify terrorist activity and prevent an operation developing. Yet you will never do so unless three factors are working in your favour: first, the public at large must be alert, and prepared to report suspicious sightings; second, they must have a simple and cost-free means of reporting information; and third, the people receiving intelligence - the police and the army – must be receptive of reports, and not treat them as a nuisance.

In considering how to combat the terrorist threat, I once again thought back to my days in the SAS, and in particular to our campaigns in Malaya and Borneo. There we had successfully used the local people as our eyes and ears – and in their knowledge of the local scene the Aborigines and the Dayaks were surely no different from the people of Deal or Dorking: what we needed to do was to harness the power of ordinary people and induce them to report any small irregularity, no matter how inconsequential it appeared – the odd behaviour of a car, the sight of heavy equipment being carried into a garage, unusual movements in rented houses, or merely suspicious activities of strangers in the street. There was, I knew, a mountain of inertia to be shifted: many people are naturally reluctant to report events which seem irrelevant, for fear that they may make fools of themselves, and many refuse to help because they do not wish to become involved with the police or with the investigation which follows a report. Nevertheless, we set up Tigerwatch, a much-publicized scheme whereby every member of every military garrison was briefed to ring a certain number if he or she saw anything suspicious (the catchy name emerged from a competition, in which I offered a small prize for the best suggestion). In my headquarters my able Chief of Staff, Brigadier Johnny Ricketts, put together a team which created a Tigerwatch cell containing not only trained telephonists, who could debrief callers sympathetically, but also analysts who would study the information coming in, collate it, and decide whether or not it contained anything meaningful.

The inception of the scheme was beset by difficulties. On the whole the police and military supported it strongly, but like any other innovation this one needed money — for special telephone exchanges, computers to record and analyse information, and so on — besides strenuous effort from myself, the five Chief Constables in the district, and senior military commanders. The goodwill and cooperation of the police were essential, for it was to local constabularies that information was passed, and it was they who had to follow up leads. We, the military, had to be careful not to turn ourselves into policemen or usurp police responsibilities.

To maintain good liaison, I used to visit all Chief Constables at least twice a year. I also held regular meetings of a counter-terrorist committee, at which John Hoddinott, the Chief Constable of Hampshire — the leading force in these matters — represented his fellow chiefs, who gave him authority to deal with me on a one-to-one basis. To keep people alert, we issued Tigerwatch cards to everyone in the district, and had notices prominently displayed on notice boards in all camps and barracks, using the daily Part One orders to drum home the need for quick and accurate reporting of untoward occurrences.

The response to the scheme was encouraging: large numbers of calls came in, and I think that the general level of alertness was raised. As to whether Tigerwatch actually achieved anything — that was difficult to say. The fact that little terrorist activity took place after the scheme had started may or may not indicate success. Yet the very absence of incidents did suggest that the new level of alertness had some effect: certainly we several times received indications that our information had forestalled a planned terrorist operation.

During my third year in the South-East I decided to make a special effort on behalf of Service charities. The stimulus was the death of two Royal Signals corporals who were beaten up and murdered by the IRA in Northern Ireland: as one of them had been my driver in the Falklands, I felt personal anger at this outrage, and published an account of precisely what had happened, so that everyone in South-East District should know the facts of the case. In the Falklands I had seen that soldiers like nothing better than raising money for a specific cause, and that they gladly organize sponsored runs and marches if they see a good target. I therefore formed a trust with the catchy name – thought up by the padre – of Soldier in Need, or, for short, SIN. At first I encountered some opposition from the Army Benevolent Fund, who feared that I was poaching on their territory, but I persuaded them that my project was an adjunct, rather than a rival, to their own activities, and I emphasized that it would run for one year only. Working with a small committee, I sent out 40,000 letters, personally addressed to every officer and soldier in my command, and in twelve months we raised a total of £62,000.

By the summer of 1990 I had decided (for the third time at least) that my army career was near its end, and I went so far as to take a demobilization course in butchery with the Army Catering Corps, to prepare for the day when I would have time to develop the retail meat outlet which my farming partner had already set up. My plans for sailing to New Zealand were also coming along, and during the winter I attended evening courses in astro-navigation. Bridget and I had arranged that in September we would go off on a week's sailing holiday together, to see how well we could manage a small boat on our own.

Then on 2 August 1990 armed forces of the Iraqi dictator Saddam Hussein invaded Kuwait, plunging the Arabian Gulf into a state of crisis. When I heard the news, a shiver went up my spine, for instinct and experience told me that aggression on this scale against an independent Arab nation would provoke a major international upheaval. Sure enough, within a week the RAF deployed Tornado and Jaguar squadrons to the Gulf, and on 15 September, as we returned from our week's sailing leave, we heard that Britain was sending 7th Armoured Brigade to join the American land forces already assembling in Saudi Arabia, while in the UK a full-scale Joint Headquarters was being set up.

These developments set my adrenalin racing. The Royal Navy was already active in the Gulf, and soon played a key role in enforcing the United Nations embargo on trade with Iraq; the RAF had just deployed; 7th Armoured Brigade was rapidly being pulled out of Germany. In other words, Britain was committing all three services to the task of containing Saddam's aggression; a triservice force would need a triservice commander – and suddenly I saw that my whole career had equipped me to be that very man. Eight years of service in Arabia, a working knowledge of colloquial Arabic, knowledge of the people and the region, and most recently fourteen months' triservice command in the Falklands: all this seemed to have shaped me for the job now imminent.

In my book *Storm Command*, a personal account of the Gulf War, I tell the full story of how I applied for, and was appointed to, the post of Commander, British Forces Middle East. Suffice it to say here that I abandoned all other plans, and after frantic briefings and personal preparations took off for Riyadh on the evening of 6 October 1990 to face the biggest challenge of my life.

CHAPTER 24

THE GULF WAR

1990–91

The bones of the Gulf campaign will be familiar to most readers. For us it began as Operation Granby; for the Americans it was Operation Desert Shield. At first the aim of the Coalition, which began to range itself against the armed forces of Iraq in September 1990, was to deter Saddam Hussein from further aggression. Then gradually, as the weeks went by, our posture changed from one of defence to one of offence: from seeking to contain the Iraqis, we swung round to the aim of driving them out of Kuwait, first by threats and finally by force. By the end of 1990 our intelligence reports suggested that Saddam had an army of half a million men established in positions of strength, with armour and artillery, in Kuwait and along the Saudi frontier. We expected, further, that he might well use the chemical and biological weapons which we believed his arsenal included. Our strategy was therefore to build up our own land forces to a level which we considered adequate before unleashing an all-out air attack, and not to engage the Iraqi troops on the ground until Allied air power had reduced their effectiveness by at least fifty per cent.

In the event, this strategy proved highly effective. After nearly four months of stand-off and preparation, the air-war was launched at 0300 local time on 17 January 1991. It continued unabated, night and day, for the next five weeks, during which Saddam's air force was grounded or dispersed, his communications severely degraded, his command centres destroyed, his biological and chemical factories put out of action, his navy eliminated and his soldiers in the desert driven to extremities of exhaustion by continual bombing. Only then, at 0400 on 24 February, did we launch our ground assault. Allied armour cut through the weakened enemy with minimal opposition, and in barely a hundred hours the war was at an end, with Coalition casualties miraculously light.

Looking back on six months which formed the climax of my career, I see that I was incredibly fortunate to have been in the right place at the right moment: it was sheer luck that at the very end of my military service I got the chance to practise all the command skills which I had built up over the years, on by far the biggest operation in which I had ever taken part. I see also that during the build-up to war my role was almost as much that of diplomat as of soldier: such were the political complexities of the Allied operation that strenuous efforts were needed to weld the thirty-four nations of the Coalition together and give them a common purpose.

Arriving in Riyadh in the early hours of 7 October, I found that the temporary commander, Air Vice Marshal Sandy Wilson, had made an efficient start by setting up a headquarters on one floor of a modern office block, the rest of which served as rear base for the US Marines. For the first few days I stayed in the five-star Sheraton Hotel, but then my Military Assistant Captain Mark Chapman rented a two-storey villa in one of the Saudi capital's expatriate compounds, and this became my home for the duration of the campaign. The situation was both unprecedented and unnerving. There we were, based in a bustling, ultra-modern Arab city, with fine new buildings and hurtling traffic, seeking to create out of thin air an immense, multi-national force with which to repel a criminal lunatic whose vast army was dug in along the frontier barely 200 miles to the north.

Within the Coalition itself the Americans were dominant from the start, and the central, unmistakable figure was that of General Norman Schwarzkopf, the US Commander-in-Chief – an outsized and formidable character, with an outstanding career behind him. In Britain there was considerable concern that the differences in style of command between the Americans and the British might lead to dissension between Norman and myself. Luckily we understood each other from the beginning, and agreed to share top-secret information freely: we also became

good friends, and have remained so since. Working with Norman, I formed the highest respect for his ability as a commander:
he stood up to colossal pressure with endurance that matched his
physical dimensions – he was six foot three inches and seventeen
stone – and he saw his plans through to fruition with a clarity
and steadfastness of purpose denied to some politicians in Washington.

Another key figure in the Coalition, HRH Prince Khalid bin
Sultan bin Abdulaziz, also became a lasting friend. A nephew of
King Fahd of Saudi Arabia, and, at the start of hostilities, Chief
of the Saudi Air Defence Force, Khalid was the Saudi officer
with whom the Allies always found it easiest to do business, and
in due course he was confirmed as overall Commander-in-Chief
of the Coalition while it remained in Saudi territory – although
it was understood that Schwarzkopf would command any attack
on Iraqi forces outside the frontiers of the Kingdom. A solidly
built, good-looking man in his forties, Khalid spoke excellent
English (the result, in part, of a spell at Sandhurst) and had a
ready sense of humour: still more important, he was broad-
minded enough to see other people's points of view.

From my long experience of Arabia, I knew that it had been
an act of high courage on the part of King Fahd of Saudi Arabia
to invite infidel forces on to Muslim soil. Merely to do this had
laid him open to attack from the traditional elements of Saudi
society, and threatened the survival of the monarchy. For this
reason alone, it was essential that the Coalition forces did everything possible to respect Arab religious beliefs and practices, and
I spread this message throughout my command. During my first
few days in theatre I visited not only Prince Sultan, brother of
the King and Saudi Defence Minister, but also Sheikh Isa, the
Emir of Bahrein, and Sheikh Zayed, the Ruler of Abu Dhabi,
reassuring all these friends of Britain that our support would
not waver.

My own paramount need was to get to know my new command. British troops quickly spread out over an immense area,
from Tabuk, the airfield in the far north-west, down to and
beyond the mouth of the Gulf in the south-east – a stretch of
more than 1500 kilometres. The only way to cover such distances was by air, and fortunately I had at my disposal a Hawker

Siddeley HS125, a seven-seater jet, with its own crew. In effect my private aircraft, this became an indispensable command tool. Not only did it enable me, for instance, to hop the 500 kilometres from Riyadh to Jubail, the port on the east coast through which 7th Armoured Brigade was coming ashore, in only an hour; it also acted as a sacrosanct flying office, in which I could talk securely and work on secret papers, away from the tyranny of the telephone.

In Riyadh itself the British Ambassador, Sir Alan Munro, quickly became a vital ally. Short, stocky, fizzing with energy, he understood the needs of the Services exceptionally well, and did all he could to help us. In Jubail, the logistics chief Colonel Martin White impressed me so strongly with his ability that I had him promoted brigadier at the first opportunity: nominally in command of the Force Maintenance Area (FMA) in which 7th Armoured Brigade was sorting itself out as it came ashore, he was in fact in charge of the entire operation of supplying the brigade's needs, from food, water and fuel to ammunition and spare parts. Nor did he have any blueprint for setting up his organization: like the rest of us, he had to improvise as he went along. (Eventually he supplied the entire British Division with equal skill.)

Another man who inspired the highest confidence was Brigadier Patrick Cordingley, commander of 7th Armoured Brigade. I had met him briefly in Germany before the deployment started, liked his friendly, open manner at once, and now admired the energy and enthusiasm with which he set about adapting his men – who had spent their careers training for war in northern Europe – to a new existence in the desert. The Brigade was initially deployed in support of the US Marines, on the eastern sector of the Coalition front, directly south of Kuwait, and Patrick reported to Lieutenant General Walt Boomer, Commander of the US Marines Expeditionary Force. From the start the two hit it off, and I had no qualms about leaving them to work together.

High among my priorities in Riyadh was the creation of a fully triservice headquarters; but this did not prove easy, as I found that the Royal Navy and Royal Air Force were at first reluctant to operate in the way I wanted. Both were used to running their own shows – and indeed the Navy had already been active in the Gulf for ten years, policing the approaches to the Straits of Hormuz with the Armilla patrol. Both Services were used to reporting directly to their own headquarters in the United Kingdom; now I had to win the loyalty of the senior commanders, make them see that I needed their active support, and show them that I, rather than their superiors in England, was the man who would be issuing orders for the duration of the campaign. This was a tricky task, but one for which my experience in the Falklands had given me useful training.

I was also exceedingly fortunate in having, as my own direct superior, Air Chief Marshal Sir Patrick Hine, the Joint Commander of Operation Granby in the United Kingdom. A former fighter pilot of exceptional intellect and ability, Paddy Hine not only understood my problems and backed me up with rare sympathy: working from the Joint Headquarters at High Wycombe, he took a heavy weight off my shoulders by standing firmly between me and the politicians and civil servants in London. (He also flew out every three weeks or so, to spend two or three days in theatre and discuss progress at first hand.)

The importance of his role as an intermediary can scarcely be exaggerated, for my own relationship with the Minister of Defence, Tom King, was not always easy. In London before the deployment King had told me that he was 'very much a hands-on man', and that in the event of war he would want to have direct access to me in the field. I had done my best to persuade him that politicians should not intervene in any military chain of command; and although he had taken my point, I knew he found it difficult not to become personally involved in day-to-day decision-making. It was therefore invaluable for me to have Paddy Hine as my first line of defence in the United Kingdom. In this command structure we had a marked advantage over the Americans, for Norman Schwarzkopf worked directly to General Colin Powell, Chairman of the US Chiefs of Staff, without any intermediary, and so was all too liable to be caught up in the surge and counter-surge of White House politics.

Learning to work with my own commanders was one thing: fitting in with the Americans, the Saudis and other members of the Coalition also demanded tact and mental agility. My close understanding with Norman Schwarzkopf soon paid dividends: Sandy Wilson had won the right for me to sit in on his 'Evening Prayers', the main briefing held for his component commanders at 1930 every night; he also granted my request that a British officer, Lieutenant-Colonel Tim Sulivan, should join his central planning team in the very heart of his headquarters. This was an exceptional privilege, which Tim handled with great good sense, as it let us in on the Americans' innermost secrets. My meetings with the Saudi leaders were less frequent; but I made a point of seeing Khalid several times a week, and when Tom King came out on an official visit, I accompanied him to an audience with King Fahd, at which both Khalid and Prince Sultan were present. As a result of our regular contacts, Khalid and I soon gained confidence in each other – and gradually the various contingents of the Coalition, instead of vying with each other to find individual roles, began to coalesce into a fully united force.

Early in November, within three weeks of arriving in Arabia, I started to press the British Government for a substantial increase in our land forces. Already Norman Schwarzkopf was calling for reinforcements from the United States, and I saw that unless we too raised our numbers, our commitment would start to look very feeble beside that of the Americans. Besides, I knew that if we put a whole armoured division into the desert, rather than one brigade, we should achieve much greater independence of manoeuvre in battle – for a division, even though part of an American corps, would be allocated a sector within which it could move freely.

Luckily for me, when I made this request through Paddy Hine and Tom King, Mrs Thatcher was still Prime Minister, and strongly supported our argument in Parliament. Within days Tom King announced that our contingent would be increased to divisional strength by the despatch of 4th Armoured Brigade, under Brigadier Chris Hammerbeck, with extra-strong artillery, logistic and engineering support. But then suddenly, on 22 November, we heard to our dismay that after a rebellion by members of the Cabinet, Mrs Thatcher had been replaced as Prime Minister by John Major. This news caused consternation in theatre, not only among the British, but among the Americans and the

Saudis, all of whom admired Mrs Thatcher's leadership and strength of character. The Saudis were particularly incredulous, finding it hard to understand how a democratic state had removed its leader without holding a general election.

Early in the deployment it had been agreed at the highest level in Whitehall that, should war break out, day-to-day tactical control of 7th Armoured Brigade would pass to Walt Boomer, provided I was satisfied with the role and tasks which the Americans had assigned us. In due course I made a formal handover – and I am aware that to a layman it may sound as though I was abandoning responsibility for my own men. In fact, since the Americans outnumbered us by ten to one, this was the only practical way of operating, and in any case I retained ultimate control through what we called the yellow card – the right to take the brigade back under my own command if things seemed to be going wrong. Furthermore, the right to decide any matter beyond the day-to-day tactics of the battlefield remained in my hands.

I was delighted to find that the officer chosen to command the British division, Major General Rupert Smith, was a man of exceptional originality, who shared my propensity for seeking unorthodox solutions to problems, and tended, when given orders, to go off and execute them on his own, without troubling his commander further. As far as he was concerned, problems were there merely to be overcome. Another first-class recruit was Commodore Chris Craig, who assumed command of the Royal Naval Task Force on 1 December: a squarely-built, dark-haired man of obvious natural authority, who had won a DSC for his conduct in command of the frigate HMS *Alacrity* in the Falklands, he brought with him a useful-sounding reputation for aggression. My third senior commander (and my own Deputy), Air Vice Marshal Bill Wratten, was equally tough and efficient: another former fighter pilot, he had commanded the RAF detachment in the Falklands immediately after the war. With three such seasoned professionals in theatre, I had every confidence that our forces would excel themselves if and when hostilities broke out.

As the Coalition forces built up through November and December, we watched and waited with growing anxiety to see what Saddam would do. We knew that he was a mass-murderer, with a contempt for his own people which knew no bounds, and that even if not clinically insane, he was certainly irrational, and therefore highly dangerous. We also knew from his military record that he was an extraordinarily bad strategist and tactician; even so, we could hardly believe that he would be idiotic enough to sit and wait while the firepower facing him rapidly increased. His shrewdest move would have been to conduct a partial with-drawal from Kuwait, perhaps retaining Bubiyan Island and the Raudhatin oilfield in the north of the state. Had he done that, he would have undermined the United Nations' resolution call-ing for his removal, and placed the Coalition in an awkward position. Equally, he could have launched pre-emptive attacks, with either aircraft or Scud missiles, before the Coalition was organized, and seriously disrupted our preparations.

In the event he did nothing, except – as we could see from aerial intelligence-gathering – pour more troops into his front line. On our side, as we came round to the idea that we would have to drive him out by force, early plans included one for a direct attack into Kuwait from the south by the US Marines, supported by an amphibious invasion from the Gulf; but gradu-ally Norman Schwarzkopf settled in favour of making these operations little more than feints, while the main punch would come in a wide left hook, which would swing in from the western desert of Iraq to hit the enemy's crack formations, the Republican Guard, from an unexpected direction.

Learning this, together with my staff I developed new ideas about where I wanted the British armour to be deployed. I now saw two objections to Norman's original plan for using the mobility and firepower of our Challenger tanks in support of the US Marines. One was that the terrain in Kuwait did not lend itself to the fast-moving, far-ranging armoured warfare at which we excelled: there were far too many obstructions, principally oil pipe-lines and other installations, for tanks to manoeuvre freely. The open, western desert of Iraq would be a far better theatre for our armour – and I felt that since, in our own terms, we were making a substantial contribution to the Allied effort, we should be given every chance to do ourselves justice. My second objection concerned casualties: because the sector of the front opposite the Marines was so heavily defended, American analysts were projecting their own casualties at seventeen per cent. This was a very high figure, but if it was watered down by being mixed in with projections for other sectors, the overall average for American ground forces came out at about five per cent, which was acceptable. The trouble was that if the whole of the British land contingent were concentrated with the US Marines, our casualties might *average* seventeen per cent. In a fighting force of 10,000 men, this would mean 1700 dead – a number I was not prepared to contemplate. I was willing to take casualties if they were essential to achieve the Coalition aim, and provided they were in proportion to the size of the forces we had committed; but I could not accept that this would be the case in the east. Finally, we deserved a major role in the main assault, as the second-largest foreign contributor to the Coalition.

Influenced by these considerations, and by the knowledge that the western desert was the place for our armour, I asked Norman to resubordinate the British division into his main attack force, coming from the west. He was not at all keen to agree: such a move did not fit in with his plans, and would necessitate major reorganization. Besides, the British and the US Marines had struck up a fine relationship: we respected the Americans' professionalism and drive, and they liked having the support of our Challengers, which could outperform any of their own equipment. (There had also been a good deal of mutually advantageous barter between the two sides: our Compo rations were so much better than the American MREs – officially Meals Ready to Eat, unofficially Meals Rejected by Ethiopians – that many of our soldiers swapped them for sleeping cots.) For several weeks Norman deferred a decision; but in the end he agreed that the British armour should be assigned to General Fred Franks, commander of the US VII Corps, and take part in the main attack.

Throughout the build-up my own life was one of non-stop activity. After early-morning exercise in the pool in our compound, I would have breakfast and be off in an unmarked Mercedes to my headquarters for the first briefing at 0745. Then, most days, I would go visiting our troops, by HS125 or helicopter or both, for I saw personal communication and the maintenance of morale as one of my key responsibilities. At the height of the campaign we had nearly 45,000 people in theatre – easily the largest operational deployment of British forces outside Europe since the Second World War – and I reckoned it my duty to show myself and talk to as many of them as possible, whether they were out in the desert or on board warships in the Gulf. These visits were no hardship for me, since I liked nothing better than to settle down with half a dozen men for a brew in the sands – a luxury which reminded me of old times in the SAS. Visits to ships out in the Gulf were also intensely rewarding, especially if the captain accorded me the privilege of addressing the crew. At RAF stations I found the airmen particularly acute at asking questions about policy and forward planning. Wherever I went, I explained the military and political situation and our plans for the future in as much detail as security considerations would allow, and thanked everyone for their efforts under exacting conditions.

Most evenings I was back in Riyadh in time for Norman Schwarzkopf's Evening Prayers, and then, after a scratch supper in our rented villa, I would launch into telephone conversations with Paddy Hine or Tom King – for Riyadh is three hours ahead of London, and 2100 local time was 1800 in England, when people were free of office pressures and able to talk at length. By 2300 or so I was usually asleep on my feet, but forced myself to write a few lines home – a practice which I had kept up throughout our married life, mainly to show Bridget that I was thinking of her and to let her know that I was alive and well. The letters had the added advantage of preserving a brief record of events, which otherwise would have disappeared in a blur.

One major burden which senior commanders of Western contingents faced was the need to cultivate Press and television. In the Falklands I had seen how strongly the media could influence public opinion for good or ill, and I had realized that it was far better to have them on our side than to antagonize them by being uncooperative. This was even more true in the Gulf, where we could use the media as a weapon, to put over a positive message, so that what we were doing would attract the support of both politicians and members of the public throughout the free world. Because the Press and television crews were equipped with the latest satellite communications, and could send despatches home instantaneously, it seemed all the more important that they should report events fairly and accurately; I therefore went to some trouble to keep the media on side, even though it meant making frequent personal appearances at Press conferences, which did not come easily to me. One persistent difficulty was the timing of news briefings: deadlines in Europe were between five and eight hours ahead of those in the United States, so that it was impossible to please everyone. The Saudis, who were used to rigid Government control, found it hard to see why we should give the media so much consideration, and the presence of nearly 1500 foreign journalists in their country made them extremely nervous. When the countdown to war began, we ourselves adopted a more Draconian attitude, and created five compact Media Reporting Teams (MRTs) and left it to individual editors to decide who should be included.

In the struggle to maintain morale, and keep all our people informed about what was happening, I had two principal weapons. One was the *Sandy Times*, a fortnightly newspaper started at my instigation, published in Riyadh and distributed free to every serviceman. The other was the radio station set up by the British Forces Broadcasting Service. Again, this was my idea, and something on which I insisted, in the face of determined opposition from civil servants in Whitehall, who maintained that it was not worth spending £750,000 on equipment which was clearly going to have a relatively short life. I was adamant that we must have a service which would entertain our troops while they waited for action, on which I could talk to them all at once, and which would combat Iraqi propaganda. After a struggle, in which Tom King supported me, only to have his own instructions ignored in Whitehall, the equipment was sanctioned, and proved a major success. I had similar battles to maintain a free supply of Blueys – in my view, vital to morale. We also got telephones installed at forward locations, so that men got a chance, every now and then, to speak to their wives and families.

As time went on, Paddy Hine and I detected an ever-increasing tendency in Whitehall to block our requests for more men or equipment. With Mrs Thatcher out of the way, the bureaucratic machine began to flex its muscles and take restrictive decisions. We became so exasperated at the obstruction that we called it 'rate-capping', and here again I relied on Paddy to fight my corner, which he did with the utmost tenacity.

The approach of Christmas caused us special concern. On the one hand we did not want to offend our devout Muslim hosts by holding Christian services and festivities; on the other, we were anxious not to depress morale among our troops by denying people any form of seasonal celebration. In the end we decided that services and parties should go ahead provided they were held out of sight: the companies of ships at sea and units out in the desert were thus relatively free to do as they wished. Morale as a whole received a high-voltage boost from the immense number of letters, cards and parcels which members of the public sent out from the United Kingdom. Hundreds came from people who had no direct connection with any member of the Services – they were simply addressed to 'A Soldier, The Gulf', or something similar – and we arranged for these to be passed to men and women without regular correspondents. It was impossible not to be moved by this spontaneous outpouring of loyalty and love – although some people found that it increased, rather than diminished, their homesickness.

I myself found Christmas emotionally difficult. I knew that at home in England the family would be gathering for carols, church-going and parties, and I decided that the best way to combat nostalgia was to arrange the fullest possible programme of visits. Thus on Christmas Day I made nine separate journeys to different units, and spent that night sleeping out on the sand with the 1st Battalion of The Staffordshire Regiment. On Boxing Day I did ten trips. Among many memorable encounters and events, the highlight was my Christmas lunch in the desert with the Queen's Royal Irish Hussars, commanded by Lieutenant-Colonel Arthur Denaro. I found he had got his tanks drawn up together in groups of three, with camouflage nets slung over their inward-facing gun barrels to form pavilions, which the crews had decorated with dangling ribbons, cards and balloons. (Such was the freedom from worry about air attack.) With typical panache and dedication the Army Catering Corps cooks had worked all night to produce a full-scale meal of turkey and plum pudding, with all the trimmings, which I helped to serve out to the men, and afterwards I spoke to the whole Regiment.

Christmas was marked by two decidedly unfestive innovations. One was the administration of vaccine against biological agents, which made us feel exceedingly ill for forty-eight hours, and the other the first launches by Iraq of Scud intercontinental ballistic missiles. The American global detection system was so acute that a launch was reported back to the United States within seconds of a rocket taking off, but a longer interval passed before the bearing and probable target of the missile could be analysed and given out – and it was this period of waiting that made launches so nerve-racking. The first three rockets all turned out to be test-firings, and went off harmlessly into the empty desert in the west of Iraq; but it was not long before Saddam Hussein began aiming at Riyadh itself, and soon the Saudi capital became known as Scud City. Whenever Riyadh came under attack, it was possible to distinguish journalists from servicemen, even though all were wearing uniform. If, during a Scud alert, you saw someone heading for the air-raid shelters, you could be sure he was a serviceman, acting under orders. Men sprinting for rooftops, in contrast, could only be journalists or cameramen in search of spectacular pictures.

By the last week of December it was obvious that war could not be delayed much longer. The United Nations had given Saddam until 15 January 1991 to pull out: after that, under the terms of Resolution 678, the Coalition would use 'all necessary force' to evict him. Another factor which made us inclined to act soon was the climate. In mid-winter the weather had become cool (and often wet), but we knew that at the end of February daytime temperatures would start to rise to levels at which combat in full NBC (nuclear, biological and chemical) kit would become physically impossible. A further consideration was that the holy month of Ramadan would begin on 15 March, after which the Muslim elements of the Coalition might well feel unable to fight.

Flying visits by Prince Charles, just before Christmas, and John Major, early in January, put fresh heart into the British contingent during those final weeks of waiting. The new Prime Minister impressed everyone with his directness and his ability to talk straight to all ranks – a skill made all the more remarkable by the fact that until then he had had scarcely any dealings with the Services. In private, he told me that we would probably unleash the air-war on 16 January – a forecast which showed how closely he had been keeping in touch with President Bush.

During the past weeks I and my senior commanders had been persistently worried by the failure of politicians to understand our need for better Rules of Engagement (ROE). Already, in the Falklands, I had seen that the natural desires of the two sides, military and civilian, were almost irreconcilable. We in the Services wanted freedom to defend ourselves before it was too late; the politicians, on the other hand, were anxious that we should not precipitate international conflict by premature reaction. In the Gulf, the danger was most acute to our aircraft and ships, any of which could, in theory, come under missile attack at any moment when on patrol.

I raised this matter with the Prime Minister during his visit, but the differences between Whitehall and the field commanders could not be resolved. Paddy Hine and I had made little progress when suddenly, on 10 January, events fanned the issue to fever pitch. At 1030 I was holding a conference in Riyadh when the Senior Naval Officer in my headquarters, Captain John Cartwright, rushed in with the news that eight Iraqi jets were heading down the Gulf towards the Type–42 destroyer HMS *Gloucester*. Chris Craig, he said, needed immediate authority to waive his normal ROE and engage them at a range of sixty kilometres. In this emergency, rather than risk losing a £120 million ship, with 300 men on board, I delegated authority immediately. In the event the enemy aircraft turned away – but my action brought agitated protests from Tom King, who demanded to know what was going on. When I had all the facts, I told him – and I believe the incident at last brought us and Whitehall closer together on this vital subject.

As time ran out, we were fully aware that last-minute diplomatic negotiations were taking place in Washington, London, Moscow, Geneva and elsewhere. Yet in theatre a sense of inevitability had built up – a feeling that after such a colossal confrontation, and such immense preparations, war had become inescapable.

The air-attack on Iraq was by far the most intense in the history of warfare – an operation of incredible complexity in which Allied aircraft flew over 3000 sorties during each twenty-four-hour period, with every aircraft coordinated to the last second. At the same time, hundreds of Tomahawk Cruise missiles, launched from US ships in the Gulf, found their way to targets in the heart of Baghdad with a precision that astonished not only the defenders, but also the Western journalists still working in the city. For me, witnessing events from Norman Schwarzkopf's War Room, two floors underground in Riyadh, there was something surreal about this terrible bombardment, which for us was represented by a continuous stream of reports coming up on two television screens. My place at the main table was next to that of Lieutenant-General Chuck Horner, the US Air Force Chief who had planned the air-war brilliantly with his assistant, Brigadier General Buster Glosson; yet even with Horner in his place beside me, and reports of hits on targets pouring in, the battle seemed far away.

Saddam Hussein's response was swift and typically devious. Although he ordered some Scuds to be fired at Riyadh, he directed his heaviest salvo at Israel, in the hope that he could provoke the Israelis into retaliation, bring them into the war and so, by their mere presence, disrupt the Arab members of the Coalition. On the night of 17 January two missiles landed in Haifa and four in Tel Aviv, causing Israel to launch a swarm of F–16 fighter-bombers on combat air patrol. 'It looks as though they are in, and will fly over Jordan,' I scribbled in a hasty note to Bridget. Only by intensive diplomatic activity was that dire consequence averted – and I believe that in the longer term the British can claim some credit for keeping Israel out of the war.

For weeks I had been discussing with Norman Schwarzkopf the possibility of deploying SAS patrols behind the Iraqi lines. At first he was sceptical, partly because of his own deep-seated mistrust of Special Forces, and partly out of his conviction that the Allies' overpowering air superiority would enable us to achieve whatever we wanted by conventional means. In due course, however, I persuaded him that the SAS could look after themselves, that they would not let him down and that they would do a valuable job interrupting Iraqi communications. Then the Scuds revealed a gap in our capabilities: partly because of low cloud, and partly because of the mobility and expert handling of the launchers, we could not find and destroy the missiles threatening Tel Aviv and other key targets in Israel.

Norman agreed that we should deploy units of the SAS, which had been training elsewhere in theatre. On the night of 22 January eight-man patrols were flown deep into Iraq by Chinook helicopter, tasked with disrupting fibre-optic communications. Almost at once they were also ordered to find the mobile Scud launchers and call in aircraft to attack them, or, if necessary, carry out the attacks themselves. One of the patrols, designated Bravo Two Zero, was bounced and scattered the next day, when it had scarcely settled into a lying-up position; but others operated with such effectiveness that no further Scuds were launched at Israel after 26 January. Once again, experience confirmed what the SAS had repeatedly demonstrated in Europe – that no amount of electronic surveillance is as effective as a pair of eyes on the ground.[1]

The opening of the air-war threw the RAF into sudden prominence. Our pilots had been flying combat air patrols for weeks, but now suddenly Tornado fighter-bomber crews were called upon to deliver their special weapon, the JP233 bomb, designed to put airfields out of action by cratering runways, taxiways and aprons. Unlike the laser-guided bombs being used with pin-point accuracy by the Americans, who could drop their weapons from medium level (10,000 feet or above), the JP233 had to be delivered from a precise altitude – which meant that pilots were called upon to attack, at night, at ultra-low level in the face of intensive anti-aircraft fire. The Tornado crews exhibited the highest courage and tenacity, but so hazardous

1. Three members of Bravo Two Zero were killed and four captured. The eighth man limped into Syria after an heroic, seven-night solo march with practically no food or water. His trek, which will go down in SAS annals as an epic of escape and evasion, was described in my own book *Storm Command*; while *Bravo Two Zero* by Andy McNab – pseudonym of the leader – gives a lively account of the adventures of the rest of the patrol. I felt deep pride in my former regiment when, after the war, Norman Schwarzkopf wrote me a personal letter praising in fulsome terms the contribution made by the SAS.

were their sorties that within a week we had lost five aircraft – a very high number in relation to our strength. Bill Wratten, with my fullest support, decided to call off low-level attacks for the time being.

By then, in any case, we had achieved air supremacy, for under the Allied assault the Iraqi air force had ceased to fly. Numerous combat planes had been destroyed inside their hardened aircraft shelters by laser-guided bombs, and many more had filtered away to the safety of Iran. Whether this was a mass defection by the pilots, or a conservation measure ordered by Saddam, we could not be sure – but in practical terms there was little difference: the enemy air force was out of business, leaving us with the freedom of the skies.

The raging air-war naturally filled the world's headlines and television screens; but beneath it non-stop activity was proceeding on land and sea as Coalition units moved up into battle positions. Norman Schwarzkopf had asked me to have the British armoured division up and running by 31 January, and thanks to the inspired direction of Rupert Smith, who had welded his disparate force together in record time, we met this deadline. By then the Tapline road – the only metalled road running north-westwards from Jubail, on the coast, into the interior – was a solid mass of vehicles ferrying men, equipment and stores up to the American depot known as Log Base Alpha, three hundred kilometres into the desert. Such was the pressure of traffic on this vital artery that places in the stream of traffic had to be booked twenty-four hours in advance, and any vehicle which broke down was bulldozed out of the way.

Our decision to subordinate the British division from east to west stretched Martin White and his logistic team to their utmost: having established one Forward Force Maintenance Area (FFMA) at Al Mish'ab, a town on the coast, he suddenly had to move everything to a new FFMA blistered on to the perimeter of Log Base Alpha, three hundred kilometres up country – a challenge to which he rose with his usual imperturbability. By then the division's supplies had reached truly colossal proportions: 24,000 tons of ammunition had been moved forward, and our munitions dump alone occupied an area of desert ten kilometres by seven.

At sea, meanwhile, the Royal Naval Task Group under Chris Craig was preparing to move northwards towards the head of the Gulf. There, its critical task was to clear a path through the minefields, so that the American battleships could move in close enough to bombard enemy positions on the coast, and thus reinforce the general deception that the main Allied assault on the Iraqis in Kuwait was coming from the east. During the past couple of weeks Chris had had some sharp arguments with the Americans, who were going to depend entirely on our five little MCMVs (mine counter-measure vessels), but did not under-stand their methods of operation. With my full support, he had vetoed one suicidal plan whereby the MCMVs would proceed close inshore, in easy range of Silkworm missiles, and then work outwards, clearing as they went. Now a better plan had been agreed, for clearing from the east, but even this carried high risks and demanded exacting levels of skill and discipline.

The British and American navies moved north on 14 Febru-ary, and began clearing a channel two days later. But at 0430 on 18 February USS *Tripoli* detonated a mine which blew a large hole in her side, fortunately without killing anyone. The explosion so unnerved the captains of other American ships that they refused to move until what Chris called his 'little coracles' led them out of danger – and as the evacuation was proceeding, a bottom-mine went up aft of USS *Princeton*, without inflicting serious damage. After these setbacks the force regrouped and worked its way in again towards the Kuwaiti coast, led by the MCMVs, which cleared as they went, until in the end the Ameri-can battleships were able to put down accurate fire from a dis-tance of only twenty kilometres.

All this time the air assault had continued unabated. For a while our Tornados dropped conventional 1000lb bombs from medium level, and Paddy Hine, Bill Wratten and I together fought off an ill-judged attempt by senior RAF officers in the United Kingdom to force the crews back to their low-level role. Millions of pounds had been spent developing the JP233 bomb, the argument went, and to abandon it at this stage would be tantamount to admitting that it had failed. In fact it had not failed, even though, for technical reasons, it had been less effec-tive against thin-skinned Iraqi runways than it would have been against Eastern bloc bases, for which it was designed. The crews had shown outstanding courage in using it to attack ferociously defended airfields; but once Saddam's pilots had ceased to fly, ultra-low-level attacks on runways were no longer needed. In any case, our crews were given new teeth by the arrival of two squadrons of Buccaneers fitted with laser-designation equipment. By flying in conjunction with these ancient but still effective workhorses, the Tornados achieved results as accurate as those of the Americans, with pin-point attacks on bridges, command centres, refineries and other high-priority targets.

For all the precision of guided bombs and missiles, some inevitably went astray, and as the air-war ground on through February, we had to steel ourselves against a rising tide of criticism, especially from America, that we were killing civilians needlessly. Saddam Hussein himself, with characteristic brutality, began trying to engineer the deaths of his own people by siting headquarters in schools, placing guns in the grounds of hospitals, and parking aircraft next to mosques, in the hope that the Allies would bomb them and alienate international opinion. In fact we took great pains to spare such targets, which were strictly off-limits to pilots – and in no previous operation had so much care been devoted to avoiding civilian casualties.

My own role in the run-up to the ground war was largely one of encouragement and exhortation, with only the gentlest touches on the tiller of a ship which by then was sailing smoothly. For better or worse, my work in directing the deployment of the British forces was complete: my job now was to foresee events, and to take action to adjust plans if this became necessary as a result of Iraqi activity. On 13 February I visited the Royal Naval minesweepers just as they were about to set off up the Gulf. On the seventeenth I called on 22 and 33 Field Hospitals, out in the desert not far from the frontier, and was heartened by their unwavering cheerfulness. 'I *hope* most of their patients will be Iraqis,' I wrote to Bridget – but like everyone else I was haunted by uncertainty about what would happen when our armour finally broke through enemy lines. On the twenty-first I paid my last visit to our Divisional Headquarters and the two brigade commanders, who by then had brought their forces up to the assembly area known as Ray, due south of the point at which the Iraqi defences were to be breached. (Their move from the east had been covered by an elaborate electronic deception, during which they themselves had maintained radio silence, but tape-recordings of earlier signal traffic had been broadcast from eastern locations.) The only place in which morale seemed low was the camp for BCRs, or battle casualty replacements, at Jubail. Remembering my own days as a BCR in Japan, I knew what it felt like, waiting to step into a dead man's shoes, so I had everyone collected together and stood on a box with a loud-hailer to tell them how closely I identified with them.

Right to the launch of the ground-war there was disagreement among the Allies over the extent to which we had degraded the Iraqis' ability and will to fight. Battle damage assessment, or BDA, is notoriously difficult, and it seemed to us in Riyadh that the Pentagon took a consistently pessimistic view of the data sent back by satellites and aircraft. Evidence trickling out directly from the front line suggested that most Iraqi soldiers had been severely demoralized by weeks of bombardment, that they were short of food and water, and that they were being kept in their positions only by the physical difficulty of escaping: wire and minefields made it almost impossible for men to cross the front line, and anyone detected trying to desert internally was shot without trial. The increasing desperation of their commanders became apparent on 16 February, when we heard of new measures for the treatment of deserters from the Iraqi III Corps: one man from each battalion was to be hung, and his body left hanging for five hours, in front of his former comrades, and the rest of those who had tried to run away were to be shot.

Eventually even Norman Schwarzkopf was satisfied, and he launched Operation Desert Sabre at 0400 on G-Day, Sunday 24 February. Meticulous preparation ensured that every facet of this colossal undertaking went according to plan, and the Iraqis suddenly found themselves threatened across the whole width of their front, from a bombardment by US warships in the far east – which was in fact part of the grand deception, but suggested that an amphibious landing was imminent – to the actual breakthrough in the far west by the main strike force. In the centre, the Islamic forces, led by the Saudis and Egyptians, breached the main Iraqi defences on the Kuwait border with determination.

The role of the British Division was to protect the right flank of General Fred Franks's VII Corps as it put in the big left hook towards the units of the Republican Guard. In our sector of the front the minefields were breached by armoured bulldozers of the US Ist Mechanized Infantry Division (known as the Big Red One), and on the cold, grey afternoon of G+1, 25 February, the Challengers of 7th Armoured Brigade led through the minefield gap. Rupert Smith's plan, which he executed perfectly, was to use his two armoured brigades like a boxer's fists, punching first with one, then with the other. His third element, the artillery, heavily reinforced by American guns and multiple rocket launchers, acted not as a separate brigade, but in direct support of the other two. His objectives, designated by names of metals – Copper, Zinc, Steel, Platinum – were not features in the desert, which was almost featureless there, but rings drawn on the map round concentrations of enemy, and his aim was never to capture ground, but to knock out enemy armour and guns, and press ahead.

For the first few hours of the assault, our people fully expected to come under gas attack, but this never materialized, and during the night it became apparent that our crews had two war-winning pieces of advanced technology: their satellite-driven global positioning systems, which told them where they were on the face of the earth to within a few metres, and their TOGS, or thermal and optical gun-sights, which enabled them to see and shoot the tanks' main armament in the dark. These devices, coupled with the fact that the enemy were drastically weakened by their ordeal over the past five weeks, meant that VII Corps could sweep forward at a speed which amazed even the most optimistic observers. So little were the Iraqis expecting an attack from the west that many of their tanks were deeply dug in facing south, and could not even turn round to face the enemy bearing down on them from a flank.

Frustrating as it was for me to be stuck in the War Room, several hundred miles from the action, it was also immensely exciting to see the British armour making such progress, and operating with the speed and flexibility which I had always hoped would distinguish it. Until the afternoon of 26 February, G+2, everything went wonderfully well for us – but then came a sickening disaster.

Soon after a 4th Brigade battle group had overrun the objective Brass, two American A–10 Thunderbolt jets mistook Warrior armoured vehicles of the Royal Regiment of Fusiliers for enemy and attacked them with missiles. Before anyone could take evasive action, two Warriors exploded and were set on fire, leaving nine men dead and eleven wounded.

News of the accident, reaching us within minutes, came as a shock but not altogether as a surprise. Throughout my career I had seen men lost in what the Americans call blue-on-blue or fratricidal incidents: in Korea alone thirty per cent of my platoon had become casualties in this way, and I knew that in war such setbacks are inevitable, especially in a battle as fluid and complex as the one we were fighting in the desert. I knew also that pilots and air-controllers were working under intense pressure, and that Norman Schwarzkopf and his generals had done everything possible to deconflict, or guard against such errors. When this traumatic event took place, I therefore knew that the worst thing I could do would be to start criticizing our American partners. Instead, at the first opportunity, I told Norman that I thought there was nothing to be gained by holding an immediate inquiry: nor was one practical, if we were not to delay the Allied advance and invite more casualties. Rather, we should press on with the war and get it finished as soon as possible. This was an important command decision, and I believe that in the circumstances it was right. Personally, of course, I felt deep sympathy for the Fusiliers, and for the families of the dead, and as soon as I could I wrote to the next of kin. I also arranged for photographs to be taken of the wrecked Warriors, and for all relevant information to be collected, so that it should be available for any inquiry that might take place later.

The Fusiliers themselves carried on in the highest traditions of their Regiment, and the headlong advance of the Coalition continued, with Iraqis surrendering by the thousand and whole formations fleeing towards the north-east. At first light on G+4 – 28 February – 7th Armoured Brigade set out on its final charge, storming eastwards across the desert at 40 kilometres per hour until it reached Objective Cobra, astride the all-important main road to Basra, a few minutes before the suspension of offensive operations was announced at 0800. By then, after three days and nights with practically no sleep, officers and men were grey-faced with exhaustion, and Rupert Smith, realizing how much people's faculties had been eroded, took to issuing all orders in written form. His division had advanced three hundred kilo-metres, destroyed most of three Iraqi armoured divisions, and taken more than seven thousand prisoners.

That evening at a televised Press conference in Riyadh I saluted the Coalition triumph and paid particular tribute to Nor-man Schwarzkopf, whom I declared to be 'Man of the Match'. I also singled out for praise Prince Khalid, and the role played by the Saudis in handling the mass influx of foreigners. I con-cluded by urging the people of Britain to ring out their church bells, 'because the British service men and women in the Gulf have won a great victory.' (Later I learnt that my words had been heeded up and down the country, not least at St Paul's Cathedral in London, where my former Chief of Staff, Brigadier Bob Acworth, had become the Registrar.)

Next morning I flew into Kuwait – and no words can describe the hell on earth that the Iraqis had created by their cruelty and wanton destruction. As we approached in one of the Hercules transports loaned by the Royal New Zealand Air Force, we saw, from miles away, an ocean of greasy black smoke given off by blazing oil wells, and as we descended into it, day turned to night. So thick was the murk that, once in it, we could no longer see our own wing-tips, and on the ground a stinking, leaden twilight prevailed. When I left the aircraft, it took me a minute to realize that the subdued roar which filled the air was the noise of oil wells burning all round the horizon. The airport itself was in ruins, littered with burnt-out planes, and the horrors which we found in Kuwait City scarcely bear recounting: after seeing some of the rooms in which the Iraqis had tortured their captives, I wrote in a letter to Bridget, 'Tenth-century behaviour, or worse.'

The same sense of evil emanated from the representatives of the Iraqi regime who met us for ceasefire talks on the desert airstrip at Safwan, just beyond the Kuwaiti frontier, on 3 March.

I took an instant dislike to the two generals, who struck me as intelligent but shifty, and I did not trust them an inch. Norman Schwarzkopf and Prince Khalid were the Coalition representatives, the rest of us merely observers, and we met in a tent amid the most stringent security I had ever seen, with a division of armour deployed all round and out to the horizon, the air full of armed helicopters, and fixed-wing aircraft on combat air patrol above them. These were not peace-talks – which would come later – but only a meeting to stabilize the position reached at the end of the fighting. At first the Iraqis appeared to be very accommodating, and agreed to meet our demands for the release of prisoners, the handover of bodies and disclosure of minefields; but then they tried to make Norman agree to move Coalition units so that they did not hold the Basra road – something which he resolutely refused to do – and when they found themselves in difficulties, said they would have to refer back to Baghdad for further instructions. Later, Norman felt that he had been 'suckered' into agreeing that the Iraqis might fly civilian helicopters, but at the time – considering the state of the country, with all main bridges down – this seemed a reasonable request, and the meeting ended on a tolerably civil note.

Ever since then I have found that one question, above all others, dominates people's curiosity about the war: should we not have gone on and captured Baghdad while we had the chance? It is certainly a very great disappointment and aggravation that, as I write three years after the event, Saddam is still in power, and still murdering his own people. Yet I firmly believed at the time, and I still do now, that the answer to that key question was 'no'.

In purely physical terms, it would have been easy to reach the Iraqi capital. We had the fuel, and our tanks could have been there within a few hours. With the greatest of ease we could have massacred tens of thousands of Iraqis as they queued at the bottlenecks created by the destruction of bridges – but none of us wanted to become involved in what the Americans were already calling a turkey hunt.

And what would we have done when we arrived in Baghdad? Saddam Hussein would not have sat and waited for us, or come out of his bunker with his hands up. The slippery devil would long since have disappeared, either into the desert, or, more likely, to some friendly nation such as Libya, where he would have set up a government-in-exile and become a martyr in the eyes of many Arabs, who saw him as a Pan-Arabian leader. We, the victors on paper, would have inherited a country in ruins, with its bridges and communications destroyed, and no one to govern it. Besides, if we had gone to Baghdad, we would have split the Coalition, for no Arab nation would have come with us. As it was, no Arab troops set foot in Iraq, except for the Safwan talks: it was only we, the Western powers, who needed elbow room to deploy our enormous forces in the Iraqi desert, and if we had gone on alone to the capital, we would have been portrayed as the aggressors in the struggle. We had no remit from the United Nations to invade Iraq: our mission was merely to free Kuwait.

For all these reasons, I believe we were right to stop the war when we did. Where I think we went wrong was in failing to demand the surrender of Saddam himself. Had we occupied Basra and the southern marshes, and refused to leave until the dictator came in person to the negotiating table, we might at least have forced him to sign a valid peace treaty that gave effective authority to UN inspection teams on future visits. This might have been a legitimate and effective move. At the time, however, politicians and military alike were so relieved that the war had ended with miraculously light Coalition casualties that we failed to see the future as clearly as we might have.

With the fighting over, everyone's keenest desire was to go home – but first there was clearing up to be done, and, for me, an unquenchable flow of very important visitors to receive. First to arrive was Tom King, who praised my role in the victory so effusively that I felt obliged to write home: 'I have to say in private that I don't feel I've done very much. It is Norman's battle, and in some ways I feel a bit bogus in taking the glory on his behalf.' Next to arrive was John Major, who flew in on 6 March, the first Western leader to reach the theatre, and the first into liberated Kuwait, where he met the Crown Prince, Sheikh Saad al Abdullah al Salem al Sabah. Hard on his heels came the Defence Committee of the House of Commons – a group of only nine, far more manageable than the eighty US Congressmen who descended on the Americans.

On 11 March, heading for retirement once again, I bade a highly charged farewell to 7th Armoured Brigade, with whom I had formed a special affinity, and I had many other goodbyes to say, not least to the Royal Navy, who had performed with exemplary skill and courage. Another enjoyable visit was to 4th Armoured Brigade, who were still stuck out in the desert beneath the pall of soot, but in high spirits nevertheless. With them I went through the whole battle, and I spent the night with the Royal Regiment of Fusiliers, deliberately making time to talk through the nightmare of the blue-on-blue. I also dropped in at as many RAF stations as time permitted, and called on the Rulers of Bahrein and Abu Dhabi, as well as on British Embassies down the Gulf.

On 17 March I received the welcome news that I was to be promoted full general, and that my service career would be extended for one more year, during which I would act as Middle East Adviser to Tom King and the British Government. With my immediate future secured, I gave my attention to writing reports and sealing off loose ends before at last, on 26 March, I set off for home. It had occurred to me that it would make an appropriate gesture if I and my senior commanders all arrived back in the United Kingdom together; my plan did not quite work out, as Bill Wratten had to travel a day earlier; but the rest of us flew together in the HS125 for an overnight stop in Italy, where the Chief of Defence Staff entertained us royally.

Eight or nine hours in the air gave me time to think back over the campaign. I saw that the Coalition had succeeded because all its members had been fired by common political and military objectives. Without these, chaos would have ensued. This thought raised in my mind the question of whether the Americans could have defeated Saddam on their own. Militarily, they were quite capable of doing so, but they could not have handled the political situation single-handed. I believe that the British role was vital to the cohesion of the whole operation, and that although the Americans outnumbered us ten to one, our contribution was much greater than those proportions suggest: because of our long association with the Middle East, the Arabs knew us well, and mutual trust oiled the machinery of Coalition business.

In retrospect, I reckoned that Norman Schwarzkopf was right to continue the air-war for as long as he did, and then to hit the Iraqi army with the heaviest possible punch. Any half measures would have resulted in heavier casualties to our own forces – and, paradoxically, to the enemy as well, for if the battle had developed into a war of attrition, many more Iraqis would have been killed. As it was, both the flat terrain and superior technology favoured us, the attackers, but the failure of the Iraqi leadership made a significant contribution to the Allied victory.

As for the British forces, I felt nothing but pride in the professionalism with which they had fought, and I saw that in future the quality of our service men and women will be more critical than ever. However much we have to reduce expenditure and therefore numbers, we must never reduce the quality of our people. Technology has assumed immense importance in modern warfare, but any weapon system, however sophisticated, is only as good as the man or woman operating it: Iraq, after all, had possessed a good deal of modern technology, but had signally failed to use it. Reflecting on the trouble which Paddy and I had had over rate-capping in Whitehall, I saw that in peacetime civil servants should certainly influence political judgment on the manning and cost of the Services. However, once it is clear that fighting is about to start, politicians must have the courage to listen primarily to the advice of their military commanders. If they fail to do this, they may easily cause an increase in the number of casualties and prejudice the conduct of operations. Furthermore, once they have taken a decision to send service men and women to fight for their country, they must commit all available resources and finance, and give the fullest political commitment, to ensure that their military forces have everything they need to win as quickly as possible.

With so much to look back on, the second leg of the journey passed quickly, and in what seemed like no time we were on the tarmac at Northolt, to find all our families assembled, together with Bill Wratten, Paddy Hine and his team from Joint Headquarters, and a champagne reception awaiting us. After nearly six months' absence, it was quite some reunion.

CHAPTER 25

MAGIC CARPET

1991–92

My forty-first and final year in the army proved a hundred times more interesting and amusing than I had any right to expect. Instead of petering out quietly, my career ended in a blaze of travel, high-level meetings and festive occasions of the most glamorous kind. For months it seemed that Bridget and I were on a magic carpet that whisked us to one exotic destination after another.

Back home in April, I found that Viscount Marchwood, the father of a school friend of Edward's and Managing Director of Moët & Chandon, had sent me a Methuselah of champagne. With this splendid gift we threw a humdinger of a family barbecue. It was spring, the garden was looking its freshest, and everyone was in ebullient form. But my leave, which was supposed to have been three weeks, shrank to two, then to one, and finally almost disappeared, such was the bombardment of telephone calls from people asking me to give lectures and make speeches.

I simply had not appreciated the extent to which, on my return, I would be thrust into public life, or the difficulties of handling it. Now, as a result of the television appearances I had made during the war, I suddenly found that I was a public figure, besieged by demands and deluged by correspondence in quantities that I could not begin to answer. Within the nation as a whole there was evidently widespread euphoria that the war had ended so quickly. Expecting the worst, people had nerved themselves to receive ghastly casualties, many disabled by chemical weapons, and when abruptly the conflict was over, with miraculously few men lost or injured, a tremendous feeling of relief swept through the community, often expressed in the form of generosity towards the Services.

For myself, this began at the top. Although no real appointment existed for me, the Chief of the General Staff, General Sir John Chapple, and Tom King had between them created one, which would last for a year and ensure that I was able to retire on a full general's pension. So I became Middle East Adviser to the Secretary of State for Defence, my task being to brief him on military affairs in general, and in particular to maintain links between Her Majesty's Government and the Gulf rulers, so that we could help the Arab nations while they restructured their defence forces and recovered from the war. The value of this role was quickly apparent, as it further enhanced the warm relationships already existing between Britain and the Gulf states.

With the best of intentions someone offered me a desk in the Ministry of Defence; but I, having managed to avoid that gloomy edifice for four decades, had no intention of spending my final year hidden away in some back corner of it. Instead, I rang my friends in the SAS and asked if they could find me space in their London Headquarters, which they obligingly did. (The room was so small that when a Harrow schoolboy came to interview me, for his school magazine, he declared that it must be the tiniest office ever occupied by a general. He was right.) I started there with nothing but two desks and a couple of chairs – not even a telephone or a typewriter – but money was squeezed out of the Chief of Defence Staff's budget to furnish the essentials of an office.

One further necessity was a car in which to travel to my continual engagements. Not only did the Royal Corps of Transport produce a vehicle: they also allowed me to retain the services of Alan Cain, and this was a huge advantage, as he knew his way around, and was well trained in security procedures.

Another invaluable asset was Captain James Hall, a Light Infantry officer who had been my ADC in Wales, and now became my AMA, or Assistant Military Assistant. Having gone out and bought telephones, an answerphone, a word-processor, paper – everything we needed – he began to answer my correspondence and organize my programme. Inexperienced though he was at dealing with senior politicians and with the top levels of the Ministry of Defence, he waded in fearlessly and did a splendid job.

I was determined not to have a large staff, but soon I saw that my little headquarters needed two branches. One was my personal staff, who ran my official life, and the other a triservice lecture and presentation team, which would put over the part played by the British in the Gulf War, both to members of our own Services, and to audiences overseas. On the personal side, I recruited a new Military Assistant, Lieutenant-Colonel Tim Spicer, who set up my office in the interval before taking up a new command; in due course he was succeeded by Lieutenant-Colonel Nick Southward, who had been my Press liaison officer in the Gulf. My new ADC, Captain Toby Tennant, had been severely wounded in the war, and now showed no mean courage in resuming work, although still on crutches. Last but not least there was my secretary, Janet Baldwin, a lively and attractive girl with a sense of humour that kept the whole office alight. The Presentation Team was led by Lieutenant-Colonel David Roberts, an officer from the Parachute Regiment, who was ably supported by Commander Tony Croke from the Navy and Wing Commander David Hamilton from the Air Force. Scrounging some offices, and carpets, curtains and furniture, they brought together a small team of draughtsmen, with a woman corporal as a secretary, and devised a graphic presentation.

News that the team was ready to travel elicited an enthusiastic response from defence attachés asking for visits, and when the show went on the road it covered thirty-six countries in nine months, giving three or four presentations in each country. It was thus a runaway success, and did Britain much good by spreading an accurate version of what had happened in the war, thus ensuring that our sizeable contribution was widely recognized.

In Britain the demand for speakers was relentless, on both formal and informal occasions. I myself had to decline the majority of invitations, because of the sheer numbers, but I steeled myself to speak as often as I could – often six times a week. I took to this new role with reluctance; yet soon I realized that my audiences were all willing listeners, not press-ganged, and that my account of the war, though increasingly well-worn and repetitive to me, came fresh and first-hand to each new gathering. For relatively informal speeches, after dinners and so on, I used notes written on cards as prompts from which I could extemporize, but for more formal presentations I relied on the visual aids prepared by my team, and stuck closely to a typed script. One of the largest such presentations, which John Chapple asked us to lay on for senior serving and retired officers, took place in the Queen Elizabeth Hall, near the Houses of Parliament, and was attended by more than a thousand people, including the Duke of Edinburgh and ex-King Constantine of Greece.

For visits to the Middle East, I was again allotted an HS125 jet, and this increased the effectiveness of my journeys enormously. Not only was it appropriate that the representative of the British Government should travel in a certain style: my ability to set my own schedule meant that I could keep my programme flexible and adjust it to maximum advantage. Moreover, the fact that there was generally a seat or two spare meant that Bridget could sometimes accompany me: throughout my Service life her lament had been that she got very little travel out of the army, and was perennially being left behind. Now she visited countries which she had never seen, but about which she had heard me talk endlessly. She found our visit to Kuwait particularly memorable: the gratitude and hospitality of the people knew no bounds, but an air of desolation hung over the battered city, and yellow flags flew to remind everyone of the missing as well as the dead.

The Gulf states had been thrown into disarray by Saddam's aggression. Now they were urgently reviewing their own defences, while still looking for help from the West, and especially from their old friend, Britain. We, for our part, wanted to keep in close touch with Arab opinion, and to join in debate about the future defence of the region. In particular, we wanted the Arab countries to take effective combined steps to defend themselves — for we had to make it clear to them that Britain might never again go to their aid on the scale of 1990. Already the Options for Change Defence Review was biting into our forces, and in future we would not have the military resources of the past. The trips were planned by Nick Southward in conjunction with the British ambassadors on the ground. I tried to take in three or four countries on every journey, and to spend three or four days in each. This meant a demanding schedule, but with the HS125 and a skilled back-up team, it was possible.

I found it a pleasure, as well as a duty, to call again on rulers whom I knew, but in circumstances more relaxed than when I had seen them last. Throughout the Gulf I was received with enormous warmth. I also went for the first time to Qatar, where I met the Ruler and the Crown Prince. The Rulers of Saudi Arabia, Kuwait, Qatar and Bahrein bestowed high honours on me – although I knew that in truth the medals represented gratitude to the British Government and Services, for their contribution to the war, rather than to me personally. I found that everyone trusted the British and the way we did things, and that the Bahreini leaders – Sheikh Isa and Crown Prince Hamad – were especially keen to develop their country's long-standing relationship with Britain.

In this country, fierce arguments developed over the venue for the national memorial service, to be held for British victims of the war. In the end the choice fell on St Mungo's Cathedral in Glasgow, Scotland being preferred to other possible locations because large numbers of the British contingent had come from the north. I believe this decision was right; the problem was that the cathedral had limited space, and no provision was made for an overflow (even a marquee would have been better than nothing). The result was that among all the politicians and dignitaries only the next-of-kin of those killed could be found places, along with a very tight selection of other servicemen. Like hundreds of other wives, Bridget had to stay at home and watch the proceedings on television.

The Queen and the Duke of Edinburgh arrived half an hour late for the service because the royal train broke down; but this did not detract from the occasion, and the most striking feature was the succession of children, of all denominations and creeds, who read short passages from the scriptures. This proved deeply moving, and showed that such occasions, temporarily transcending all the normal problems of politics and religion, can bring people together in a way that symbolizes the new world order which President Bush had talked about, and raise genuine hopes for peace in our time. Nevertheless, there was a widespread feeling among Service wives that they had missed out. Bridget herself was distressed that she did not have a chance to meet the bereaved families. The memorial service would have been the natural occasion for her to do so, and, having not been present then, she had to wait until another service took place in Cardiff, to which only a few of the families could come.

Sometime in May the Americans invited the British to send a contingent of Service men and women, led by myself, to take part in the ticker-tape Victory Parade, planned for New York on 10 June. Thanks to the persuasive advocacy of Tim Spicer, British Airways generously produced four return tickets on Concorde – two for him and his fiancée, two for myself and Bridget. Arriving at the Concorde lounge at Heathrow on the morning of 9 June, we were immediately presented with a bottle of champagne, which gave an extra edge to the special treatment we were receiving. The journey was very comfortable, and the service so good that the flight seemed to be over almost before it started. (Bridget was particularly thrilled to see the magic legend MACH 2 come up on the screen at the front of the cabin.) We arrived in New York in time for breakfast, and stayed with the Consul-General, Gordon Jewkes: as he had been Governor of the Falkland Islands immediately after Rex Hunt, we were never stuck for conversation.

Of many memorable days that summer, 10 June was the least forgettable. Festivities began with a giant breakfast at Merrill Lynch, the investment house, to which all the leading personalities had been invited. Norman Schwarzkopf was presented with a five-star general's hat, and – there being no five-star generals in the American army – got in a characteristically quick crack, saying that he hoped the bank could afford his five-star salary. Then Bridget was shepherded to a stand next to the saluting base, where she had been allocated a seat beside Sir Anthony Acland, the British Ambassador in Washington, and his wife Jennifer. I, meanwhile, met the rest of the British contingent, which was seventy strong and included a band; for myself, there was a Range Rover, provided by the firm, with its roof cut away, so that I could ride standing up throughout the proceedings.

The contingents formed up in alphabetical order, and because we were listed as 'United Kingdom', we came near the end. Before we set off, I was issued with a steel plate, which I could hold over my head if people started to pelt us with ball-bearings or anything heavier than paper – but we need not have worried. Under a blazing sun, the intensity of goodwill and the sheer enthusiasm of the crowds were beyond anything I had ever experienced. If this was triumphalism, I was all for it – and behind the thunderous roars of excitement one could sense unbounded relief: relief that this war had not turned into another Vietnam, but had come to such a speedy, successful conclusion.

The cavalcade was so vast that it took several hours to pass any one point, and we thought that by the time the United Kingdom came along, enthusiasm might have waned. Not a bit of it: at the sight of us, the crowds burst into fresh roars, and paper of all kinds fluttered down into the concrete canyons of the city. On the saluting base, Norman and Colin Powell had been taking turns: by the time I drew level, Norman had returned specially to the dais, and with a thrill of pride I saw Bridget standing between him and Brenda. Altogether the occasion was not just profoundly moving, but fantastically invigorating as well.

That night our boys went out on the town – and never paid for a thing. The moment anyone discovered they were British, all drink and food were free. So indeed were they for us, since we were invited to a phenomenal dinner and firework party by the millionaire tycoon Robert Maxwell. Dinner took place on the *Peking*, a sailing barque moored in the old harbour on the Hudson river, and everything was done on a lavish scale, with vintage champagne, whole lobsters galore, a full symphony orchestra playing, and many leading New York personalities present. The fireworks, financed by Coca-Cola and the *New York Daily News* (then owned by Maxwell), were stupendous, and we dined at beautifully laid tables on the open deck, looking down on a throng of people milling about on the quay; but Maxwell himself, though friendly and solicitous, was also extraordinarily restless. He was supposed to be placed next to us at table, but when we sat down he did not appear: at last he did come and sit down, but after one bite he leapt up again and vanished. The only time he settled down was when I asked him to tell me how he had won his Military Cross. At that, he took me off to an upper deck, away from the crowd, and became fully composed as he reminisced about his wartime experiences. Looking back, I see that he was all nerves – as well he might be, with his financial affairs in rapidly worsening chaos. At the time we little realized that it may have been the *Daily Mirror* pension fund, rather than our host himself, which was financing such profligate entertainment.[1]

Coming home, I had the fascinating experience of sitting behind the pilots on the flight-deck as Concorde took off. Back in England, debate was raging as to whether we too should hold a victory parade. Some people felt that, ten years earlier, Margaret Thatcher had overplayed our victory in the Falklands, and that the scenes of triumphalism which took place then should not be repeated. Others believed that a parade was not only desirable, but was positively owed to all who took part in the Gulf War, as a public exhibition of thanks and an acknowledgment of what had been achieved. I myself, naturally shying away from parades of all kinds, was against the idea at the time, but now, looking back, I believe I was wrong. The war had, after all, been a triumph for our forces: all the British Services had contributed, and they deserved proper recognition.

In the event, a parade of sorts was authorized. Thanks to the generosity of the City of London, who sponsored the occasion, it took place in the heart of the capital. The Ministry of Defence coordinated the details, but policy was to keep the show small and short, and for that reason it fell flat. In my view it should either have been done magnificently, or not at all; instead, we went for a middle-of-the-road celebration, which left a luke-warm impression.

For Service families, the worst feature of the day was the fact that wives and children of participants were denied the opportunity of attending – an extraordinary decision on the part of the authorities, and one which hurt people deeply. I, for instance, was given a numbered seat in the main stand, and there right in front of me I found the Prime Minister and Norma Major, together with the Crown Prince of Kuwait, Neil and

1. Four months later, on 5 November 1991, Maxwell was lost overboard from his yacht *Lady Ghislaine* off Gran Canaria. He was later found to have embezzled more than £700 million, principally from the *Mirror* pension fund.

Glenys Kinnock, and other politicians and their wives. Bridget, in contrast, had not been invited; nor had Melissa Cordingley, Patrick's wife, or his mother. Luckily Annabel Chapple (wife of the CGS) introduced them to Henry Keswick, Chairman of Matheson & Co., and he generously offered them places in his office windows – otherwise they would have had no vantage point from which to watch the parade. Wives and families should not have been excluded in this way. They had played a major role in backing up their men during the war: without their active support, we would have found it infinitely harder to sustain morale over the long months of waiting – and now the families felt badly let down.

A few days later, I was driving home for the weekend when a call came through on the car telephone. It was the Ministry of Defence, saying that the Prime Minister wanted to see me at 10 Downing Street at 1800 on Sunday, 14 July. A call to the Prime Minister's office elicited the fact that President Bush was in London, and wanted to present me with a medal on behalf of the American people. Having expressed my gratitude, I asked if I might bring members of my family, including my son-in-law, to the ceremony. The answer was 'yes', so we quickly summoned Andrew and Nicola from Brussels, and Sunday evening saw the entire de la Billière tribe bearing down on Number 10, myself wearing a frock coat, my most formal uniform.

For a few minutes we were agreeably entertained by the staff in a small but beautifully furnished drawing room; then John and Norma Major arrived with the President and Barbara Bush, all together. After a flurry of introductions, we chatted before moving into a larger room. There Press and television cameramen were lined up, and the President formally presented me with the Legion of Merit, Grade Chief Commander – the highest award given to people outside the United States – and read out the following address:

> I am pleased to mark my visit to Great Britain by honouring one of Her Majesty's finest soldiers, Sir Peter de la Billière, for his many contributions to the Coalition victory in the Gulf. General, under your leadership, in the midst of the most daunting tasks, never once did Britain hesitate or waver. Always, Britain was there, steadfast and strong. Sir,

let me say to you and to the forces under your command: America is honoured to be your ally. In recognition of your courage and accomplishment, it is a privilege and pleasure to present you with the Legion of Merit, Degree of Chief Commander.

After Bush had spoken, a United States Lieutenant Commander read out the full text of the citation. With grand and generous words of commendation for our country ringing in our ears, we repaired to the smaller room, where bottles of champagne were cracked, and formality disappeared in a buzz of friendly conversation, in which the family found it easy to join, so that a jovial atmosphere developed. Later I found that on the bottom of his typewritten speech, the President had added in his own hand: 'I was very pleased to do the honour, well deserved and earned. George Bush.'

Our magic carpet remained inspired throughout July. On the sixteenth it bore us to Buckingham Palace, where national leaders had dined after the G7 Summit meeting. More guests like ourselves were invited to join the company for fireworks and a laser show once the meal was over. Thus we arrived in evening dress at 2200, and after a cordial reception from the royal family, went out on to balconies in the inner courtyard to watch fireworks being set off from the roofs.

Nobody entertained us more handsomely than the Prime Minister and Norma Major, who invited us to lunch at Chequers on 21 July as the principal guests in a distinguished gathering which included Fatima Whitbread, the Olympic javelin thrower, Helen Sharman, the astronaut, Sir Peter Ustinov, Sir Robin Day, and other outstanding personalities. Our hosts skilfully induced a friendly, informal atmosphere, which made the occasion particularly memorable.

Two days later, on 23 July, we were at Buckingham Palace again, on the occasion of a state banquet given by the Queen in honour of President Mubarak of Egypt. I had seen the inside of the Palace several times before, when receiving awards, but never had I known it lit up in full array for a state occasion. Many of the Royal Family were present, including the Queen and Prince Philip, the Queen Mother, the Prince and Princess of Wales,

Princess Anne, the Duke and Duchess of York, and the guests numbered three or four hundred. As we gathered for dinner, the scene was as magnificent as only the British can lay on: gold plate and cutlery, brilliant crystal glass, wonderful porcelain, waiters in eighteenth-century livery, a Brigade of Guards orchestra playing in the gallery, and trumpeters sounding a fanfare as the Royal Family and principal guests came in. After dinner and speeches, we adjourned to neighbouring rooms, and Bridget and I felt particularly privileged when the Queen Mother asked to see us: being Colonel-in-Chief of the Light Infantry, she wanted, as always, to hear news of them. We also met Prince Charles, and I had a long conversation with President Mubarak – a straightforward, sincere man, with whom it was easy to talk about the contribution which Egyptian forces had made to the war.

Immediately after that, at the invitation of the Chief of the Defence Staff, Field Marshal Sir Richard Vincent, Norman Schwarzkopf came over to join Tom King in taking the salute at the Royal Tournament at Earl's Court. Between his other official engagements I managed to kidnap him for a few hours. After a briefing at SAS Headquarters, we went for a foray into the borders of England and Wales, as I was determined that he should see a little of our countryside. Having survived one crash in a helicopter, Norman is none too keen on that form of transport; but by taking two aircraft (in case one should break down) I persuaded him to fly to Goodrich, a ruined castle south of Ross-on-Wye. We landed in a field and were met by the farmer, with his wife and their small baby, and after a local Press photographer had taken a picture of Norman holding the infant, we were given an informative tour of the castle by a representative of English Heritage. Then we flew on to Llanthony Priory, in the Black Mountains, where the RAF had negotiated to land the helicopters on a stretch of moor close to the ruins. The farmer there was not in the least impressed by the arrival of a brace of airborne generals: he was delighted to see us, he said, but it would cost £50 every time a helicopter touched down. So the RAF were obliged to shell out £100, while we had our tour and tea in the little restaurant.

On the way back I got our pilot to drop me off in a field at home; but after this landing Norman's bad vibrations about helicopters were suddenly vindicated. The aircraft in which he was travelling took off again, but abruptly dropped out of the sky with total hydraulic failure. Luckily it had been airborne for only a few seconds: if the breakdown had happened two or three minutes later, the crash might well have been fatal. In the event, the second helicopter took Norman – not a little shaken – on to London, where he had an appointment, but the sick aircraft was in such a poor way that it could not be repaired *in situ*: a team of engineers had to come and strip it down, loading the rotor blades on to a lorry. Even then the body could not be taken away by road because the lanes were so narrow, and it had to be lifted out by a Chinook, which flew the corpse away, dangling on a cable over the sleepy countryside.

At the Royal Tournament, on 25 July, Norman, Tom King and I were the official guests. I waited to receive him, and when he arrived, driving straight to the centre of the arena, the place erupted in a standing ovation, to which he played up splendidly.

October proved a particularly nostalgic month for me, because on a visit to Oman I returned to the Jebel Akhdar and the scene of the life-and-death SAS patrols of 1958–59. In three decades the country had changed out of all recognition. In place of a poverty-stricken, medieval desert kingdom I found a thriving, ultra-modern Arab state, with new buildings of the boldest design, flourishing agriculture, the latest communications, and fine roads running in all directions – not only on the coastal plains, but also up and over the Green Mountain that had tested us to our limits. Unlike most other Arab countries, Oman has made sure that new buildings reflect national culture, with the result that elements of traditional atmosphere have been retained. Thanks to the generosity of a former SAS officer who was serving in the Sultan's special forces, a helicopter lifted me effortlessly up over the slabs of baking rock and set me down near the summit for which Johnny Watts and I had raced as dawn came up that morning thirty-two years ago. Once again I walked about the spot at which we had come over the lip on to the plateau – but so much had changed that I found it difficult to recognize any features of the terrain. It was extraordinary to think how young and fit and wild we had been, and how the whole of the Gulf had developed since then.

In mid-November Prince Khalid came to England to receive his KCB in a private audience with the Queen. Acting as his host during his stay, I escorted him to the Palace – where he appeared in national dress, looking very fine – and then took him to lunch at Admiralty House with the CDS. Afterwards, spurning our official cars on a lovely afternoon, we walked through Whitehall to the Ministry of Defence, where Tom King, whom we saw next, was surprised to find our vehicles arriving empty. Later in the afternoon we flew by helicopter to my home in the country, where we had laid on a dinner party. This went well, as Khalid, looking immaculate in a well-cut dinner jacket, relaxed and enjoyed himself. In the morning I took him to SAS Headquarters in Hereford, and then on to the Eastnor Castle estate, where he enjoyed himself driving a Discovery Land Rover on the circuit of hair-raising slopes and mud wallows which Ben Hervey-Bathurst created in his woods for the testing of Rover four-wheel-drive vehicles.

Later that month I took Bridget with me on another of our magic-carpet tours, to Egypt, Syria and Jordan. All were fascinating, but none more so than Syria, which I was the first British officer to visit for several decades. My trip was seen as an opportunity for some form of *rapprochement* between our two governments, after Syria's long allegiance to the Soviet bloc and its involvement in terrorist activities. We stayed with the British Ambassador, Andrew Green, and I met, among many others, General Mustapha Tallas, the Minister of Defence, a close associate of President Assad. I was also taken on a tour of the villages overrun and destroyed by the Israelis.

In Jordan I saw the Prime Minister, the Chief of Defence Staff and King Hussein, all in the same day. All made it clear that they were eager for Jordan's traditional friendship with Britain to be re-established, and my visit was widely reported on local television and in the Press. Patrick Eyers, the British Ambassador, with whom we were staying, was amazed at the warmth of the reception I received – and there was no doubt that it symbolized the Government's desire for a *rapprochement*. On a personal level, I enjoyed meeting the King again, and my old friend from the Royal College of Defence Studies, General Salem al Turk, now Chief of Staff. The Gulf War had put Jordan in an exceedingly difficult position: the King had done his best to persuade Saddam Hussein to withdraw from Kuwait, but throughout the conflict his own conduct had been driven by the need to keep Jordan's large Palestinian population on his side. As always, the Jordanians' hospitality was lavish: they took us down to Petra by helicopter, and then, after a tour of the site, during which we rode through the famous gorge on horses, they flew us back up the Wadi Rum, where the scenery in the afternoon light was as magnificent as any I have seen.

All winter I continued to travel – to Germany (where I saw Rupert Smith, Patrick Cordingley and others), to Norway, Holland, Belgium, Naples, Paris. Between these trips there were continual speaking engagements at lunches and dinners up and down the country, both civilian and military. One evening, after a dinner for six hundred people given by the Southampton Master Mariners' Club (of which I had been made an honorary member), my car failed to appear on schedule to pick me up. This caused a considerable disturbance, and I eventually had to ask the police to launch a search. An hour after everyone else had departed, the vehicle at last appeared – but by then I was in the police station, wearing full uniform and being given coffee as the evening's prisoners were brought down to the cells.

On my last official trip to the Gulf, in February 1992, I took along Mike Wilkes, who was to succeed me as Middle East Adviser. Our first stop was Kuwait, which had been efficiently cleared up since I last saw it, and I was glad to find Michael Weston, the British Ambassador, in excellent spirits. After meeting the Kuwaiti Defence Minister, Sheikh Ali Sabah, we had a half-hour audience with the Emir, who presented me with the Kuwaiti Medal, First Class. Then we went by helicopter to meet members of the United Nations observation force at their outposts on the frontier with Iraq, and later visited units of the Kuwaiti Navy, Army and Air Force. Our most memorable sight was that of captured Iraqi weapons and vehicles corralled in a special arena for the public to inspect them. An incredible array of tanks, artillery pieces, anti-aircraft guns, self-propelled guns, medical vehicles, personnel carriers, chemical tankers and soft-skinned vehicles was massed together so tightly that Mike and I could clamber over the tanks, stepping from one to another.

The assembly brought home to me the scale of the Iraqi defeat as nothing had before.

From Kuwait we went on to Saudi Arabia, Abu Dhabi, Dubai and Qatar, where the Crown Prince, His Highness Hamad bin Khalifa al Thani, presented me with the Qatar Sash of Merit in a phenomenal palace lined with marble, and sporting oak entrance doors forty feet high, alleged to weigh forty tons apiece. In Bahrein once more, at an audience with the Ruler, I again felt the warmth of that little state's affection for Britain, and afterwards I noted: 'I shall be sorry to leave the Bahreinis, who have been great friends all the way through. I hope I shall return.'

In Oman we were accompanied by Sir Terence Clark, the British Ambassador, and the high point of our stay was an audience with Sultan Qaboos, holding his annual *majlis*, or court, way out in the desert at a site which I described in contemporary notes as 'truly amazing':

> Hundreds if not thousands of Bedu camped beside their Toyotas, with rugs and food laid out on the sand in the middle of nowhere. Camels sitting in the backs of Toyotas – latest Arab practice! About a mile further on, the royal camp of six hundred vehicles, with tents erected and body-guard in position, backed by picturesque, five-hundred-foot sand dunes.

After lunch in our own tent – served on tables, with silver cutlery – we were summoned to the royal presence. An aide met us at the entrance, and as we were hesitating over whether or not to take off our shoes, the Sultan himself called out from inside, 'Don't bother!' He was wearing dark robes, suitable for the desert, and he had discarded his own sandals. When I introduced Mike as my successor, Qaboos gave him a cordial welcome, and then in a relaxed talk lasting an hour and a half ranged over current political problems, clearly seeing a role for himself as a leading mediator for peace in the region. It was an impressive performance by an impressive man.

In March a quick-fire lecture tour in America took Bridget and myself to Florida, where we dined with Norman and Brenda Schwarzkopf at their local country club. Then in swift succession we went on to Washington, New York, Chicago and back to

Washington. For me the most notable events of a packed fortnight were meetings with Colin Powell, Chairman of the United States Chiefs of Staff, and Prince Bandar, the Saudi Ambassador to the United States. With both I held useful post-mortems on the war, and discussed the intractable problem of how to deal with Saddam Hussein.

In England, lectures and after-dinner speeches continued apace, but my time in the army was fast running out, and I knew I must make provision for my retirement. I was lucky enough to be appointed a non-executive Main Board Director of Robert Fleming, the only merchant bank with offices in the Gulf, which they had kept open throughout the war. The job would entail travel in the Middle and Far East. Banking was something new to me, and clearly would present a considerable challenge; but at least I would be specializing in an area of the world with which I was already familiar. At the same time, after considering many other charitable organizations, I joined FARM Africa, a charity which seeks to improve the productivity of agriculture in remote areas of the continent by increasing output without changing people's traditional methods or way of life. This attracted me partly because of my own farming background, and partly because the work – banishing poverty and starvation through community projects – was exactly what the SAS had pioneered at Salala twenty years earlier.

I also wanted to do something for the Services, and my chance came one day when my old friend and colleague from the DLI and Korea, Bob Macgregor-Oakford, walked into the office. By then he was Secretary of the Army Cadet Force, and he approached me on behalf of his council to ask if I would become President. Since I had always wanted to provide young people with opportunities for adventure and excitement which they would not otherwise get, I felt glad and privileged to accept.

Looking back over my career, I realize that all my life I have enjoyed a great deal of luck. Often by sheer good fortune I have been in the right place at the right moment; yet I believe that I have also benefited from a simple belief about luck and how to handle it. Everybody needs luck – but luck will get you only so far. Luck, in my experience, presents you with a series of opportunities, that come past as if on an endless conveyor belt. As each opportunity passes, you have a short time in which to inspect it and decide whether to grab it or let it go by. This means that you have to take both decisions and risks: if you are slow to make your mind up, you may lose an opportunity through failing to react in time; and you run the risk, if you pick the wrong opportunity, of setting back your whole career.

In almost all my career decisions I have been extraordinarily fortunate. At the end of my tour in Malaya, in 1958, I grabbed at the opportunity of fighting on the Jebel Akhdar, and that worked out well. In seizing the chance of serving in Aden in 1963, I again landed on my feet. In committing the SAS to Oman in the early 1970s, I hit on a political situation ripe for intervention. In postponing retirement and volunteering for the Gulf in 1990, I obtained a command in which all my past service and experience came together. Every one of these decisions involved risks, whether of physical injury or of failure to measure up to the task in hand.

My greatest good fortune has been the quality of the people I have had to work with me, and particularly my subordinates in the chain of command. I, if anyone, am the living embodiment of the 'toothpaste' theory: all along, it has been the competence of the people working for me that has squeezed me out at the top.

As will be clear by now, most of my career has been with the SAS, and if I had to pinpoint the secret of the Regiment's success, I should identify it as the willingness of its officers and men to look ahead, to seek change, and to adapt to an ever-shifting threat. This sense of endless quest, which has shaped my life, is memorably expressed in the lines from James Elroy Flecker's *The Golden Road to Samarkand* inscribed on the base of the Regiment's memorial clock tower in Hereford, along with the names of the dead lost on operations or exercises since the Second World War:

> We are the Pilgrims, master; we shall go
> Always a little farther: it may be
> Beyond that last blue mountain barred with snow,
> Across that angry or that glimmering sea.

INDEX